INDIVIDUAL DIFFERENCES
IN THEORY OF MIND

Macquarie Monographs in Cognitive Science
General Editor: MAX COLTHEART

The newly launched Macquarie Monographs in Cognitive Science series will publish original monographs dealing with any aspect of cognitive science. Each volume in the series will cover a circumscribed topic, and will provide readers with a summary of the current state of the art in that field. A primary aim of the volumes is also to advance research and knowledge in the field through discussion of new theoretical and experimental advances.

Published titles

Routes to Reading Success and Failure: Toward an Integrative Cognitive Psychology of Atypical Reading, Nancy Ewald Jackson & Max Coltheart

Cognitive Neuropsychological Approaches to Spoken Word Production, Lyndsey Nickels (Ed.)

Rehabilitation of Spoken Word Production in Aphasia, Lyndsey Nickels (Ed.)

Masked Priming: The State of the Art, Sachiko Kinoshita & Stephen J. Lupker (Eds.)

Individual Differences in Theory of Mind: Implications for Typical and Atypical Development, Betty Repacholi & Virginia Slaughter (Eds.)

Forthcoming titles

From Mating to Mentality: Evaluating Evolutionary Psychology, Kim Sterelny & Julie Fitness (Eds.)

Subsequent volumes are planned on various topics in cognitive science, including visual cognition and modeling of visual word recognition.

Macquarie Monographs in Cognitive Science

INDIVIDUAL DIFFERENCES IN THEORY OF MIND

Implications for Typical and Atypical Development

Betty Repacholi
University of Washington

and

Virginia Slaughter
University of Queensland

PSYCHOLOGY PRESS

New York and Hove

Published in 2003 by
Psychology Press
29 West 35th Street
New York, NY 10001
www.psypress.com

Published in Great Britain by
Psychology Press
27 Church Road
Hove, East Sussex
BN3 2FA
www.psypress.co.uk

Copyright © 2003 by Taylor & Francis Books

Psychology Press, is an imprint of the Taylor & Francis Group.
Printed in the United States of America on acid-free paper.

10 9 8 7 6 5 4

Library of Congress Cataloging-in-Publication Data

Individual differences in theory of mind : implications for typical and atypical development /
    edited by Betty Repacholi and Virginia Slaughter.
        p. cm. — (Macquarie monographs in cognitive science)
    Includes bibliographical references and index.
    ISBN 1-84169-093-7
    1. Philosophy of mind in children. 2. Individual differences in children. I. Repacholi,
Betty. II. Slaughter, Virginia. III. Series.

BF723.P48I53 2003
155.4'13—dc21

2003040459

*This book is dedicated to the memory of Linda Mealey,
Professor of Psychology at St. Benedict's College
in St. Cloud, Minnesota, and Adjunct Professor of Psychology
at the University of Queensland, Australia.
Linda's death at the age of 46 from colon and liver cancer
was a great loss for the field. She was a pioneer
in her thinking about the potential impact
of individual differences in theory of mind.*

Contents

About the Editors

Betty Repacholi is a developmental psychologist with a broad interest in so-cial-cognitive development, especially during infancy and early childhood. After training as a Clinical Psychologist in Australia, she completed a PhD at the University of California–Berkeley in 1996. She was a tenured lecturer in psychology at Macquarie University (Sydney, Australia) until relocating to Seattle in 2001. Betty is now an Assistant Professor at the University of Washington and director of the Social and Emotional Development Laboratory.

Virginia Slaughter is a developmental psychologist specializing in social-cognitive development in infancy and early childhood. She earned her PhD from the University of California, Berkeley in 1994 and has been at the University of Queensland since 1996, where she is codirector of the Early Cognitive Development Unit in the School of Psychology.

Contributors

Janet Wilde Astington
University of Toronto, Canada

Robert J. R. Blair
Mood and Anxiety Program,
National Institute of Mental Health,
London, UK

Martin Davies
Research School of Social Sciences,
Australian National University

Cheryl Dissanayake
School of Psychological Science,
LaTrobe University, Australia

Philip Gerrans
University of Adelaide, Australia

Vicki Gibbs
Department of Psychology,
Macquarie University, Australia

Thomas Keenan
University of Canterbury,
New Zealand

Robyn Langdon
Macquarie Centre for Cognitive Science,
Macquarie University, Australia

Kathleen Macintosh
School of Psychological Science,
LaTrobe University, Australia

Victoria McGeer
Research School of Social Sciences,
Australian National University

Doris McIlwain
Department of Psychology,
Macquarie University, Australia

Candida C. Peterson
School of Psychology,
University of Queensland, Australia

Michelle Pritchard
School of Psychology,
University of Queensland, Australia

Tony Stone
Department of Psychology,
South Bank University, London, UK

Jon Sutton
The British Psychological Society,
Leicester, UK

Helen Tager-Flusberg
Boston University, USA

1

Introduction:
Individual Differences
in Theory of Mind
What Are We Investigating?

VIRGINIA SLAUGHTER
School of Psychology, University of Queensland
BETTY REPACHOLI
Psychology Department, University of Washington

S ince the early 1980s, the acquisition of a theory of mind, defined as the ability to predict and explain people's behavior with reference to mental states, has been seen as a crucial watershed in social-cognitive development: one that changes the toddler from a literal observer of human behavior to a folk psychologist, capable of making complex mental-state attributions, engaging in elaborate social and communicative games, and even deception. Theory of mind ability, variously referred to as mentalizing, mind reading, or belief-desire psychology, has traditionally been viewed as the foundation for our adultlike understanding of the social world. As Wellman (1990) expressed it:

> Why is achievement of a theory of mind important? . . . belief-desire psychology is our framework theory of persons. As a framework theory it dictates our basic ontology, our parsing of personal action and thought into its most basic categories. And it dictates our causal-explanatory infrastructure, our basic grasp of how to go about making sense of ourselves and others. In short, belief-desire psychology frames our worldview. (p. 328)

Thus, individual differences in theory of mind ability presumably have important implications for children's and adults' everyday social interactions. This view is

1

most strongly stated in the theory of mind deficit account of autism (e.g., Baron-Cohen, Leslie, & Frith, 1985; Baron-Cohen, Tager-Flusberg, & Cohen, 1993), where it is argued that the atypical social and communicative behavior of individuals with autism results from their failure to acquire a theory of mind.

Given the centrality of theory of mind as a construct in developmental psychology over the last 15 years, it seems natural that the field should turn to investigations of how it relates to other aspects of development, and indeed, there is already a substantial body of research that does just that (see Bartsch & Estes, 1996, for an early review). This research literature suggests that there are measurable individual differences in the mind-reading abilities of young children, and that these individual differences are correlated in theoretically predictable ways with other variables. We can identify at least three major classes of individual differences studies: those that examine the role of family variables in theory of mind development; those exploring the connection between theory of mind and other cognitive constructs; and those that link theory of mind with various social outcome measures (see Bartsch & Estes, 1996, and Keenan, this volume, for a somewhat different way of classifying this literature).

Studies that have linked theory of mind ability with family variables often focus on identifying predictors of mindreading ability. This class of studies has demonstrated relations between elements of family structure or interaction and mind-reading ability in children, with theory of mind skill being predicted by such variables as family talk about mental states (Dunn, Brown, Slomkowski, Tesla, & Youngblade, 1991; Meins, Fernyhough, Wainwright, Gupta, Fradley, & Tuckey, 2002); number of siblings (Perner, Ruffman, & Leekam, 1994; Ruffman, Perner, Naito, Parkin, & Clements, 1998); socioeconomic status (Holmes, Black, & Miller, 1996; Hughes, Deater-Deckard, & Cutting, 1999); maternal education (Cutting & Dunn, 1999); parenting styles (Ruffman, Perner, & Parkin, 1999; Vinden, 1997); and attachment security (Meins, Fernyhough, Russell, & Clark-Carter, 1998; Symons & Clark, 2000). In general, these studies suggest that children's theory of mind development is enhanced when their family environment somehow draws attention to the fact that people's behavior is based on mental states like belief, desire, and emotions, and that such mental states are unique to individuals.

Mind-reading ability has also been shown to correlate with various cognitive constructs. For instance, significant relations have been obtained between theory of mind and executive functioning (Carlson & Moses, 2001; Frye, Zelazo, & Palfai, 1995; Hughes, 1998; Perner & Lang, 1999), creativity (Suddendorf & Fletcher-Flinn, 1999), fantasy (Taylor & Carlson, 1997), and moral reasoning (Dunn, Cutting, & Demetriou, 2000). In general, children who score highly on measures of theory of mind also perform positively on these other cognitive measures. The most robust relation, replicated across numerous studies, is that between theory of mind and language (Astington & Jenkins, 1999; Cutting & Dunn, 1999; Eisenmajer & Prior, 1991; Jenkins & Astington, 1996; Happé, 1995;

Hughes & Cutting, 1999). Some evidence has been found for a minimum threshold of verbal ability that is necessary for children to pass one or more theory of mind tasks (Jenkins & Astington, 1996). Consistent with this finding, children with autism who pass theory of mind tasks tend to have higher levels of verbal ability than those who fail such tasks (Eisenmajer & Prior, 1991; Happé, 1995). The nature of the link between theory of mind and language is not entirely clear, but it is unlikely that this association is simply due to the linguistic demands of the mind-reading tasks (Jenkins & Astington, 1996). Moreover, Astington and Jenkins (1999) recently provided evidence suggesting that language plays a fundamental role in the development of a theory of mind. In their longitudinal study, earlier language ability predicted later theory of mind performance (controlling for earlier theory of mind), but earlier theory of mind did not predict later language ability (controlling for earlier language).

Another class of studies has linked theory of mind to various social outcome measures, including social behavior and other indicators of social competence. These studies demonstrated associations between mind-reading ability and socially competent behavior (Lalonde & Chandler, 1995; Spatz & Cassidy, 1999), the quality of children's peer relationships (see reviews in Sutton and Repacholi et al., this volume), and clinical status (Baron-Cohen, Tager-Flusberg, & Cohen, 2000; Charman, Carroll, & Sturge, 2001; Happé & Frith, 1996; Hughes, Dunn, & White, 1998). This body of research suggests that children with relatively good mind-reading skills enjoy more successful social relationships than those who are less adept mind readers. However, in recent years, evidence has been accumulating (see Sutton and Repacholi et al., this volume) that an advanced theory of mind does not guarantee social success. Indeed, some children (e.g., ringleader bullies; Sutton, Smith, & Swettenham, 1999) and adults (e.g., psychopaths; Blair et al., 1996) consistently use their mind-reading skills for antisocial purposes. Thus, the relationship between theory of mind and social outcome measures is much more complex than previously thought.

So what is it that we are investigating when we try to understand individual variability in theory of mind? What do we mean by "individual differences" in this developmental domain? Presumably, we want to capture something about the way(s) in which individuals vary as mind readers: how they differ in their prediction and explanation of behavior based on mental states. To date, researchers have tended to rely on experimental tasks to assess individual differences in theory of mind, with the bulk of the research focusing on 3- to 5-year-old children or individuals (children and adults) diagnosed with some form of autistic spectrum disorder. This work has generated a wide variety of experimental tasks designed to tap participants' understanding of an array of mental states and related constructs, including visual perspectives, desires, intentions, pretense and imagination, states of knowledge and degrees of knowledge certainty, remembering and forgetting, recognition of appearances versus reality, understanding of verbal ambiguity, and understanding of deception. Many of these tasks follow a standard structure: Participants are presented with a scenario in which a protagonist is described in some situation, and then they are asked to explain or predict the protagonist's behavior (based on an inferred mental state) or to directly report the protagonist's mental state. Because there is a clear developmental sequence in the typically developing child's acquisition of a theory of mind between the ages of 2½ and 5, the majority of tasks target this age range. Preschoolers' capacity to correctly infer mental states in these tasks serves as the basis for measuring individual differences in mind reading.

The most widely used theory of mind measure is the false-belief task, in which accurate predictions about another person's behavior can be derived by referring to that person's mental (mis)representation (i.e., their false belief). This task is often referred to as the "litmus test" for assessing children's understanding of the mind, although a number of authors have noted its limitations and called for a reduction in its use (Astington, 2001; Bloom & German, 2000; Chandler & Hala, 1994; Gopnik, Slaughter, & Meltzoff, 1994). Putting these criticisms aside for the moment, the false-belief task has some admirable characteristics that deserve mention. First, it is quick and easy to administer and it is engaging for children. These features are not trivial, particularly when studying individual differences in theory of mind where research protocols demand assessments of multiple constructs. Second, a recent meta-analysis (Wellman, Cross, & Watson, 2001) demonstrated that the task is psychometrically sound. For instance, it is now well standardized. The Wellman et al. (2001) meta-analysis of the false-belief task performance of thousands of children across seven different countries demonstrated a strong age effect whereby the majority of children failed the task at age 3 but passed by age 4½ . Furthermore, the task has acceptable reliability, with test–retest and alternate forms reliabilities as high as .80 (Hughes et al., 2000; Wellman et al., 2001). There has been a good deal of debate about the validity of the false belief task. While some have suggested that it is not a valid measure of theory of mind ability (Bloom & German, 2000; Chandler & Hala, 1994; Leslie, 2000), the task appears to have good construct validity, having been developed out of a philosophical analysis of the conditions under which one could be certain that an individual was appealing to mental states when predicting human behavior (Dennett, 1978; Wimmer & Perner, 1983). In addition, as noted before, false-belief task performance has been shown to be correlated in predictable ways with a number of cognitive constructs (e.g., creativity—Suddendorf & Fletcher-Flinn, 1999), behavioral (e.g., social skills—Lalonde & Chandler, 1995), and other variables (e.g., popularity within the peer group—Peterson & Siegal, 2002), thereby demonstrating some concurrent and predictive validity.

In addition to the standard false-belief task and similar tools measuring preschoolers' ability to attribute other types of mental states (e.g., desires, emotions, etc.), there is also a large literature that analyzes mental state term usage in naturalistic language transcripts as indicators of individual children's theory of mind (Bartsch & Wellman, 1995). To date, however, only a few measures have been developed to assess mind reading in older children. Perhaps the most well known of these is the "second-order" false-belief task, which requires prediction of behavior or a mental state based on what a story protagonist thinks another person thinks (Perner & Wimmer, 1985). This task is not passed by typically developing children until age 7 or 8, and is therefore considered to be an advanced test of theory of mind. Although these are the most widely used theory of mind measures, a number of other tools have been developed over the past 15 years, and many of these have come from the autism literature (see Baron-Cohen, 2001, for a review). Examples include interpreting or sequencing cartoon pictures that portray a mind-reading episode (Baron-Cohen, Leslie, & Frith, 1986); interpreting utterances in terms of the intention behind them (Baron-Cohen, O'Riordan, Stone, Jones, & Plaisted, 1999); creating or identifying deception (Hala, Chandler, & Fritz, 1991); interpreting facial expression, direction of eye gaze, or voice modulation in terms of the underlying mental state (Baron-Cohen, Wheelwright, Hill, Raste, & Plumb, 2001; Rutherford, Baron-Cohen, & Wheelwright, 2002); and making mentalistic attributions about the behavior of moving geometric forms (Abell, Happé, & Frith, 2000). As with the standard false-belief task and the like, these measures typically provide information about individual differences in terms of correct versus incorrect attribution of mental states. Some (e.g., Abell et al., 2000) also provide information about the extent to which individuals appeal to different types of mental states, thereby providing richer information about differences in mind reading.

In summary, then, there are many techniques currently available to assess theory of mind. However, a number of issues related to measuring and conceptualizing theory of mind, issues that are particularly relevant to the project of studying individual differences, have been recently noted and deserve discussion. The standard false-belief task and the various other tasks mentioned here typically capture a developmental trend such that younger children either fail or perform at chance levels, whereas older children pass the task, giving an adultlike answer at better than chance levels. In other words, what has traditionally been measured is simply earlier versus later acquisition of the ability to predict another person's mental state or to explain behavior with reference to mental states. Thus, individual differences are captured in age of onset of the particular mind-reading skill measured by a given task. More recently, researchers have moved in the direction of theory of mind test batteries that include multiple tasks, assess understanding of a variety of mental states, and enable a composite score to be created (see both Peterson and Tager-Flusberg, this volume, for comprehensive developmental assessments using a range of theory of mind tasks). However, even in these designs, it is still the case that the dependent variable is age of onset. Although age of onset provides useful information that allows us to understand when basic theory of mind concepts are mastered, from the perspective of investigating individual differences it is quite limited. All we can do is measure variation in the extent to which individuals pass tasks relatively early or late.

The fact that children's performance on false-belief and similar mental-state attribution tasks is highly reliable suggests that we do a good job assessing this aspect of mind reading. However, all of the tasks, both standard and advanced measures, are plagued by ceiling effects in samples where mind-reading skill is relatively good. For typically developing children above the age of 7 or 8, and for adults, there are as yet few assessments that reveal significant and meaningful individual differences in mind reading (Happé's Advanced Test of Theory of Mind [Happé, 1994] and Baron-Cohen's various mind-reading test batteries [see Baron-Cohen, 2001, for an overview], all initially developed for use with high-functioning autistic individuals, are notable exceptions). This is partly because few researchers have speculated about the changes that might occur in mentalizing ability during middle to late childhood (see, however, Bosacki & Astington, 1999, and O'Connor & Hirsch, 1999), and also because there is a lack of consensus as to what constitutes a mature theory of mind. On the other hand, it is obvious from our everyday social interactions that even adults differ in their mentalizing skills, so devising appropriate theory of mind measures for older children and adults should be a high priority. Having said that, we need to be very careful about relying on any one measure; mind reading is not a unidimensional construct, and it would be shortsighted to believe that one type of task could capture all of its complexity.

The majority of mind-reading tasks assess what individuals are capable of doing in a specific experimental context but the results are generalized to everyday life. For instance, younger children who fail the standard false-belief task are considered by some to be incapable of predicting behavior based on a false belief, whereas older children who pass the task are thought to have acquired this capacity. This conclusion is not shared by all researchers. There is a large literature that hypothesizes early theory of mind competence, arguing that the standard false-belief task is unnecessarily complex and masks children's genuine ability (e.g., Chandler, 1988; Leslie, 2000; Siegal, 1997). These authors note a competence/performance distinction, arguing that the false-belief task conflates the two: Children have the competence (i.e., the capacity to reason about mental states), but performance factors (e.g., task complexity, memory requirements, etc.) obscure that basic ability in the experimental task. We would like to highlight another type of competence/performance distinction that has been discussed in the autism literature (Boucher, 1989; Bowler, 1992) and is particularly relevant for the study of individual differences more generally: that is, the distinction between competence, defined as what an individual *can do* when presented with an experimental theory of mind task, and performance, defined as what an individual *will do* when facing real-life situations that call for theory of mind reasoning. Theory of mind tasks may provide a picture of what individuals are capable of with respect to reasoning about mental states (that is, if the task is deemed valid), but it does not provide any insight into the spontaneous mind reading that we engage in on a daily basis. This point is demonstrated in some of the research conducted with high-functioning individuals with autism. Some of these individuals can pass standard false-belief tasks but their relatively deficient social and communicative skills in everyday life suggest that they do not necessarily utilize this ability when dealing with other people (Bowler, 1992; also see Dissanayake & Macintosh, this volume).

Given the need to assess theory of mind more comprehensively, it seems worthwhile to ask the question: What is it that we do in our everyday social reasoning that is different from what we assess with standard and higher level mental state attribution tasks? Several dimensions of difference between laboratory theory of mind tasks and everyday social reasoning spring to mind. For instance, in everyday mind reading, we compute mental states online, and often act on those computations. It would seem rare for us to explicitly reflect on the mental state attributions we make in the course of social interactions; instead, we are much more likely to act on those attributions with an immediate behavioral or linguistic response. Our everyday mind reading happens quickly (and may seem almost automatic); multiple attributions take place in parallel; our typical social experiences may involve several people at once; and environmental elements of the social situation that inform our attributions can change quite rapidly. It seems likely that social dysfunction may sometimes by characterized as an inability to keep up; someone who can compute mental states, but only 3 minutes after everyone else does, is likely to be perceived as a social oaf. Perhaps this issue of reaction time goes part of the way to explaining why some high-functioning autistic individuals who can pass even advanced theory of mind tasks are still judged to have social interaction deficits (Bowler, 1992). Furthermore, the social cues that inform our mind reading in everyday interactions are multifaceted, as we simultaneously take note of other people's eyes, body language, voice modulation, situational constraints and whatever information we may have gleaned from any prior encounters with a particular individual. And finally, everyday mind reading is highly fluid and constant, as we move in and out of multiple social interactions throughout the day.

If we are serious about investigating individual differences in theory of mind, then we need to design assessments that (1) are more complex, better approximating our everyday mind reading and (2) can go beyond age-of-emergence or pass/fail data and begin to capture more qualitative differences in theory of mind ability. Some of the tasks that have been used in the autism literature have begun to move in this direction; for instance, Happé's (1994) story interpretation task provides relatively rich information about the story protagonists' motivations and the relevant situational constraints. In addition, this task can be scored according to the presence/absence of mental state attributions as well as the appropriateness of these attributions. Others have extended such tasks by introducing reaction time measurements and other variations designed to capture subtle individual differences in mind reading (e.g., Kaland et al., 2002). It has already been demonstrated that some adults are more likely than others to talk about mental states in conversation with their children, and that such variation in parental conversational style predicts the emergence of children's mind-reading skills (Dunn et al., 1991; Meins et al., 2002). It is worth considering, then, that children can also be described as being more or less "mind-minded," to use Elizabeth Meins's (1997) terminology. Indeed, there is some preliminary evidence that variation in the tendency to appeal to mental states in everyday social reasoning may constitute an important individual difference variable. For example, Bosacki and Astington (1999) explored individual differences in preadolescents' mentalizing ability as evidenced in their interpretation of stories about ambiguous social situations. Rather than scoring participants' verbal responses as right or wrong, Bosacki and Astington (1999) devised a coding scheme that reflected the cognitive complexity of their responses, "moving from simple, obvious ('surface') characteristics to the interaction of several different abstract psychological concepts and the integration of multiple and paradoxical perspectives" (p. 241). Mentalizing scores were positively correlated with peer-rated social skills (even after controlling for language), thereby providing evidence for the construct validity of this mentalizing measure. Along similar lines, O'Connor and Hirsch (1999) presented young adolescents with vignettes based on common teacher–student experiences (e.g., the student was not called on by the teacher even though she had her hand up). Once again, by virtue of the ambiguity of these social situations, it was possible to measure the level or degree of mentalizing that was evident in adolescents' interpretation of these stories (also see Repacholi et al., this volume, who use a similar technique with 10- to 12-year-old children). Theoretically predictable correlations were once again obtained between participants' mentalizing scores and indicators of their social adjustment (e.g., friendship quality). Taken together, these two studies provide some preliminary support for the notions that individual differences in theory of mind continue to exist beyond age 7 or 8; that this variation can be captured in experimental tasks; and that such differences are meaningful in so far as they appear to be related to real-world behavior.

Besides the degree to which an individual engages in mental-state reasoning, there are other stylistic variations that could potentially be assessed. In a much-quoted passage, Happé and Frith (1996) suggested that conduct-disordered children in their study who passed standard theory of mind tasks but scored below a control group on a measure of everyday social functioning "have intact but skewed theory of mind—perhaps a theory of nasty minds" (p. 395). This quote suggests that there may be significant individual differences in theory of mind that can be captured by assessments focusing on the types of mental states children attribute to others (i.e., the content of their mentalizing), rather than simply whether or not they refer to mental states (see Blair and Repacholi et al., this volume, for further discussion of this point).

Finally, it may be that a move toward investigating theory of mind styles will force us to consider whether these individual differences are best viewed as continuous variance along a single dimension (e.g., a tendency to appeal to mental states in reasoning about social situations), or whether there are other ways of conceptualizing such variation. For instance, there may be multiple dimensions of variation in mind reading, similar to the multiple factors that are measured in personality research (McCrae & Costa, 1997). This sort of analysis could include the dimensions of mind-reading variation that we already assess very well—for example, identifying individuals whose mental state reasoning is highly engaged (those who perform well on standard tasks and also readily/frequently appeal to mental states in predicting and explaining everyday social events) and those whose theory of mind is relatively disengaged (at the extreme, high-functioning autistic individuals who pass standard theory of mind tasks). At the same time, there may be other intersecting mind-reading dimensions that reflect stylistic variations in how individuals conceive of others' minds, along the lines of Happé and Frith's (1996) theory of nasty versus kind minds. Other potential individual differences in mentalizing might capture variation in the extent to which such reasoning is based on "hot" (perhaps reflected in levels of empathy) versus "cold" cognitive processing when trying to make sense of others' experiences. A related distinction has already emerged in the autism literature, where some able autistic individuals have been characterized as developing strategies for "hacking out" appropriate responses in mind-reading tasks (Bowler, 1992; also see Dissanayake & Macintosh, this volume). Finally, it may be worth considering that there are mind-reading "types" who share a basic theory of mind capacity but use it in such different ways (e.g., for antisocial vs. prosocial purposes) that they constitute distinct groups of individuals (Mealey, 1995).

This volume represents the first collection of work that focuses on individual differences in theory of mind, in both typically and nontypically developing samples. It brings together a variety of papers that consider interrelations between mind-reading ability and other aspects of mind and behavior, including empathy, aggression, social competence, peer acceptance, personality, psychopathology (e.g., psychopathy, schizophrenia), and communication skills (see Davies and Stone, this volume, for a comprehensive summary and discussion of these chapters). As such, it makes a valuable contribution to our understanding of the construct of theory of mind, as well as providing avenues for further study. As we follow those avenues, we may want to consider expanding our conceptualizations of what it means to talk about, and measure, individual differences in this developmental domain.

ACKNOWLEDGMENTS

We thank all the participants in the Macquarie Centre for Cognitive Sciences workshop on Mindreading and Behaviour held in Sydney, July 2001, for an enthusiastic and inspiring workshop experience. We also thank Stuart Kinner and Linda Mealey for valuable input to some of the ideas presented in this chapter.

REFERENCES

Abell, F., Happé, F., & Frith, U. (2000). Do triangles play tricks? Attribution of mental states to animated shapes in normal and abnormal development. *Cognitive Development, 15,* 1–16.

Astington, J. (2001). The future of theory of mind research: Understanding motivational states, the role of language and real world consequences. *Child Development, 72,* 685–687.

Astington, J. W., & Jenkins, J. (1999). A longitudinal study of the relation between language and theory of mind development. *Developmental Psychology, 35,* 1311–1320.

Baron-Cohen, H., Tager-Flusberg, H. & Cohen, D. (1993) *Understanding other minds: Perspectives from autism.* Oxford: Oxford University Press.

Baron-Cohen, H., Tager-Flusberg, H., & Cohen, D. (Eds.). (2000). *Understanding other minds: Perspectives from developmental cognitive neuroscience* (2nd ed.). Oxford: Oxford University Press.

Baron-Cohen, S. (2001). Autism: A review. *International Review of Research in Mental Retardation, 23,* 169–184.

Baron-Cohen, S., Leslie, A. M., & Frith, U. (1985). Does the autistic child have theory of mind? *Cognition, 21,* 37–46.

Baron-Cohen, S., Leslie, A. M., & Frith, U. (1986). Mechanical, behavioural and intentional understanding of picture stories in autistic children. *British Journal of Developmental Psychology, 4,* 113–125.

Baron-Cohen, S., O'Riordan, M., Stone, V., Jones, R., & Plaisted, K. (1999). Recognition of faux pas by normally developing children and children with Asperger syndrome or high-functioning autism. *Journal of Autism and Developmental Disorders, 29,* 407–418.

Baron-Cohen, S., Wheelwright, S., Hill, J., Raste, Y., & Plumb, I. (2001). The "Reading the Mind in the Eyes" Test revised version: A study with normal adults, and adults with Asperger syndrome or high-functioning autism. *Journal of Child Psychology and Psychiatry, 42,* 241–251.

Bartsch, K., & Estes, D. (1996). Individual differences in children's developing theory of mind and implications for metacognition. *Learning and Individual Differences, 8,* 281–304.

Bartsch, K., & Wellman, H. M. (1995). *Children talk about the mind.* New York: Oxford University Press.

Blair, J., Sellars, C., Strickland, I., Clark, F., Williams, A., Smith, M., & Jones, L. (1996). Theory of mind in the psychopath. *Journal of Forensic Psychiatry, 7,* 15–25.

Bloom, P., & German, T. (2000). Two reasons to abandon the false belief task as a test of theory of mind. *Cognition, 77,* B25–B31.

Bosacki, S., & Astington, J. W. (1999). Theory of mind in preadolescence: relations between social understanding and social competence. *Social Development, 8,* 237–255.

Boucher, J. (1989). The theory of mind hypothesis of autism: Explanation, evidence and assessment. *British Journal of Disorders of Communication, 24,* 181–198.

Bowler, D. (1992). "Theory of mind" in Asperger's syndrome. *Journal of Child Psychology and Psychiatry and Allied Disciplines, 33,* 877–893.

Carlson, S., & Moses, L. (2001). Individual differences in inhibitory control and children's theory of mind. *Child Development, 72,* 1032–1053.

Chandler, M. (1988). Doubt and developing theories of mind. In J. Astington, P. Harris, & D. Olson (Eds.) *Developing theories of mind* (pp. 387–413). Cambridge: Cambridge University Press.

Chandler, M., & Hala, S. (1994). The role of personal involvement in the assessment of early false belief skills. In C. Lewis & P. Mitchell (Eds.), *Children's early understanding of mind: Origins and development* (pp. 403–425). Hillsdale, NJ, England: Lawrence Erlbaum Associates.

Charman, T., Carroll, F., & Sturge, C. (2001). Theory of mind, executive function and social competence in boys with ADHD. *Emotional and Behavioural Difficulties, 6,* 31–49.

Cutting, A., & Dunn, J. (1999). Theory of mind, emotion understanding, language and family background: Individual differences and interrelations. *Child Development, 70,* 853–865.

Dennett, D. (1978). Beliefs about beliefs. *Behavioural and Brain Sciences, 1,* 568–570.

Dunn, J., Brown, J., Slomkowski, C., Tesla, C., & Youngblade, L. (1991). Young children's understanding of other people's feelings and beliefs: Individual differences and their antecedents. *Child Development, 62,* 1352–1366.

Dunn, J., Cutting, A. L., & Demetriou, H. (2000). Moral sensibility, understanding others, and children's friendship interactions in the preschool period. *British Journal of Developmental Psychology, 18,* 159–177.

Eisenmajer, R., & Prior, M. (1991). Cognitive and linguistic correlates of theory of mind ability in autistic children. *British Journal of Developmental Psychology, 9,* 351–364.

Frye, D., Zelazo, P., & Palfai, T. (1995). Theory of mind and rule-based reasoning. *Cognitive Development, 10,* 483–527.

Gopnik, A., Slaughter, V., & Meltzoff, A. (1994). Changing your views: How understanding visual perception can lead to a new theory of mind. In C. Lewis & P. Mitchell (Eds.), *Origins of a theory of mind* (pp. 157–182). Hillsdale, NJ: Lawrence Erlbaum Associates.

Hala, S., Chandler, M., & Fritz, A. (1991). Fledgling theories of mind: Deception as a marker of 3-year-olds' understanding of false belief. *Child Development, 61,* 83–97.

Happé, F. G. (1994). An advanced test of theory of mind. Understanding of story characters thoughts and feelings by able autistic mentally handicapped, and normal children and adults. *Journal of Autism Developmental Disorders, 24,* 129–154.

Happé, F. (1995). The role of age and verbal ability in the theory of mind task performance of subjects with autism. *Child Development, 66,* 843–855.

Happé, F., & Frith, U. (1996). Theory of mind and social impairment in children with conduct disorder. *British Journal of Developmental Psychology, 14,* 385–398.

Holmes, H. A., Black, C., & Miller, S.A. (1996). A cross-task comparison of false belief understanding in a head start population. *Journal of Experimental Child Psychology, 63,* 263–285.

Hughes, C. (1998). Executive function in preschoolers: Links with theory of mind and verbal ability. *British Journal of Developmental Psychology, 16,* 233–253.

Hughes, C., Adlam, A., Happé, F., Jackson, J., Taylor, A., & Caspi, A. (2000). Good test-retest reliability for standard and advanced false-belief tasks across a wide range of abilities. *Journal of Child Psychology and Psychiatry, 41,* 483–490.

Hughes, C., & Cutting, A. (1999). Nature, nurture and individual differences in early understanding of mind. *Psychological Science, 10,* 429–432.

Hughes, C., Deater-Deckard, K., & Cutting, A. L. (1999). "Speak roughly to your little boy?" Sex differences in the relations between parenting and preschoolers' understanding of mind. *Social Development, 8,* 143–159.

Hughes, C., Dunn, J., & White, A. (1998). Trick or treat?: Uneven understanding of mind and emotion and executive function among "hard to manage" preschoolers. *Journal of Child Psychology and Psychiatry, 39,* 981–994.

Jenkins, J., & Astington, J. W. (1996). Cognitive factors and family structure associated with theory of mind development in young children. *Developmental Psychology, 32,* 70–78.

Kaland, N., Moller-Nielsen, A., Callesen, K., Mortensen, E., Gottlieb, D., & Smith, L. (2002). A new "advanced" test of theory of mind: Evidence from children and adolescents with Asperger syndrome. *Journal of Child Psychology and Psychiatry and Allied Disciplines, 43,* 517–528.

Lalonde, C. E., & Chandler, M. J. (1995). False belief understanding goes to school: On the social-emotional consequences of coming early or late to a first theory of mind. *Cognition and Emotion, 9,* 167–185.

Leslie, A. (2000). How to acquire a "representational theory of mind." In D. Sperber (Ed.), *Metarepresentations: A multi-disciplinary perspective* (pp. 197–223). Oxford: Oxford University Press.

McCrae, R., & Costa, P. (1997). Personality trait structure as a human universal. *American Psychologist, 52*, 509–516.

Mealey, L. (1995). The socio-biology of sociopathy: An integrated evolutionary model. *Behavioral and Brain Sciences, 18*, 523–541.

Meins, E. (1997). *Security of attachment and the social development of cognition.* Hove, UK: Psychology Press.

Meins, E., Fernyhough, C., Russell, J., & Clark-Carter, D. (1998). Security of attachment as a predictor of symbolic and mentalising abilities: A longitudinal study. *Social Development, 7*, 1–24.

Meins, E., Fernyhough, C., Wainwright, Gupta, Fradley, & Tuckey, M. (2002). Maternal mind-mindedness and attachment security as predictors of theory of mind understanding. *Child Development, 73*, 1715–1726.

O'Connor, T. G., & Hirsch, N. (1999). Intraindividual differences and relationship-specificity of mentalising in early adolescence. *Social Development, 8*, 256–274.

Perner, J., & Lang, B. (1999). Development of theory of mind and executive control. *Trends in Cognitive Sciences, 3*, 337–344.

Perner, J., Ruffman, T., & Leekam, S. R. (1994). Theory of mind is contagious: You catch it from your sibs. *Child Development, 65*, 1228–1238.

Perner, J., & Wimmer, H. (1985). John thinks that Mary thinks that: Attribution of second order beliefs by 5-year-old to 10-year-old children. *Journal of Experimental Child Psychology, 39*, 437–471.

Peterson, C. C., & Siegal, M. (2002). Mindreading and moral awareness in popular and rejected preschoolers. *British Journal of Developmental Psychology, 20*, 205–224.

Ruffman, T., Perner, J., & Parkin, L. (1999). How parenting style affects false belief understanding. *Social Development, 8*, 395–411.

Ruffman, T., Perner, J., Naito, M., Parkin, L., & Clements, W. (1998). Older (but not younger) siblings facilitate false belief understanding. *Developmental Psychology, 34*, 171–171.

Rutherford, M., Baron-Cohen S., & Wheelwright, S. (2002). Reading the mind in the voice: A study with normal adults and adults with Asperger syndrome and high functioning autism. *Journal of Autism and Developmental Disorders, 32*, 189–194.

Siegal, M. (1997). *Knowing children: Experiments in conversation and cognition* (2nd ed.). Hove, UK: Lawrence Erlbaum Associates.

Spatz, J., & Cassidy, K. (1999, April). *Theory of mind and prosocial behaviour in preschool children.* Poster presented at the Biennial Meeting of the Society for Research in Child Development, Albuquerque, NM.

Suddendorf, T., & Fletcher-Flinn, C.M. (1999). Children's divergent thinking improves when they understand false beliefs. *Creativity Research Journal, 12*, 115–128.

Sutton, J., Smith, P., & Swettenham, J. (1999). Social cognition and bullying: Social inadequacy or skilled manipulation? *British Journal of Developmental Psychology, 17*, 435–450.

Symons, D. K., & Clark, S. E. (2000). A longitudinal study of mother–child relationships and theory of mind in the preschool period. *Social Development, 9*, 3–23.

Taylor, M., & Carlson, S. (1997). The relation between individual differences in fantasy and theory of mind. *Child Development, 68*, 436–455.

Vinden, P. (1997, April). *Parenting and theory of mind.* Paper presented at the Biennial Meeting of the Society for Research in Child Development, Washington DC.

Wellman, H. (1990). *The child's theory of mind.* Cambridge, MA: MIT Press.

Wellman, H., Cross, D., & Watson, J. (2001). Meta-analysis of theory of mind development: The truth about false belief. *Child Development, 72*, 655–684.

Wimmer, H., & Perner, J. (1983) Beliefs about beliefs: Representation and constraining function of wrong beliefs in young children's understanding of deception. *Cognition, 13*, 103–128.

2

Sometimes Necessary, Never Sufficient

False-Belief Understanding and Social Competence

JANET WILDE ASTINGTON

University of Toronto

*I*n this chapter I address the question of whether a theory of mind, in particular false-belief understanding, is needed for socially competent interaction. First, I discuss theory of mind and social functioning, and consider the paradoxical relation between children's everyday behavior and their laboratory task performance. Second, I review research literature addressing the issue of relations between false-belief understanding and social competence. Third, I present findings pertinent to this issue from research conducted by my collaborators and myself. Fourth and finally, I attempt to resolve the paradox in light of the research findings.

THEORY OF MIND AND SOCIAL FUNCTIONING

Theory of mind has been a lively area of research in developmental psychology for the last 20 years or so but, surprisingly, the topic of its relation to social development has only recently come to the fore. Nonetheless, even early on, it was acknowledged as an important issue. In a 1988 workshop convened at Yale University to consider the implications of theory of mind development, the organizers argued that "a theory of mind, is firstly and most obviously, a powerful social tool. It allows the explanation, prediction, and manipulation of the behavior of others" (Moore & Frye, 1991, pp. 2–3). However, they went on to say, "secondly, acquiring a theory of mind may well be instrumental in the development of particular forms of reasoning and, as such, may represent a significant step in cognitive development" (Moore & Frye, 1991, pp. 2–3). It is noteworthy that it is this second item that has been primary on the research agenda for a majority of the field, at least until recently. Nonetheless, almost from the start of investigation in this area, it was apparent that the social consequences of theory of mind development are striking in their absence, as suggested by studies of children with autism (Baron-Cohen, Leslie, & Frith, 1985). It is only more recently, however, that the field has turned its attention to the social consequences of theory of mind development in the lives of typically developing children. Yet this is not to suggest that no one was investigating the issue earlier on, as will soon become apparent.

Theory of mind is a broad term, referring to the intentional stance (Dennett, 1987) that characterizes human social interaction. We attribute intentional states (i.e., mental states) to other people in order to interpret their behavior. Various mental states all have importance within the theory—for example, perception, attention, belief, desire, intention, emotion, and more. The core of the theory is that we assume that people's actions are motivated by their desires in light of their beliefs. However, this is by no means all that there is to it. Desires influence beliefs, as do attention, perception, and emotion; in addition, desires are themselves influenced by emotions and beliefs, and beliefs and desires influence intention, and so on. That is to say, a theory of mind has to take into account an interconnected network of mental states. It might seem obvious that understanding this interconnected network is fundamental to social functioning. Without it, we would not be able to interpret the actions of our fellow humans, or rather, we would be left trying to understand them by considering their physical movements and the outcomes they cause, and we would be left trying to understand the literal meaning of everything they say. Thus, it seems obvious that a theory of mind is fundamental to social functioning. However, seeming obvious is one thing—showing it to be true is something else, and much more difficult.

THE PROBLEM: A PARADOX

Despite the fact that many researchers have only recently begun to consider the social consequences of theory of mind development, others have long focused on this issue. Dunn's (e.g., 1988) work is an obvious and important example. At the Yale meeting mentioned earlier, Dunn pointed to a paradox that is at the heart of the issue. It is this: Babies and toddlers are fundamentally social creatures, who are tuned in to other people and seemingly well aware of other people's behavior and emotional reactions. Yet until the end of the preschool years, children typically fail experimental tasks that are designed to assess their understanding of another person's point of view. "This growing sophistication about the social world, documented in babies who have hardly begun to talk, stands in notable contrast to the limitations in much older children's understanding of other minds, which have been revealed by experimental research" (Dunn, 1991, p. 98).

Possible Solutions

How should the paradox be resolved? It is nothing so simple as the problem of comparing naturalistic and experimental observations, although one should keep that particular problem in mind while considering the more fundamental issues. A possible response is to say that there is no real paradox, but rather, that there just appears to be one because of the multifaceted nature of theory of mind understanding—the network referred to earlier—and the fact that naturalistic and experimental observations are focusing on different aspects of this network. This argument has some substance to it. The primary focus of Dunn's (1988, 1991) observations is on children's understanding of, and talk about, other people's motives and emotions, not their beliefs and mistakes, whereas in the experimental work, it is children's understanding of false belief that shows the clearest developmental change between 3 and 5 years of age. In the classic false-belief task (Wimmer & Perner, 1983), the child has to predict where someone will look for an object when the child, but not the other person, has seen it moved to a new location. In another frequently used task (Perner, Leekam, & Wimmer, 1987) the child has to predict what someone will say is inside a familiar container, such as a candy box, when the child knows that the box contains pencils, but the other person has not yet seen inside the box. It is not until about age 4 that children can take the perspective of the ignorant or misinformed other person and correctly predict what they will do or say.

However, the children who fail false-belief tests do not have a problem with other kinds of perspective taking. They can take another person's perspective in the case of desires and emotions. For example, in experimental tasks similar in form to false-belief tasks, older 2- and 3-year-old children can predict that another person will act to get what he or she wants, even when it is different from what the children themselves might want (Wellman & Woolley, 1990). Moreover, they can recognize how someone will feel, in cases where that person's desire is either satisfied or not satisfied (Wellman & Banerjee, 1991). Such young children can also recognize how someone will feel even in a situation where they would probably feel different (Denham, 1986). More strikingly, toddlers only 18 months of age can recognize that someone might want something that they themselves do not want and will give it to them in a forced-choice task situation (Repacholi & Gopnik, 1997).

Thus, 2- and 3-year-olds are successful in experimental tasks assessing their understanding of desire and emotion, and these appear to be the mental states that they are most aware of in everyday life. However, these 3-year-old children fail false-belief tasks and in everyday life they do not think about other people's knowledge and beliefs, or so the argument goes. Thus, it is claimed that 3-year-olds cannot keep secrets, play tricks, tell lies, and so on (Perner, 1991; Peskin & Ardino, in press; Sodian, 1994). Lying is deliberately deceiving someone, deliberately creating a false belief in another, and without understanding false belief, it would seem that this could not be achieved. Perner (1991, pp. 192–193) dismissed examples of lying in 3-year-olds as "pseudo-lies," that is, routines that children use to get what they want or to avoid what they do not want. He argued that these "lies" are not the intentional manipulation of another person's beliefs—because children do not have the ability to perform such manipulations until they are old enough to pass false-belief tests. There seems to be a certain circularity in this argument, although it does appear to resolve the paradox. However, I do not think that it is the solution we seek.

Deception and False Belief

For one thing, even though Dunn (1988) focused on motives and emotions in examining 2-year-olds' interactions with their mothers and siblings, there is some discussion of such young children's excuses, deceits, evasions, and tricks. That is, there is evidence that children much younger than 4 years of age do take an interest in what others know and do not know. Further, there is evidence from natural language production that children talk about what people think, know, guess, and so on before the age at which they are typically able to pass false-belief tests (Bartsch & Wellman, 1995; Bretherton, 1991). Moreover, these are not data from a few precocious individuals who talk about mental states early on, and who might well have passed the false-belief test if one had been given to them; nor is it merely mindless imitative usage (Astington, 2000).

A recent study provided even more striking evidence that illustrates the paradoxical nature of young children's competent social interactions and their incompetent false-belief task performance (Newton, Reddy, & Bull, 2000). The study explicitly compares children's false-belief task performance with deceptive behavior naturalistically observed. In this longitudinal study, the children ($n = 24$) ranged in age from young 3-year-olds to young 4-year-olds at the start of the investigation. There were three periods of observation, each 1 month long, at the beginning, middle, and end of a 7-month time-span. Mothers, following careful instructions, kept notes of their child's deceptive behaviors for each of the observation periods. The families were visited twice during each of the three periods. In these visits, mothers were interviewed to discuss their diary records and the children were given two false-belief tests (i.e., 12 in all). Thus, the data to be compared are mothers' records of apparent deception and children's false-belief scores across a 7-month period. Three groups of children were formed: Failers, who passed none or just one of the false-belief tasks during the 7-month period; Passers, who passed 10 or more of these tasks; and Developers, children who moved up at least two points on their false-belief test score from one time period to the next.

The striking findings in this study are the range of forms, and the frequency of occurrence of deceptive behavior shown by all children in all three groups, not just those who passed the false belief tasks. The children all denied doing things that they had in fact done, frequently in response to a question asking if they had done it or asking who had done it. However, many other deceptions were produced, not in response to a question or accusation, but as genuinely spontaneous acts, such as false excuses, produced in an attempt to avoid an unwanted outcome or to bring about a desired one. All but one child made such false excuses. A slightly less frequent but still common form of spontaneous deception involved tricking, seemingly designed to amuse, but still attempting at the beginning of the episode to conceal the fact that it was a trick. Again, children in all three groups were reported to engage in such trickery. Further, there was no evidence that those who failed the false-belief tasks were just engaging in learned deceptive routines. In sum, the overall finding was a complete lack of any relation between false-belief understanding and the form or frequency of deceptive behavior. These findings strongly suggest that the paradox stands. Children's experimental task performance is not reflected in their social interaction naturalistically observed.

NARROWING THE FOCUS: FALSE-BELIEF UNDERSTANDING AND SOCIAL COMPETENCE

My attack on the problem that the paradox raises will be to focus on typically developing children's false-belief understanding and to consider whether the development of this understanding has any bearing on their social competence. I focus on false-belief understanding for the following reasons. First, the paradox referred to is highlighted when we consider false-belief task performance and everyday deceptive behavior, as in the Newton et al. (2000) study. Second, false-belief understanding is central to theory of mind development, and it has a well-documented developmental history. Third, and most important, there is a huge body of research investigating children's understanding of false belief, and false-belief tasks are frequently used in studies that investigate the link between theory of mind and social functioning.

Research Relating False-Belief Understanding to Social Competence

Newton et al. (2000) notwithstanding, there are some suggestions in the literature that some aspects of children's social functioning are related to their theory of mind development when this is assessed using false-belief tasks. I have already mentioned the case of children with autism, whose social development is unlike that of typically developing children, and who have great difficulty understanding false belief (Baron-Cohen et al., 1985). However, some children with autism do pass false-belief tasks, usually at an age older than 4 years. Frith, Happé, and Siddons (1994) examined the relation between false-belief task performance and real-life social behavior, assessed by caregivers using the Vineland Adaptive Behavior Scale (VABS; Sparrow, Bala, & Cichetti, 1984). The VABS was supplemented with additional items to distinguish between learned social routines and insightful behavior that requires thought about another person's mental states. Three groups were tested: 7- to 19-year-olds with autism, 7- to 10-year-old learning-disabled children, and typically developing 4-year-olds. For the autistic individuals, but not for the other two groups, there was a relation between false-belief understanding and social behavior. That is, only those autistic individuals who passed false-belief tasks showed the insightful behaviors whereas those who failed false-belief tasks did not, even though they were capable of routine social behavior. Importantly, and this is a point I pursue later in the chapter, those who understood false belief and showed the insightful behaviors had better verbal ability. Another study (Fombonne, Siddons, Achard, & Frith, 1994) produced similar results—that is, there was a relation between false-belief task performance and insightful social behavior in individuals with autism. However, in this study, the relation was no longer significant when language ability was controlled.

My focus is on typically developing children's false-belief understanding and its relation to their social competence. It is worth noting that Frith et al. (1994) found no relation between false-belief task performance and social behavior in typically developing 4-year-olds. However, Lalonde and Chandler (1995) did find such a relation using a similar type of questionnaire based on the VABS and the Portage Checklist (Bluma, Shearer, Frohman, & Hilliard, 1976). In a sample of forty 3-year-olds, false-belief task performance was related to teacher ratings of social behavior that required thought about another person's mental states, but it was not related to ratings of conventionally appropriate behaviors. This is an important pioneering investigation, although with shortcomings that I discuss later when describing an attempt to replicate it. One limitation is that both false-belief task performance and social behavior ratings were related to age, but age was not controlled for. Of course, age is only a proxy for some maturational variable, perhaps language, which is known to play an important role in the development of false-belief understanding (Astington & Jenkins, 1999) and also in competent social behavior (Duck, 1989). Nonetheless, there is some evidence from other studies that false-belief understanding and social competence are related even when differences due to age and language ability are taken into account (Watson, Nixon, Wilson, & Capage, 1999). In a study of fifty-two 3- to 6-year-olds, Watson et al. found that false-belief understanding was related to teacher ratings of social skills (using Harter's [1979] Perceived Competence Scale for Children) even when age and language ability were controlled. However, false belief did not relate, independently of language, to teacher ratings of children's popularity.

Dunn's Research on Children's Relationships

By far the most comprehensive investigation of the relation between social competence and theory of mind development is found in a number of longitudinal studies conducted by Judy Dunn and her colleagues in Pennsylvania and in London. In their entirety, these studies provide an extensive set of findings on contemporaneous relations among various aspects of theory of mind development and social behavior, as well as richly informative accounts of the antecedents and sequelae of development in the two domains. The samples recruited for these studies reflect the importance Dunn ascribes to studying how theory of mind and its relation to behavior actually affects children's social relationships (Dunn, 1996). The Pennsylvanian children were all second-born, studied in interaction with their older siblings, as well as with their mothers and friends. In the London studies, children were recruited as pairs of close friends; the nature of their friendship is an important focus of the investigation.

The Pennsylvania Study of Social Understanding. Fifty children were followed from toddlerhood (mean age = 2-9 [years-months]) to first grade (mean age = 6-3), with three intermediate data collection points at 3-4, 3-11, and 5-8 (Dunn, 1998). In this study, children's emotion understanding was assessed more comprehensively than their belief understanding. To assess belief understanding at 3-4, children were asked both to predict and to explain a puppet's false belief (as in Bartsch & Wellman, 1989). In the prediction task, the child is shown two boxes: for instance, an empty Band-Aids box and a plain box with Band-Aids inside. An injured puppet appears. The child is told he wants a Band-Aid, and is then asked where the puppet will look for Band-Aids. In the explanation version of the task, rather than asking the child where the puppet will look, the experimenter walks the puppet toward the empty Band-Aids box and starts to open it, and then asks the child why the puppet is looking in there. The child might respond correctly that the puppet thinks the box has Band-Aids in it, but is more likely to say, not incorrectly, that he wants a Band-Aid. The experimenter then prompts, "What does he think?" All children failed the prediction task, so the data used are their responses, prompted or not, in the explanation task. This is somewhat controversial—the task is sometimes regarded as an inadequate measure of children's false-belief understanding (Perner, 1991, pp. 309–310). However, I think it is fair to say that it is a measure of nascent, albeit scaffolded (Astington, 1996), understanding of belief in young 3-year-olds.

At 3-11, the children were given two simplified false-belief prediction tasks,

in which they were told where an object is located and also that a story character who wants the object thinks it is in a different location. Children were then
asked where the character would look for the object (Wellman & Bartsch, 1988).
In addition to assessing children's belief understanding, the following measures
were also used over the five test periods: emotion-understanding task (Denham,
1986), understanding of conflicting-emotions task (based on Gordis, Rosen, &
Grand, 1989), moral-sensibilities task (Kochanska, 1991), and response to teacher
criticism task (Heyman, Dweck, & Cain, 1992). The children were also interviewed to determine their perceptions of school, and they were observed at
home and in play with a friend, allowing for assessment of their interaction with
mothers, siblings, and peers.

The complexity of this data set reflects the complexity of the network of
understandings, referred to earlier, that makes up a theory of mind, and allows
for the assessment of complex relations over time. For example, Dunn (1995,
2000) showed that emotion understanding and belief understanding are not
closely related in young 3-year-olds and, further, that there are different sequelae in each domain. Early false-belief understanding predicts sensitivity to
teacher criticism and negative perceptions of school at the time of school entry,
whereas early emotion understanding predicts positive perceptions of school
experiences with peers, and also predicts the understanding of mixed emotions
and moral sensibility. The early understanding of belief in young 3-year-olds
was also related to connected communication with friends at age 4 (Slomkowski
& Dunn, 1996), more frequent self-disclosure in conversation with friends at
age 6, and more frequent pretend play with friends at age 6 (Maguire & Dunn,
1997). In addition, false-belief understanding assessed as the children were turning 4 was related to conflict resolution strategies 2 years later. That is to say,
children who passed the false-belief tasks at age 4 were more likely at age 6 to
request clarification of another's point of view, and to use distraction strategies
in trying to settle an argument (Dunn & Herrera, 1997).

The London Studies. There are three longitudinal studies conducted in
London by Dunn and her colleagues, and false-belief understanding is much
more comprehensively assessed in these studies. The first is a longitudinal study
of 50 children, recruited as 25 pairs of friends, observed and assessed when
they were 4, 4-6, and 5 years of age. At each time point, children were given a
battery of theory-of-mind tasks, including four standard false-belief prediction
tasks, three false-belief explanation tasks, two deception tasks, and a task that
required predicting emotion based on false belief (Harris, Johnson, Hutton,
Andrews, & Cooke, 1989). Emotion understanding was also assessed at each
time point, and pairs of friends were videotaped as they played together.

A finding from this study relevant to the issue of the social implications of
theory of mind development is that, although there were no gender differences
in performance on the theory of mind battery (understanding belief and emo-

tion), girls showed more frequent and more developed talk about mental states than did boys when playing with friends. "This suggests that although laboratory tasks provide a quick method of assessing children's social insight, they are less likely to prove especially sensitive to individual differences in how children apply their understanding of mind to the everyday social world" (Hughes & Dunn, 1998, p. 1035). One important difference in this study's findings from those in the Pennsylvania study is that belief understanding and emotion understanding were closely related (Dunn & Hughes, 1998; Hughes & Dunn, 1998). The difference may be due to the fact that belief understanding was more comprehensively assessed in the present study, yielding a broad range of scores in comparison to 0/1 in the Pennsylvania study.

The second and third London studies are parallel longitudinal investigations, following children from 4 to 6 years of age, across the transition to school. One study involves 128 typically developing children (64 pairs of friends) from a range of social-class backgrounds (Cutting & Dunn, 1999), whereas the other employs similar measures to assess the development of a group of 40 children with behavioral problems (Hughes, Dunn, & White, 1998). Again, an enormously rich set of data was collected over the period of investigation: observations at home and at school; interviews with teachers and parents; videotaped sessions with the friend pairs playing together; and experimental task performance assessed individually. Again, in these studies, false-belief understanding was comprehensively assessed. At age 4, the battery included an unexpected identity task that required memory for one's own false belief and prediction of another's false belief; unexpected location tasks that required prediction and explanation of a puppet's actions; an emotion false-belief prediction task (Harris et al., 1989) for both a nice and a nasty surprise; and a verbal and nonverbal deception task. At age 6, second-order false-belief tasks were used (Perner & Wimmer, 1985), assessing awareness of the possibility of false belief about another person's belief. In addition, emotion-understanding tasks, moral-sensibility tasks, executive-function tasks, and language assessments were administered.

In the study of typically developing children (Cutting & Dunn, 1999), their understanding of belief was related to emotion understanding, as in the study by Hughes and Dunn (1998) that was just reported. However, in Cutting and Dunn's study, the relation between the two domains was not independent of age, language ability, and family background. This fact, like the finding in the Pennsylvania study that the long-term sequelae of belief and emotion understanding are different, illustrates the importance of treating false belief and emotion understanding as separate aspects of theory of mind development.

Children's false-belief understanding was related to various aspects of their interaction with a friend in the videotaped play sessions (Dunn & Cutting, 1999). It was positively related to frequency of shared pretend play and total amount of talk between the friends, and negatively related to conflict between the friends and failures in communication. That is, "those who frequently created make-believe worlds together were less likely to quarrel, or to fail in communication with each other" (Dunn & Cutting, 1999, p. 215). Although not all the relations with false belief were independent of emotion understanding and language ability, false-belief understanding was clearly related to the quality of the friendship.

Children's moral sensibility was assessed by their judgment of whether trangressions, such as excluding a friend from play, were permissible or not, and their justifications for their responses (Dunn, Cutting, & Demetriou, 2000). False-belief understanding was related both to more sophisticated moral judgments and to more sophisticated justifications, although for judgments, this was not independent of emotion understanding and language ability. Interestingly, for boys' justifications, false-belief understanding contributed independently of these other variables, whereas for girls, it was emotion understanding that made an independent contribution to the sophistication of their moral justifications.

As mentioned, the same measures that were used to assess the typically developing children were also administered in a longitudinal study to 40 children who were diagnosed as "hard-to-manage" (using Goodman's [1994] Strengths and Difficulties Questionnaire), and at risk for attention-deficit hyperactivity disorder (ADHD) and other conduct disorder problems in the early school years (Hughes, Cutting, & Dunn, 2001; Hughes & Dunn, 2000; Hughes et al., 1998; Hughes, White, Sharpen, & Dunn, 2000). It has long been known that school-age children with conduct disorder are more likely to mistakenly attribute hostile intentions to others and to respond inappropriately in a hostile manner (Dodge, 1980). Further and more recently, Happé and Frith (1996) assessed a sample of such children, using similar measures as in the Frith et al. (1994) study, and suggested that the children's theory of mind, although intact, may be skewed toward antisocial understanding. The London "hard-to-manage" study, conducted by Hughes and Dunn, made a tremendous contribution to this area by identifying preschool children who are at risk for behavioral problems in the school years, assessing multiple aspects of their cognition and behavior, and following them across the transition to school. However, I do not explore the rich set of findings from this study, partly because my focus is on typically developing children's false-belief understanding and its relation to their social competence, and also because other contributors to the present volume (e.g., Sutton) take up the topic in much more detail.

An important finding that emerges from all of the studies, conducted in Pennsylvania and in London, concerns the complexity of the relations between theory of mind and social behavior over time. That is, it is not simply the case that variability in theory of mind task performance is associated with later variability in measures of social behavior. There are also relations between earlier assessments of social behavior and later assessment of theory of mind. That is, not only does theory of mind have implications for social behavior, but reciprocally, interactions in the social world provide a context in which theory of mind skills are developed. These interactions are within the family and with peers, and involve such experiences as engaging in pretend play, talking about inner states, constructing collaborative narratives, arguing about disagreements, and being exposed to and engaging in deception (Dunn, 2000). It is likely that there are bidirectional causal effects, that is, reciprocal bootstrapping interactions between social understanding and social competence as development proceeds.

A second important finding is that the relation between children's theory of mind and their social behavior varies across their different relationships. The way in which children use their understanding of mind to talk about mental states, to engage in pretend play, and to settle arguments differs depending on whether they are interacting with mother, sibling, or friend (Dunn, 1996). "The key point suggested by these findings is that whether children use their understanding of other people's inner states depends on the nature of their relationship with the other" (Dunn, 2000, p. 143). This differential use of understanding adds a further complexity to the already complex relation between theory of mind and social behavior (see Keenan, this volume, for further discussion of intraindividual differences).

FALSE BELIEF, LANGUAGE, AND SOCIAL COMPETENCE

In this section, I report research conducted in Toronto over the past decade in collaboration with Jennifer Jenkins, Janette Pelletier, and Trudy James. My initial interest, inspired by Jenkins, was to investigate the real-world consequences of theory of mind development. Partly because of the findings from our research (Astington & Jenkins, 1999; Jenkins & Astington, 1996), my subsequent and current interest is in the fundamental role that language plays in theory of mind development and in social functioning.

False-Belief Understanding and Social Behavior

In a cross-sectional study involving sixty-eight 3- to 5-year-old children (mean age 4-1), we aimed to investigate the impact that understanding false belief might have in their everyday lives (Astington & Jenkins, 1995; Jenkins & Astington, 1996). We employed three different measures to examine possible social correlates of false-belief understanding. First, empathy, popularity, and aggression were assessed using a sociometric rating task (Denham, McKinley, Couchoud, & Holt, 1990). Second, communicative competence was assessed in a referential communication task (Krauss & Glucksberg, 1969). Third, approximately half the sample was videotaped during pretend play in order to measure overall levels of pretending, engagement in role assignment, and carrying out joint planning with other children. In addition, all the children were given four standard false-belief prediction tasks, the Test of Early Language Development (TELD; Hresko, Reid, & Hammill, 1981), and a verbal memory measure (subtest of the Stanford-Binet).

Our plan was to look for differences in the social behaviors of children who did and who did not pass false-belief tasks, given equal language ability. We soon discovered this to be an unworkable aim. We found that false-belief understanding is strongly related to language ability, even when age is controlled for (Jenkins & Astington, 1996). This result has now been replicated many times (e.g., Astington & Jenkins, 1999; Cutting & Dunn, 1999; de Villiers, 2000; Hughes, 1998; Ruffman, Slade, & Crowe, 2002), highlighting the importance of controlling for language ability when investigating links between false-belief understanding and social competence.

Empathy, Popularity, and Aggression. There are suggestions in the literature that false-belief understanding is necessary for certain kinds of cooperative behavior (Moore & Frye, 1991) For instance, we might expect to see a relation between false-belief understanding and altruistic or empathic behaviors, because these kinds of help and comforting seem to depend on the ability to see another's point of view. Children who have this perspective-taking ability might also more likely be popular with others, and less likely to engage in aggressive acts against others. Thus, we hypothesized that false-belief understanding would be positively associated with empathy and popularity, and negatively associated with aggression.

The children were shown photographs of their classmates and asked to pick three they liked to play with, three who fought a lot, and three who were kind when others were sad (Denham et al., 1990). This gave us a measure of each child's popularity, aggressive behavior, and empathy, as rated by their peers. Somewhat to our surprise, we found no relation between these sociometric ratings and children's false-belief task scores. Given Dunn's findings (Cutting & Dunn, 1999; Dunn, 1995, 2000) that children's understanding of beliefs and their understanding of emotions are not necessarily closely related, perhaps we should not have expected a close association between false-belief understanding, which is a cognitive measure, and an affective measure such as empathy. However, Moore (2001) did find such a relation in a study with a large sample ($n = 120$) of 3- and 4-year-olds, although the relation was significant only for the 4-year-old group. Sociometric ratings of empathy and popularity were related to false-belief understanding and also to an experimental measure of altruism (Moore, Barresi, & Thompson, 1998). Possibly the difference between Moore's findings and ours is due to the fact that he had a larger sample size and a broader range of false-belief scores.

On the other hand, perhaps there is no important relation between false-belief understanding and empathy. Children might respond empathically at a behavioral level—for example, by comforting a crying friend without understanding the mental state underlying the friend's behavior and without explicitly taking his or her point of view. That is to say, even very young children may learn social routines, such as, when someone cries, you should comfort them and then they will stop crying. In addition or alternatively, children with a greater understanding of their peers' mental states may not in fact use this understanding to provide comfort. Awareness of others' mental states may also be required to annoy, tease, and deceive others (Moore & Frye, 1991). Furthermore, possessing an understanding of another's mental state is only part of the reason why one might either comfort or annoy. That is, as well as understanding a person's needs, one also has to have the motivation to help or to harm (Moore, 2001). These two, the understanding and the motivation, are not necessarily related.

Communicative Competence. An important part of social competence is the pragmatic ability to communicate effectively (Duck, 1989), which depends in part on being aware of and keeping track of the beliefs and intentions of one's conversational partner. Thus, communicative competence would seem to be necessarily related to theory of mind, and indeed, false-belief task performance was found to be related to scores on a test of pragmatic ability in a sample of children with autism (Eisenmajer & Prior, 1991). In addition, Frith et al. (1994) included items requiring pragmatic skill in their measure of real-life social adaptation and found this to be associated with false-belief task performance in a group of children with autism, but not in comparison groups of typically developing and learning-disabled children. However, in both Dunn's Pennsylvania and London longitudinal studies, false-belief understanding in typically developing children was related to connected and successful communication between friends in a naturalistic play situation (Dunn & Cutting, 1999; Slomkowski & Dunn, 1996).

In our study, we used the traditional referential communication game (Krauss & Glucksberg, 1969; Robinson, 1986) to measure children's communicative competence. In this task, the child and an experimenter each have an identical set of pictures; there is a screen between them so that they can see only their own set. The pictures differ from one another in small details. The child has to choose a picture without showing it to the experimenter and describe it so that she can pick exactly the same one from her set. This task has frequently been used as a measure of communicative competence because the child has to realize that the experimenter cannot see the picture and will not know how to make a match unless given a precise description. Children received a composite score that took account of how informative they were and how much prompting they needed, over three trials. Performance on this task was significantly related to false-belief task scores. Unfortunately, however, the communication task was too easy for our sample and the ceiling on the measure reduced the correlation to the extent that it was not significant after controlling for age and general language ability (using TELD scores). However, after excluding those children who performed at ceiling, 53 children remained and their communicative competence was significantly related to false-belief understanding, controlling for both age and general language ability.

Recently, James (2001) adapted this standard referential communication paradigm to devise a task that is more like a natural conversation and more motivating for child participants. James's task resembles a real-world communication episode where a child is giving information to a person in another room. In her task, children were required to choose stickers and then describe them, in order to receive a set for themselves from an experimenter in an adjacent office cubicle. Pairs of stickers, which shared three attributes and differed on one, were shown to the children by a second experimenter in a series of four trials. For successful communication, children needed to keep in mind that the experimenter in the next room was looking at the same sticker pairs, but did not know exactly which sticker the child had chosen. The children were given neutral prompts, if needed, although they were generally motivated to communicate as much information as possible because they wanted the stickers.

James (2001) administered this modified task to fifty-three 3- and 4-year-olds, along with three false-belief tasks, the Peabody Picture Vocabulary Test (Dunn & Dunn, 1981), and the traditional referential communication task just described. After controlling for age and language, she found that children's false-belief understanding was related to their performance on the new task. That is, children who passed the false-belief tasks were more likely to communicate critical referent information to the experimenter in the other room. However, there was no relation between false-belief task scores and performance on the traditional referential communication task, after controlling for age and language. This suggests that one not only needs the cognitive competence provided by the development of false-belief understanding, but one also needs the motivation to employ that competence in an experimental task situation.

Pretend Play, Joint Plans, and Role Assignments. The third aspect of children's social behavior that we investigated in the cross-sectional study was pretend play (Astington & Jenkins, 1995). A relation between false belief and pretence has often been proposed, although for a variety of different reasons (Harris, 1991; Leslie, 1988; Lillard, 1993; Perner, Baker, & Hutton, 1994), and indeed Dunn's studies revealed a relation between false-belief understanding and the frequency of pretend play (Dunn & Cutting, 1999; Maguire & Dunn, 1997). We hypothesized that high levels of engagement in pretend play would be related to false-belief understanding. Further, we hypothesized that particular aspects of pretend play would be associated with this understanding—specifically, making joint plans and assigning roles to the self and others. Pretend play takes place in an imaginative hypothetical world. Children who understand false belief are more likely to be aware that their own thoughts about this pretend world may be different from those of their friends. They would therefore see the need to make their version of the pretend world explicit, and thus would be more likely to offer explicit joint plans and to assign roles explicitly to the self or to another child.

Thirty of the children in the cross-sectional study were videotaped in groups of three or four as they played in the house center in their daycare or nursery. The videotapes were transcribed and the frequency of pretend play turns and frequency of turns involving joint plans or role assignments were coded for each child (see Astington & Jenkins, 1995). We found no relation between false-belief task performance and frequency of pretend play, but we did find relations, independent of age and language ability, between false-belief task performance and the two specific measures: assigning roles to self and other, and making joint plans for the play.

To summarize, these studies showed that empathy, popularity, aggression, and frequency of pretend play were not related to false-belief understanding. However, role assignment and joint planning in pretend play, and communicative competence in a modified referential communication task, were related to false-belief understanding, independent of age and language ability. These latter three behaviors have in common the need to consider the ambiguity of a situation, and to recognize that others do not necessarily know what you are thinking, and therefore need you to communicate this information to them.

Longitudinal Investigation of Relations. In a follow-up study (Astington & Jenkins, 1999; Jenkins & Astington, 2000), we investigated relations over time among false belief, language, and social behaviors in pretend play. Our aim was to investigate causal directions in the correlations we had found in the cross-sectional study. We gave false-belief and language tests (TELD) to 3-year-old children, and videotaped their pretend play, at the start, midpoint, and end of a 7-month period. We found that earlier language scores predicted later false-belief understanding, controlling for earlier false belief, but that earlier false-belief scores did not predict later language ability, controlling for earlier language ability. We also found that earlier false-belief scores predicted later role assignment frequency (controlling for earlier role assignment, age and language), but earlier role assignment frequency did not predict later false-belief understanding. Similarly, earlier false-belief scores predicted later joint planning frequency (controlling for earlier joint planning, age and language), but earlier joint planning frequency did not predict later false-belief understanding. These findings support, although they do not prove, two causal arguments. First, language is causally related to the development of false-belief understanding. Second, independent of language ability, the development of false-belief understanding is causally related to behaviors that help to disambiguate the play situation; that is, joint plans and role assignments. This second finding is important for two reasons. It shows that the development of false-belief understanding is more than a change in language ability, and furthermore, the development of false-belief understanding brings about changes in real-world behavior.

False-Belief Understanding and Success in School

A subsequent longitudinal study, conducted in collaboration with Janette Pelletier and Trudy James, aimed to explore the relations among children's theory of mind, metacognitive language abilities, and school performance, controlling for general language ability and family background, in order to determine whether children's understanding of mind makes a difference to their success in school (Astington & Pelletier, 1997; James, Astington, & Pelletier, 2000; Pelletier & Astington, 1999). Academic and social competence are both important to children's school success. Given the focus of the present chapter, I summarize only our findings on relations between children's false-belief task performance and their social behavior.

We followed two groups of children, 74 in total, for 2 years during the transition to school. At the start of the project, the mean age of the younger group was 4-4 and that of the older group was 5-4. Children were tested once each term over the 2 years (i.e., six times in all) on a variety of measures. Most relevant here are the false-belief tests given at the start of the first year and second-order false-belief tests given at the end of the second year. Children also completed a story retelling task in the middle of the second year, which assessed their metacognitive language production. In addition, their general language ability was measured using the TELD (Hresko et al., 1981) at the start of each year.

First Teacher Rating of Social Behavior. In the middle of the first year of the project, we used Lalonde and Chandler's (1995) rating scale to assess the children's social competence. This is a 40-item questionnaire that asks teachers to rate children as "never," "sometimes," or "usually" displaying each behavioral item. As mentioned earlier, Lalonde and Chandler found that false-belief task performance was significantly related to total score on the questionnaire in a sample of 3-year-olds ($n = 40$). However, false belief was also correlated with age, and the age-partialed correlation is not given. In our sample of seventy-four 4- to 5-year-olds, false-belief task performance was significantly related to social competence, controlling for age. However, after controlling for language, the relation was no longer significant.

Lalonde and Chandler divided the 40 items in their questionnaire into two sets: 20 "Social Convention" and 20 "Intentionality" items. The first set of items assesses children's ability to follow social conventions and to control their own impulses. The second set assesses their ability to attend to, recognize, and take into account other people's mental states. Lalonde and Chandler found that false-belief understanding was significantly related to the Intention score but not to the Convention score, although age was not taken into account. They conclude that false-belief understanding relates only to those aspects of social behavior that require understanding others' minds, and not to the ability to behave in a conventionally appropriate manner. Our findings were somewhat different from theirs, although supporting their result. We found that false-belief understanding was significantly related to both the Intention and the Convention scores, but when language ability was controlled for, only the relation with the Intention score was significant.

One concern with Lalonde and Chandler's (1995) measure is the way in which items were assigned to the Intention and Convention categories. The division was made on conceptual grounds by Lalonde and Chandler and confirmed with two other raters. However, our research group disagreed with quite a few of their assignments. We attempted to validate the scale (as in Frith et al., 1994) with adult students who were training as kindergarten and elementary teachers. For each item, we asked them to judge whether it required thinking about other people's point of view—that is, their thoughts, or wants, or feelings, or whether the child could just follow appropriate social conventions. Based on these ratings we again formed two groups of items—Intention and Convention—but excluded 13 items that had low agreement among the raters. This recoding did not map closely onto Lalonde and Chandler's scheme. Even so, we replicated their findings. Before controlling for language ability, both social competence subscales were related to false-belief understanding, but after controlling for language, the relation between false belief and the ability to follow social conventions was no longer significant. However, there was a relation, independent of language ability, between false-belief understanding and aspects of social competence that involve an awareness of others' mental states. This result, like that of Watson et al. (1999), provides clear evidence of a relation between false belief and real-world behavior as judged by classroom teachers.

Second Teacher Rating of Social Behavior. At the end of the second year of the project, the children were in new classes with a different set of teachers, who completed a different rating scale (Cassidy & Asher, 1992), which includes 12 items that can be used to assess children on four behavioral dimensions: prosocial, aggressive, disruptive, and shy/withdrawn. We computed a composite measure of social competence, giving equal weight to social competence items (prosocial) and to social incompetence items (aggressive, disruptive, shy/withdrawn), and counting competence items as positive and incompetence items as negative. A composite false-belief measure was also computed using children's scores on the first-order false-belief tasks given at the start of the first year and the second-order false-belief tasks given at the end of the second year. In addition, we had a measure of children's spontaneous use of metacognitive terms (e.g., think, know, remember) from the story retelling task given in the middle of the second year, and a measure of their general language ability using the TELD (Hresko et al., 1981) at the start of the second year.

In order to assess the contribution of false-belief understanding to social competence, we performed a hierarchical regression analysis with the teacher rating of social competence as the dependent variable. We found that children's social competence at the end of the second year was predicted by their false-belief task performance, controlling for age and language ability. In the regression analysis, age and language ability accounted for 10% of the variance in the teacher rating of social competence and false-belief understanding accounted for an additional unique 8%. Beyond this, however, children's spontaneous production of metacognitive terms in the story retelling task explained an additional 10% of the variance in the social competence scores. It may be that this sort of language makes children appear competent to teachers. More importantly, it may be that metacognitive language helps children integrate first- and third-person perspectives (Astington, 1996), which then contributes to their social competence. Metacognitive language may also play a useful role in resolving conflicts in a manner that socially competent children use (e.g., "He didn't know you thought it was my turn").

When researchers investigate individual differences in false-belief understanding and social competence, they tend to focus on the preschool years, when there is variability in false-belief scores. However, an important question is whether there are consequences of an early understanding of false belief that endure and that are apparent later on, at an age when all children have developed false-belief understanding (Astington, 2001). As noted previously, Dunn's longitudinal studies address this question. We can also address it in the present data set, by examining the relationship between first-order false-belief task performance, assessed at the beginning of the project, and teacher rating of social competence 20 months later. Children who were below ceiling on the first-order false-belief test were retested at subsequent test times until they reached ceiling. At the end of the second year, nine children still did not reach ceiling. By excluding them from the analysis, we can investigate whether there are any consequences of an early understanding of false belief in a group of children who are all now at ceiling on first-order false belief. Hierarchical regression analysis, with the teacher rating of social competence at the end of the second year as the dependent variable, showed that first-order false-belief performance, assessed 20 months earlier, accounts for 9% of the variance in the teacher ratings of social competence, independent of the effects of age and language ability. This is an important finding because it highlights the enduring consequences of earlier development of false-belief understanding.

Children's Own Perceptions of their School Experience. As well as being rated by their teachers at the end of the second year of the project, the children themselves were interviewed by an experimenter whom they had come to know over the 2 years of the project (James et al., 2000). A semistructured interview was developed (based on Donelan-McCall & Dunn, 1997) to tap children's perceptions of schoolwork, teacher–child interaction, and peer relations. The questions were open-ended and children's initial responses were followed up in a conversational manner. Sample questions were: "What do you like about school?"; "What don't you like?"; and "If a new kid came to your class, what would you tell them about what school is like?" Children's responses, both initial and prompted, were coded for affective content, with separate scores for positive (weak/strong), negative (weak/strong), and neutral comments to each question. This distinguishes truly neutral children from those with both positive and negative feelings, and gives a sense of the emotional tone of the child's school experience.

Children's reports of positive experiences were positively related to the contemporaneous measure of false-belief understanding, that is, second-order false belief, independent of language ability. Similarly and reciprocally, their reports of negative experiences were negatively related to second-order false belief, independent of language ability, and also were negatively related to first-order false belief, assessed at the start of the project—again, independent of language ability. Children's reports were also consistent with the teacher ratings of social behavior. That is, children who reported positive school experiences were more likely to be rated socially competent by their teachers, and children who had more negative perceptions of school life were less likely to be judged by teachers as socially competent.

Interestingly, scores from the children's own reports make a contribution to variance in the teacher rating of social competence that is independent of age, language ability, and false-belief understanding. In a hierarchical regression analysis with the teacher rating of social competence as the dependent variable, age and language ability once again account for 10% of the variance in the teacher rating of social competence, and false-belief understanding accounts for an additional 8%. Children's positive or negative interview comments account for an additional 7% of the variance in the teacher rating of social competence. These findings suggest that children may be viewed as accurate reporters of their own experience, because of the coincidence between child and teacher reports. However, it is important to note that these correlations come from one time point and cannot suggest a causal direction. Moreover, the children's positive and negative comments were not significantly related to the ratings made by a different set of teachers at the end of the first year of the project, although they were in the same general direction. This may be because the relations were attenuated over time, or it may be the effect of a specific teacher–child relationship. That is, we cannot say whether children who are happy at school are generally seen as more socially competent than those who are less happy, or whether children whose teachers judge them to be more socially competent are happier at school. It seems obvious anyway that these two factors would be related.

In sum, in this longitudinal study, we showed relations, independent of age and language ability, between children's false-belief understanding (both first- and second-order) and their social competence, judged by two different sets of teachers using two different rating scales. We also showed a relation between false-belief understanding and children's own report of satisfaction or dissatisfaction with their school experience, which included their social relationships with peers and teachers.

TOWARD A RESOLUTION OF THE PARADOX

There is a fundamental assumption underlying all of the research reported in this chapter, which is this: False-belief tests have ecological validity, such that individual differences in false-belief task performance will relate to individual differences in social behavior in the real world. However, the false-belief test situation is quite unlike children's social interaction in the real world, and this fact may help to resolve the paradox introduced at the beginning of the chapter. Nonetheless, first it must be acknowledged that false-belief tests do appear to be ecologically valid—that is, as the research review demonstrates, differences in false-belief understanding do mark real differences in social behavior; false-belief understanding is sometimes needed for competent social performance.

Sometimes Necessary

Although there are some disparities among the studies reported, overall there is clear evidence that false-belief understanding is related to some aspects of social functioning. Briefly, referring back to the research review, these are: communication abilities, as seen in more connected and more informative conversation; imaginative abilities, as seen in more frequent and more sophisticated pretend play (assigning roles and joint planning); ability to resolve conflicts and to maintain harmony and intimacy in friendships; teacher ratings of global social competence (on a variety of rating scales); contentedness in school; and peer-rated empathy and popularity (at least in one study). Importantly, in most if not all cases, these relations are independent of age and language ability. Thus, the findings show that individual differences in false-belief understanding are associated with actual differences in behavior in the social world.

One is tempted to say that it is the development of false-belief understanding that brings about the changes in social behavior. However, much of the evidence for the relation between them is based on correlations among contemporaneous variables, so that claims cannot be made about causal direction. Even when false-belief tests are given earlier in time than the social behaviors that they are related to, one cannot make causal claims with any certainty. Nonetheless, this claim is strengthened by demonstrating that, independent of age and language ability, false-belief understanding contributes to change in the social behavior, by taking into account the earlier level of performance of the behavior (cf. Jenkins & Astington, 2000). The causal claim would be further strengthened by training studies teaching children to understand false belief and showing concomitant changes in targeted social behaviors. Such studies have been conducted, but only—to my knowledge—with autistic children as participants (Hadwin, Baron-Cohen, Howlin, & Hill, 1997; Ozonoff & Miller, 1995). Furthermore, although it is possible to teach false-belief understanding at least to some of these children, its effect on social behavior is much more difficult to achieve.

Never Sufficient

Finally, I turn to the attempt to resolve the paradox introduced at the beginning of the chapter—that is, the discrepancy between preschool children's evident social competence and their incompetent performance on theory of mind tasks, especially those assessing false-belief understanding. Even though we can claim that false-belief tests have ecological validity because differences in false-belief understanding mark real differences in social behavior, it is still important to consider how false-belief tests differ from social behavior in the real world, because this may help to explain the paradox. The false-belief task is imposed by an experimenter who questions the child about unknown others: story characters or puppets. The experimenter formulates the problem, which is clearly defined and may hold little interest for the child. All the information needed is provided in the task, which has a single correct response that the child is asked to produce on his or her own. This is obviously very different from the sort of interactions children engage in and the problems that they encounter in their everyday social lives. Children's real-world social behavior occurs in familiar settings that have huge emotional significance for them. Further, and importantly, social functioning is, by definition, not a solo performance. It occurs in relation to another person, indeed, to various others, such that it may vary across relationships. These facts may help explain why children show competent social behavior alongside incompetent false-belief task performance, and also why, although false-belief understanding is necessary for some social behaviors, it is never sufficient to guarantee the performance of such behavior.

First, social behavior is interactional, and young children's interactions are often with people older than themselves—parents, teachers, older siblings, and so on. Thus, much of young children's social behavior is supported by more competent others. The standard false-belief prediction test is designed to assess an individual child's cognitive abilities. But consider the nonstandard and easier false-belief explanation task (Bartsch & Wellman, 1989): After the child has said that the puppet is looking in an empty Band-Aids box because he wants a Band-Aid, the adult asks, "What does he think?"—it is easy for the child to then reply that the puppet thinks there are Band-Aids in there. From a Vygotskian perspective, the child's performance is "scaffolded" by the adult's leading question

(Astington, 1996). Somewhat similarly, Sullivan and Winner (1993) showed that the standard "smarties" false-belief task is easier if the experimenter and child together play a trick on someone else, perhaps because the emotional involvement in a shared social situation scaffolds the child's performance. It is likely that much real-world social behavior is supported in this way because the child is playing only one part in the social drama.

Second, the fact that emotional involvement in a situation affects performance suggests why knowing that a child understands false belief is not sufficient to explain how that child will behave in a particular social situation. Understanding another's mental state and thus being aware of how to behave toward them is only part of the picture. Beyond that, one also has to have the motivation to act in an appropriate manner. This is seen, for example, in James's (2001) study of communicative competence, where children not only needed the cognitive ability (marked by the development of false-belief understanding) to realize that someone who could not see what they were looking at would not know all of the details, but they also needed the motivation of obtaining stickers for themselves, in order to employ their ability in the experimental situation. Furthermore, emotional understanding is important in addition to emotional involvement. Our finding that empathy was not related to false-belief understanding (Astington & Jenkins, 1995) and Dunn's findings that emotion understanding is different from belief understanding (Cutting & Dunn, 1999; Dunn, 1995) show that understanding cognitive states, such as realizing that someone is ignorant or mistaken, is insufficient to determine how to behave toward the person. One also needs to understand how they feel about the situation.

Conclusion: Theory of Mind, Social Behavior, and Language

There is rapid development in many areas during the preschool period, linked to neurological maturation and social experience. Three of these areas are theory of mind, social behavior, and language, as this chapter illustrates. Theory of mind, at least as assessed by false-belief understanding, is strongly related to language ability (Astington & Jenkins, 1999), and language is undoubtedly important to children's developing social abilities. Thus, as I have emphasized in this chapter, it is important to control for language when investigating relations between false-belief understanding and social behavior. However, I am afraid that partialing language out of the relation is in some ways throwing out the baby with the bath water. In statistical terms, we are discounting the overlapping variance of the three factors, in order to measure the shared variance of false belief and social competence. All well and good, yet the most interesting story may be the one that is to be told in this overlapping area. To my mind, what is most in need of explanation is the fundamental relation between these three aspects of preschool development: theory of mind, social behavior, and language. But that must be left for another time.

ACKNOWLEDGMENTS

I am grateful to my research collaborators Jennifer Jenkins, Janette Pelletier, and Trudy James. I am also grateful to the Natural Sciences and Engineering Research Council of Canada and the Social Sciences and Humanities Research Council of Canada for financial support for the research reported here.

REFERENCES

Astington, J. (1996). What is theoretical about the child's theory of mind? A Vygotskian view of its development. In P. Carruthers & P. K. Smith (Eds.), *Theories of theories of mind* (pp. 184–199). Cambridge, UK: Cambridge University Press.

Astington, J. W. (2000). Language and metalanguage in children's understanding of mind. In J. W. Astington (Ed.), *Minds in the making: Essays in honor of David R. Olson* (pp. 267–284). Oxford, UK: Blackwell.

Astington, J. W. (2001). The future of theory-of-mind research: Understanding motivational states, the role of language, and real-world consequences. *Child Development, 72*, 685–687.

Astington, J. W., & Jenkins, J. M. (1995). Theory of mind and social understanding. *Cognition and Emotion, 9*, 151–165.

Astington, J. W., & Jenkins, J. M. (1999). A longitudinal study of the relation between language and theory of mind development. *Developmental Psychology, 35*, 1311–1320.

Astington, J. W., & Pelletier, J. (1997, April). *Young children's theory of mind and its relation to their success in school*. Paper presented at the Biennial Meeting of the Society for Research in Child Development, Washington, DC.

Baron-Cohen, S., Leslie, A. M., & Frith, U. (1985). Does the autistic child have a "theory of mind"? *Cognition, 21*, 37–46.

Bartsch, K., & Wellman, H. M. (1989). Young children's attribution of action to beliefs and desires. *Child Development, 60*, 946–964.

Bartsch, K., & Wellman, H. M. (1995). *Children talk about the mind*. New York: Oxford University Press.

Bluma, S., Shearer, M., Frohman, A., & Hilliard, J. (1976). *The Portage guide to early education checklist*. Portage, WI: Portage Project Co-operative Educational Service Agency 12.

Bretherton, I. (1991). Intentional communication and the development of an understanding of mind. In D. Frye & C. Moore (Eds.), *Children's theories of mind* (pp. 49–75). Hillsdale, NJ: Lawrence Erlbaum Associates.

Cassidy, J., & Asher, S. (1992). Loneliness and peer relations in young children. *Child Development, 63*, 350–365.

Cutting, A. L., & Dunn, J. (1999). Theory of mind, emotion understanding, language and family background: Individual differences and interrelations. *Child Development, 70*, 853–865.

Denham, S. A. (1986). Social cognition, prosocial behavior, and emotion in preschoolers: Contextual validation. *Child Development, 57*, 194–201.

Denham, S. A., McKinley, M., Couchoud, E. A., & Holt, R. (1990). Emotional and behavioral prediction of preschool peer ratings. *Child Development, 61*, 1145–1152.

Dennett, D. C. (1987). *The intentional stance*. Cambridge, MA: Bradford Books/MIT Press.

de Villiers, J. G. (2000). Language and theory of mind: What are the developmental relationships? In S. Baron-Cohen, H. Tager-Flusberg, & D. J. Cohen (Eds.), *Understanding other minds: Perspectives from developmental cognitive neuroscience* (pp. 83–123). Oxford: Oxford University Press.

Dodge, K. A. (1980). Social cognition and children's aggressive behavior. *Child Development, 51*, 162–170.

Donelan-McCall, N., & Dunn, J. (1997). School work, teachers, and peers: The world of first grade. *International Journal of Behavioral Development, 21,* 155–178.

Duck, S. (1989). Socially competent communication and relationships development. In B. H. Schneider, G. Attili, & J. Nadel (Eds.), *Social competence in developmental perspective* (pp. 91–106). Dordrecht, the Netherlands: Kluwer.

Dunn, J. (1988). *The beginnings of social understanding.* Cambridge, MA: Harvard University Press.

Dunn, J. (1991). Young children's understanding of other people: Evidence from observations within the family. In D. Frye & C. Moore (Eds.), *Children's theories of mind* (pp. 97–114). Hillsdale, NJ: Lawrence Erlbaum Associates.

Dunn, J. (1995). Children as psychologists: The later correlates of individual differences in understanding of emotions and other minds. *Cognition and Emotion, 9,* 187–201.

Dunn, J. (1996). Children's relationships: Bridging the divide between cognitive and social development (The Emmanuel Miller Memorial Lecture 1995). *Journal of Child Psychology and Psychiatry, 37,* 507–518.

Dunn, J. (1998). Siblings, emotion and the development of understanding. In S. Braten (Ed.), *Intersubjective communication and emotion in early ontogeny* (pp. 158–168). New York: Cambridge University Press.

Dunn, J. (2000). Mind-reading, emotion understanding, and relationships. *International Journal of Behavioral Development, 24,* 142–144.

Dunn, J., & Cutting, A. L. (1999). Understanding others, and individual differences in friendship interactions in young children. *Social Development, 8,* 201–219.

Dunn, J., Cutting, A. L., & Demetriou, H. (2000). Moral sensibility, understanding others, and children's friendship interactions in the preschool period. *British Journal of Developmental Psychology, 18,* 159–177.

Dunn, J., & Herrera, C. (1997). Conflict resolution with friends, siblings, and mothers: A developmental perspective. *Aggressive Behavior, 23,* 343–357.

Dunn, J., & Hughes, C. (1998). Young children's understanding of emotions in close relationships. *Cognition and Emotion, 12,* 171–190.

Dunn, L. M., & Dunn, L. M. (1981). *Peabody Picture Vocabulary Test—Revised manual for forms L and M.* Circle Pines, MN: American Guidance Service.

Eisenmajer, R., & Prior, M. (1991). Cognitive linguistic correlates of "theory of mind" ability in autistic children. *British Journal of Developmental Psychology, 9,* 351–364.

Fombonne, E., Siddons, F., Achard, S., & Frith, U. (1994). Adaptive behavior and theory of mind in autism. *European Child and Adolescent Psychiatry, 3,* 176–186.

Frith, U., Happé, F., & Siddons, F. (1994). Autism and theory of mind in everyday life. *Social Development, 3,* 108–123.

Goodman, R. (1994). A modified version of the Rutter Parent Questionnaire including extra items on children's strengths: A research note. *Journal of Child Psychology and Psychiatry, 35,* 1483–1494.

Gordis, F. W., Rosen, A. B., & Grand, S. (1989, April). *Young children's understanding of simultaneous conflicting emotions.* Paper presented at the Biennial Meeting of the Society for Research in Child Development, Kansas City, MO.

Hadwin, J., Baron-Cohen, S., Howlin, P., & Hill, K. (1997). Does teaching theory of mind have an effect on the ability to develop conversation in children with autism? *Journal of Autism and Developmental Disorders, 27,* 519–537.

Happé, F., & Frith, U. (1996). Theory of mind and social impairment in children with conduct disorder. *British Journal of Developmental Psychology, 14,* 385–398.

Harris, P. L. (1991). The work of the imagination. In A. Whiten (Ed.), *Natural theories of mind: Evolution, development and simulation of everyday mindreading* (pp. 283–304). Oxford: Basil Blackwell.

Harris, P. L., Johnson, C. N., Hutton, D., Andrews, G., & Cooke, T. (1989). Young children's theory of mind and emotion. *Cognition and Emotion, 3,* 379–400.

Harter, S. (1979). *Perceived Competence Scale for Children: Manual.* Denver, CO: University of Denver.

Heyman, G. D., Dweck, C. S., & Cain, K. M.

(1992). Young children's vulnerability to self-blame and helplessness: Relationship to beliefs about goodness. *Child Development, 63*, 401–415.

Hresko, W. P., Reid, D. K., & Hammill, D. D. (1981). *The Test of Early Language Development (TELD)*. Austin, TX: Pro-Ed.

Hughes, C. (1998). Executive function in preschoolers: Links with theory of mind and verbal ability. *British Journal of Developmental Psychology, 16*, 233–253.

Hughes, C., Cutting, A. L., & Dunn, J. (2001). Acting nasty in the face of failure? Longitudinal observations of "hard-to-manage" children playing a rigged competitive game with a friend. *Journal of Abnormal Child Psychology, 29*, 403–416.

Hughes, C., & Dunn, J. (1998). Understanding mind and emotion: Longitudinal associations with mental-state talk between young friends. *Developmental Psychology, 34*, 1026–1037.

Hughes, C., & Dunn, J. (2000). Hedonism or empathy? Hard-to-manage children's moral awareness and links with cognitive and maternal characteristics. *British Journal of Developmental Psychology, 18*, 227–245.

Hughes, C., Dunn, J., & White, A. (1998). Trick or treat?: Uneven understanding of mind and emotion and executive dysfunction in "hard to manage" preschoolers. *Journal of Child Psychology and Psychiatry, 39*, 981–994.

Hughes, C., White, A., Sharpen, J., & Dunn, J. (2000). Antisocial, angry and unsympathetic: "Hard to manage" preschoolers' peer problems, and possible cognitive influences. *Journal of Child Psychology and Psychiatry and Allied Disciplines, 41*, 169–179.

James, T. (2001). *Relations between pragmatic development and theory of mind in young children*. Unpublished doctoral dissertation, University of Toronto.

James, T., Astington, J. W., & Pelletier, J. (2000, May). *Children's perception of school: Relations to theory of mind, school performance and family life*. Paper presented at the Development 2000, Conference of Developmental Section of Canadian Psychological Association, Waterloo, Canada.

Jenkins, J. M., & Astington, J. W. (1996). Cognitive factors and family structure associated with theory of mind development in young children. *Developmental Psychology, 32*, 70–78.

Jenkins, J. M., & Astington, J. W. (2000). Theory of mind and social behavior: Causal models tested in a longitudinal study. *Merrill-Palmer Quarterly, 46*, 203–220.

Kochanska, G. (1991). Socialization and temperament in the development of guilt and conscience. *Child Development, 62*, 1379–1392.

Krauss, R. M., & Glucksberg, S. (1969). The development of communication: Competence as a function of age. *Child Development, 42*, 255–266.

Lalonde, C. E., & Chandler, M. (1995). False belief understanding goes to school: On the social-emotional consequences of coming early or late to a first theory of mind. *Cognition and Emotion, 9*, 167–185.

Leslie, A. M. (1988). Some implications of pretense for mechanisms underlying the child's theory of mind. In J. W. Astington, P. L. Harris, & D. R. Olson (Eds.), *Developing theories of mind* (pp. 19–46). New York: Cambridge University Press.

Lillard, A. S. (1993). Pretend play skills and the child's theory of mind. *Child Development, 64*, 348–371.

Maguire, M. C., & Dunn, J. (1997). Friendships in early childhood, and social understanding. *International Journal of Behavioral Development, 21*, 669–686.

Moore, C. (2001, April). *Theory of mind and social competence in the preschool years*. Paper presented at the Biennial Meeting of the Society for Research in Child Development, Minneapolis, MN.

Moore, C., Barresi, J., & Thompson, C. (1998). The cognitive basis of future-oriented prosocial behavior. *Social Development, 7*, 198–218.

Moore, C., & Frye, D. (1991). The acquisition and utility of theories of mind. In D. Frye & C. Moore (Eds.), *Children's theories of mind* (pp. 1–14). Hillsdale, NJ: Lawrence Erlbaum Associates.

Newton, P., Reddy, V., & Bull, R. (2000). Children's everyday deception and performance on false-belief tasks. *British Journal of Developmental Psychology, 18*, 297–317.

Ozonoff, S., & Miller, J. (1995). Teaching theory of mind: A new approach to social skills training for individuals with autism. *Journal of Autism and Developmental Disorders, 25,* 415–433.

Pelletier, J., & Astington, J. W. (1999, April). *Theory of mind and representational understanding in early childhood education.* Paper presented at the Annual Meeting of the American Educational Research Association, Montreal, Canada.

Perner, J. (1991). *Understanding the representational mind.* Cambridge, MA: Bradford Books/MIT Press.

Perner, J., Baker, S., & Hutton, D. (1994). *Prelief:* The conceptual origins of belief and pretence. In C. Lewis & P. Mitchell (Eds.), *Children's early understanding of mind* (pp. 261–286). Hove, UK: Lawrence Erlbaum Associates.

Perner, J., Leekam, S., & Wimmer, H. (1987). Three-year-olds' difficulty with false belief: The case for a conceptual deficit. *British Journal of Developmental Psychology, 5,* 125–137.

Perner, J., & Wimmer, H. (1985). "John *thinks* that Mary *thinks* that . . . " Attribution of second-order beliefs by 5- to 10-year-old children. *Journal of Experimental Child Psychology, 39,* 437–471.

Peskin, J. & Ardino, V. (in press). Representing the mental world in children's social behaviour: Playing hide-and-seek and keeping a secret. *Social Development.*

Repacholi, B. M., & Gopnik, A. (1997). Early reasoning about desires: Evidence from 14- and 18-month-olds. *Developmental Psychology, 33,* 12–21.

Robinson, W. P. (1986). Children's understanding of the distinction between messages and meanings: Emergence and implications. In M. Richards & P. Light (Eds.), *Children of social worlds* (pp. 213–232). Cambridge: Polity Press.

Ruffman, T., Slade, L., & Crowe, E. (2002). The relation between children's and mothers' mental state language and theory-of-mind understanding. *Child Development, 73,* 734–751.

Slomkowski, C., & Dunn, J. (1996). Young children's understanding of other people's beliefs and feelings and their connected communication with friends. *Developmental Psychology, 32,* 442–447.

Sodian, B. (1994). Early deception and the conceptual continuity claim. In C. Lewis & P. Mitchell (Eds.), *Children's early understanding of mind* (pp. 385–401). Hove, UK: Lawrence Erlbaum Associates.

Sparrow, S., Bala, D., & Cichetti, D. (1984). *Vineland Adaptive Behavior Scales (survey form).* Circle Pines: MN: American Guidance Services.

Sullivan, K., & Winner, E. (1993). Three-year-olds' understanding of mental states: The influence of trickery. *Journal of Experimental Child Psychology, 56,* 135–148.

Watson, A. C., Nixon, C. L., Wilson, A., & Capage, L. (1999). Social interaction skills and theory of mind in young children. *Developmental Psychology, 35,* 386–391.

Wellman, H., & Woolley, J. (1990). From simple desires to ordinary beliefs: The early development of everyday psychology. *Cognition, 35,* 245–275.

Wellman, H. M., & Banerjee, M. (1991). Mind and emotion: Children's understanding of the emotional consequences of beliefs and desires. *British Journal of Developmental Psychology, 9,* 191–214.

Wellman, H. M., & Bartsch, K. (1988). Young children's reasoning about beliefs. *Cognition, 30,* 239–277.

Wimmer, H., & Perner, J. (1983). Beliefs about beliefs: Representation and constraining function of wrong beliefs in young children's understanding of deception. *Cognition, 13,* 103–128.

3

Bypassing Empathy
A Machiavellian Theory of Mind and Sneaky Power

DORIS McILWAIN
Department of Psychology, Macquarie University

DISCERNING NEEDS AND THE EXERCISE OF SNEAKY POWER

*B*eing good at discerning what another person needs doesn't mean that you will necessarily meet those needs. No personality style illustrates this more powerfully than the Machiavellian, where empathy is either lacking or bypassed. In such a person, skill in mapping the intentional states of others, that is, having a good theory of mind (ToM), is a basis for the exercise of sneaky power. Lacking, it seems, moment-to-moment sensitivity to the affective states of another, more cognitive processes seem to suffice. The Machiavellian (Mach) worldview targets the human weaknesses and lack of insight that leave others open to tactical manipulation. It seems that the Mach worldview does a stand-in for the online reading of others' affective states, suggesting that one does not need to use affective processes to discern affective processes in another. The Mach's tactics set up a power imbalance, restricting the other's awareness of relevant facts and cues, intensifying motivational and emotional states, playing on or priming normatively held false beliefs the Mach does not share. The gap between the Mach's worldview and that normatively held by others gives her a darkly charismatic edge. The person whose mind is read may be manipulated against her best interests.

The personality style of Machiavellianism is chosen here as a case study relevant to ToM, because Machs are strategic manipulators who are able to map the intentional states of others. Yet there is a puzzle at the heart of Mach manipulative abilities. To successfully manipulate another, that is, to align her motivation with one's own goals, one needs to discern the beliefs, affective states, and need states of that other, in order to influence them to one's own advantage. Yet research suggests that those high in Mach tendencies not only lack empathy, but lack skill in correctly recognizing the expressive cues of others (Simon, Francis, & Lombardo, 1990). How then are the beliefs, affective states, and need states of others discerned? The ability to map such states is central to ToM concerns. Machs seem to be able to map even affective states without using affective processes. What are the consequences for development of a disorder of empathy in conjunction with an intact ToM?

Let me set up my line of argument. First, I make a case for the relevance of individual differences to theory of mind. Machs exemplify two kinds of individual differences with implications for theory of mind research. The Mach's individual differences in belief systems require us to extend the concept of theory in ToM to include shared understandings (rather than a more restrictive account of "theory" as epigenetically unfolding module). Taking seriously differences in empathic functioning (exemplified by Machs) broadens our research concerns to include the mapping of affective states in addition to beliefs, and the manner in which this is achieved.

Since not everyone who is steeped in the ToM literature is as familiar with the Machiavellian literature, I give a thumbnail sketch of the views and tactics that the Mach scales measure and discuss definitions of empathy. I then use Machiavellianism as a case study of a disorder of empathy. By selectively considering such individuals, it is almost as though one had experimentally diminished the capacity for vicarious, compassionate arousal in response to the affective state of another. The developmental literature shows that young Machs are good at behavioral manipulation, lack compassionate empathy as a correlative of exploitation, and fail to help another in evident need. While it is a developmental achievement in ToM acquisition to realize that another may not have access to all the information that you do (perspective-taking), I show that young Machs may actively use tactics to restrict access to information, the better to manipulate others.

Legendary for using foxy cunning, do Machs reveal their actorly skills in controlled empirical studies? Are they skilled in observing the emotional cues of others? I discuss their impression-management skills, noting their capacity to split being from seeming, and the ToM skills required for such discretion and deception. I discuss contexts in which such skills may be put to prosocial use and form part of a civilized and highly subtle use of ToM.

Given that Machs can manipulate, but seem to have no moment-to-moment sensitivity to the states of others, I then consider the possibility that rather than lacking empathy, Machs do experience vicarious affective arousal, but bypass it in some way. Relevant to this is the prevalence of an external attributional bias in Machiavellians. Such a bias apportions to others and to chance causal responsibility and blame. It's a kind of "it wasn't me" attributional style. I suggest it may in fact have an affective-management function; some Machs may feel some guilt and anxiety over their exploitative tendencies, and have to deal with it. In this scenario, any affect that may arise as a result of the shoddy treatment of others is dealt with by an external attribution bias where the world, chance, powerful others, anyone but the Mach herself is attributed causal responsibility. The worldview itself may function as a cognitive schema that further minimizes affective responsivity to the plight of another, since that other is cynically viewed as likely to do the very same thing if given the chance. In summary, I contend the Mach worldview may well have a dual function: to diminish discomfort via the cognitive modification of empathic tendencies (and I show how this is possible even in non-Machs), and to point out weaknesses ripe for exploitation. The Mach worldview maps prevalent human weaknesses; the tactics maximize those weaknesses, with an eye to situational contingencies. The lack of sustained, vicariously aroused affect on behalf of another means that the Mach manipulator never gets sidetracked or loses focus on the goal, while she maximizes the distraction of the other to create a power imbalance ripe for manipulative victory.

I then consider the possibility that a lack of empathy for others actually has a causal role in the development of a theory of nasty minds. Does a Machiavellian theory of nasty minds arise via externalizing responsibility for one's own actions and coming to view others with contempt and disdain after the fact of having exploited them? A close look at the data suggests cynicism, some early mistrust, and affective blunting might characterize the young Mach very early on.

Despite the affective blunting that seems to characterize Machs, there are limits to the Machiavellian cool. They do still have affective responses to others, if not of the compassionate, vicarious variety as is shown in pilot data concerning their experiences of rage. In conclusion, I consider whether a primary and secondary subtype of Mach depends on the developmental starting point regarding affective responsivity. I note finally the limits to empathy in coming to take the perspective of another, and suggest that it does take cognitive skills to map the intentional states of markedly different others.

THEORY OF MIND:
ROOM FOR INDIVIDUAL DIFFERENCES?

Theory of mind research has not been an obvious intellectual context for those of us interested in individual differences in personality. Most theory of mind research until recently has addressed species-general human capacities. Looking for universals is congenial to an austere, sparse conception of what constitutes a theory in ToM research and sits well with assuming an innate, epigenetically developing, but largely preprogrammed, module. This stance does not readily bring within one's research ambit the role of individual experiences, or cultural differences.

Many propose that a person's ToM develops as the result of an informationally encapsulated module. Meltzoff (1999) noted that modularity can't explain qualitative change in development, other than by the triggering of something preprogrammed. He took the position that although there may be an innate structure, the qualitative reorganization in children's thought occurs on the basis of input from people and things in their culture. Experience makes a difference to the acquisition of ToM, which entails qualitative shifts in a child's reasoning about the inferences another will make based on the evidence the child realizes is available to that other. It is a remarkable developmental achievement when a child comes to realize that the evidence another has may be more restricted than the information possessed by the child, representing a marked qualitative shift in ability. Hobson (1990) suggested that experiences and abilities arising from complex interpersonal exchanges (particularly of a shared, affective nature) form the experiential basis of ToM. It is possible that systematic differences in these interpersonal exchanges will have systematic influence on the acquisition of ToM. Whether or not social and individual difference factors arising from differential life experience influence the acquisition of theory of mind, this chapter attempts to show that they certainly influence the use made of ToM. It is not ToM as ascription of beliefs and desires alone, but beliefs and desires in the context of affects and needs. First we must address whether a case can be made for the significance of within-culture differences in social functioning and ToM.

A Robust Role for Experience in ToM: The Case of Cross-Cultural Differences

Although cross-cultural differences in the concepts and processes involved in the acquisition and functioning of a theory of mind have been explored (Lillard, 1998), a case has not been explicitly made for within-cultural differences in mind-reading abilities. Lillard argued that culture (like language) might be seen to function as "a continual priming effect, getting people to think about certain concepts and not others, thereby influencing the inferences people draw" (1998, p. 6). From her point of view, culture "makes its way into the mind-reading processes much more than theories have described" (p. 23). She suggested a terminology by which "theory of mind" may consist of core beliefs, and "folk psychology" may be noncore, built on top of that and influenced by culture. Whether or not between-culture variation does truly complicate the search for universals in the processes and concepts involved in an intentional mapping of others, one's folk psychology in this wider sense is likely to shape the manner in which a ToM shapes social functioning.

Within-Cultural Variation: Individual Differences

Within-culture variation of an individual difference form has been addressed in the theory of mind literature regarding autism (Baron-Cohen, 1995; Baron-Cohen, Tager-Flusberg, & Cohen, 1994). This chapter broadens the consideration to include personality differences that occur as a matter of degree within the general population. The child-as-scientist model promoted by researchers such as Gopnik (1996), Gopnik and Wellman (1992), and Meltzoff (1999) already allows a robust role for the world in the formation of a theory of mind. This world we bump up against is a social and cultural world, with affectively charged relationships (see Hobson, 1990, in his reply to Leslie, 1987, and see also Preston & de Waal, in press). Because it is already accorded causal role in the formation of ToM, it is a small step to acknowledge its *differential* effect on certain individuals. Such differences might be relevant to the development of the component processes of ToM itself: for example, having an inherent disorder of the component abilities that promote the development of empathy, or a lack of relevant, optimal early life experiences (see Saltaris, 2002).

Or if ToM does prove to be innate/modular, or a result of preprogrammed processes unfolding contingently from a world structured by Gibsonian affordances in a highly invariable way (Leslie, 1987), then such differences might be relevant at least to the implications of ToM for social functioning. In short, whatever theory of theory of mind you prefer, individual differences matter. Social factors might influence performance rather than competence in theory of mind, and may be downstream from more modular ToM processes that provide input to competent performance (Currie & Sterelny, 2000). Currie and Sterelny (2000) noted that as Machiavellian reasoning seems to depend on integrating information from a wide variety of sources, it is unlikely that such social judgments are produced by an encapsulated mechanism (p.153). Such theoretical models may be postponed while we show the phenomena to be taken seriously. Before presenting the case study of the Machiavellian personality, here is a word about the use of terms.

Extending the Meaning of Theory in ToM: Shared Understandings and Affective Processes

Performance in the wider world relevant to ToM may be shaped by individual differences, and may result in individual differences in the subtlety of theory of mind use. "Theory" here is used in a broad sense, as a system of interconnected understandings, which may show cultural and within-cultural variability. In examining within-cultural variability, the relevance of social, developmental, and personality factors to ToM becomes apparent.

ToM and Empathy: Do We Need to Feel Emotion to Discern Emotion?

Empathy and role-taking abilities enable us to suppress our own perspective and entertain that of another person. Individual differences in perspective taking and empathy are relevant to the intentional mapping of the beliefs and desires of another. Perspective taking is the ability to recognize the experience of another *without* experiencing vicariously that person's emotional state. Affective perspective taking involves an understanding of another's internal affective state; empathic concern does not. Empathic concern, in contrast, is the tendency to experience the specific emotional reaction of sympathy/compassion in response to another's misfortune (Davis & Kraus, 1991). This latter empathic resonancing or "hot" empathy also shapes what use is made of the information gained about the state of another, whether it is used to help another person, or to exploit them.

Contemporary ToM researchers have placed more emphasis on discerning the beliefs of another (rather than affects/emotions/desires). Affects are more readily read off the expressive facial and bodily displays and the behavior of another person (Hobson, 1990; Tomkins, 1962). Affective experience is not as private as belief states. A person undergoing an emotional experience does not have the same privileged access to their state. Others may in fact discern a person's state more rapidly than the person herself does. As Simmel (1950) so eloquently noted, "To the man with the psychologically fine ear, people innumerable times betray their most secret thoughts and qualities, not only *although* but often *because* they anxiously guard them" (original emphasis, pp. 323–324). Simmel was at pains to point out that it is not indiscreet in itself to acquire such knowledge—it is, for some, virtually automatically read off the behavior of others. "Conclusions happen so quickly that no power over this skill, no normative position is possible, it is a matter of individual decision."

Possessing a psychologically fine ear may consist of the cognitive ability to understand the affective perspective of another, which is different from actually experiencing the affect of the other person. Let's take a moment to clarify affective perspective taking and empathy.

Preston and De Waal (in press) defined empathy as "any process where the attended perception of the object's state generates a state in the subject that is more applicable to the object's state of situation than to the subject's own prior state or situation" (p. 8). Empathy and role taking are two ways we can pick up on the needs of others. Empathy is usually seen as multidimensional, involving cognitive and emotional abilities, usually complexly interacting. The "cold" and "hot" distinction between the more cognitive elements and the more emotional resonancing elements fits well with le Doux's two systems for processing emotional stimuli, as Preston and de Waal (in press) noted. Empathy processes "likely contain fast reflexive sub-cortical processes (directly from sensory cortices to thalamas to amygdala to response) and slower cortical processes (from thalamas to cortex to amygdala to response). These roughly map onto contagious or cognitive forms of empathy respectively" (Preston & de Waal, in press, p. 251).

Self-report measures sustain the distinction between hot and cold empathy. The Interpersonal Reactivity Index (IRI; Davis, 1980) is a multidimensional measure of empathy that assesses separately both emotional (hot/contagious) and cognitive (cold) aspects. Hot empathy is reliably assessed by the IRI subscale "Empathic Concern" (an affective response to the distressed other). The more cognitive features of empathy are addressed by the subscales of Fantasy (the tendency to place oneself in the life situation of fictitious others) and Perspective Taking (the cognitive ability to understand another's affective state).

Cold, or cognitive, empathy refers to the ability to understand the need state of another. This undergoes dramatic changes developmentally since it depends in part on the level at which a person is aware of other people as entities separate from herself. Hoffman (1978) noted that young children will offer their own mother as comforter to another child in distress, even when that child's own mother is available. What we know about others may alter the very quality of experience of any particular affect. Cognitive empathy is one way of discerning the need state of another where we may obtain the knowledge we seek, but there is no guarantee that we will behave altruistically (Krebs & Russell, 1981). The experience of the warmer features of empathy, namely, emotional resonancing, makes us more likely to help when another's need is obvious or when asked (Barnett & Thompson, 1985). Altruistic action may be promoted by the feeling of kinship that may arise in some observers from the sharing of affective states, via the vicarious arousal of one's own bodily and emotional states as a result of observing a person's situation. Such emotional resonancing may give highly exact information about another's state, which theoretically may be used for manipulation. Empirically, though, it has been found that those who manipulate, or who don't help another, tend not to have this aspect of empathy.

MACHIAVELLIANISM: CASE STUDY AS NATURAL EXPERIMENT

Machs seemingly lack all empathy and thus provide us with a natural experiment; without invoking the wrath of any ethics committee, we can see what happens to ToM use if empathy is excised from a personality. First, we offer a general portrait of Machs, then a few words about what the Mach scales measure (because there is more to Machiavellianism than a lack of empathy), and lastly a discussion of the relevance to ToM of the Machs' lack of empathy or capacity to bypass it.

Portrait of a Mach: Sneaky Power and Deceptive Self-Presentation

Simmel (1950) saw as uniquely human the split between "being" and "seeming" that so perturbs us in the skilled Machiavellian. He noted: "No other object of knowledge can reveal or hide itself in the same way, because no other object of knowledge modifies its behavior in view of the fact it is recognized" (p. 310). Whiten's research suggests that other species may in fact share this ability.

These abilities perturb us in Machs, yet the same abilities underpin discretion and deception. Although the difference between them is a matter of degree, the attitude we take to each is also shaped by the goals served, and whether we share those goals. In discretion we artfully do not reveal all that we know about the other (or at least conceal all that has not been expressly told to us by the other) to smooth social exchanges, and not to intrude upon the privacy of another person. Yet Simmel noted "all of human intercourse rests on the fact that everybody knows somewhat more about the other than the other voluntarily reveals to him, and those things he knows are frequently matters whose knowledge the other person (were he aware of it) would find undesirable" (p. 323). So not revealing all that we know, using skilled sending abilities (to use the language of impression-management research), involves an element of deception. Yet this is not seen as antisocial in that it is required for civilized society. The art as outlined by Machiavelli himself was to conceal the self and to avoid identifying too fully with "the enemy." There are parallels here with the art of hostage negotiation, where negotiators must identify sufficiently with terrorists to be trusted by them, but not sufficiently to slip into true allegiance (see Serrano & Rodriguez, 1993). Very few negotiators are ever thanked by the victims, who can be forgiven in the circumstances for not understanding the subtlety of the process and are usually just screaming, "Give them the helicopter and the $16 million."

So deceptive self-presentation, one of the hallmarks of Machiavellianism, to conceal artfully and reveal ruthlessly, is not per se antisocial. The goals and worldview of the manipulator shape our views of his or her behavior. The truncation in empathy felt for the terrorists on the part of the hostage negotiator arises as a function of the negotiator not identifying with the goals of the terrorists. The negotiator holds a worldview that sees the sacrifice of the lives of terrorists as a necessary evil should the success of his or her own mission require it. From a morally neutral perspective, this is using those others against their own interests. Arguably a negotiator does this not merely for personal gain, but for collectively (although rarely universally) agreed-upon good.

Subtlety of theory of mind is required for skilled deceptive manipulation. One must be able to discern needs, affective states, and beliefs of the to-be-manipulated other although that individual herself may not know her own true intentional state, nor her implicit beliefs. Further, one must avoid alerting the to-be-manipulated other that one has discerned his intentional state until (if ever) it is in one's interests to do so. This requires considerable stagecraft.

Splitting Being and Seeming: Are Machs Good Actors?

Machiavellians and high self-monitors are immune to cognitive dissonance type pressures because they are quite able to partition off what they "really feel and believe" from what the situation requires. This "role distance," the ability to separate "self" from "role" (Ickes et al., 1986; Goffman, 1961), enables them to "distinguish their more stable and enduring dispositions (attitudes, values, sentiments) from those that they are only temporarily espousing in order to create a desired impression" (Ickes et al., 1986, footnote, p. 61).

Machs have high poise and high competence in expressive performance. Cerulnik, Way, Ames, and Hutto (1981) note that high Machs were never seen as irritating or cold in their experiment. Yet Mach is inversely linked with emotional expressivity or the ability to send emotional displays (as measured by Kring, Smith, & Neal's 1994 Emotional Expressivity Scale) (McHoskey, 1997, cited in McHoskey, Worlzel, & Szyarto, 1998, p. 197). Further, Mach is unrelated to the spontaneous affective displays assessed by extraversion ($r = .02$, ns, Riggio & Friedman, 1982), whereas it is slightly positively related to the more measured acting ability implied in "posed sending" skills ($r = .23$, $p < .05$; Riggio & Friedman, 1982).

What the Mach Scales Measure: A Multidimensional Personality Style

The Machiavellian scales used in current research are predominantly the Christie and Geiss (1970) Mach IV (a Likert scale), the Kiddie-Mach, and the Mach V, a forced-choice scale where subjects must choose one item from among three. In the Mach V, of the three options per item, one is the socially desirable response. Of the latter two, although both are equally socially undesirable, only one is indicative of a Machiavellian response. The Mach V has been plagued by reliability problems, however, so many use the Mach IV. It is very difficult to interpret much of the literature uncritically, as many use sample-specific median splits to determine high and low Machs (whereas Christie and Geiss required an absolute cutoff). This means that sometimes the same researcher is using a different criterion for what constitutes a high-Mach person across different samples within the same study.

Machiavellianism is characterized by a set of attitudes toward the interpersonal world, and by a preparedness to use exploitative tactics. This distinction between "tactics" and "views" was made by Christie and Geis (1970) and has proved robust enough (see Fehr, Samson, & Paulhus, 1992, for a review). Hunter, Gerbing, and Boster's (1982) study produced a four-cluster model: "Tactics" split into Deceit (dishonesty in social relationships) and Flattery (telling people what they want to hear), and "Views" split into Immorality and Cynicism (clusters that correspond closely to Christie and Lehman's [1970] "Distrust in People" and "Affirmative Negativism" factors). Although correlations between the clusters are all positive, other evidence they present (showing the clusters relate differentially to other personality dimensions) suggests we must embrace the finding that Machiavellianism is multidimensional in nature. What this means is that having a Machiavellian style is likely to be not only a matter of degree. Using the total score on a Mach scale may be a rather blunt measure for research aims addressing individual differences among those classed as high Machs. There are subtler profile differences. For instance, some have the views without the tactics, like the cynical but moral student protestors studied by Gold et al. (1976, cited in Martinez, 1989, p. 50). Some Machs may experience anxiety and socialized affects like guilt. Drake (1995) suggested there are high Machs who also score highly on the guilt questionnaire by Mosher (1988). However, Drake used a score of 60 as the cutoff for high Machs, which is extremely low by comparison with other studies. It may be that such Machs who experience anxiety and the socialized affects of guilt and shame are secondary Machs. McHoskey et al. (1998) claimed that current Mach scales confound two styles as distinct as primary and secondary psychopathy, an issue I return to later.

For some purposes, taking seriously the different components of the personality style is preferable to aiming for unidimensionality. Much that is relevant to ToM gets lost in more behaviorally oriented self-report measures such as that of Allsopp, Eysenck, and Eysenck (1991). Mudrack and Mason (1995) noted that while the Christie and Geis and Allsopp et al. measures correlate at .57 ($p < .001$), the Allsopp et al. measure is unrelated to external locus of control, a feature robustly associated with Machiavellianism that we discuss in detail later. Further, Mudrack and Mason noted "Subtlety . . . is largely absent in the Allsopp scale, which seems to capture a more direct and straightforward orientation" (p. 197), which they suggested might be more related to dominance than Machiavellianism. If it is sneaky power that concerns us, then we must wrestle with the more multidimensional scales.

Over and above the views and tactics (assessed by the scales) that make them such smooth operators, Machs have the "cool syndrome" (Christie & Geiss, 1970). This is not directly assessed by the Mach scales, but is invariably associated with Machs' real-world performance. They betray little spontaneous affect, and thus are good deceivers; they respond little to the emotional situation of others, and thus are exceptional at exploitation. As children and as adults, they lack empathy. They do not report being vicariously compassionately aroused by the emotional experience of others. This makes them almost a natural experiment. It is as if they are the experimental group where empathy is excluded from operation so we can see what difference this lack makes to ToM use. It may seem obvious at a commonsense level that to discern the affective and need states of a person one would use empathy or skill in correctly recognizing the expressive cues of others. Let's see whether the evidence on Machs bears out this assumption.

EMPATHY AND SNEAKY POWER

We know Machs are competent manipulators from an early age. Even before the budding Mach has an articulated worldview, those identified as Machiavellian are willing to use and are adept at using manipulative tactics and give "explanations" to the deceived others that are plausible, if wide of the full truth (Braginsky, 1970; Barnett & Thompson, 1985). They are certainly behaviorally skilled at getting compliance, and it seems they do not suffer from expressive leakage of emotion because others do not detect their deceit. In Braginsky's (1970) experiment, children were required to get a fellow student to eat quinine-soaked biscuits, with reward to the manipulator being contingent on the number eaten. It was the young Mach who manipulated successfully and (particularly the young girl Mach) left the experimental situation with the full trust of the manipulated other, and good relations intact (Braginsky, 1970). Braginsky likened the boy Machs to used-car salespeople, who sought one-off success, whereas the young girl Machs rather resembled life-insurance salespeople.

Affective coolness is there by age 10 in the form of an absence of the emotionally based, empathic concern dimension of empathy. Thompson and Barnett (1985) found among fourth and fifth graders that low-empathy children had higher Mach scores. Those who were Machiavellian were high in affective perspective-taking abilities (the cognitive capacity to accurately identify and infer the emotional state of another) and low in empathic concern. These were the children least likely to behave prosocially, in that they were less helpful when another's need was clear than were their peers. Thompson and Barnett (1985) suggested that Machs may have a heightened awareness of the feelings of others, yet be insensitive to the feelings of others. It is as if a Mach knows the words but not the music of emotion (John & Quay, 1962, cited in Saltaris, 2002, p.736). To be motivated to help another, Thompson and Barnett suggested one needs to be affectively, empathically aroused, and to anticipate the cessation of mutually experienced personal distress. So hot empathy seems to block exploitation and promote helping. Although it may fine-tune our information about the emotions being experienced by another, it seems to diminish the likelihood that we will harm or exploit that other.

The developmental findings that young Machs are low in this vital dimension of hot empathy, "empathic concern," have also been demonstrated in adult Machs. Pellarini (2001) found that high levels of Machiavellianism were associated with low empathic concern (path = −.43, p < .01) and high levels of Fantasy (path = .27, p < .05). There were no paths from either Personal Distress or Perspective Taking to Machiavellianism. Pellarini used Davis's multidimensional measure of empathy (the IRI) and the Mach IV in a path analysis examining the simultaneous influences of personality and empathy in 64 university students. She noted, "The tendency of Machiavellians to callously engage in interpersonal exploitation is enhanced by their cold, cognitive empathy style, which enables them to imagine another's position (Fantasy), without the buffering warmth of Empathic Concern" (p. 48). Using the same scales, on a student sample of 109, Lauria (2002) found significant negative correlations between Machiavellianism and the following features of empathy: Perspective Taking (r = −.22, p < .02), Empathic Concern (r = −.27, p < .004), and Fantasy (r = −.24, p < .01). She found no correlation between Machiavellianism and Personal Distress (r = −.06, ns). The Tactics cluster of Machiavellianism was significantly negatively related to all dimensions of empathy—Perspective Taking (r = −.25, p < .001), Empathic Concern (r = −.38, p < .001), and Fantasy (r = −.277, p < .05)—whereas the Views cluster of Machiavellianism was only significantly negatively related to Empathic Concern (r = −.20, p < .001) and to Fantasy (r = −.25, p < .02). A lack of both hot and cold empathy is broadly linked with a willingness to use Machiavellian tactics, and with a high endorsement of the Mach worldview.

Machiavellians are famously described as having the "cool syndrome" and one wonders how they could go on to exploit others if they did have any aspect of hot empathy. It is possible, however, that current empathy scales are overly loaded with what for the Mach would feel like socially desirable, morally inflected, touchy-feely nuances that she cannot bring herself to endorse. Twenty-two of the 26 items in the IRI include the word "feel" even though the scale ostensibly measures cold empathy as well as hot. If this bias toward the language of feeling turns Machs off, preventing their endorsement of the items even when they do have the relevant abilities, then the scales will not pick up on some very real skills the Mach has. The scales may fail to tap skills that are relevant to detecting and understanding the feeling and need states of others, independently of experiencing vicariously those same states, or feeling compassionately about the plight of another.

As case study, Machiavellianism seems to suggest that affective processes need not be involved in mapping the affective state of another. In short, Machs' manipulative success suggests it may not be essential to *use* emotional processes to *discern* emotional, need-state processes. Thus Machs enable us to explore what is involved in the competent use of theory of mind—namely, what are the component processes involved in discerning the intentional state of another? Being deprived of certain features of empathy may not hinder Machiavellians' mind-reading ability—not if they are skilled readers of subtle cues.

Readers of Subtle Cues: Do Machs Have Skilled Receptive Abilities?

Considering the experimental literature on the receptive abilities of Machs, the short story is . . . they don't seem to have them. A general receptivity to the expressive influence of others was found to discriminate high Machs from low Machs in Madonna, Wesley, and Anderson's (1989) study, but this general receptivity does not seem to extend to accurate recognition of the particular emotion portrayed—quite the reverse. (Blair's work on psychopathy, in this volume, is relevant here, and see also McHoskey et al., 1998.) Simon et al. (1990) found that decoding accuracy and Mach V scores were significantly and negatively linked ($r = -.23$, $p < .03$); the link seemed to come from the Machiavellian women's relative lack of emotional decoding ability. For Machiavellian individuals, the correlation between decoding accuracy and masculinity was $-.15$ (ns) and for women $-.31$ ($p < .01$). Their study used the Profile of Mood States (POMS) and had Machs decode from still photos in which emotional expression was being shown. They suggested that the decoding task may not have been particularly challenging because the POMS usually requires sound, motion-picture scenarios that are much more complex than the still photographs used in this research. And, may I add, there was nothing to gain by accuracy for the Machs. However, given the finding of differential inaccuracy across genders, Simon et al. suggested the possibility that "women who are capable of effective interpersonal manipulation must actively suppress their sensitivity to and subsequently their detachment from others" (p. 246).

BYPASSING EMPATHY: THE COGNITIVE TRANSFORMATION OF AFFECTIVE STATES

This comment about suppressing sensitivity to others raises the possibility that Machs (or at least some Machs) do have the emotional accompaniments of empathic resonancing to the observed emotional states of others. They may experience them just long enough to get the information relevant to manipulation and then "turn them off" or "block them from awareness" in some way, the better to exploit the other person. The worldview may be responsible for diminishing empathic response.

Hoffman (1978) noted that it is possible to transform empathic distress into some sort of derogatory feeling toward the other, if causal attributions made result in one feeling responsible for the origin or continuation of another's distress, such as when one could have helped but did not. This may suggest that a theory of nasty minds may arise as a result of the mistreatment of others through behavioral exploitation if one attributes agentic responsibility to oneself for the plight of the other. However, far from having dismissive and contemptuous views of the manipulated others, the high-Mach girls in Braginsky's study were concerned with maintaining good, ongoing relations, which is shown in the strategies they selected: omissive lying, the money-split bribe, and external attribution of power to the experimenter. Further, high-Mach girls increased their liking of the manipulated other more than low-Mach girls, whereas low-Mach boys tended to increase their liking more than high-Mach boys. It doesn't seem a clear case for suggesting that "a person may convince himself that the people to whom he lies are not worth liking" (p. 93). The cynicism about others must be sought elsewhere than mere post hoc justification of manipulative actions. Hunter et al. (1982) would of course suggest that the cynicism predated the behavioral manipulation.

However, Hoffman's point about the transformation of empathy is not really refuted by this evidence because Braginsky's research evidence suggests that the Mach children were not taking responsibility for the manipulation. Braginsky (1970) noted the tendency of the high-Mach children to attribute responsibility externally to the experimenter or to the experimental situation. This may be one early way of dealing with whatever anxiety or discomfort may arise for some from the use of others for one's own aims, or it may simply have been the child's perception of the experimental setup. Certainly, an external locus of control is robustly associated with Machiavellianism in the adult literature.

It Wasn't Me: Managing Affect via an External Attributional Bias Invoking Powerful Others and Chance

One of the hallmarks of Machiavelli's writings is a belief that as humans we are subject to Fortune (La Fortuna . . . a woman). Hannah Pitkin, in her book *Fortune is a Woman,* noted of Machiavelli that he was entirely disenchanted with religion, and believed one's fate to be controlled by the wheel of fortune, "which grimly turns," and by "the fleeting maiden, opportunity." Satisfyingly enough, contemporary research reveals that Christie and Geiss managed to retain the richness of his dark philosophy in their items to the extent that those high in Machiavellianism are very much oriented toward having an external locus of control.

Although an external attributional style is not a psychometric feature of Machiavellianism, it seems to be robustly associated with the personality style. Mudrack (1990) noted that "Machiavellianism does indeed seem associated with an external locus of control" (p. 125). His meta-analysis was based on results of 20 separate studies that investigated Machiavellianism and locus of control (with most researchers using the Mach IV or Mach V scales, and some variant of the Rotter, 1966, Internal-External locus-of-control scale). He noted that all of the studies were from Western European or North American populations, and queried how robust the relationship might be in other cultural contexts. The

Machiavellianism–locus of control correlation was .38 after correcting for both sampling error and attenuation resulting from unreliability. A 93% confidence interval surrounding this estimate was bounded on the upper end by .55 and on the lower end by .22. It is because this interval does not span a zero point that Mudrack suggests Machiavellianism is associated with an external locus of control. "The use of manipulation, deception or ingratiation tactics may thus reflect an attempt on the part of the Machiavellian to assert some influence over a hostile environment that subverts the efficacy of more internally oriented approaches, such as hard work " (p. 126).

In fact, on closer analysis, an external attributional style is linked only to the flattery (tactics) and cynicism (worldview) components of Mach. Let me run through the findings. There are two elements to an external locus of control, believing that outcomes are reliant on chance or on the actions of powerful others. Hunter et al. (1982) noted that although the two components (powerful others and chance) of external control only correlate .72 with each other, they have similar correlations with all other variables, which suggests that they are consequent variables to the same factor, which Hunter et al. named Fatalism. There are clear links between Fatalism and Mach. "External control, in terms of both powerful others and chance is moderately correlated with the Mach IV scale (r = .45 and r = .33, respectively)" (p. 1301). At the level of correlations, there is a clearly differentiated pattern of relationships among the subcomponents of Mach. The Fatalism variable (powerful others and chance combined) is correlated moderately with the Flattery (r = .65) and Cynicism (r = .72) components of Machiavellianism, and to a much lesser degree with Deceit (.27) and Immorality (.13), which contribute little. So Fatalism is powerfully linked with the preparedness to use tactics of flattery and the cynical views of others espoused as part of the Mach worldview, and weakly linked to the immorality or preparedness to deceive components of the Mach IV scale. "Those who perceive themselves under the control of powerful others and subjected to the whims of fate perceive others as cynical (r =.59 and r =.64 respectively) and recommend the use of flattery (r = .70 and r = .41)" (Hunter et al., 1982, p. 1301).

The Hunter et al. analysis does not rest at the level of demonstrating associations between variables; it does not merely demonstrate correlations. They were able to suggest a pattern or process that relates the variables to each other, and suggested that the development of Cynicism comes before an exploitative, competitive stance. In their path analysis, Hunter et al. (1982) suggested that "those who develop a cynical worldview towards others, especially if they are not religious, tend to adopt a competitive stance towards others. Those who develop a cynical view of others but who reject competition and are religious develop highly dogmatic abstract philosophies of life" (p. 1302).

CYNICALLY MAPPING HUMAN FRAILTY: THE MACH WORLDVIEW

In concert with a cynical, underlying basic distrust of others, attributional bias is linked to a preparedness to use the tactics of flattery. Yet one must know where to aim one's flattery. To manipulate, one needs to know something of the material one is working with, specifically the manipulable features of the other's motivational system. Wrightsman (1991) spoke of the perverse trust of the Machiavellian that we can all be manipulated. The Machiavellian worldview assumes that we are all more or less vulnerable to manipulation. Kligman and Culver (1992) cited an array of features of human's motivational system making them ripe for manipulation: "playing on human weaknesses, exploiting a character flaw, pandering to human frailty" (p. 190). If one were to read many of the items of the Mach scales, the worldview components are a litany of such human tendencies. One does not need to be alive to the moment-to-moment need state of another via mind-reading ability if human weaknesses are prevalent, or can be intensified through the strategic portrayal of the situation and its possible outcomes. Human weakness is more prevalent than we might like to think, with some suggesting it is "a universal tendency to indulge one's lower tastes in defiance of one's governing standards" (Feinberg, 1980, cited in Kligman & Culver, 1992, p. 190). In such a case "the victim acts not against his will, but against his better judgment and his initial disposition." Listing common character flaws leaves us in no doubt that to someone with a willingness to manipulate, there are plenty of openings: "insecurity, gullibility, fear, vanity, curiosity, (morbid) superstitiousness, sentimentality, misplaced anger or wishful thinking" (Kligman & Culver, 1992, pp. 190–191).

Giving Machs the Charismatic Edge: Normatively Held Self-Deceptive False Beliefs

Learning the tacit rules of culture, being able to be discreet, to present ourselves in the best light means that we sometimes are neither accurate nor ruthlessly honest with ourselves about what we are likely to do in competitive, zero-sum situations. Self-presentational concerns, presenting a less than accurate picture of oneself to others, may come to blur with self-deception. It is common to hold more favorable attitudes about our likely actions than our actual behavior warrants. False beliefs about oneself and about one's action propensities are quite widely shared within Western cultures. This discrepancy may become a weakness or foible that leaves us open to manipulation by flattery, and to those who might enable us to enact our baser motives without having to confront the fact that we are doing so (which La Barre, 1980, suggested is one aspect of charisma). That many self-deceive is precisely the point at which the Mach's exploitation of others can begin. To think better of oneself than one can live up to is a modern operationalization of a character weakness central to those with narcissistic tendencies (Bushman & Baumeister, 1996). It is the root of vanity, conceit, complacency, and insecurity—a stunning list of character weaknesses exploitable by Machs.

It is possible that self-deceptive, flattering beliefs are a chink in the human folk psychological armor and precisely what the Mach does not share. Machs are prepared to be almost psychopathically honest about their capabilities; a striking feature of a Mach's worldview is that her cynical belief that others are untrustworthy does not exclude herself. There is little self-deception at this level. Machiavellianism is robustly negatively correlated with social desirability (Fehr et al., 1992; Ray & Ray, 1982). However, although a Mach is psychopathically honest and clear about what she is prepared to do (see Ray & Ray, 1982, and McHoskey et al., 1998, for a discussion of the overlap between psychopathy and Machiavellianism), from the Mach's point of view, others have cherished, self-serving false beliefs about themselves. The weakness the Mach exploits in those others is that, unlike the Mach, they do not recognize clearly the discrepancy between their avowed beliefs and what they are prepared to do. Thus from the Mach's point of view, others endorse a folk psychological notion that avowed beliefs predict actions—that people are as good as their word. The Mach is more like a social scientist knowing that attitudes and actions are poorly correlated (in the range of .3). The Mach takes a very dark view of the direction of that discrepancy, cynically expecting the worst of others, and getting in first. This basic distrust in people and affirmative negativism is perhaps the earliest hallmark of a Machiavellian worldview (Erik Erikson, 1950, take a bow). This distrust may be inchoate in young Machs, featuring as a behavioral preparedness to manipulate rather than a fully articulated set of beliefs (Sutton & Keogh, 2000). The combination may selectively elicit negative responses from others, operating as a self-fulfilling schema in that the tactics and attitudes used in competitive situations by a Mach may bring out and intensify the worst features of others. Thus, the budding Mach may mature past contingent behavioral manipulation based on a basic distrust to acquire a more fully articulated, jaded view of human nature. Sutton and Keogh (2000) found an increasing lack of faith in others with age, particularly in boys.

The Mach's cynical beliefs about others mark out likely points of weakness at which to aim their tactics. The Machiavellian worldview demarcates human weakness and provides a theory–theory basis for effective manipulation. What is central to manipulation and exploitation is that the manipulator sets up a power imbalance, and does not regard the object of manipulation as an equal negotiating partner. Using persuasion in relation to attitudes, seduction in relation to actions, one can gain seamless obedience or cooperation as one can more deeply discern the needs of others. One can augment those needs and weaknesses by appealing to "a baser nature rather than to a higher morality" (Kligman & Culver, 1992). If there is a continuum from rational persuasion through manipulation to coercion (Kligman & Culver, 1992, p. 185), the middle ground is where the Machs are. High scorers on the scale are "cynical, suspicious, motivated primarily by self-interest and expediency and are relatively unconcerned with considerations of interpersonal attachment, ethics and conventional morality" (Mudrack & Mason, 1995).

Manipulation, it seems, requires a detailed and accurate view of aspects of others, yet the Machiavellian worldview is one that many of us would shun as a compelling portrait of humanity. For the Machiavellians, their worldview is a theory of the way humans really operate, as opposed to the ways they believe they operate. For them, it is because the populace lacks insight into its true motives and views, because people don't know themselves but ascribe to a folk psychology laced with false, self-serving beliefs, that is a far more flattering view of themselves than their actual behavior suggests that they can be manipulated. The evidence suggests that faced with a Machiavellian, many can be manipulated, at least on a one-off basis.

The Machiavellian worldview may also be seen as bypassing hot, empathic, moment-to-moment sensitivity to the states of others in order to exercise sneaky power over others. It may also deflect any residual self-sanction like shame and guilt in those who are Mach manipulators. Who could feel shame for exploiting those who prove themselves time and again to be worthy of contempt and disdain? This may come to perpetuate the cool syndrome, the lack of empathy that promotes exploitation, the lack of affect that permits deception.

Can Worldview Modify Online Empathy?

It seems that the fully articulated Machiavellian worldview develops later than earlier Mach propensities, as the findings by Sutton and Keogh (2000) suggest. The worldview or theory of nasty minds may have a dual function within the system of skills and beliefs that make up Machiavellian functioning. It serves to further diminish any residual discomfort felt at exploitative manipulation, and it points out where the weaknesses lie in others, at which to aim tactics of flattery. The worldview hinges on a cynical view of others; felt anxiety or remorse is pointless because, as a Mach, one is merely doing what one believes others would readily do given the chance.

Even non-Mach people can change their level of empathy via following instructions to take a detached view. As Hoffman (1978) noted "If the observer's set is to fragment the victim or make him the object of intellectual scrutiny, this set will put a distance between him and the victim, or at least distract him from the victim's affective state thereby reducing the observer's empathic response" (p. 232). Assessing whether this occurs would require a more experimental paradigm and monitoring of physiological indicators indicative of affective arousal (see Blair, this volume). Historical accounts of Machiavelli's character are intriguing on the issue of a more cold or cognitive relationship to affective experience. He is reputed to have had "a flair for the dramatic coupled with a wry self-awareness; a temperament that allowed the fullest rein to intellectual enthusiasms, while never fully releasing personal ones" (Hale, 1972, p. 4). Hale (1972) noted that there was some self-conscious inhibitor at work that prevented his feelings from having free and natural play. The tendency toward a more intellectual control of affective display and a more intellectual understanding of others would predispose a person to manipulative success.

Whatever affective impact manipulation does have on Machs' personal experience may be further dealt with by the relativistic morality that is also a feature of the personality style. This relativistic morality endorses the necessity for lying in certain situations, suggesting that "right" behavior does not always lead to good consequences (Leary, Knight, & Barnes, 1986).

Discerning Intentional States or Intensifying and Creating Manipulation?

Given that Machs lack empathy or can bypass it, and lack subtle cue-detection skills regarding the emotional states of others, how do they manage to manipulate? Perhaps they don't need to pick up on the specific state of another. Perhaps the worldview and tactics are a winning combination. The tactics enable a smooth operator to capitalize on existing need states and intensify the common foibles and character weaknesses of the to-be-manipulated other demarcated by the cynical worldview of the Machiavellian. Such tactics may thus promote in the manipulated other actions against his or her initial better judgment (as in the case of seduction) or the adoption of beliefs he or she might initially have rejected or disputed (as in the case of persuasion).

The Mach thus uses tactics to create or intensify the affective/need states of another. The tactics the Mach uses function to restrict the to-be-manipulated other's awareness of vital situational contingencies. Flattery plays on the weaknesses and (even) strengths or virtues of others in manipulating them. For instance, lacking much experience of guilt themselves, Machs nonetheless do not hesitate to use guilt induction as a manipulative strategy (Vangelisti, Daly, & Rudnick, 1991, cited in McHoskey et al., 1998, p. 196). So Machs can create the relevant state they need in the other to be successful manipulators. Their worldview seems to point them in the direction of where weak points might lie. It may be that they use this more "sedimented" awareness of the minds and proclivities of others as a basis for manipulation rather than a moment-to-moment sensitivity to the needs of others.

A DEVELOPMENTAL TRAJECTORY: DOES AFFECTIVE BLUNTING RESULT IN A THEORY OF NASTY MINDS?

Which features of the full Machiavellian mosaic arise first developmentally? Research has shown that while there is an ability to deceive from an early age, and links have been shown between Mach and willingness to engage in and success in behavioral manipulation, the full articulation of the worldview components may arrive much later. Sutton and Keogh (2000) found using the Kiddie-Mach with 9- to 12-year-olds that "lack of faith in human nature was negatively correlated with age, suggesting that children get more cynical as they get older" (p. 143). Sutton and Keogh also suggested that the belief components of Mach clustered more tightly in boys than in girls; "dishonesty and distrust were significantly more positively correlated in boys than girls ($p < .05$) as were both lack of faith in human nature/P[sychoticism] ($p < .01$) and dishonesty/P[sychoticism] ($p < .001$)" (p. 145). This confirms sex differences in Mach and its relationship to personality. Sutton and Keogh (2000) noted:

> Mealey (1997) points out that males are more susceptible than females to the environmental conditions of their early years, and boys are subsequently more likely than girls to respond to competitive disadvantage by associating with delinquent peers and adopting an anti-social lifestyle. A range of factors such as socioeconomic status, intelligence, physical attractiveness and social skills may lead a competitively disadvantaged boy to "make the best of a bad job by seeking a social environment in which they may be less handicapped or even superior. (Sutton & Keogh, 2000, p. 147)

Dien and Fujisawa (1979) showed that because of the disparate pressures on girls and boys in Japanese culture, girls may learn to espouse a more socially desirable worldview than boys, although nonetheless being predisposed to acquire Mach tactics to fend for themselves. Sneaky power may be more of a requirement for girls in a situation where they have less culturally endorsed access to power. Dien and Fujisawa suggested that there might be a greater belief/behavior divide in girls than in boys. They found suggestive evidence of this in that girls were significantly lower on Mach scores than boys, but cheated the same amount. This chimes with Sutton and Keogh's finding that lack of faith in human nature was correlated with age, especially for boys. Girls may acquire a readiness to use the tactics, but because they retain a less cynical view of others may have a lower score on Machiavellianism.

It seems that the behavioral preparedness to use manipulative tactics is the first feature readily detected developmentally (Sutton & Keogh, 2000), and there seems to be early success in this (Braginsky, 1970), particularly when combined with the cognitive ability of affective perspective taking (Barnett & Thompson, 1985). However, although manipulative behavioral and persuasive tactics may be the first sign detected, the sheer preparedness to manipulate that character-ized the young Mach suggests an underlying distrust or cynicism toward others, and that cynicism should come first is consonant with the statistical path analy-ses of Hunter et al. (1982). I am suggesting that there are two features here that may be the first features of the nascent Machiavellian and they may or may not be linked. First, there is a basic if inchoate distrust in others early on, and sec-ond, a cool syndrome. What contributes to a basic sense of distrust in others may be a less-than-optimal experience of receptivity, matching, and its conse-quences for self-soothing (Gerrans & McGeer, this volume; Preston & de Waal, in press; Saltaris, 2002). Disruptions in these processes may be an early precur-sor of the cynicism that Hunter et al. (1982) deemed so central to the develop-ment of Machiavellianism.

There is indirect evidence of the cool syndrome being an early feature of Mach. The skill in manipulation shown in the developmental studies attest to a reduced level of emotionality that otherwise may betray the budding Mach in her attempts to manipulate. That there is an early absence of "empathic con-cern" for others already (Barnett & Thompson, 1985) shows a reduced capacity for the vicarious arousal of affect. Although Braginsky (1970) noted that the successful young girl Machs experienced discomfort, it did not hinder their performance. The cool syndrome may be innate or may arise from early attenu-ation in affective expressiveness (in the range and intensity of affects expressed), which I call affective blunting. Tomkins (1962) suggested emotional expression is intimately linked with the proprioceptive experiencing of the emotion central to the very formation of an affect. So not expressing emotion may in fact hinder the formation of it. Such affective blunting seems central to the Mach's tactical abilities in deceiving and exploiting. Consider for a moment an undated poem by Niccolo Machiavelli himself:

> I hope and hoping feeds my pain
> I weep and weeping feeds my failing heart
> I laugh but the laughter does not pass within
> I burn but the burning leaves no mark outside. (cited in Hale, 1972, p. 9)

Such an affective style would make one a good exploiter and deceiver. If affective responses do not pass within, one is not emotionally concerned. There is no emotional resonancing to events, to the feelings of others . . . this would make one a good exploiter. Not feeling strongly the proprioceptive effects of emotion, one is not hindered in one's willingness to exploit, not revealing or expressing much emotion one is thus a consummate deceiver. It is perhaps the affective coolness that may permit the development of successful tactics, ma-nipulation, and deceit. The worldview that characterizes the personality style may be a later development.

However, what this analysis shows is that even at the level of behavioral tactics, we are talking sneaky power, implicating abilities relevant to ToM. Machiavellian behavioral tactics are not synonymous with the open use of dominant problem-solving strategies. It is not a straightforward use of power. Deception is a component from the start. Manipulative goals are pursued at the expense of another, without the consent of another right from the start. This means that even at the behavioral level, the skills involved are those relevant to ToM. To advance one's own aims entails persuading or manipulating another into complicity (intentional or otherwise), and this requires some insight into that person's weaknesses, if not an ongoing awareness of the affective state and needs of another, in order manipulate them.

In teasing apart the component features of Machiavellianism, center stage is the disorder of affective experience, of which empathy is a part. The central feature of the Machiavellian "to conceal artfully and ruthlessly to reveal" (Pitkin, 1984) may arise from an innate or early-acquired diminished emotional expressivity and responsivity—an affective blunting. Research is required as to whether the deficits Machs evidence in relation to empathy generalize to their affective experience in general, or are unique to vicarious affective experience.

Intolerability of Intense Affect

It is possible that there is something intolerable about intense affect for the Machiavellian. It may be difficult to sustain impression management under conditions of intense affective arousal. Machs may deal with it so that it will not be seen by observers to be a sign, an uncontrolled emanation of what matters (as it were). From a Machiavellian point of view, this would be to leave oneself open to having one's needs/desires read and thus ripe for manipulation. Machs never seem to imagine that someone might meet their needs rather than exploit them and this may be a function of the basic distrust or cynicism research suggests underpins their worldview and is linked with their flattering tactics. It is as if they want to have no spontaneous expressive participation in society (because its meaning can't be controlled). Highly willing to use deceit and flattery, their cynical worldview makes them inviolate to the same tactics. In this regard they are like the protagonist in the novel *Perfume* (1987), by Patrick Susskind, who could triumph over others via his preternatural capacity for the detection of smell yet he did not have a signature, personal location on that very sensory dimension.

The affective mutability of the Machiavellian can perhaps only be achieved at low intensities, since high intensity emotion may be less controllable. Recent pilot research by McIlwain and Asciak (2001), content-analyzing interviews of Machiavellians' and Narcissists' experiences of rage, shows that their profile is quite similar on certain dimensions. High narcissists and high Machs were similar in terms of ego threat felt, tendency toward outward aggression, the instantaneity of rage in response to a trigger, and their sense of entitlement. High Machs reported a higher frequency of aggression toward the trigger of their rage than did high narcissists, and although there was less mention of shame in their accounts than in those of narcissists, it was more than the general population. Machs show higher affective intensity of rage experience than do those high in narcissism. Given the sound findings of narcissists' defensive self-esteem, proneness to ego-threat, and ease of being shamed into rage (Bushman & Baumeister, 1996; Rhodewalt & Morf, 1998; Tangney, Wagner, Fletcher, & Gramzow, 1992; Watson, Hickman & Morris, 1996), this represents a serious chink in the affective armor of the Machiavellian. As yet these are only pilot data based on a community group subsample of 107 people (59 males and 48 females) with a mean age of 30.3. Narcissism was assessed using the Narcissistic Personality Inventory (Raskin & Hall, 1979) and Machiavellianism was assessed using the Mach IV with a relatively low cutoff of 81.

Primary and Secondary Machiavellianism: Does the Developmental Starting Point Differ?

It is not possible to say which feature of the Mach personality style arises first and predisposes the person to develop others. However, because Mach is not a single construct but a cluster of views and tactics that co-occur in some people, a developmental story is required as to when and how these features come to exist together. I map a very tentative picture based on developmental and social literature as to the timing of when particular features might arise, and how one feature might predispose a person to developing others in the Machiavellian cluster.

I emphasize a disorder of affective sensibility (inherited or acquired) and a lack of basic trust in others as initial predispositions. The lack of affective expressivity is likely to make behavioral manipulation contingently successful; the lack of affective resonance to another minimizes the internal sanction of shame, guilt, and anxiety. The legendary coolness in affective style may be innate in some (primary) Machs, acquired in others. There is certainly evidence that taken as a group these largely cool people still experience anxiety (see Fehr et al., 1992), are not ubiquitously manipulative (Barber, 1994), and have narcissistic-like vulnerabilities that mean that of all the strategies they will use, they will not play dumb (Shepperd & Socherman, 1997). The group called high Machs in the literature may shelter a confounded subtype: some who are more like the classic portrait of the secondary psychopath rather than the primary that shows no such tendency toward anxiety and neuroticism. Those who still show anxiety, and discomfort at manipulation, may be differentially more endorsing of an external attributional style to lay the blame elsewhere. This style, where "powerful others" and "chance" are seen as the causal locus of events (Mudrack, 1990), may deflect or cope with any residual felt discomfort at manipulation (Braginsky, 1970). Residual affective experience thus might predispose a person to an external attributional bias.

For others, the affective style may be the result of a temperamental differ-ence that contingently promotes success in behavioral manipulation due to an absence of "give-away" discernable, spontaneous emotional reactions. Those who have no emotional resonancing from the start may be primary Machiavel-lians (as it were). This distinction between innate or early-acquired affective attenuation may be crucial in discerning a primary/secondary Machiavellianism parallel to that found in recent work on psychopathy (McHoskey et al., 1998). Primary psychopathy is a more dispositional characterization of which emo-tional detachment is one feature (along with grandiosity, and glibness or super-ficial charm), whereas secondary psychopathy is seen as similar at a behavioral level but "motivated by different dispositions" (McHoskey et al., 1998), such as neurotic conflict. Imagine there were (primary) Machs born without the more simulation-like empathic resonancing; they would never have had vicariously felt access to the emotional states of others, and they would treat people from the start as "thinking objects" (Graham, 1996, p. 68). They might also lack the discomfort at manipulation found by Braginsky, and the anxiety that research finds to be related to some Machs, and thus not proceed to develop an external attributional bias. Nor might they develop the highly articulated and contemp-tuous worldview of the adult Mach, and score more highly due to a willingness to use tactics.

Postulating such a subtype raises questions of methodology. Our current methodologies do not enable us to discern whether there is an inherent or ac-quired disorder of the component abilities and experiences that promote the development of empathy, or whether Machs actually do fleetingly experience vicarious affective arousal, but bypass it in some way. Are vicariously aroused affects fleetingly experienced by Machs, only to be "turned off" in some manner? Cognitively or otherwise? To answer this we need to expand our consideration from self-reported empathy as currently operationalized, to include additional measures that are less focused on feeling terms and without such prosocial over-tones. We need to select individuals on a detailed profile basis, checking that they are high (or low) in all of the relevant dimensions of Machiavellianism. We also need to use performance-based measures where there is something at stake for the Machiavellian, for without something that tweaks self-interest, they don't perform and the relevant abilities may not be manifest. Machiavellianism as overall style may subsume real differences in personality profile at the level of the etiology of components, and their organization with other features of the personality style. More detailed research may reveal systematic real-world be-havioral and affective differences that are currently confounded.

Given that from the evidence available Machs can manipulate perfectly well without empathy, we need to look more closely at what skills they do have in observing and theorizing about others. We need to explore longitudinally how a theory of nasty minds arises, and whether and how early distrust in others might predispose a child to behavioral exploitation, external attributional bias, and the exercise of sneaky power. It may be that this is the only form of power available to them due to other aspects of social disadvantage (Mealey, 1995). It may be their preferred form of power, if they manage to get others to do the more hands-on exercise of power for them (see Sutton, this volume) and thus escape further the affective consequences of manipulating others against their interests. Machs as case study reveal how an excessively cognitive use of ToM, split off from tempering affective processes, may predispose a person to atypical development. The Mach style may actively shape the nature of interactions with others and create a subculture of distrust. The Mach may selectively attend to and recall evidence of others as self-serving and two-faced. The Mach's treatment of others in setting up power imbalances and always having an eye for the main chance may selectively elicit reciprocity of distrust and suspicion. In this way the Mach maximizes in others the cynical tendencies he or she ascribes to them.

LIMITS TO EMPATHY

Empathy can only help us feel our way into the intentional life space of relevantly similar others. For most of us, that won't give us a strong grasp on the intentionality of the psychopath or the Machiavellian. We need theory to get us there. In trying to understand another person's point of view or experience, we use a more cognitively based understanding where the other is too radically different from us for simulation to give us reliable results. Currie and Sterelny (2000) noted, "our basic grip on the social world depends on our being able to see our fellows as motivated by beliefs and desires we sometimes share and sometimes do not" (p. 145). They perhaps meant this as being able to see people as having beliefs and being motivated by desires in a given moment that we, at that moment, may or may not share. There is another sense of mapping dissimilar others central to the consideration of personality and ToM; that is, being able to map intentional states, common to certain personalities, that we may never share, such as a psychopath's pleasure in harming another for no reason. Thus, where others are radically disanalogous to ourselves, we need a coordinated set of beliefs to understand their perspectives and predict their actions. Many a clinician has dreamed as much. For Machiavellians, lacking perhaps the moment-to-moment sensitivity to the ongoing experience of another, their worldview is central to their mind-reading ability, to their ability to discern the desires and need states of another that their tactics can intensify or mold. What this case study shows is how ToM manifests itself in behavior is influenced by individual differences in the attitudes taken toward others, tactics used to promote self-gain, and by a capacity "not to feel" for others.

REFERENCES

Allsopp, J., Eysenck, H. J., & Eysenck, S. B. G. (1991). Machiavellianism as a component in psychoticism and extraversion. *Personality and Individual Differences, 12,* 29–41.

Barber, N. (1994). Machiavellianism and altruism: Effect of relatedness of target person on Machiavellian and helping attitudes. *Psychological Reports, 75,* 403–422.

Barnett, M. A., & Thompson, S. (1985). The role of perspective-taking and empathy in children's Machiavellianism, prosocial behavior and motive for helping. *Journal of Genetic Psychology, 146*(3), 295–305.

Baron-Cohen, S. (1995). *Mindblindness: An essay on autism and theory of mind.* Cambridge, MA: MIT Press.

Baron-Cohen, S., Tager-Flusberg, H., & Cohen, D. J. (1994). *Understanding other minds: Persepectives from autism.* Oxford University Press.

Braginsky, D. D. (1970). Machiavellianism and manipulative interpersonal behaviour in children. *Journal of Experimental Social Psychology, 6,* 77–99.

Bushman, B. J., & Baumeister, R. F. (1996). Threatened egotism, narcissism, self-esteem, and direct and displaced aggression: Does self-love or self-hate lead to violence? *Journal of Personality and Social Psychology, 75*(1), 219–229.

Cherulnik, P. D., Way, J. H., Ames, S., & Hutto, D. B. (1981). Impressions of high and low Machiavellian men. *Journal of Personality, 49*(4), 388–400.

Christie, R., & Geis, F. L. (Eds.). (1970). *Studies in Machiavellianism.* London: Academic Press.

Currie, G., & Sterelny, K. (2000). How to think about the modularity of mind-reading. *Philosophical Quarterly, 50*(199), 145–160.

Davis, M. H. (1980). A multi-dimensional approach to individual differences in empathy. *JSAS Catalog of Selected Documents in Psychology, 10,* 85.

Davis, M. H., & Kraus, L. A. (1991). Dispositional empathy and social relationships. *Advances in Personal Relationships, 3,* 75–115.

Dien, D. S., & Fujisawa, H. (1979). Machiavellianism in Japan. *Journal of Cross-cultural Psychology, 10*(4), 508–516.

Drake, D.S. (1995). Assessing Machiavellianism and morality conscience-guilt. *Psychological Reports, 77,* 1355–1359.

Erickson, E. H. (1950). *Childhood and society.* New York: Norton.

Fehr, B., Samson, D., & Paulhus, D. L. (1992). The construct of Machiavellianism: Twenty years later. In C. D. Spielberger & J. N. Butcher (Eds.), *Advances in personality assessment* (Vol. 9, pp. 77–116). Hillsdale, NJ: Lawrence Erlbaum Associates.

Goffman, E. (1961). *Asylums: Essays on the social situation of mental patients and other inmates.* Oxford, England: Aldine.

Gopnik, A. (1996). The scientist as child. *Philosophical Psychology, 63*(4), 485–514.

Gopnik, A., & Wellman, H. M. (1992). Why the child's theory of mind is a theory. *Mind and Language, 1–2,* 145–171.

Graham, H. (1996). Machiavellian project managers: Do they perform better? *International Journal of Project Management, 14*(2), 67–74.

Hale, J. R. (1972) *Machiavelli and Renaissance Italy.* Middlessex, England: Penguin.

Hobson, R. P. (1990). On acquiring knowledge about people and the capacity to pretend: Response to Leslie (1987). *Psychological Review, 97*(1), 114–121.

Hoffman, M. (1978). Toward a theory of empathic arousal and development. In M. Lewis & L. Rosenbaum (Eds.), *The development of affect* (pp. 227–256). New York & London: Plenum Press.

Hoffman, M. L. (1977) Empathy, its development and prosocial implications. In C. B. Keasey (Ed.), *Nebraska Symposium on Motivation* (Vol. 25, pp. 169–217). Lincoln: University of Nebraska Press.

Hunter, J. E., Gerbing, D. W., & Boster, F. J. (1982). Machiavellian beliefs and personality: Construct invalidity of the Machiavellian dimension. *Journal of Personality and Social Psychology, 43,* 1293–1305.

Ickes, W., Reidhead, S., & Patterson, M. (1986). Machiavellianism and self-monitoring: As different as "me" and "you." *Social Cognition, 4*(1), 58–74.

Kligman, M., & Culver, C. M. (1992). An Analysis of interpersonal manipulation. *The*

Journal of Medicine and Philosophy, 17, 173–197.

Krebs, D., & Russell, C. (1981). Role-taking and Altruism: When you put yourself in the shoes of another, will they take you to the owner's aid? In J. P. Rushton & R. M. Sorrentino (Eds.), *Altruism and helping behavior* (pp. 137–165). Hillsdale, NJ: Erlbaum.

Kring, A., Smith, D., & Neale, J. (1994). Individual-differences in dispositional expressiveness: Development and validation of the emotional expressivity scale. *Journal of Personality and Social Psychology, 66*(5), 934–949.

La Barre, W. (1980). *Culture in context.* Durham, NC: Duke University Press.

Lauria, J. (2002). *Psychopathy and Machiavellianism: Relationships between subscale components and personality.* Unpublished manuscript, Department of Psychology, Macquarie University, Sydney, Australia.

Leary, M. R., Knight, P. D., & Barnes, B.,D. (1986). Ethical ideologies of the Machiavellian. *Personality and Social Psychology Bulletin, 12,* 75–80.

Leslie, A. M. (1987). Pretense and representation: The origins of "theory of mind." *Psychological Review, 94*(4) 412–426.

Lillard, A. (1998). Ethnopsychologies: Cultural variations in theories of mind. *Psychological Bulletin, 123*(1), 3–32.

Machiavelli, N. (1979). *The prince.* Oxford: Oxford University Press. (Original work published 1532.)

Madonna, S., Wesley, A. L., & Anderson, H. N. (1989). Situational and dispositional social cues that define Machiavellian orientation. *The Journal of Social Psychology, 129*(1), 79–83.

Martinez, D. (1989). On the morality of Machiavellian deceivers. *Psychology: A Quarterly Journal of Human Behaviour, 24*(4), 47–56.

McHoskey, J. W., Worlzel, W., & Szyarto, C. (1998). Machiavellianism and psychopathy. *Journal of Personality and Social Psychology, 74*(1), 192–210.

McIlwain, D., & Asciak, C. (2001). *Just rage: An affective profile of narcissists and Machiavellians.* Unpublished manuscript, Macquarie University, Sydney, Australia.

Mealey, L. (1995). The socio-biology of sociopathy: An integrated evolutionary model. *Behavioral and Brain Sciences, 18,* 523–541.

Meltzoff, A. N. (1999). Origin of theory of mind, cognition and communication. *Journal of Communication Disorders, 32,* 251–269.

Mosher, D. L. (1988). Measurement of guilt in females by self-report inventory. *Journal of Consulting and Clinical Psychology, 29,* 690–695.

Mudrack, P. E. (1990). Machiavellianism and locus of control: A meta-analytic review. *Journal of Social Psychology, 130,* 125–126.

Mudrack, P. E., & Mason, E. S. (1995). Extending the Machiavellianism construct: A brief measure and some unexplored relationships. *Journal of Social Behaviour and Personality, 10*(1), 187–200.

Pellarini, D. (2001). *The charismatic relationship: Leader attributes in the eyes of the follower.* Unpublished manuscript, Department of Psychology, Macquarie University, Sydney, Australia.

Pitkin, H. (1984). *Fortune is a woman: Gender and politics in the thought of Niccolo Machiavelli.* Los Angeles: University of California Press.

Preston, S. D., & de Waal, F. B. M. (in press). Empathy: Its ultimate and proximate bases. *Behavioral & Brain & Sciences.*

Raskin, R., & Hall, C. (1979). A narcissistic personality inventory. *Psychological Reports, 45*(2), 590–603.

Ray, J. J., & Ray, J. A. B. (1982). Some apparent advantages of subclinical psychopathy. *Journal of Social Psychology, 117,* 135–142.

Rhodewalt, F. R., & Morf, C. C. (1998). On self-aggrandizement and anger: A temporal analysis of narcissism and affective reactions to success and failure. *Journal of Personality and Social Psychology, 74*(3), 672–685.

Riggio, R., & Friedman, H. (1982). The interrelationships of self-monitoring factors, personality traits and nonverbal social skills. *Journal of Non-verbal Behaviour, 7*(1), 33–45.

Rotter, J. P. (1966). Generalized expectancies for internal versus external control of reinforcement. *Psychological Monographs, 80*(No. 609).

Saltaris, C. (2002). Psychopathy in juvenile

offenders: Can temperament and attachment be considered as robust developmental precursors? *Clinical Psychology Review, 22,* 729–752.

Serrano, G., & Rodriguez, D. (1993). Individual characteristics of successful negotiators. *Boletin de Psicologia, 40,* 53–65.

Sheppherd, J. A., & Socherman, R. E. (1997). On the manipulative behaviour of low Machiavellians: Feigning incompentence to "sandbag" an opponent. *Journal of Personality and Social Psychology, 72*(6), 1448–1459.

Simmel, G. (1950). *The sociology of Georg Simmel* (K. H. Wolff, Trans. Ed.). New York: Macmillan.

Simon, L. J., Francis, P. L., & Lombardo, J. P. (1990). Sex, sex-role and Machiavellianism as correlates of decoding ability. *Perceptual and Motor Skills, 71*(1), 243–247.

Snyder, M. (1974). Self-monitoring of expressive behavior. *Journal of Personality and Social Psychology, 30,* 526–537.

Susskind, P. (1987). *Perfume: The story of a murderer.* London: Penguin.

Sutton, J., & Keogh, E. (2000). Components of Machiavellian beliefs in children: relationships with personality. *Personality and Individual Differences, 30,* 137–148.

Tangney, J. P., Wagner, P., Fletcher, C., & Gramzow, R. (1992). Shamed into anger? The relation of shame and guilt to anger and self-reported aggression. *Journal of Personality and Social Psychology, 62*(4), 669–675.

Thompson, M. A., & Barnett, S. T. (1985). The role of perspective-taking and empathy in children's Machiavellianism, prosocial behaviour and motive for helping. *Journal of Genetic Psychology, 148*(3), 295–305.

Tomkins, S. S. (1962). *Affect, imagery and consciousness* (Vols. I and II). New York: Springer.

Watson, P. J., Hickman, S. E., & Morris, R. J. (1996). Self-reported narcissism and shame: Testing the defensive self-esteen and continuum hypothesis. *Personality and Individual Differences, 21*(2), 253–259.

Wrightsman, L. S. (1991). Interpersonal trust and attitudes towards human nature. *Measures of Personality and Social Psychological Attitudes* (pp. 373–412). New York: Academic Press.

4

Theory of Mind, Machiavellianism, and Social Functioning in Childhood

BETTY REPACHOLI
Department of Psychology, University of Washington

VIRGINIA SLAUGHTER
MICHELLE PRITCHARD
School of Psychology, University of Queensland, Australia

VICKI GIBBS
Department of Psychology, Macquarie University, Australia

An issue of central interest to developmental psychologists has been whether and how children's social understanding is related to their social functioning. That is, how does children's knowledge about self and other as social beings reflect or affect different aspects of their social lives? Do children who have a good understanding of the social world also demonstrate high levels of social functioning, or are social knowledge and social functioning relatively distinct? It makes intuitive sense that children who know more about the social world should be best equipped to function in that world. However, it is also evident that social knowledge and social functioning are both complex constructs (Bosacki & Astington, 1999), and therefore the links between them are likely to be quite intricate.

SOCIAL FUNCTIONING

The quality of children's social functioning is reflected in various aspects of their social lives, including their behavior (e.g., socially skilled/unskilled

behavior), their attitudes (e.g., self-esteem, well-being), and more objective indicators (e.g., peer relationships, school achievement) (Schaffer, 1996). There
is a long history of research looking specifically at peer relationships as indices
of children's social functioning. In itself, this construct is multifaceted, because
peer relationships can be measured both qualitatively and quantitatively, with
variables including children's number of friends, their placement within the
peer group, the quality of their friendships, and the specific social roles they
take within the peer group. Furthermore, all of these variables can be measured through diverse means, including self-report, teacher or parent ratings,
peer nominations, and observation. Some of these peer-relationship measures
are related, but they have also been shown to reflect distinct aspects of children's
peer experience (Gest, Graham-Bermann, & Hartup, 2001).

One of the most widely used measures of children's peer relationships is
the sociometric status classification system developed by Coie, Dodge, and
Coppotelli (1982). Within this system, children are assigned to one of five categories reflecting the degree to which they are liked and accepted as a member
of a peer group (Williams & Gilmour, 1994). To use this peer acceptance measure, all children within the peer group are required to make positive and negative peer nominations. Two scores are calculated from these nominations: social
preference, which refers to the extent to which children are liked or disliked by
their peers, and social impact, which reflects the degree to which children are
noticed by their peers (Coie et al., 1982). Based on these scores, children's
status within their peer group can then be classified as popular, controversial,
average, neglected, or rejected.

The research literature has demonstrated reliable links between children's
sociometric status and other aspects of their social functioning, including amount
of aggressive and prosocial behavior, isolation and withdrawal from peers, off-task
activity in the classroom, amount of rough play, and style of social approach (see
Coie, Dodge, & Kupersmidt, 1990, for a review). Children who are classified as
popular are generally well liked by their peers. In addition, they have been
shown to engage in high levels of prosocial behavior and low levels of aggressive
and disruptive behavior. Rejected children, who have low levels of peer acceptance and are actively disliked by their peers, demonstrate the opposite pattern.
An interesting and little-studied group consists of those children who are classified as controversial—that is, those who are simultaneously liked and disliked
by their peers. These children have been found to engage in high levels of
aggressive and disruptive behavior, as well as relatively high levels of prosocial
behavior (e.g., cooperation) (Coie & Dodge, 1988).

In general, there appears to be a clear link between socially skilled behaviors and positive peer relationships in childhood. But there is evidence that
cognitive variables, such as children's intelligence, language ability, and perspective taking, also influence peer relationships (Coie et al., 1990). For instance, Dekovic and Gerris (1994) found a significant association between

children's social-cognitive abilities (e.g., affective perspective-taking, prosocial moral reasoning) and their sociometric status, but this relation appeared to be mediated by prosocial behavior. Such findings highlight the potential importance and complexity of exploring the relations between children's social-cognitive understanding and their social functioning.

THEORY OF MIND AND CHILDREN'S SOCIAL FUNCTIONING

Theory of mind (or "mind reading") refers to our uniquely human ability to predict and explain behavior with reference to internal, mental states. More specifically, it involves understanding a constellation of different mental states, including emotions, percepts, intentions, desires and beliefs, and the interrelations between them (e.g., how perception may signal desire) (Baron-Cohen, 1994; Lee, Eskritt, Symons, & Muir, 1998). It is hypothesized that this tendency to view self and other as mental agents underpins human social interactions beginning in the late toddler period (Wellman, 1990).

A number of recent studies provide evidence that individual differences in children's theory of mind abilities are linked to particular aspects of their social functioning (also see Astington, this volume). For example, Lalonde and Chandler (1995) reported that children's performance on false-belief tasks was positively related to those socially competent behaviors that appear to rely on an understanding of mental states (e.g., "engages in simple make-believe with others"; "plays cooperatively with a small group of children"). Dunn and colleagues (Dunn, 1996; Hughes & Dunn, 1997; Macguire & Dunn, 1997) have likewise shown that children who perform well on theory of mind tasks have relatively positive peer interactions. For example, they tend to play in a coordinated fashion and display highly connected communication with their friends (Slomkowski & Dunn, 1996). Research by Moore, Barresi, and Thompson (1998) revealed a correlation between young children's theory of mind and their tendency to delay immediate gratification for themselves in order to share with another person at a later date. In two different studies, Watson, Nixon, Wilson, and Capage (1999) found that 4- to 6-year-old children's theory of mind was positively correlated with teacher-rated social competence, even after controlling for age and language. However, theory of mind ability was not related to teacher ratings of children's popularity. Finally, Bosacki and Astington (1999) reported a significant correlation between adolescents' theory of mind and peer-rated social competence, even after partialing out verbal ability. In contrast, the relationship between theory of mind and peer-rated likeability was not significant once verbal ability was controlled.

More recent research has included sociometric status as an index of children's social functioning. For instance, in a sample of 4- to 6-year-old Spanish children, popular girls were significantly better than average or neglected girls on a deception task, although performance on several other theory of mind tasks did not vary with peer acceptance (Badenes, Estevan, & Bacete, 2000). The rejected boys in this study performed significantly worse than their peers on one theory of mind task and also demonstrated more hostile attributions in tasks requiring explanations of other people's behavior. Slaughter, Dennis, and Pritchard (2002) also explored the relations between sociometric status, prosocial and aggressive behaviors, and theory of mind in preschoolers. In two separate samples, they found a developmental trend whereby theory of mind ability was the best predictor of popularity for children over age 5. In children under age 5, however, amounts of prosocial behavior and aggression were the best predictors of peer popularity. In line with these other studies, Peterson and Siegal (2002) reported that popular preschoolers obtained higher theory of mind scores than those who were rejected by the peer group. Moreover, the presence of a stable mutual friendship made an independent contribution to children's theory of mind scores. Thus, popular children with at least one mutual friendship obtained the highest theory of mind scores, whereas rejected children without such friendships received the lowest scores.

In summary, these investigations have all revealed some type of positive relation between theory of mind and social functioning in samples of typically developing children. Similar patterns are also apparent in non-typical populations. Hughes, Dunn, and White (1998) reported that "hard-to-manage" preschoolers (identified by disturbances in their social relationships) received lower scores on a series of theory of mind tasks than matched control children. They were also more likely to understand false beliefs in the context of an unpleasant, rather than a pleasant, surprise which is contrary to the typical developmental pattern (Wellman & Banerjee, 1991). Similarly, Strange and Nixon (2001) reported that children diagnosed with attention deficit hyperactivity disorder (ADHD) were delayed in their theory of mind development in comparison to their peers. Furthermore, those ADHD children who were rated as more socially competent by their teachers were also found to have higher theory of mind scores.

These sorts of findings have been used to support the argument that an intact, well-functioning theory of mind promotes social competence, and, as a corollary, that a delay in theory of mind development is detrimental to children's social functioning. This position has been further bolstered by the discovery that individuals with autism have a specific theory of mind deficit—one that can apparently account for their diverse range of social problems (Baron-Cohen, Leslie, & Frith, 1985). However, it is impossible to confirm such a causal pathway in either typically developing or atypical children, given the correlational nature of the data. Thus, it is necessary to consider the alternative—that is, children's social experiences (e.g., friendships) provide the necessary input for an increasingly mature theory of mind. Consistent with this, numerous studies have reported a positive relationship between number of siblings and preschoolers' understanding of false beliefs, even after controlling for language ability (e.g., Jenkins & Astington, 1996; Ruffman, Perner, Naito, Parkin, & Clements, 1998). Like peers, siblings may provide the opportunity for interactions in activities that are relevant to acquiring a theory of mind. However, when considering causal direction, any associations between peer relationships and mind reading pose more interpretive difficulties than those involving sibling relationships. In addition, common sense would suggest that it is inappropriate to describe social experiences as formative for later mind reading, without also emphasizing how mind reading can impact later social functioning (Macguire & Dunn, 1997). For instance, there is some evidence that the link between the two becomes stronger over time (e.g., Badenes et al., 2000; Dekovic & Gerris, 1994; Slaughter et al., 2002). It appears that children with poor theory of mind skills may miss out on some forms of social interaction, which in turn limits their ability to further develop their social-cognitive skills. Thus, the relationship between theory of mind and social functioning is probably most accurately characterized as bidirectional.

Traditionally, the association between mind reading and social functioning has been conceptualized as a positive one: A well-functioning theory of mind should be linked to good social outcomes (e.g., popularity). But there is mounting evidence that superior mind reading is not always associated with positive, let alone superior, social functioning. For example, Astington and Jenkins (1995) reported that 3- to 5-year-old children who had a better understanding of false beliefs failed to show greater empathic concern toward their peers. Although children may need a degree of insight into the minds of their peers in order to be empathic, it is apparent that this knowledge is not always acted upon. Moreover, Dunn (1995) found that the transition to school was more difficult for those children who, at 40 months of age, had demonstrated an advanced understanding of false beliefs. These early mind readers were more likely to indicate that they were experiencing difficulties with teachers, school activities, and their peers at the start of kindergarten relative to other children. Finally, in a recent study by Cuming and Repacholi (1999), children with few or no mutual friends at preschool were more successful on false-belief tasks than those with many such friendships. Thus, an advanced theory of mind did not guarantee that these preschoolers would be able to form and maintain a large circle of friends.

Such findings are not limited to early childhood. Sutton, Smith, and Swettenham (1999) reported that 7- to 10-year-old ringleader bullies had higher theory of mind scores than followers, victims, or defenders of victims. Teacher ratings were also obtained to assess the type of bullying that was carried out and whether this was differentially linked to children's social cognition scores. Neither indirect (e.g., the spreading of rumors/lies, social exclusion) nor physical bullying (e.g., hitting) was related to children's mind-reading ability. However, even after controlling for age, verbal ability, and the other types of bullying, there was a significant positive relationship between verbal bullying (e.g., name calling, ridiculing, teasing), and children's social cognition scores. In contrast, indirect aggression (peer estimated) in a sample of 10- to 14-year-old Finnish children was found to be positively correlated with social intelligence (Kaukiainen et al., 1999). Interestingly, this peer-estimated measure of social competence was not associated with more direct forms of aggression (i.e., physical attack, verbal threats). Despite their differences, both of these studies suggest that being able to accurately read another person's mind is useful for knowing how to effectively hurt someone with words (e.g., gossip, lies, name calling).

Similar studies with atypical populations have reinforced the idea that poor social functioning does not necessarily imply a mind-reading deficit (also see Blair, this volume). Sutton, Reeves, and Keogh (2000) tested theory of mind in 11- to 13-year-old children diagnosed with disruptive behavior disorder (DBD) using the "eyes" task (Baron-Cohen, Jollife, Mortimore, & Robertson, 1997), in which another person's mental state is inferred from the expression in their eyes. They found that children with DBD performed at typical levels on this task. This finding is in accordance with previous work by Happé and Frith (1996). In their study, 6- to 12-year-old children with conduct disorder (CD) performed as well as a matched control group on theory of mind tasks, despite having significantly lower social functioning scores. Happé and Frith (1996) proposed that children with CD may have an intact but atypical theory of mind that biases them to focus on negative elements of social interactions (i.e., a "theory of nasty minds"). Finally, Blair et al. (1996) administered Happé's (1994) advanced test of theory of mind to a group of incarcerated psychopaths and non-psychopaths, matched on age and IQ. There were no significant differences between the two groups in the number of correct inferences about the underlying cause of a story character's behavior, nor in the frequency with which they referred to mental states.

It has become increasingly apparent that the relation between theory of mind and social functioning is not necessarily a positive one. Due to motivational and other factors, children and adults may not always competently use the mind-reading skills that they have at their disposal (see O'Connor & Hirsch, 1999, for a similar point). More importantly, however, there are some individuals who competently use this knowledge, but do so to achieve antisocial goals (e.g., teasing, deceiving, or manipulating others). Thus, social-cognitive abilities like mind reading are probably best viewed as "neutral social tools" (Kaukiainen et al., 1999) and researchers need to turn their attention to the factors that determine when and how these skills are used. Such variables could include situational features (e.g., a familiar vs. unfamiliar context), the individual's relationship with the other person (e.g., liked vs. disliked peer), empathic disposition, and personality.

MACHIAVELLIANISM—AN OVERVIEW

One personality characteristic that may determine whether individuals use their mind-reading skills to achieve positive or negative social outcomes is Machiavellianism (Mach; see McIlwain, this volume, for further discussion). The Machiavellian believes that other people can be manipulated in interpersonal situations and actively engages in manipulative, exploitative behavior for his or her own personal gain (Wilson, Near, & Miller, 1996). This manipulative tendency appears to be accompanied by a cool detachment in interpersonal relations and an indifference to conventional standards of morality (Christie, 1970a). Machiavellian adults have traditionally been identified using self-report questionnaires, with the majority of researchers employing Christie's (1970b) Mach IV scale. The scale items are designed to measure an individual's cynical perception of other people as weak and untrustworthy (e.g., "Generally speaking, people won't work hard unless they're forced to do so") and the strategies they use when dealing with interpersonal situations (e.g., "Never tell anyone the real reason you did something unless it is useful to do so"). The remaining items tap what Christie (1970b) refers to as abstract or generalized morality (e.g., "All in all, it is better to be humble and honest than important and dishonest").

Using these types of scales, researchers have demonstrated that individuals with high Mach scores are extremely successful manipulators. It should be kept in mind, however, that much of this research involves short-term, laboratory-based social interactions. For example, high Machs have been rated as more charming and intelligent than low Machs by other experimental subjects as well as by the researchers themselves (Cherulnik, Way, Ames, & Hutto, 1981). They are also more successful than low Machs at winning games that involve bargaining and the formation of alliances (e.g., Geis, 1970). High Machs frequently outperform low Machs in experimental situations that require participants to steal, lie, or cheat (Harrell & Hartnagel, 1976) or to persuade others to engage in these behaviors (Bogart, Geis, Levy, & Zimbardo, 1970; Exline, Thaibut, Hickey, & Gumpert, 1970). Their skills of persuasion have also been noted in mock courtroom situations (Sheppard & Vidmar, 1980). Given these findings, it comes as no surprise that high Machs are also less likely to help another individual when it is of no benefit to themselves (Wolfson, 1981). Little research has been conducted to determine how high Mach adults fare in the real world and, to date, the results have been highly inconsistent (see Wilson et al., 1996, for a detailed review).

Researchers (e.g., Allsopp, Eysenck, & Eysenck, 1991) frequently report that males receive higher scores on the Mach scale than females. However, scores on the Mach IV tend to be correlated with measures of social desirability

(Christie, 1970b), with high Machs being more willing to endorse socially un-desirable items. Thus, the Mach gender difference may simply reflect the fact that females are more concerned with being accepted by others and typically display higher levels of socially desirable responding than males. The Mach V (a forced-choice version of the Mach IV) was constructed by Christie (1970b) to eliminate the effects of social desirability. Although the two scales are highly correlated and there is some evidence that mean Mach V scores are roughly equivalent across the sexes (e.g., O'Connor & Simms, 1990), few researchers have adopted this version of the scale. Concerns have also been raised by Brown and Guy (1983) that these scales underestimate Machiavellianism in females, because they are insensitive to the different manipulative behaviors that can be employed. For example, O'Connor and Simms's (1990) research suggests that high-Mach females are more likely to use self-disclosure as a manipulative strat-egy than low-Mach females. Among males, however, there appears to be no link between Machiavellianism and strategic disclosure. Further research is sorely needed to determine how males and females differ and the areas of overlap in their manipulative behaviors. Such knowledge can then be used to construct new scales that are more sensitive to the behavior styles of both male and fe-male Machiavellians.

Braginsky (1966, cited in Christie, 1970c) and Nachamie (1969, cited in Christie, 1970c) independently modified the Mach IV so that it could be used with children as young as 9 years of age and adults with little education. Consis-tent with the adult literature, a number of studies have reported that boys ob-tain higher Mach scores than girls (e.g., Dien & Fujisawa, 1979; Sutton & Keogh, 2001). There is also some evidence (Sutton & Keogh, 2001) that, like the Mach IV, Nachamie's Kiddie-Mach scale is negatively correlated with social desirabil-ity. To date, only a few studies have examined the behavioral correlates of these child Mach scales and the findings have been somewhat mixed.

Braginsky (1970) examined the ability of high- and low-Mach 10-year-old children to entice a same-sex, middle-Mach child to eat crackers unpleasantly flavored with quinine. Children were told that they would receive money for every cracker that the other child ate. The pairs were matched for age, IQ, and parental socioeconomic states (SES). The high-Mach children used manipula-tive strategies more frequently and were more successful at manipulating than the low Machs. Neutral adult observers also judged the high-Mach children to be more skillful and effective than low Machs. Interestingly, high-Mach boys and girls displayed quite different manipulative styles. The girls used more subtle, evasive strategies (e.g., withholding of information, attributing responsibility to the experimenter), whereas the boys were more direct in their approach (e.g., using more commissive lies).

Nachamie (1969, cited in Christie, 1970c) studied the behavior of 11-year-old high- and low-Mach children in a bluffing game. Children rolled two dice and won candy if they could deceive their opponent about the outcome of the roll or if they were able to see through their opponent's bluffs. A payoff matrix was constructed that encouraged successful bluffing and challenging. Each pair consisted of one high- and one low-Mach child, matched for gender and ethnicity. High-Mach children were more able to distinguish lying from truth-telling in their opponents, and were also more adept at deceiving. Nachamie's procedures were replicated by Kraut and Price (1976), but they failed to find a significant correlation between children's Mach scores and the amount of candy they had won by the end of the game. Significant correlations were found, however, between parental Mach scores and children's performance. Children who were more successful in this game had parents with higher Mach scores. The authors concluded that Mach beliefs and behaviors develop separately and that it is not until sometime later in development that the two converge. Without additional information about the Mach scores of children in the high versus low groups, it is difficult to interpret these contradictory results. For example, if the high-Mach children had lower scores than those in the original study, this may well explain the failure to replicate Nachamie's findings. Comparison is further hampered by the use of different dependent variables and analyses. For instance, Kraut and Price (1976) did not report how many low- versus high-Mach children won the game.

Interpretive difficulties also arise in Dien and Fujisawa's (1979) longitudinal study of Japanese children. At age 4, children's cheating was measured in a game where they were required to roll a ball toward a target tray containing three holes. Children received two tokens (later exchanged for stickers) if the ball rolled into the red hole, one token when it went into the other two holes, and none if they missed all three holes. Children were left alone to play the game and were unobtrusively observed via closed-circuit television. At age 11, these children completed a Japanese translation of the Kiddie-Mach scale. Regardless of gender, Mach scores were not correlated with earlier cheating behavior. However, no descriptive data were supplied about children's Mach or cheating scores. Thus, once again, the possibility cannot be discounted that their sample included few children with truly high (or low) Mach scores. In addition, it was reported (see Dien, 1974) that a few children cheated very often, but most of the sample cheated infrequently. Thus, a skewed distribution in the cheating scores may well account for these null findings. Finally, although the Kiddie-Mach has been translated into various languages, the cross-cultural appropriateness of this measure remains unknown.

Two very recent studies support Christie's (1970c) claim that a Machiavellian orientation can be measured in older children and that this personality disposition is also expressed at the behavioral level. Sutton and Keogh (2000), for instance, found that 9- to 12-year-old children who identified themselves as bullies had significantly higher Kiddie-Mach scores than control children. Consistent with this finding, children with high Mach scores were generally less sympathetic toward victims of bullying relative to those with lower Mach scores.

Similar findings emerged in a sample of 8- to 12-year-old Greek children (Andreou, 2000). Children who reported that they both bullied others and were bullied themselves (i.e., bully victims) had significantly higher Kiddie-Mach scores than bullies, victims, and control children. These bully victims also had low levels of social acceptance and negative self-esteem. These studies suggest that childhood Machiavellianism does indeed translate into real-world, inter-personal behavior and is not simply associated with short-term, laboratory-based interactions. But do these findings mean that all or most bullies are high Machs? We would argue that they are not necessarily one and the same. First of all, having a higher Mach score than one's peers may indicate Machiavellian ten-dencies, but does not necessarily mean that the individual is a high Mach. For instance, those bullies who engage in physical aggression and/or verbal intimi-dation may obtain relatively high scores simply because they share the high Mach's negative perceptions of others. On the other hand, some bullies use "indirect" or "relational" forms of aggression such as social exclusion and the spreading of false rumors (Crick & Grotpeter, 1995). These more subtle and calculating behaviors are similar to the manipulative tactics that a Machiavel-lian might employ. However, to successfully exploit and manipulate others, a person must be able to disguise their true intentions and present themselves favorably to others. It is conceivable, then, that high Machs are bullies, but extremely accomplished ones. In addition to the type of antisocial act, the un-derlying intentions and motivations of the bully and the high-Mach child may often be quite different. For example, Olweus (1993) argues that bullies are motivated by a strong desire for power and dominance. Although their aggres-sion frequently has an instrumental component (e.g., coercing victims to hand over money, food, or homework), bullies appear to derive satisfaction from the distress that they produce in their victims, along with the sense of power that such acts engender (Olweus, 1993). Unlike the bully, the Machiavellian's ac-tions are not specifically focused on causing suffering in others. Any hurt that is inflicted is more often the unfortunate by-product of the Machiavellian having used that person in order to achieve some other goal. On occasions, the out-come might be a sense of power, but unlike the bully, it is probably not their only or their usual goal. Of course, this is all extremely speculative given how little is currently known about the Machiavellian child. However, whether a distinction can be made between bullies and Machiavellians is an issue that theoreticians and researchers will ultimately need to address.

MIND READING AND MACHIAVELLIANISM—HOW MIGHT THEY BE RELATED?

So, what enables the high Mach to successfully manipulate other people? The Machiavellian individual must not only view others as open to manipulation, but must also be able to accurately read the social situation and know how to influence other people's thoughts, feelings, and actions. Thus, one of the essential skills for the aspiring Machiavellian is a well-functioning theory of mind. The Blair et al. (1996) finding of an intact theory of mind in adult psychopaths is particularly pertinent here. Machiavellianism has been theoretically (e.g., McHoskey, Worzel, & Szyarto, 1998; Mealey, 1995) and empirically (e.g., Allsopp et al., 1991; McHoskey et al., 1998) linked to a subclinical form of psychopathy. Moreover, recent evidence from Sutton and Keogh (2001) suggests that this conceptualization of Machiavellianism is also applicable to children. It is conceivable, then, that like the psychopath, the Machiavellian's performance on theory of mind tasks could be quite average (i.e., similar to other individuals of the same mental age). Although the high- and low-Mach individual may not differ in the degree or quantity of mind reading, the quality of their mind reading may instead be the crucial factor. For example, the high Mach may have some general mind-reading bias (akin to Happé & Frith's 1996 "theory of nasty minds"), whereby their cynical attitudes about people tend to color their interpretation of another's behavior and their specific mental state attributions. These biases may then be partly responsible for the deployment of manipulative interpersonal strategies.

On the other hand, Machiavellians are *not* psychopaths, nor are they conduct-disordered in the clinical sense. Moreover, at least in the short-term, high Machs are successful in their antisocial endeavors and able to frame their manipulative intentions in a favorable light. What differentiates them from many other individuals may be their possession of superior mind-reading skills. The Machiavellian must outwit other mind readers in order to successfully manipulate them. Although possible, there is no evidence to suggest that the high Mach only preys on those individuals with a below-average or defective theory of mind. In addition, their mind-reading skills may be further enhanced by virtue of engaging in frequent bouts of manipulation. The reported association between verbal forms of bullying and higher social-cognition scores (Kaukiainen et al., 1999; Sutton et al., 1999) is consistent with this view of the Machiavellian as a superior mind reader. Two studies are discussed next that explore the association between Machiavellianism and theory of mind in children.

MACHIAVELLIANISM, THEORY OF MIND, AND SOCIOMETRIC STATUS IN PRESCHOOLERS

To date, there has been no measure of Machiavellianism for children under age 9. There are two potential reasons for this—one practical and the other theoretical. Practically, it may be too difficult to develop such a measure for young children, given the complex definition of Mach in the adult literature as both a prevailing attitude and a pattern of behavior (Christie, 1970b). For older children and adults, these aspects of Machiavellianism are assessed through self-reports, in which participants are asked to endorse statements that reflect manipulative, self-serving beliefs and practices. This format is clearly inappropriate for young children, who may not have the test wisdom or self-understanding to reliably endorse attitudinal statements or even identify their behavioral strategies (Siegal, 1997). Thus, it may be that there are no Mach scales for children under 9 years of age simply because they are too young to be assessed with a self-report instrument. On the other hand, it is possible that, theoretically, Mach does not emerge until middle childhood. Children of preschool and/or early school age may not yet have developed consistent beliefs about others or the behavioral strategies that exemplify Mach. In particular, the attitudinal component of the Mach construct may be hard to identify in young children, because the tendency to conceptualize other people in terms of mental or personality constructs does not develop until sometime in middle childhood (Damon, 1988; Wellman, 1990). Thus, the cardinal Mach belief that other people are "manipulable" or "gullible" may not develop before age 9 or so. It does seem possible, however, that precursors to classic Machiavellian attitudes and behaviors emerge as soon as children begin to regularly engage in social interactions with peers, such as during preschool or first grade. It may be that children who are too young to verbally agree that "the best way to handle people is to tell them what they want to hear" may still demonstrate a tendency toward behavior that we would label as relatively Machiavellian, for instance "by lying when cornered." Thus, there may be measurable individual differences in the extent to which children's behavior tends toward Machiavellianism, even if, as yet, they do not identify or endorse their own tendencies to manipulate others in social situations and to behave in a self-serving manner.

In a first attempt to measure Machiavellianism in young children, Slaughter and Pritchard (2000) developed a 12-item rating scale that could be used by adult informants who were familiar with the child's behavior within the peer group (e.g., teachers). Following previous developers of Mach scales for children, the items were constructed with reference to the Mach IV for adults. The scale (see Table 4.1) was constructed to fit into a standard behavior rating format, with the 12 items depicting a Mach orientation and specific Mach behaviors to be rated on a 3-point scale (0 = *rarely applies*; 1 = *applies somewhat*; 2 = *certainly applies*).

This new Mach scale for young children was initially administered in the context of a larger study investigating the interrelations among various cognitive and behavioral variables, including verbal ability, theory of mind, aggressive and prosocial behaviors, and sociometric status (Slaughter et al., 2002). Only the results relevant to the Machiavellian scale are presented here. On the basis of previous studies of Mach in school-aged children, several predictions were made. First, it was hypothesized that relations between Machiavellianism and aspects of behavior in preschool-aged children would parallel findings from

TABLE 4.1. 12-Item Machiavellian Rating Scale
for Young Children

1. Lies if cornered
2. Is trusting (reverse scored)
3. Is manipulative
4. Has a sense of right and wrong (reverse scored)
5. Is self-absorbed
6. Is generous (reverse scored)
7. Understands social hierarchies
8. Seeks popularity
9. Is a flatterer
10. Tends to put others' needs before his/her own (reverse scored)
11. Will use any means to achieve what he/she wants
12. Is "out for number 1"

studies with older children. Thus, Mach ratings should be negatively related to ratings of prosocial behavior and positively related to ratings of aggression (Barnett & Thompson, 1985). Second, it was hypothesized that there would be a positive correlation between ratings of Machiavellianism and children's theory of mind ability. This correlation was expected to be relatively high, given the theoretical relation between a capacity for interpersonal manipulation and successful mind reading. However, it was also acknowledged that high-Mach children might simply be average in their theory of mind ability, which would be reflected in a low (nonsignificant) correlation. Finally, it was hypothesized that children who were controversial in their peer group, that is, highly noticed (positively and negatively), would be relatively high on Mach compared to their peers. This hypothesis followed from previous research on controversial children, who have been shown to engage in high levels of prosocial and aggressive behavior. This pattern suggests that controversial children may change their behavioral strategies from situation to situation, perhaps in an effort to gain power and control over their peers. Controversial status is determined by high social impact scores; that is, a high number of both positive and negative nominations. This noticeability of controversial children may be analogous to the noticeability of adult social "cheaters," who are more likely to be remembered than "noncheaters" (Mealey, Daood, & Krage, 1996). If there is a link between a tendency toward social manipulation and social impact within one's peer group, the prediction follows that children who are high on Machiavellianism would be more likely than their peers to be classified as controversial within the peer group, and further, that there would be a predictive relation between Machiavellianism and social impact as measured by the peer-nomination procedure.

Eighty-seven children (46 boys, 41 girls) between the ages of 4 years, 0 months; and 6 years, 7 months participated in the study. The children attended classes in five different child-care centers from middle-class suburbs of a large Australian city. All children had been known by their teachers for a minimum of 3 months at the time of testing. Children were tested individually by a female experimenter for a total of approximately 40 minutes per child over three occasions. On the first testing occasion, children completed two theory-of-mind tasks and a test of verbal ability. On the second testing occasion, children were given two more theory-of-mind tasks as well as the peer nomination task, which was used to determine peer status. On the final testing occasion, children completed the peer-nomination task again so as to calculate reliability for the peer status classifications.

Children's verbal ability was assessed through the administration of the Peabody Picture Vocabulary Test–Revised (Dunn & Dunn, 1981). To assess theory-of-mind ability, two false-belief tasks were administered to children on the first and second testing occasions. The standard change in location task (Wimmer & Perner, 1983) and an unexpected contents task (Gopnik & Astingon, 1988) were used, with the materials varied across testing occasions. Children obtained passing scores for the theory-of-mind tasks if they correctly answered all control and test questions, with total theory of mind scores ranging from 0 to 4.

The head teacher of each classroom group filled out a Behavioral Questionnaire for all children involved in the study. This 57-item questionnaire asked teachers to rate children on prosocial behavior, aggression, and Machiavellianism. A 3-point rating scale was used (i.e., 0–2), and for each construct a total score was calculated by summing the ratings for all relevant items. The 20 items assessing prosocial behavior were taken from the Prosocial Behavior Questionnaire (Weir & Duveen, 1981). Example items include: "Will clap or smile if someone else does something well in class"; "Comforts a child who is crying or upset"; and "Will invite bystanders to join in a game." The possible range for prosocial behavior scores was 0–40. The 25 items assessing children's level of aggressive behavior were taken from the aggression subscale of the Child Behavior Checklist (Achenbach & Edelbrock, 1983). Example items include: "Destroys property belonging to others"; "Threatens people"; and "Temper tantrums or hot temper." This score could range from 0 to 50. The 12 items listed in Table 4.1 were used to assess children's level of Machiavellianism. The Mach score could range from 0 to 24.

Children's sociometric status was determined using the method described by Coie and Dodge (1983). Children were requested to nominate the three children in their respective classroom groups that they liked to play with the most (like most, LM) as well as the three children they did not like to play with very much (like least, LL). These LM and LL nominations were standardized within each individual classroom group. The standardized LM and LL scores were then used to calculate a social-preference (SP) and a social-impact (SI) score for each child. Social-preference scores, which reflect the extent to which children are well-liked by their peer group, were calculated by subtracting children's individual standardized LL score from their standardized LM score (SP = LM − LL). Social impact scores, which reflect the extent to which children are noticed within their peer group, were calculated by adding each child's individual standardized LM score to their individual standardized LL score (SI = LM + LL). Based on these scores, children were classified into one of five sociometric status groups (Coie & Dodge, 1983).[1]

A reliability analysis on the four false-belief tasks revealed a Cronbach's alpha of .75, indicating good internal consistency for the theory of mind measure. The 12-item Mach scale had acceptable internal consistency, with a Cronbach's alpha of .68. The Pearson correlations for children's SI and SP scores derived from nominations made on the second and third testing occasions were $r(85) = .65$ and $r(85) = .77$, respectively. These test–retest reliabilities are similar to those reported by Sanderson and Siegal (1995), who used a similar measure and a comparable sample of children.

Simple correlations between Mach scores and the various cognitive and behavioral measures are presented in Table 4.2. Verbal ability was found to be negatively correlated with Mach, so the correlation coefficients were recomputed with PPVT scores partialed out. The pattern of results was unchanged after removing the effects of verbal ability. Mach scores were negatively correlated with prosocial behavior scores and positively correlated with aggression scores. There was no relation between Mach scores and theory of mind ability. Mach scores were not correlated with social preference scores, but were significantly related to social impact scores, supporting the hypothesis that Machiavellianism may be related to social impact within the peer group.

Next, the relation between Machiavellianism and controversial status was investigated. Table 4.3 shows the number of children classified into each of the five peer status groups, together with their ages and average Mach scores. Nine children could not be classified into any status group. The pattern shows that children classified as controversial had the highest Mach scores in the sample. In order to test the hypothesis that controversial children would be relatively high Machs, we conducted a planned complex comparison of the mean Mach scores of controversial children versus the mean Mach scores of all the other

TABLE 4.2. Relations Between Mach Scores and Other Variables in Preschoolers ($n = 87$)

	PPVT Score	Theory of Mind Score	Prosocial Behavior Score	Aggressive Behavior Score	Social Preference Score	Social Impact Score
1. Mach	−.26°	−.11	−.30°	.79°°	−.13	.26°°
2. PPVT partialled out		−.03	−.23°	.78°°	−.08	.24°

Note. Line 1 shows the zero-order correlations and line 2 shows the partial correlations with the effects of verbal ability (PPVT score) removed. Significance: ° $p < .05$, °° $p < .01$ (all tests two-tailed).

TABLE 4.3. Mean Machiavellian Rating Scores for Children
in the Five Sociometric Status Groups (*n* = 78)

Peer status	*n*	Age (in months)		Mach score (0–24)	
		Mean	(SD)	Mean	(SD)
Popular	19	61.5	(6.2)	6.63	(3.55)
Controversial	9	61.6	(6.4)	10.33	(4.00)
Average	16	61.1	(6.0)	6.63	(3.42)
Neglected	14	60.5	(6.2)	7.36	(3.41)
Rejected	20	59.4	(6.0)	8.60	(4.27)

groups combined. This analysis revealed a significant difference, with controversial children obtaining significantly higher Mach scores, $t(76) = 2.24$, $p < .05$.

Finally, a multiple regression analysis was conducted to investigate the relative importance of Machiavellianism for children's social impact within the peer group. For this analysis, the continuous social impact scores were used as the dependent variable, and all of the other cognitive and behavioral variable scores were entered as predictors. The total R^2 for the model was computed at .105, which was not significant, $F(5, 81) = 1.91$, $p > .10$. However, examination of the individual beta weights for the regression revealed that Machiavellianism scores were a significant predictor of social impact scores (see Table 4.4).

This study represents the first to attempt to measure Machiavellianism in children under age 9. Although the Mach rating scale requires further work to establish its reliability and validity, the pattern of results obtained in this first study is promising. This scale, although only consisting of 12 items, was shown to have acceptable internal reliability. Moreover, children's Mach scores were related to aspects of their cognitions, behavior, and social functioning in the predicted, or at least in interpretable, ways.

Two competing hypotheses regarding the relation between Machiavellianism and theory of mind were explored. First, it was suggested that high

TABLE 4.4. Multiple Regression of Cognitive and Behavioral
Variables on Social Impact Scores (*n* = 87)

Variable	Regression beta
PPVT score	−.04
False belief score	.03
Prosocial behavior score	−.08
Aggressive behavior score	−.33
Mach score	.49**

Note. Significance: ** $p < .01$, two-tailed

Machs might also be high on theory-of-mind ability, given the hypothesized relation between mind reading and successful manipulation. Alternatively, successful manipulation may not require superior theory-of-mind skills. Instead, these children might use their average theory-of-mind skills in a specifically Machiavellian style for Machiavellian purposes. The results were consistent with this second hypothesis. In this sample of preschool-aged children, in which there was a good deal of variance in theory-of-mind scores, there was no link between teacher-rated Machiavellian tendencies and children's theory-of-mind ability. This finding supports the proposal that Machiavellianism is a distinct interpersonal behavioral style that develops separately from the cognitive prerequisite—theory of mind—that supports it.

Machiavellianism was found to be significantly related to children's verbal ability, and to their rated levels of prosocial and aggressive behavior. The correlations between Mach and the behavioral variables remained even when verbal ability was partialed out. This pattern of results parallels findings from studies with older children, in which Machiavellianism has been shown to be negatively correlated with prosocial behavior and positively correlated with aggressive behavior (Barnett & Thompson, 1985). The very high correlation between Mach and aggression scores found in this study may lead to the concern that in preschool children, Mach and aggression are one and the same. This conclusion is untenable, however, given the results of the regression analysis, in which Machiavellianism, but not aggression, significantly predicted children's social impact. It may be the case that teachers, when asked to rate children on aggression and Machiavellianism, adopt a generally negative stance toward those children who are relatively disruptive in the classroom. Thus, children who are high on aggression may also be rated as being "out for number 1" or "self-absorbed," which would give them a relatively high Mach score. Future users of this child-Mach scale might consider administering it separately from other behavior rating scales, in order to avoid a general negative or positive response set from raters.

Overall, the pattern of results obtained in this study suggest several avenues for future research. First, this new Mach-rating scale appears to be a promising tool for assessing Machiavellian tendencies in young children. It must be noted, however, that the scale items reflect the overt behavioral, but not the subjective attitudinal, components of the Mach construct. As such, it is quite different from the Mach IV, and may or may not tap the same personality construct that represents adult Machiavellianism. Second, validation studies are needed to confirm several things—for instance, whether scores derived from this new Mach scale correlate with later scores on the Kiddie-Mach, a scale that more closely resembles the Mach IV and has also been validated with observational data.[2] Scores on this new Mach scale should also be independently validated with objective behavioral observations in naturalistic and experimental situations, and with other indicators of social functioning, such as bully status in the peer group (Andreou, 2000; Sutton & Keogh, 2000). Finally, the results of this study highlight the need for more detailed study of controversial status children, as well as further investigation of the relation between Machiavellianism and social impact within the peer group, particularly in older school-aged children.

MACHIAVELLIANISM AND MIND READING IN PREADOLESCENTS

Repacholi and Gibbs (2000) recently explored whether Machiavellianism in 9- to 12-year-old children was related to theory of mind, attributional style, and/or empathic disposition. It was expected that high Machs would possess a well-functioning theory of mind and that, in certain contexts, they might exhibit superior mind reading relative to low Machs. In the adult literature (e.g., Schultz, 1993; Wilson et al., 1996), there is some suggestion that Machiavellians are not successful in all social situations and do not consistently outperform low Machs. There is also growing recognition (e.g., O'Connor & Hirsch, 1999; Repacholi & Trapolini, submitted) that, depending on the social context, children may be more or less motivated to accurately read and reflect on other people's mental states. Machiavellians appear to be preoccupied with the pursuit of instrumental goals and are willing to exploit social relationships in order to achieve these. Thus, it was hypothesized that high Machs would demonstrate more advanced mind reading than low Machs when the social situation involves an instrumental, rather than relational, goal.

Regardless of whether Machiavellians have an average or superior theory of mind, one of the factors that may enable them to use this ability for antisocial purposes is the existence of a social-cognitive bias. Aggressive children are more likely to attribute hostile intent to others than their nonaggressive peers, particularly in ambiguous social situations (Crick & Dodge, 1996). This hostile attributional bias also operates in depressed children (Quiggle, Garber, Panak, & Dodge, 1992) and those with paranoid personalities (Turkat, Keane, & Thompson-Pope, 1990). Thus, by itself, this bias is not sufficient to cause aggression, but may contribute to children's interpersonal difficulties. More recently, Nelson and Crick (1999) explored whether some children have a benign attributional bias that then predisposes them to very high levels of prosocial behavior. In their study, prosocial 10- to 12-year-old children were more likely to perceive benign intent behind a provocation and tended to expect more favorable outcomes in conflict situations relative to control group peers (i.e., children who were neither highly aggressive nor highly prosocial). It is possible that high Machs also have specific social-cognitive biases that support their antisocial behavior. In particular, we expected that high Machs would attribute negative intent to the actions of another person in an ambiguous social situation and would be more likely to report negative outcomes than low Machs.

The adult Machiavellian is frequently characterized as having a "cool detachment that makes them less emotionally involved with other people" (Wrightsman, 1991, p. 378). Thus, low empathic disposition may also be a crucial part of the equation. Empathy includes both the ability to understand another person's emotional state and a degree of emotional responsiveness to that state (Hoffman, 1988). It has been argued throughout this chapter that Machiavellians are adept at reading others' minds; consequently, they should not be deficient with regard to the cognitive component of empathy. Instead, what they may be lacking is the affective element. The Machiavellians presumably know how their manipulative behavior will impact another person's feelings, but this knowledge is not accompanied by any feelings of concern, sympathy, or compassion. Without this emotional arousal, antisocial behavior is less likely to be inhibited (Miller & Eisenberg, 1988; Richardson, Hammock, Smith, Gardner, & Manuel, 1994) and high Machs can readily apply their mind-reading skills to obtain what they need from other people.

Barnett and Thompson (1985) examined Machiavellianism in relationship to 10- to 12-year-old children's affective perspective-taking ability (i.e., the cognitive component of empathy) and their affective responsiveness to other people's feelings. Children with high affective perspective-taking (APT) skills and low empathy obtained higher Kiddie-Mach scores than all the other groups (high APT/high empathy; low APT/high empathy; low APT/low empathy). There were no significant differences in the Mach scores of these latter three groups. In addition, children with high APT/low empathy tended to be rated by their teachers as less likely than the other three groups to help another child when their need was obvious (e.g., the child has dropped an armful of school books in a puddle). These findings are consistent with the suggestion that the ability to vicariously experience another's affect is central to the enactment of altruistic and prosocial behavior (Hoffman, 1988). Thus, we predicted that children with high Mach scores would report lower levels of empathic affect than those with low Mach scores.

A total of 137 children (78 males, 59 females), with a mean age of 10 years 9 months (SD = 8.10 months, range = 9;4–12;3), participated in the initial part of the study. All of the children completed Nachamie's Kiddie-Mach scale (1969, cited in Christie, 1970c) and Bryant's (1982) Empathy Index, which measures the emotional component of empathy. The Children's Social Desirability Scale (CSDS; Crandall, Crandall, & Katkovsky, 1965) was employed to exclude participants whose responses on the other two questionnaires might be invalid, due to their extreme fear of disapproval. About 6.5% (5 males, 4 females) of the sample were subsequently excluded on the basis of their CSDS scores.

Table 4.5 presents the intercorrelations between age, gender, Machiavellianism, Empathy, and Social Desirability. Females obtained higher Empathy and lower Mach scores than males. There was also a tendency, albeit nonsignificant, for females to receive higher scores on the Social Desirability

TABLE 4.5. Intercorrelations Between All Variables (n = 128)

Measure	2.	3.	4.	5.
1. Age	−.06	.01	−.04	−.12
2. Gender		−.34[d]	.38[d]	.16[a]
3. Mach			−.22[b]	−.24[c]
4. Empathy				.02
5. Social Desirability				

[a]p < .10, [b]p < .05, [c]p < .01, [d]p < .001.

scale than males. As predicted, Mach and Empathy were significantly correlated, with those scoring higher on the Mach scale being less empathic. However, the correlation between these two measures was no longer significant once the effects of gender were removed, partial r = −.10. When separate gender analyses were carried out, there were likewise no significant correlations between Mach and Empathy scores (all ps > .05). Social Desirability was significantly correlated with children's Mach scores, even after controlling for gender, partial r = −.20, p < .05. Thus, children with lower Mach scores were more concerned with seeking social approval than those with higher Mach scores.

Only children with Mach scores in the upper and lower quartiles were eligible for participation in the second part of the study. The majority of these children were recruited and the final sample consisted of 27 low and 29 high Machs. Each child participated in a 40-minute testing session. A 12-item picture-sequencing task (Langdon & Coltheart, 1999) was employed as a non-verbal measure of mind-reading ability. Each sequence consisted of four black-and-white, cartoon-style drawings. There were four picture sequences for each of three card types. The *mechanical* (ME) cards depicted physical cause–effect sequences and children were required to infer causal relations. Everyday social routines were presented in the *social-script* (SS) cards. These sequences required the use of logic and social-script knowledge. In the *false-belief* (FB) cards, story characters were depicted as being unaware that a particular event had occurred. To obtain the correct sequence, children had to be able to predict that the character would act according to a false belief. A score of 1 was given for each correct sequence, with possible scores for each card type ranging from 0 to 4. The time taken to complete each sequence was recorded and an average time (in seconds) was calculated for each card type.

Children were also given a verbal mind-reading task in which four vignettes were orally presented by the experimenter. Each vignette involved an ambiguous social situation based on common childhood experiences. For example: "Jane and Anne are best friends. They are going on a school excursion and Jane asks Anne to mind the seat next to her on the bus. When Jane gets on the bus, she sees that Anne is sitting next to someone else." The wording of these vignettes was slightly different for boys and girls but the key aspects of the situations remained the same. Two of the vignettes were based on relational goals (e.g., getting to sit next to your best friend on the bus) and two involved intrumental goals (e.g., obtaining a rare collector's card). At the end of each vignette, children were asked: (1) Why did this happen?; (2) What did X think?; (3) What did Y think?; (4) What did X feel?; (5) What did Y feel?; and (6) What happens next?

To assess children's mind-reading ability, answers to each question were given a score ranging from 0 to 2, using the qualitative coding system described by O'Connor and Hirsch (1999). These scores were summed to produce a total *mind-reading* score ranging from 0 to 48, which represented the degree of mentalizing evident in children's responses. A second, blind coder independently scored the responses of 14 participants (i.e., 25% of the sample). Interrater agreement was very high (92–96%) and Cohen's kappa ranged from .73 to .84. Children's responses to questions 1 and 2 for stories 1, 2, and 4 were scored in order to assess *intent attributions* (story 3 was omitted because all children gave similar responses). A score of 0 was given for responses indicating that the behavior of the other person was accidental or resulted from a benign intent. Responses suggesting that the intention behind the actions of the agent in the story was to hurt, trick, or ignore (i.e., negative intent) received a score of 2. A score of 1 was given when both benign/accidental and negative intent were specified. Scores were summed to produce a total intent attribution score with a possible range of 0–12. To assess *outcome expectations,* children's responses to question 6 ("What do you think will happen next?") in each of the four stories were scored. Responses indicating that the outcome would be positive or neutral received a score of 0. A score of 2 was given when responses indicated that a negative outcome would ensue. A score of 1 was given when both neutral/positive and negative outcomes were mentioned. Scores were summed across the four stories to produce a total outcome expectation score with a possible range of 0–8. Once again, 25% of the responses were scored by a second coder. Cohen's kappa ranged from .79 to .84 (86–89% agreement) for intention attributions and .90 to .94 (84–88% agreement) for outcome expectations.

A number of researchers have reported that language ability is highly correlated with children's performance on social-understanding tasks (e.g., Astington & Jenkins, 1999; Cutting & Dunn, 1999). Children's receptive language development was measured using the Peabody Picture Vocabulary Test (PPVT–R; Dunn & Dunn, 1981). Expressive language ability was estimated by administering a test of verbal fluency (adapted from O'Connor & Hirsch, 1999). Children were simply asked to name foods, words beginning with the letter S, and animals. They were given 30 seconds to generate as many words as possible for each category. The average number of words generated over the three categories was then calculated. Finally, children's performance on the theory of mind measures, particularly the picture-sequencing task, might also be influenced by their level of inhibitory control (Carlson & Moses, 2001). Therefore, the Stroop Color and Word Task (Golden, 1978) was included as an index of this ability.

Table 4.6 presents the age and gender breakdown for the high- and low-Mach groups, along with group means for the questionnaire and control measures. The groups were similar in age, but there were more boys in the high- than the low-Mach group. There was a significant difference between the two groups in their mean Mach scores, $t(54) = 20.07$, $p < .001$. Consistent with the correlational analysis in part 1, the low Machs obtained higher Social Desirability scores than the high Machs, $t(54) = 2.67$, $p = .01$. High Machs had slightly lower Empathy scores than low Machs, but this difference was not significant when gender was entered as a covariate, $F(1, 53) = .58$, $p > .10$. Inhibitory control and verbal fluency were not significantly correlated with age or gender (all $p > .05$). VMA was unrelated to gender but was positively correlated with age, $r(54) = .47$, $p < .001$, and verbal fluency, $r(54) = .30$, $p < .05$. There were no significant differences between the high- and low-Mach groups for any of the control measures (all $ps > .05$), so these variables were excluded from subsequent analyses.

Gender was not significantly related to children's verbal theory of mind score or the two subscores ($ps > .10$) and was therefore not included in subsequent analyses. As illustrated in Table 4.7, there was no significant difference between the high and low Machs in their overall mind-reading score ($p > .10$) Subscores were created to determine whether children's performance differed when the situation involved an instrumental versus a relational goal. A mixed factorial analysis of variance (ANOVA) yielded a significant story-type effect, $F(1, 53) = 4.69$, $p < .05$, but no main effect of Mach group and no story-type × group interaction. Thus, children tended to obtain somewhat higher mind-reading scores for instrumental compared to relational stories.

Mean card-sequencing scores are also presented in Table 4.7. A mixed factorial analysis of covariance was conducted with card type as a within-subjects

TABLE 4.6. Group Characteristics—Age, Gender, Questionnaires, and Control Measures

Variables	High Machs ($n = 29$) (23 males, 6 females)		Low Machs ($n = 27$) (9 males, 18 females)	
	Mean	(SD)	Mean	(SD)
Age (in months)	32.93	(8.03)	131.42	(8.36)
Kiddie-Mach	63.86	(5.06)	39.41	(3.94)
Empathy	70.79	(16.28)	78.43	(13.77)
Social desirability	11.20	(6.07)	15.97	(7.13)
PPVT	126.86	(15.68)	121.44	(14.54)
Verbal fluency	12.47	(2.49)	11.58	(2.05)
Inhibitory control	49.62	(4.65)	50.30	(5.27)

TABLE 4.7. Verbal and Nonverbal Theory of Mind Scores
for High Versus Low Machs

Theory-of-mind scores	High Machs (n = 29)		Low Machs (n = 27)	
	Mean	(SD)	Mean	(SD)
Verbal Task				
Overall mind-reading ability	10.48	(2.38)	11.19	(2.00)
Relational goal	5.03	(1.35)	5.45	(1.37)
Instrumental goal	5.45	(1.35)	5.74	(.92)
Nonverbal task				
Number of correct ME sequences	3.59	(.63)	3.78	(.42)
Number of correct SS sequences	3.66	(.48)	3.63	(.56)
Number of correct FB sequences	3.14	(.74)	3.22	(.75)
Time (in seconds) to sequence ME cards	16.34	(4.09)	18.16	(4.14)
Time (in seconds) to sequence SS cards	15.29	(3.49)	15.29	(3.95)
Time (in seconds) to sequence FB cards	20.39	(4.96)	20.27	(4.49)

Note. ME, mechanical; SS, social script; FB, false belief.

factor and Mach group as a between-subjects factor. Gender was included as a covariate because it was associated with performance on the social-script cards. This analysis only revealed a significant main effect for card type, $F(2, 106)$ = 10.05, p < .001. Post hoc analyses, controlling for gender, indicated that children were less accurate in sequencing false-belief cards relative to mechanical, $F(1, 53)$ = 12.24, p < .01, and social-script cards, $F(1, 53)$ = 13.37, p < .01. Children were equally adept at sequencing the latter two types of cards.

Across all card types, males tended to be faster at sequencing the cards than females (all ps < .10). Mean card-sequencing times (in seconds) for the low and high Machs are presented at the bottom of Table 4.7. A mixed factorial analysis of covariance yielded a significant main effect for card type, $F(2,106)$ = 28.53, p < .001. Post hoc analyses, controlling for gender, indicated that children took significantly longer to sequence the false-belief cards in comparison to the other two card sets (both ps < .001). In addition, children took less time to sequence the social-script cards relative to the mechanical ones, $F(1, 53)$ = 4.73, p < .05.

Gender was not related to children's intent attributions or their outcome expectations (all ps > .10) and was therefore not included in any of the subsequent analyses. The high Machs produced more negative intent attributions (M = 2.14, SD = 2.10) than the low Machs (M = 1.00, SD = 1.41), adjusted $t(49)$ = 2.39, p < .05. In line with this, the high Machs were also more likely to predict negative outcomes in the vignettes (M = 3.14, SD = 2.63) than the low Machs (M = 1.78, SD = 2.04), adjusted $t(52)$ = 2.17, p < .05.

In summary, it appears that high-Mach preadolescents have an intact theory of mind but are no more skilled in this cognitive domain than their low-Mach peers. However, it remains unclear whether high and low Machs are "average" or "extremely skilled" mind readers. For example, high and low Machs may both possess a superior theory of mind, with one group using it primarily for antisocial purposes and the other using it to support highly prosocial endeavors. Consequently, the "average" theory of mind might be demonstrated in those children who are neither high nor low in their Machiavellian orientation. It should also be noted that, as in other studies of Machiavellianism, those in the high-Mach group were high relative to all the other children surveyed in the study. Therefore, the objection could be raised that these children were not true high Machs and that superior mind-reading ability only exists at the extreme end of the Machiavellian continuum. Normative data, taking into account gender and age, will ultimately be needed if researchers are to continue using the Kiddie-Mach scale to select low- and high-Mach children.

It has been argued (Dunn, 1996; O'Connor & Hirsch, 1999) that our mind-reading skills are not fixed per se, but are contextually sensitive. Thus, it was possible that the high-Mach children would only display superior mind reading in certain contexts. This hypothesis was tested in the current study but was not supported. Instead, both high and low Machs obtained higher mind-reading scores for the instrumental compared to relational stories. Furthermore, it remains unclear whether it was the goal type or some other factor inherent in these stories (e.g., more realistic or familiar) that resulted in higher scores across both groups. This finding provides some preliminary support for the notion that contextual factors may inhibit (or facilitate) an individual's basic mind-reading ability (O'Connor & Hirsch, 1999). Further studies are needed, however, to determine whether there are any particular social contexts in which high Machs demonstrate more advanced mind-reading than low Machs.

If high-Mach children merely possess average mind-reading skills, how do we explain their success in the realms of social manipulation and exploitation? One possibility explored here is that some type of social-cognitive bias might be involved. In the present study, high Machs tended to make more negative attributions about story characters in ambiguous social situations than their low-Mach counterparts. For example, they were more likely to report that the other person's behavior involved trickery, selfishness, or rejection. High Machs were also more likely to predict that these social situations would lead to negative outcomes (e.g., arguments, termination of the friendship). In contrast, the low Machs provided much more charitable explanations for the story characters' behavior and also concluded that the outcomes would be more positive. These differences in social-cognitive style may account for some of the reported differences in the interpersonal behavior of high- and low-Mach children. For instance, children who perceive negative intent behind the actions of others may then feel that this justifies their own antisocial behavior. However, whether male and female Machiavellians have similar biases remains unknown. There is some evidence (e.g., Braginsky, 1970) that the two sexes use different forms of manipulation, and it is possible that these strategies are supported by qualitative differences in the content of their mind reading. Unfortunately, this issue could not be explored in the present study due to the extremely small number of females in the high-Mach group. The negative social-cognitive bias exhibited by the high-Mach group suggests that, even if they were not true Machiavellians, these were not ordinary children. For example, such biases are evident in a range of childhood disorders, including aggression, depression, and paranoia. Of these, however, only aggression (in the form of bullying) has been linked with Machiavellianism. In the absence of additional information about their social functioning, it is not known whether some or all of these high-Mach children were bullies.

It was hypothesized that one of the other factors enabling Machiavellians to use their theory of mind differently from other children is an inability to share another's emotions. However, the negative correlation between the Kiddie-Mach and empathic disposition was not significant once the effects of gender were partialed out. This finding is difficult to reconcile with the traditional view of the cold-hearted social manipulator. One possibility is that measures like the Empathy Index are prone to self-report biases. However, in the present study, there was no correlation between children's social desirability and empathy scores. Moreover, the high Machs were less likely to endorse socially desirable attributes than the low Machs. Thus, an alternative view deserves consideration. Machiavellians may not lack empathic affect but instead may be more adept at regulating such feelings, especially when these are liable to interfere with personal goals. Moreover, any empathic response might be tempered by the positive affect associated with the attainment of such goals. It is also likely that the Machiavellian can minimize related negative feelings, like guilt and remorse, by virtue of the self-justifications they create for their antisocial actions (e.g., "I'm sorry he got hurt, but he would have done the same thing to me"). Regardless, more direct measures of empathic responsiveness (e.g., children's facial or physiological response to another person's negative affect) are clearly needed to explore how emotion processes are involved in Machiavellianism.

CONCLUSIONS

The review of the existing literature and the two new studies presented in this chapter suggest that the theoretical link between theory of mind ability and social competence is not always empirically borne out. Though there is some evidence for such a link, this is clearly an oversimplification. For example, a number of studies (e.g., Blair et al., 1996; Kaukiainen et al., 1999; Sutton et al., 1999) have indicated that an intact theory of mind is sometimes related to negative social behaviors. And others (e.g., Astington & Jenkins, 1995; Cuming & Repacholi, 1999) have failed to find the expected link between theory of mind and certain positive social outcomes. The two studies described here add to this growing body of research. Using very different age groups and measures, both studies found that Machiavellian children, who are characterized as skillful social manipulators, were neither impaired nor more advanced in their theory of mind development relative to their agemates. Although Machiavellian children appear to possess a well-functioning theory of mind, by late childhood, their mental state attributions are prone to a negative social-cognitive bias. Thus, it appears to be the quality or content of older children's theory of mind that is crucial to their social functioning. In other words, the lens through which an individual views a social situation may be more important in predicting interpersonal behavior than simply whether the person can or cannot accurately read another person's mind. It remains to be determined whether this is also the case for the adult Machiavellian.

Evidence was also presented that, at least during the preschool years, Machiavellian tendencies are related to controversial peer status. Such children share features of both the popular and the rejected sociometric categories. Despite their antisocial behaviors (e.g., elevated levels of aggression), controversial children are not perceived by their peers as highly uncooperative; they behave prosocially at least some of the time, and are often viewed as group leaders (Coie et al., 1982). Thus, even though some of their peers dislike them, they have sufficient positive qualities that they are liked by others and not excluded from the peer group (Newcomb, Bukowski, & Pattee, 1993). This description is in line with how we might imagine Machiavellians to operate. As long as it doesn't jeopardize their own self-interests, Machs can presumably engage in prosocial behavior, thereby eliciting trust and acceptance within the social group. Indeed, such actions may be a very calculated impression management strategy that enables them, at least in the short term, to avoid detection. Children who dislike the Machiavellian may consequently be those members of the peer group who are aware that they and/or others have been subject to manipulation and exploitation.

The two studies presented here are only a first step in exploring what may ultimately be a complex relationship between Machiavellianism and theory of mind. Mind reading is not a unidimensional capacity, and using just one type of measure (e.g., the false-belief task) is unlikely to capture all of its complexity, even in the preschool years. Moreover, high- and low-Mach preadolescents differed not in their basic ability to read another person's mind, but in the quality or content of their mind reading. Thus, one challenge for researchers is to devise a range of measures that reflect the diverse components of our mind-reading capacity, as well as its more qualitative aspects. This may be particularly difficult in the case of older children and adults because, as yet, there is no consensus as to what constitutes a "mature" theory of mind. However, once valid and age-appropriate instruments are available, researchers will be in a much better position to explore not only how mind reading is related to Machiavellianism but also how it supports social functioning more generally.

Researchers should also be alert to the possibility that an individual's task performance, especially that of the Machiavellian, may not represent their optimal level of mind reading. It may only be in real-life interpersonal situations, where they are pursuing a personal goal or there is some personal payoff involved, that Machiavellians will fully engage their theory of mind. Given all of these measurement issues, it would be premature to conclude that high Machs are merely average mind readers. Moreover, Machiavellianism, as an emerging personality attribute in children, may only be one of many variables that determine how a theory of mind is used in peer relationships and other forms of social interaction.

NOTES

1. Popular children were those children who had an SP score greater than +1, a standardized LM score greater than the mean of zero, and a standardized LL score less than the mean of zero. Controversial children were those who had an SI score greater than +1, and had standardized LM and LL scores greater than the mean of zero. Average children were those with an SP score between –0.5 and +0.5. Neglected children were those children who had an SI score less than –1, and standardized LM and LL scores below the mean of zero. Finally, rejected children were those with an SP score below –1, a standardized LM score below the mean of zero, and a standardized LL score above the mean of zero.
2. A recent pilot study with 37 fifth- and seventh-graders investigated the relation between scores on the 12-item Mach scale (filled out by parents) and concurrent Kiddie-Mach scores. This analysis revealed a Pearson's correlation coefficient of .53. Although preliminary, this initial attempt at validation suggests fairly good correspondence between the two measures of Machiavellianism in young children.

REFERENCES

Achenbach T., & Edelbrock, C. (1983). *Manual for the Child Behavior Checklist and Revised Child Behavior Profile.* Burlington, VT: Department of Psychology, University of Vermont.

Allsopp, J., Eysenck, H. J., & Eysenck, S. B. (1991). Machiavellianism as a component in psychoticism and extraversion. *Personality and Individual Differences, 12,* 29–41.

Andreou, E. (2000). Bully/victim problems and their association with psychological constructs in 8- to 12-year-old Greek schoolchildren. *Aggressive Behavior, 26,* 49–56.

Astington, J. W., & Jenkins, J. M. (1995). Theory of mind development and social understanding. *Cognition and Emotion, 9,* 151–165.

Astington, J. W., & Jenkins, J. M. (1999). A longitudinal study of the relation between language and theory-of-mind development. *Developmental Psychology, 35,* 1311–1320.

Badenes, L. V., Estevan, R. A. C., & Bacete, F. J. G. (2000). Theory of mind and peer rejection at school. *Social Development, 9,* 271–283.

Barnett, M. A., & Thompson, S. (1985). The role of perspective taking and empathy in children's Machiavellianism, prosocial behavior, and motive for helping. *Journal of Genetic Psychology, 146,* 295–305.

Baron-Cohen, S. (1994). How to build a baby that can read minds. *Current Psychology of Cognition, 13,* 513–552.

Baron-Cohen, S., Jolliffe, T., Mortimore, C.,

& Robertson, M. (1997). Another advanced test of theory of mind: Evidence from very high functioning adults with autism or Asperger syndrome. *Journal of Child Psychology and Psychiatry, 38*, 813–822.

Baron-Cohen, S., Leslie, A. M., & Frith, U. (1985). Does the autistic child have a "theory of mind"? *Cognition, 21*, 37–46.

Blair, J., Sellars, C., Strickland, I., Clark, F., Williams, A., Smith, M., & Jones, L. (1996). Theory of mind in the psychopath. *Journal of Forensic Psychiatry, 7*, 15–25.

Bogart, K., Geis, F., Levy, P., & Zimbardo, P. (1970). No dissonance for Machiavellians. In R. Christie & F. Geis (Eds.), *Studies in Machiavellianism* (pp. 236–259). New York: Academic Press.

Bosacki, S., & Astington, J. W. (1999). Theory of mind in preadolescence: Relations between social understanding and social competence. *Social Development, 8*, 238–255.

Braginsky, D. D. (1970). Machiavellianism and manipulative interpersonal behavior in children. *Journal of Experimental Social Psychology, 6*, 77–99.

Brown, E. C., & Guy, R. F. (1983). The effects of sex and Machiavellianism on self-disclosure patterns. *Social Behavior and Personality, 11*, 93–96.

Bryant, B. K. (1982). An index of empathy for children and adolescents. *Child Development, 53*, 413–425.

Carlson, S. M., & Moses, L. J. (2001). Individual differences in inhibitory control and children's theory of mind. *Child Development, 72*, 1032–1053.

Cherulnik, P. D., Way, J. H., Ames, S., & Hutto, D. B. (1981). Impressions of high and low Machiavellian men. *Journal of Personality, 49*, 388–400.

Christie, R. (1970a). Why Machiavelli? In R. Christie & F. L. Geis (Eds.), *Studies in Machiavellianism* (pp. 1–9). New York: Academic Press.

Christie, R. (1970b). Scale construction. In R. Christie & F. L. Geis (Eds.), *Studies in Machiavellianism* (pp. 10–34). New York: Academic Press.

Christie, R. (1970c). Social correlates of Machiavellianism. In R. Christie & F. L. Geis (Eds.), *Studies in Machiavellianism* (pp. 314–338). New York: Academic Press.

Coie, J. D., & Dodge, K. A. (1983). Continuities and changes in children's social status: A five year longitudinal study. *Merrill-Palmer Quarterly, 29*, 261–282.

Coie, J. D., & Dodge, K. A. (1988). Multiple sources of data on social behavior and social status in the school: A cross-age comparison. *Child Development, 59*, 815–829.

Coie, J. D., Dodge, K. A., & Coppotelli, H. (1982). Dimensions and types of social status: A cross-age perspective. *Developmental Psychology, 18*, 557–570.

Coie, J.D., Dodge, K.A., & Kupersmidt, J. (1990). Peer group behavior and social status. In S. R. Asher & J. D. Coie (Eds.), *Peer rejection in childhood* (pp. 17–59). New York: Cambridge University Press.

Crandall, V. C., Crandall, V. J., & Katkovsky, W. (1965). A children's social desirability questionnaire. *Journal of Consulting and Clinical Psychology, 29*, 27–36.

Crick, N. R., & Dodge, K. A. (1996). Social information processing mechanisms in reactive and proactive aggression. *Child Development, 67*, 993–1002.

Crick, N. R., & Grotpeter, J. K. (1995). Relational aggression, gender, and social-psychological adjustment. *Child Development, 54*, 1396–1399.

Cuming, S., & Repacholi, B. (1999, July). *Is there a link between children's peer relationships and their theory of mind?* Poster presentation at the 11th Australasian Human Development Association Conference, Sydney, Australia.

Cutting, A. L., & Dunn, J. (1999). Theory of mind, emotion understanding, language, and family background: Individual differences and interrelations. *Child Development, 70*, 853–865.

Damon, W. (1988). *The moral child.* New York: Free Press.

Dekovic, M., & Gerris, J. R. M. (1994). Developmental analysis of social cognitive and behavioral differences between popular and rejected children. *Journal of Applied Developmental Psychology, 15*, 367–386.

Dien, D. S. (1974). Parental Machiavellianism and children's cheating in Japan. *Journal of Cross Cultural Psychology, 5*, 259–270.

Dien, D. S., & Fujisawa, H. (1979). Machiavellianism in Japan: A longitudinal study.

Journal of Cross Cultural Psychology, 10, 508–516.

Dunn, J. (1995). Children as psychologists: The later correlates of individual differences in understanding emotions and other minds. *Cognition and Emotion, 9,* 187–201.

Dunn, J. (1996). The Emmanuel Miller Memorial Lecture 1995. Children's relationships: Bridging the divide between cognitive and social development. *Journal of Child Psychology and Psychiatry, 37,* 507–518.

Dunn, L. M., & Dunn, L. M. (1981). *Peabody Picture Vocabulary Test–Revised (PPVT–R).* Circle Pines, MN: American Guidance Service.

Exline, R. V., Thiabaut, J., Hickey, C. B., & Gumpert, P. (1970). Visual interaction in relation to Machiavellianism. In R. Christie & F. Geis (Eds.), *Studies in Machiavellianism* (pp. 53–76). New York: Academic Press.

Geis, F. (1970). The con game. In R. Christie & F. Geis (Eds.), *Studies in Machiavellianism* (pp. 106–129). New York: Academic Press.

Gest, S., Graham-Bermann, S., & Hartup, W. (2001). Peer experience: Common and unique features of number of friendships, social network centrality, and sociometric status. *Social Development, 10,* 23–40.

Golden, C. J. (1978). *Stroop color and word test.* Wood Dale, IL: Stoelting.

Gopnik, A., & Astington, J. W. (1988). Children's understanding of representational change and its relation to the understanding of false belief and the appearance-reality distinction. *Child Development, 59,* 1–14.

Happé, F. (1994). An advanced test of theory of mind: Understanding of story character's thoughts and feelings by able autistic, mentally handicapped, and normal children and adults. *Journal of Autism and Developmental Disorders, 24,* 129–154.

Happé, F., & Frith, U. (1996). Theory of mind and social impairment in children with conduct disorder. *British Journal of Developmental Psychology, 14,* 385–398.

Harrell, W. A., & Hartnagel, T. (1976). The impact of Machiavellianism and the trustfulness of the victim on laboratory theft. *Sociometry, 39,* 157–165.

Hoffman, M. L. (1988). Interaction of affect and cognition in empathy. In C. E. Izard & J. Kagan (Eds.), *Emotions, cognition, and behavior* (pp. 103-131). New York: Cambridge University Press.

Hughes, C., & Dunn, J. (1997). "Pretend you didn't know": Preschoolers' talk about mental states in pretend play. *Cognitive Development, 12,* 381–403.

Hughes, C., Dunn, J., & White, A. (1998). Trick or treat? Uneven understanding of mind and emotion and executive dysfunction in "hard to manage" preschoolers. *Journal of Child Psychology and Psychiatry, 39,* 981–994.

Jenkins, J. M., & Astington, J. W. (1996). Cognitive factors and family structure associated with theory of mind development in young children. *Developmental Psychology, 32,* 70–78.

Kaukiainen, A., Bjorkqvist, K., Lagerspetz, K., Osterman, K., Salmivalli, C., Rothberg, S., & Ahlbom, A. (1999). The relationships between social intelligence, empathy, and three types of aggression. *Aggressive Behavior, 25,* 81–89.

Kraut, R. E., & Price, J. D. (1976). Machiavellianism in parents and their children. *Journal of Personality and Social Psychology, 33,* 782–786.

Lalonde, C. E., & Chandler, M. J. (1995). False belief understanding goes to school: On the social-emotional consequences of coming early or late to a first theory of mind. *Cognition and Emotion, 9,* 167–185.

Langdon, R., & Coltheart, M. (1999). Mentalizing, schizotypy, and schizophrenia. *Cognition, 71,* 43–71.

Lee, K., Eskritt, M., Symons, L., & Muir, D. (1998). Children's use of triadic eye gaze information for "mindreading." *Developmental Psychology, 34,* 525–539.

Macguire, M. C., & Dunn, J. (1997). Friendships in early childhood and social understanding. *International Journal of Behavioral Development, 21,* 669–686.

McHoskey, J. W., Worzel, W., & Szyarto, C. (1998). Machiavellianism and psychopathy. *Journal of Personality and Social Psychology, 74,* 192–210.

Mealey, L. (1995). The sociobiology of sociopathy: An integrated evolutionary model. *Behavioral and Brain Sciences, 18,* 523–599.

Mealey, L., Daood, C., & Krage, M. (1996).

Enhanced memory for faces of cheaters. *Ethology & Sociobiology, 17,* 119–128.

Miller, P., & Eisenberg, N. (1988). The relation of empathy to aggressive and externalizing/antisocial behaviour. *Psychological Bulletin, 103,* 324–344.

Moore, C., Barresi, J., & Thompson, C. (1998). The cognitive basis of future-oriented prosocial behavior. *Social Development, 7,* 198–218.

Nelson, D. A., & Crick, N. R. (1999). Rose-colored glasses: Examining the social information processing of prosocial young adolescents. *Journal of Early Adolescence, 19,* 17–38.

Newcomb, A. F., Bukowksi, W. M., & Pattee, L. (1993). Children's peer relations: A meta-analytic review of popular, rejected, neglected, controversial, and average sociometric status. *Psychological Bulletin, 113,* 99–128.

O'Connor, T. G., & Hirsch, N. (1999). Intra-individual differences and relationship-specificity of mentalising in early adolescence. *Social Development, 8,* 256–274.

O'Connor, E. M., & Simms, C. M. (1990). Self revelation as manipulation: The effects of sex and Machiavellianism on self-disclosure. *Social Behavior and Personality, 18,* 95–100.

Olweus, D. (1993). *Bullying at school.* Cambridge, MA: Blackwell.

Peterson, C. C., & Siegal, M. (2002). Mind-reading and moral awareness in popular and rejected preschoolers. *British Journal of Developmental Psychology, 20,* 205–224.

Quiggle, N. L., Garber, J., Panak, W. F., & Dodge, K. A. (1992). Social information processing in aggressive and depressed children. *Child Development, 63,* 1305–1320.

Repacholi, B., & Gibbs, V. (2000). *Machiavellianism in children: Is it related to empathy, social-cognitive ability and parenting?* Unpublished manuscript, Macquarie University.

Repacholi, B., & Trapolini, T. (submitted). *Individual differences in children's social understanding: The role of person identity and attachment.*

Richardson, D., Hammock, G., Smith, S., Gardner, W., & Manuel, S. (1994). Empathy as a cognitive inhibitor of interpersonal aggression. *Aggressive Behavior, 20,* 275–289.

Ruffman, T., Perner, J., Naito, M., Parkin, L., & Clements, W. (1998). Older (but not younger) siblings facilitate false belief understanding. *Developmental Psychology, 34,* 161–174.

Sanderson, J. A., & Siegal, M. (1995). Loneliness and stable friendship in rejected and non-rejected preschoolers. *Journal of Applied Developmental Psychology, 16,* 555–567.

Schaffer, R. (1996). *Social development.* Oxford, UK: Blackwell.

Schultz, J.S. (1993). Situational and dispositional predictions of performance: A test of the hypothesized Machiavellianism X structure interaction among sales persons. *Journal of Applied Social Psychology, 23,* 478–498.

Sheppard, B. H., & Vidmar, N. (1980). Adversary pretrial procedures and testimonial evidence: Effects of lawyer's role and Machiavellianism. *Journal of Personality and Social Psychology, 39,* 320–332.

Siegal, M. (1997). *Knowing children: Experiments in conversation and cognition.* Hove, UK: Psychology Press.

Slaughter, V., Dennis, M. J., & Pritchard, M. (2002). Theory of mind and peer acceptance in preschool children. *British Journal of Developmental Psychology, 20,* 545–564.

Slaughter, V., & Pritchard, M. (2000). *Determining peer acceptance amongst preschool children.* Unpublished manuscript, University of Queensland.

Slomkowski, C., & Dunn, J. (1996). Young children's understanding of other people's beliefs and feelings and their connected communication with friends. *Developmental Psychology, 32,* 442–447.

Strange, A., & Nixon, C. (2001, April). *Social competence and theory of mind understanding in elementary school children with attention deficits.* Poster presented at the biennial meeting of the Society for Research in Child Development, Minneapolis, MN.

Sutton, J., & Keogh, E. (2000). Social competition in school: Relationships with bullying, Machiavellianism and personality. *British Journal of Educational Psychology, 70,* 443–456.

Sutton, J., & Keogh, E. (2001). Components of Machiavellian beliefs in children: Relationships with personality. *Personality and Individual Differences, 30,* 137–148.

Sutton, J., Reeves, M., & Keogh, E. (2000). Disruptive behaviour, avoidance of responsibility and theory of mind. *British Journal of Developmental Psychology, 18,* 1–11.

Sutton, J., Smith, P. K., & Swettenham, J. (1999). Social cognition and bullying—Social inadequacy or skilled manipulation? *British Journal of Developmental Psychology, 17,* 435–450.

Turkat, I. D., Keane, S. P., & Thompson-Pope, S. K. (1990). Social processing errors among paranoid personalities. Special issues: DSM-IV and the psychology literature. *Journal of Psychopathology and Behavioral Assessment, 12,* 263–269.

Watson, A. C., Nixon, C. L., Wilson, A., & Capage, L. (1999). Social interaction skills and theory of mind in young children. *Developmental Psychology, 35,* 386–391.

Weir, K., & Duveen, G., (1981). Further development and validation of the prosocial behavior questionnaire for use by teachers. *Journal of Child Psychology and Psychiatry, 22,* 357–374.

Wellman, H. M. (1990). *The child's theory of mind.* Cambridge, MA: MIT Press.

Wellman, H. M., & Banerjee, M. (1991). Mind and emotion: Children's understanding of the emotional consequences of beliefs and desires. *British Journal of Developmental Psychology, 9,* 191–214.

Williams, B. T. R., & Gilmour, J. D. (1994). Annotation: Sociometry and peer relationships. *Journal of Child Psychology and Psychiatry, 35,* 997–1013.

Wilson, D. S., Near, D., & Miller, R. R. (1996). Machiavellianism: A synthesis of the evolutionary and psychological literatures. *Psychological Bulletin, 119,* 285–299.

Wimmer, H., & Perner, J. (1983). Beliefs about beliefs: Representations and constraining function of wrong beliefs in young children's understanding of deception. *Cognition, 13,* 103–128.

Wolfson, S. L. (1981). Effects of Machiavellianism and communication on helping behaviour during an emergency. *British Journal of Social Psychology, 4,* 328–332.

Wrightsman, L. S. (1991). Interpersonal trust and attitudes towards human nature. In J. P. Robinson, P. R. Shaver, & L. S. Wrightsman (Eds.), *Measures of personality and social psychological attitudes* (pp. 373–385). New York: Academic Press.

5

ToM Goes to School
Social Cognition and Social Values in Bullying

JON SUTTON

The British Psychological Society, Leicester, UK

M any of you will have been bullied. A recent United Kingdom (UK) survey found that 12% of 10- to 14-year-olds reported being bullied "at least two or three times a month" over the last 6 months (Smith & Shu, 2000) and Rayner (1997) found that 53% of a large sample of part-time university students reported they had been bullied at some point in their working lives. There is no doubt that this is an unpleasant experience. Victims suffer from low self-esteem (Boulton & Smith, 1994), may play truant in order to avoid the bullying (Sharp & Thompson, 1992), and in extreme cases may take their own lives: Around ten suicides a year in the UK alone are linked to persistent bullying. The effects are long lasting: Victimization during middle school predicts depression and low self-esteem 10 years later (Olweus, 1993).

Now conjure up a picture in your head of the bully. Were they the stereotypical "oafs of literature tormenting the school swot" (Besag, 1989, p. 15), "Dennis the Menace" to your "Walter the Softy" (from the children's comic *The Beano*), the thuggish "Gripper" to your fat, bespectacled victim Roland (from the 1980s UK TV program *Grange Hill*)? Use your own "theory of mind" (ToM) to take the mental leap into their thoughts, to consider their beliefs, desires, and intentions. Surely they must have been mentally or socially deficient in some way, to put you through that torment?

Or are you getting a more complex picture? Is it in fact you looming into view, with the odd throwaway but devastating putdown, because you believed that the situation demanded it? Deliberately excluding a classmate or spreading rumors about them because it helped you to clamber one more rung up the classroom hierarchy?

In this chapter, I argue that the negative effects of bullying are always lurking in the background when we consider the topic, even as supposedly detached scientific investigators. Perhaps we feel protected by assuming that bullying is an unusual behavior that has a cause located squarely within the individual, whether that cause is low self-esteem, a deprived family background, or poor social cognition. This attributional bias is common across many domains of behavior (see Hewstone, 1983) and does serve important psychological functions. But as tempting as it may be simply to demonize the individuals involved, greater understanding will only arise from scientific study of the sociocultural and interpersonal factors and the motivations to bully they create.

To build this kind of picture, we need a new canvas. Antisocial behavior becomes social behavior, often carried out for perfectly understandable reasons such as to win friends by creating a powerful reputation. Social cognition deficits become social cognition differences, often realistic responses to experience or a particular social environment. And as we paint the picture of social cognition in bullying, we discover that ToM is just one brush stroke within it, albeit a central one. Other elements are added to the canvas—emotional understanding and empathy, Machiavellianism, social competition, self-esteem, and a whole host of reputation-enhancement strategies. Finally, as we draw back from the picture we see that it is not an unusual one—that when ToM goes to school it often finds the right conditions for bullying. Is it time for a reassessment of what is socially competent, "normal" development? Can a ToM used to bully others really be considered "superior"?

TAKING THE "ANTI" OUT OF ANTISOCIAL BEHAVIOR

Over the last 20 years, bullying among young children has expanded considerably as a research issue (see Smith & Brain, 2000). It is now recognized as a global problem, with investigation originating in Norway (Olweus, 1978) and spreading to Japan (Kikkawa, 1987), Australia (Rigby & Slee, 1991), England (Smith & Thompson, 1991), Canada (Pepler, Craig, Zeigler, & Charach, 1993), and the United States (Ross, 1996). Although intervention projects have had some success (Olweus, 1993; Smith & Sharp, 1994), none of these school-based programs have reduced reported bullying by more than about 50%. Evidence from individual schools and reports from teachers in such projects (e.g., Eslea & Smith, 1998) suggest that there may be a "hard core" of children who bully, and some may even be stimulated to bully in association with the interventions (Randall, 1996). Academics and practitioners may need to consider in more detail the cognitive style and skills associated with such persistent bullying or victimization, or they may need to consider what it is about the school environment that allows bullying to continue to flourish, even when awareness of the problem is raised. I hope to show that these questions are linked by, and can benefit from, a ToM/social cognition approach.

The first step in tackling problem behavior is to define it. This has not proved to be a simple task: Ross (1996) reviewed the debate on definitions of bullying and concluded that the field was "in a state of disarray by the early 1990s" (p. 24) as a result of inconsistencies in definition. Unfortunately a consensus may not be forthcoming, particularly as an all-inclusive definition may seem appealing for intervention and antibullying policy, whereas a more restricted and operationalized definition would be more suitable for research purposes. For our purposes, to discuss a link with social cognition, I believe it is important to emphasize the differences between bullying and aggression. There is no doubt that aggression, whether it is physical, verbal, or psychological, is a key component of bullying. But bullying is more than aggression—it is the "systematic abuse of power" (Smith & Sharp, 1994). Olweus (1991, 1994) also highlights the key elements of intention, repetition, and asymmetry of power. The implications for ToM and social cognition are immediately clear—this is not a simple case of, for example, hitting out in response to provocation.

Now consider the context in which bullying often takes place. Bullying has been referred to as violence in a group context in which pupils reinforce others' behavior in their interaction (Pikas, 1975), and the collective character and importance of social relationships are often emphasized (Lagerspetz, Bjorkqvist, Berts, & King, 1982). It tends to take place in a social setting: peers are present in 85% of bullying episodes (Pepler & Craig, 1995). One half of female-to-female and one third of male-to-male bullying takes place within a friendship network (Salmivalli, Huttenen, & Lagerspetz, 1997).

Within this social context, bullying often uses social and indirect methods. Bullies leave people out of groups or spread nasty gossip, and with the natural age progression toward more sophisticated and indirect bullying (Rivers & Smith, 1994) methods can even include creating "furtive alliances" and the use of entrapment (inviting someone to commit themselves to a course of action that is already known by the abuser to be flawed; Thomas-Peter, 1997).

It is when we consider bullying as social behavior in this way that social cognition becomes absolutely vital in understanding and addressing it. The clue was there in the first definition of ToM: "the ability to understand *and manipulate* the mental states of others" (Premack & Woodruff, 1978, my italics). Children are constantly making that mental leap into someone else's head that is central to a first-order ToM and belief-desire reasoning. They are thinking about what other children are thinking, and from there it is a small step to manipulating these thoughts: a useful skill in some forms of bullying, particularly so-called "relational aggression" (Crick, 1996). Here the bully attempts to harm others through the damage and manipulation of peer relationships (Crick & Grotpeter, 1995). Children may often use their ToM to think about whether another child wants to be in their gang, and whether the child believes that it is possible that he or she could be. Such thoughts can easily lead to indirect bullying through social exclusion.

This type of bullying can occur almost as a by-product of reputation enhancement strategies, and a sophisticated ToM is quite a string to your bow here. What other children think of you can make or break your schooldays. Mike is thinking "if Tony thinks that I think Bill is a teacher's pet and that I don't like him and don't want to play with him, then Tony will like me. And if other children in the class think that Tony likes me then they will like me too, because I know most of the other children like Tony and think he's cool. So I need to make the other children think that I don't like Bill, even though I really do." What I think you think I think can be the difference between sitting alone at lunch or being leader of a gang—it is survival of the fittest in the playground and ToM is a vital weapon.

Even if a child is only bullying physically, the child may be planting false beliefs in the minds of the teachers to avoid detection or punishment, or choosing the most effective time and method for each situation in terms of maximizing the impact on the victim while simultaneously minimizing chances of detection or hurt to themselves—Bjorkqvist, Österman, and Kaukiainen's (1992) "effect-danger ratio theory." The child must ponder which particular insult will cause the maximum impact on their victim, and select from a multitude of emotions such as scared, upset, angry, or indifferent in judging the victim's response. The child may be persuading other children to take part in the bullying, to reinforce their power.

But the fact that the conditions appear to be right for ToM skills to play a part in bullying does not necessarily mean that they do. In fact, most research has hypothesized that a lack of social understanding is a cause of aggression. The assumption that this will extend to bullying has been a pervasive one: Children bully because they don't have the social skills to interact properly, and they are forced to rely on aggression to get their own way. Although this view may certainly explain *some* bullying, I have argued (for more detailed reviews of the debate see Sutton, Smith, & Swettenham, 1999a, 1999b, 1999c, 2001) that there is little empirical evidence to support the popular stereotype of a bully as physically powerful yet intellectually simple or backward. Both antibullying interventions and social cognition research may be hampered by a tendency to behavior the bully and his or her cognitive style. Let's consider the evidence.

A LACK OF ToM?

Randall (1997a, p. 23) claimed that "bullies do not process social information accurately and seem unable to make realistic judgments about the intentions of other people." They "fail to understand the feelings of others" and "have little awareness of what other children actually think of them . . . a symptom of their social blindness." Hazler (1996) suggested that to stop bullying, bullies "need to recognize information about how others perceive the situation" (p. 98).

But views of children who bully as lacking in social perspective-taking skills have not been based on empirical work involving bullies; instead, the foundations are largely theory and equivocal evidence from research using mostly male samples of aggressive or conduct-disordered children. For example, the social-skills model of aggression (Dodge, Pettit, McClaskey, & Brown, 1986; updated by Crick & Dodge, 1994) has been influential in explaining childhood aggression in terms of social information processing biases or deficits at one or more of the following points in a five-stage process of assessing and responding to social situations: social perception, interpretation of social cues perceived, goal selection, response-strategy generation, and response decisions. Several studies have found that aggressive children tend to attribute hostile intent to the actions of others more frequently than non-aggressive children (Dodge, Petit, Bates, & Valente, 1995; Feldman & Dodge, 1987; Gibbins & Craig, 1997; Guerra & Slaby, 1989; Steinberg & Dodge, 1983).

However, Dodge (1991) distinguished between reactive aggression (occurring in the context of a negatively affectively charged, high-conflict relationship) and proactive aggression (coercive behavior observed in one boy's dominance of a peer), and hypothesized that "the processing patterns at each step might be more strongly associated with one type of aggression than the other" (Dodge, 1991, p. 211). Crick and Dodge (1996) noted that proactive aggressors are not particularly vulnerable to attributional biases, and Boulton and Smith (1994) noted that it is only proactive aggression that includes bullying.

In terms of ToM specifically, several investigators have hypothesized (but not necessarily found) ToM deficits in relation to antisocial behavior. Happé and Frith (1996) found that children with conduct disorder passed two standard first-order false-belief tasks but showed impairments of social insight in real-life behavior as measured by the Vineland Adaptive Behavior Scale (Sparrow, Balla, & Cicchetti, 1984). Hughes, Dunn, and White (1998) reported that "hard to manage" preschoolers performed worse than matched peers on false-belief tasks. Blair et al. (1996) predicted, but failed to find, significant differences in correct inferences or references to mental states in an advanced test of ToM with incarcerated psychopaths and controls.

But children who bully are not psychopaths. They are not all conduct disordered, and they are not even all "hard to manage." As discussed earlier, they have a context and methods that would seem to benefit from superior ToM skills. So is there any evidence of such superiority?

A SUPERIOR ToM?

The inequality of power inherent in bullying implies dominance, and (in contrast to the more general field of aggression) dominance is often associated with social skills and manipulation of belief. For example, Keating and Heltman (1994) found that preschool children who deceived successfully (were judged as honest by adult researchers when persuading another child that a nasty-tasting drink was pleasant) also tended to be those who terrorized the playground and were rated as dominant. The element of repetition in bullying may also imply planning, which could well involve ToM: In fact, Happé and Frith (1996) found that the conduct-disordered children in their study most clearly showed their mentalizing abilities in the domains of lying, cheating, teasing, and bullying.

But we will not achieve a reliable picture of the applicability of the ToM or social information processing approach until various measures are used with a range of subgroups of bullying children who might be expected to use social cognition in their behavior. Little research has attempted this approach, although social intelligence has been found to be positively and most strongly related to indirect forms of aggression (Bjorkqvist, Österman, & Kauikainen, 2000; Kauikiainen et al., 1999). In unpublished data by Kaukiainen, Peltonen, and Sippola (2002), the bullies' scores on peer-rated social intelligence were found to be significantly higher than the victims' corresponding scores (although not significantly different from the scores of children not involved in bullying). In another recent study, cluster analysis identified a group of bullies with good skills in learning, average scores on social intelligence, and an extremely positive view of self (Kaukiainen, Salmivalli, Lagerspetz, Tamminen, Vauras, Maki, and Poskiparta, 2002). Thinking more specifically about ToM, a theoretical link is suggested by the fact that indirect bullying is also relatively more frequent in girls than boys (Bjorkqvist et al., 1992; Rivers & Smith, 1994), and a ToM superiority has been demonstrated among girls (Baron-Cohen & Hammer, 1996).

Just as it is important to recognize that children with conduct problems are a notoriously heterogeneous group, we should also avoid treating social skills or mentalizing as a unitary concept. Children may have a very good "theory of nasty minds" (Happé & Frith, 1996), or "cold cognition" (Mealey, 1995): a gap between understanding thoughts and feelings. This is a familiar concept within the field of Machiavellianism (the high Machiavellian "appraises a situation logically and cognitively rather than emotionally": Christie & Geis, 1970, p. 85), and also psychopathy. Although not all bullies are budding psychopaths, the possibility of emotionless manipulators is obviously a serious one in a school environment (see McIlwain and Repacholi et al., this volume).

In Sutton et al. (1999c), we investigated the cognitive/emotion distinction in a ToM framework. Because it was important to address the social context of bullying rather than focusing on an artificial bully/victim dichotomy, we also addressed the other roles peers may take on. They may help the bully (Assistant), for example, by holding the victim as they are assaulted. They may reinforce the bully through watching, laughing, and shouting encouragement (Reinforcer). Alternatively, they may stick up for or comfort the victim (Defender), or remain resolutely uninvolved (Outsider). Using this Participant Role Scale approach (PRS), Salmivalli, Lagerspetz, Bjorkqvist, Österman, and

Kaukiainen (1996) found that it was possible to assign one of these roles to 87% of 11- to 13-year-old Finnish children. Having a grasp of the internal mental states of those involved, along with an ability to manipulate these thoughts and beliefs, may be crucial for the bully in developing and maintaining such inter-role relations. A Bully would be at a social advantage if he or she were to possess social cognition skills that were superior to those of the Followers (Assistants and Reinforcers) and the Victims.

There were 193 children (102 girls and 91 boys) in the study, aged between 7 years 7 months and 10 years 8 months (mean 9 years) old. Using a shortened version of the PRS (see Sutton & Smith, 1999), each child had six continuous role scores, reflecting level of involvement in each behavior (Bully, Assistant, Reinforcer, Defender, Outsider, and Victim), and one main Participant Role, reflecting what they did most. A child was considered a Victim if he or she was nominated in "gets bullied" by 30% or more of his or her same-sex classmates. These scores and roles were then related to performance on a set of 11 stories assessing understanding of false beliefs or false belief-based emotion (see Sutton et al., 1999c, for details). See the example of an emotion story that follows, as well as Figure 5.1.

Emotion Story.

Mike wants to go out with his friends, but he has a really bad tummy ache. He knows that if his Mum notices he is ill, she won't let him go out to play. Mike goes downstairs and asks his Mum "can I go out to play please?"

Which picture shows how Mike will look when he talks to his Mum?
Control question: Which picture shows how Mike really feels?

To get full marks, a child would say that although Mike feels really ill (top right) he will look happy or at least neutral (bottom pictures) when he talks to his Mum, so that she doesn't know he's ill. This would show the child can understand that an appropriate display of emotion can create a belief in another that differs from reality. (See Figure 5.1 for story pictures.)

Participant Role had a significant effect on total social cognition score, after controlling for age and verbal ability. Bullies scored higher than any other group: significantly higher than Victims, Followers, and Defenders. The significant difference between Bullies and Defenders seems particularly worthy of further research: Although at first glance we might consider Defenders to be socially skilled children, these skills may involve assertiveness and empathy more than the manipulation thought to involve the skills assessed with the stories in this study.

In addition to the categorical Participant Role results, there were interesting associations between social cognition score and level of involvement in bullying. The continuous Bully role score was positively correlated with total social

FIGURE 5.1. Emotion story pictures: Top left, Angry Mike; top right, Sick Mike; bottom left, Happy Mike; bottom Right, Neutral Mike.

cognition score, cognitive score, and (perhaps surprisingly) with emotion score. In contrast, Victim score was negatively correlated with total social cognition score—perhaps it is the victims' lack of mentalizing ability that puts them at the bottom of the pecking order.

ToM GROWS UP, AND GETS NASTY

The present knowledge base linking ToM to bullying is limited, and the few studies that have been carried out do not paint a consistent picture; for example, Monks, Smith, and Swettenham (submitted) found that 4- to 6-year-olds involved in bullying did not show superior ToM skills, perhaps suggesting that it is only as bullying becomes more indirect and relational that more sophisticated ToM skills are used. Investigation of developmental trends, placing social cognition in bullying in a life-span perspective, may be a fruitful avenue for research.

One key question for both bullying and ToM research is whether there is a reciprocal relationship between the two. It is widely accepted that children's social experiences provide the necessary input for an increasingly mature ToM. Siblings appear to be beneficial, with several studies reporting a relationship between number of siblings and preschoolers' understanding of false beliefs, even after controlling for language ability (e.g., Jenkins & Astington, 1996; Ruffman, Perner, Naito, Parkin, & Clements, 1998). Dunn, Brown, Slomkowski, Tesla, and Youngblade (1991) suggested that "being in close and positive relationships motivates children to become interested in and responsive to the behavior and thoughts/feelings of others." But read that sentence again, substituting "bullying" for "close and positive." Is it not possible that involvement in bullying could also boost ToM? A bully and the victim often appear to have a bizarre dyadic relationship (Randall, 1997a), in which there may be more consideration of mind than is immediately evident in the bully's behavior. The "interest" may be motivated by personal gain and the child may therefore be "responsive" to the behavior and thoughts/feelings in an undesirable way, but this remains a plausible way for ToM to become honed over time. Indeed, the strategic planning and execution of deceptive acts have been found to facilitate false-belief understanding in 3-year-olds (Hala & Chandler, 1996).

So how would a bully's ToM develop? It could be argued that if the input to the system continues to be skewed in favor of abusive relationships and predominantly negative emotions on the part of others, the output will also be skewed in terms of better understanding and manipulation of negative mental states. Such a process could start early: Although studying "hard to manage" preschoolers rather than bullies, Hughes et al. (1998) found that understanding of false belief was better in the context of an unpleasant rather than a pleasant surprise. The ideal test would, of course, be longitudinal study of the understanding of positive and negative emotions in relation to concurrent bullying behavior.

And what does the end result of a theory of nasty minds look like in terms of behavior? Although reported bullying generally declines with age, there is specific continuity in bullying superimposed on the general continuity in aggression: Bullying at the age of 14 predicts bullying at the age of 32, independently of the tendency of aggression at one age to predict aggression at another age (Farrington, 1993). Jacobson (1992) identified two types of domestic violence possibly reflecting earlier forms of bullying based on the absence or presence of a sophisticated ToM: a hot-headed, reactive type, and a proactive, cool, calculated aggression that is part of a more general subjugation of the partner.

An increasingly sophisticated adult ToM can enable bullying to continue unchecked in a workplace, passed off as an "autocratic style." At an extreme level, the kind of social control sometimes seen in the workplace has been likened to a cult (O'Reilly & Chatman, 1996), and there may be common elements between cult leaders, managers, and 10-year-old bullies. All may use their ToM skills in a controlled, efficient, proactively aggressive form in an environment that allows it to flourish, often carefully choosing to punish those who are not valued and even disliked by the peer group.

It is also interesting to consider what type of families socially skilled bullies might come from. Contributory family factors in the development of social cognition could be integrated with existing knowledge of bullying and the family, possibly investigating the links between "internal working models" (Bowlby, 1988) and ToM in bullying. For example, the families of children who bully are often characterized by a lack of cohesion and an imbalance of power between the parents (Bowers, Smith, & Binney, 1992), and ringleader bullying appears to be associated with insecure attachment (Myron-Wilson, Sutton, & Smith, submitted). Is this style of relationship internalized in children, providing a model for a cold, manipulative way of thinking?

Some preliminary evidence comes from Sutton (1998). Here, the family factors of neglect, overprotection, and punitive parenting (as measured by the parental style questionnaire: Bowers, Smith, & Binney, 1994) were all strongly negatively correlated with ToM performance in the group of bullies, but not in the rest of the sample. In fact, punitive parenting was significantly positively correlated with ToM in the victims. This perhaps suggests that punishment *style* is very important in mental understanding. Perhaps the harsh, inconsistent discipline more common in the families of bullies (Olweus, 1993) is less effective in teaching empathy and understanding than inductive discipline is. There may be a big difference in terms of implications for ToM development and resultant emotional style between "Go to your room" and "Go to your room and think how would you feel if someone did that to you."

EMOTION UNDERSTANDING

In Sutton et al. (1999c), we found that level of involvement in bullying was positively correlated with understanding of emotion-related false belief. This was an unexpected finding—it suggested that bullies had a good understanding of the emotions they were causing but went ahead anyway. In fact, there was an even more interesting result (Sutton, 1998): Emotion understanding was also positively correlated [$r = .48$, $p < .01$] with teacher ratings to the statement "This child bullies because they enjoy seeing the victim suffer, and subsequently think of ingenious ways to cause this suffering." It is as if some children who bully understand the emotions their actions cause and go ahead not only despite that, but because of that.

Studies using a wider range of social cognition tests may cast some light on the distinction between emotion recognition, emotion understanding, and empathy in children who bully. Such a study could utilize stories, self-report questionnaires of empathic concern (e.g., Bryant, 1982), and even physiological measures of arousal. Do those bullies with a good ToM show this in all kinds of mentalizing, or do they still show deficits in specific areas, in particular on ToM and false-belief tasks involving the moral emotions (e.g., guilt, love, remorse, sympathy, and shame)? Do they understand these emotions but just not share them—in other words, lack empathy? It is certainly the case that young bullies frequently ignore the submissive behavior of their victims and carry on inflicting pain (Dodge, Price, Coie, & Christopoulous, 1990). It is possible that a child who displays a heightened awareness of the feelings of others but also demonstrates an inability or unwillingness to share those feelings (i.e., low empathic disposition) would be especially manipulative in his or her dealings with others (Hoffman, 1975; Staub, 1979). Randall (1997a) noted (but fails to test empirically) that proactive aggressors are "not easily upset emotionally . . . their emotions do not interfere with their social cognition" (p. 29). In a small sample of clinic-referred children, Frick, O'Brien, Wootton, and McBurnett (1994) identified the factor of "selfish, callous, and remorseless use of others": familiar behavior to victims of bullying.

Similarly, in Sutton, Reeves, and Keogh (2000), ToM performance (as measured by a version of the "eyes task": Baron-Cohen, Jolliffe, Mortimore, & Robertson, 1997) was associated with a factor on an "avoidance of responsibility" measure called "denial/lack of remorse." This involved children reporting that when they got in trouble they didn't feel guilty and would argue that they didn't do it; the correlation with performance on the eyes task suggests that this type of persuasion might be facilitated by a good understanding of the mental states and emotions of others. Perhaps some bullies have "affective social competence" (Halberstadt, Denham, & Dunsmore, 2001), including efficacious communication of their own affect, and successful interpretation and response to others' affective communications. "Successful" can again be judged from a variety of perspectives: Halberstadt et al. noted that affective social competence may be used for different purposes, and that "some school-age children express anger on the playground to assert dominance, and within the schoolyard peer culture this works quite well" (p. 89).

Is the emotional style of bullies rooted in a Machiavellian but often realistic appraisal of interpersonal relationships? I have also found that children categorized as bullies scored significantly higher than controls on a "Kiddie-Mach" questionnaire, measuring the belief that others are not to be trusted or are there to be manipulated for your own gain (Sutton & Keogh, 2000). In a subsequent study (Sutton & Keogh, 2001), we found that a "lack of faith in human nature" was positively correlated with age (more so in boys)—children get more cynical. Perhaps bullies are particularly prone to this, as a response to experience of an imbalance in power relationships at home or in school.

WHY DO CHILDREN BULLY? HOW ToM PLAYS A PART IN THE SEARCH FOR POWER

If the emotional style and ToM skills are in place to allow bullying, a child still needs to make the decision to use them in that way. In terms of Crick and Dodge's (1994) social skills model, bullies may perceive and interpret social cues very accurately (the first two stages), but may differ in goal selection, response strategy generation, and response decisions. Such differences may reflect past experiences and strategies that have worked rather than demonstrating an "error." The difference may lie in their values, or the content of the cognitions rather than the accuracy. Arsenio and Lemerise (2001) noted that "most of the unique features of proactively aggressive children converge on their 'values' and 'valuing processes' regarding aggression, namely 'it's easy, it works, and it makes me feel good'" (p. 64). Considering motivations like these within the social cognition framework might provide clearer theoretical understanding of bullying, and ultimately lead to a more effective set of techniques for dealing with it. The "it's easy" step is largely beyond the scope of this chapter (some comment can be found in Sutton, 2001), but the "it works" and "it makes me feel good" steps are closely linked and both may involve a ToM.

A cold, manipulative attitude to interpersonal relationships in school would clearly have impact upon a child's goals. Dodge, Lochman, Harnish, Bates, and Pettit (1997) found that proactively aggressive children expected aggression to be an easy and effective social strategy, and that they would feel more emotionally positive than all other children after initiating aggression. Aggressive children also attach more value (or importance) to the rewarding outcomes of aggression and less value to the negative outcomes than do nonaggressive children (Boldizar, Perry, & Perry, 1989). Findings such as these are absolutely vital in understanding how social cognition operates in a competitive social environment, rather than divorced from social reality in a lab-based false-belief task.

Using ToM skills in bullying may be just one of a range of interrelated strategies available for children to create a powerful reputation. Looking more generally at social competition in school (Sutton & Keogh, 2000), I found that probullying and Machiavellian attitudes were both correlated with a "desire for social success" factor that incorporated a deliberate lack of effort or hiding of effort in class. This correlation remained even after removing the effects of various other interpersonal attitudes. It appears that the attitude "nobody likes a teacher's pet" incorporates attitudes toward both bullying and academic achievement—and it may be a particularly prevalent and disruptive one, especially among boys (who scored significantly higher than girls on both the "desire for social success" factor and the probullying measure).

So the positive valuation of the outcomes of aggression and the manipulation of social relationships through self-presentation appear common. An intervention that could make it as uncool to be a bully as it generally is to be a telltale, a swot, or a victim would be a successful strategy indeed. Attempting this may involve consideration of a potential link between ToM and self-esteem in bullying.

The "standard" view over the years in the literature, interestingly mirroring the deficiency perspective in the social cognition and aggression research, has been that bullying and aggression are associated with a lack of self-esteem (for examples, see Baumeister, 1997, pp. 135–136). However, according to Baumeister, Smart, and Boden (1996), this view suffers from ambiguities, inconsistencies, and contradictory empirical evidence. They argued that aggression and violent behavior are related to positive, rather than negative, self-appraisals.

A particular form of high self-esteem may be important in understanding bullying and, once again, in understanding how ToM may be an important brush stroke on the canvas in our picture of why children bully. According to the "threatened egotism" hypothesis, a combination of highly favorable self-appraisals and ego threat (e.g., some person or circumstance challenging or denying the individual's own favorable appraisals) may lead to aggression toward the source of the threat (Baumeister et al., 1996; Bushman & Baumeister, 1998). Salmivalli (2001) reviewed the evidence for this hypothesis in relation to bullying, reporting her own study that operationalized defensive egotism through peer evaluations of three items describing (1) an individual's need to be constantly in the center of attention, (2) a tendency to think too highly of him/herself, and (3) an inability to face criticism. Bullying was most typical of those adolescents identified by cluster analysis as high in defensive self-esteem. This finding dovetails nicely with clinical observations of bullying in the workplace (e.g., Randall, 2001), where the narcissistic bully is characterized by a tendency to deride the abilities and accomplishments of others while being preoccupied with fantasies of their own success, power, and value to society.

I am not aware of any research linking ToM skills and threatened egotism in relation to bullying. But a highly "active" ToM (as evidenced, for example, by frequent reference to the mental states of self and others in natural language accounts) may well operate in tandem with fragile self-esteem to maintain a child, at least in his or her own mind, as "center of attention." It would certainly be interesting to test empirically whether children who bully might be found to be particularly "tuned in" to perceived slights on their reputation, without necessarily assuming that this indicates a hostile attribution bias. There is a fine line between paranoia and an accurate perception of the negative views of others, which children who bully may then attempt to eradicate through various reputation-enhancement strategies—including bullying.

USING ToM IN INTERVENTIONS

If certain types of bully are indeed found to have high-level social cognition, this has implications for intervention strategies. These bullies, being cold, manipulative masters of a social situation, may resist traditional antibullying policies and curriculum work. For example, the "No Blame" approach (see Robinson & Maines, 1997) relies heavily on empathy on the part of the bully. Considerable success has been reported using this method in terms of the reports of victims, but further research would be needed to determine if this success is greatest in the most empathic bullies, and whether the bully is also changed by the intervention.

The empathic capacity of bullies is particularly important: Bullies may perform well on stories assessing understanding of emotions (Sutton et al., 1999c), but if they do not actually share these emotions, then intervention strategies may inadvertently hone the skills of an already emotionally manipulative bully. Hare (1993) proposed a similar thing in his work with psychopaths, noting increased recidivism after intervention studies and commenting, "Programs of this sort merely provide the psychopath with better ways of manipulating, deceiving, and using people" (p. 243). The suggestion that ToM training should be provided for young bullies (Randall, 1997b) should therefore be treated with caution.

Emphasis should instead be placed on finding other ways to defuse bullying situations that don't necessarily demonize the bully or take their perceived power away from them (activating their "threatened egotism" discussed earlier). Perhaps rather than asking children "How would you feel if someone did that to you?," interventions could address "How would you feel if you did something else instead?" Are there any other ways (e.g., using humor) that a child who bullies could come out of the situation with his or her reputation and someone else's feelings both intact? If ringleader bullies do indeed have a superior ToM and a deep concern with reputation enhancement, they should be imaginative in thinking of such solutions.

Admittedly, children with conduct problems are a notoriously heterogeneous group (Hinshaw, Lahey, & Hart, 1993) and it is possible that no "blanket" technique will be completely effective. But the "popular stereotype" of bullies as lacking in intelligence and social skills may be guiding antibullying policy away from individuals who do not fit this picture, and confronting such individuals may depend on a much clearer understanding of the psychological weapons that some may use in causing distress to others.

Alternatively, the focus could be shifted toward the way that a ToM could be used by others as a psychological defence. In Sutton et al. (1999c), Bullies did not score significantly higher in terms of social cognition than Outsiders. Further research is needed to determine what prevents these children from becoming involved in bullying, and also how their ToM skills could be used in prosocial ways to combat bullying. These children could be a useful resource in antibullying work, as could Defenders. The Participant Role approach could be used in combination with sociometry, identifying popular Defenders and Outsiders and encouraging them to play an active role in reducing bullying in the school. This could involve training them as peer mediators or counselors (Cowie & Sharp, 1996) in order to use their accurate perception of the thoughts and feelings of others to good effect, or asking them to talk to Assistants and Reinforcers about bullying and the effects it may have. Targeting the social support of bullies in this way may isolate them, and ultimately be more effective than attempting to change the more entrenched cognitive style and behavior of the bully or victim.

Given the low scores of Victims and the negative correlations found between victim score and ToM performance in Sutton et al. (1999c), one possibility for interventions to keep in mind is a deficit in the social cognition skills of victims contributing to their experience. Does this leave them more open to manipulation by others? Interventions could possibly use ToM training alongside assertiveness training to give victims added skills in assessing and responding to bullying, although clearly such a course of action would need to be carefully monitored and empathy also emphasized to avoid the potential problem of victims turning into bullies. As Lazarus (1973) noted, "There is little to be gained (and much to be lost) from the acquisition of abrasive and obnoxious behaviors in the guise of 'assertiveness training'" (p. 698). Or as a child once reported to me: "I stood up to him, and shouted 'You're just a stupid coward and I'm not scared of you.' He thumped me." It is just possible that a better ToM would have allowed this child to assess what the bully was thinking, identify the high but fragile self-esteem, and come up with better ways to defuse the situation.

The school culture is also clearly important in understanding the uses to which ToM skills are put: If some bullies are indeed skilled in "psychological warfare," it may be necessary to change the battleground as well as the weapons used. Askew (1989) suggested that schools that value competitiveness may tacitly encourage bullying, and Olweus (1991) and Smith and Sharp (1994) demonstrated the positive effects of a warm and participative school environment. Even more crucial may be the fit between a child's particular ToM skills and the environment in which they find themselves. For example, in groups of autistic children, who usually have a poor ToM, those individuals who do exhibit second-order ToM skills appear to put it to use in sophisticated bullying (S. Johnson, personal communication, October 6, 2001). To use a rather crude metaphor, in the kingdom of the blind the one-eyed man is king.

DIVORCING SOCIAL VALUES FROM SOCIAL COGNITION

Even if we accept that at least some bullies may have a good ToM, we need to add more brush strokes to the picture of bullying for it to be a useful one. ToM is not a sufficient condition for bullying—children who bully also need an intention to cause harm to others. But not only is ToM at least one important part of how we understand and tackle bullying—bullying can also teach us important lessons about how we study ToM.

One important aspect of this is the relationship between social cognition and social values. Even if we accept that at least some children who bully might be considered "socially skilled" in terms of ToM performance, could this use of ToM be considered "socially competent"? Much of the debate with Crick and Dodge (Sutton et al., 1999a, 1999b) and Arsenio and Lemerise (Sutton et al., 2001) centers around this question. Crick and Dodge (1999, p. 131) rejected the notion that "competent social cognitions can result in incompetent behaviors." Such a view has very important implications for how we think about social cognition and ToM: We might infer that social cognitions are, by association, being defined as competent or incompetent on the basis of the social desirability of the resultant behavior, rather than its competence in a particular social situation.

Arsenio and Lemerise (2001, p. 62) also introduced social desirability into their discussion of social competence. They argued that being socially competent involves maximizing shared standards concerning what is "fair" or "right." This might be "social conformity," "socially acceptable behavior," or even "moral behavior," but can it really be considered "social competence?" A "socially conforming" behavior taking account of "shared standards" might include shooting prisoners in Nazi concentration camps (conforming to Gestapo shared standards) or imprisoning suffragettes (conforming to society standards at the turn of the century). Such persons might or might not be "socially competent." Gandhi did not conform to "shared standards" in his protests—but was he not "socially competent?" Couldn't someone who was excellent at worming their way into another's affections in order to con them out of money be described as socially competent? Is a ringleader bully, widely feared or even admired in class and consistently getting his or her own way in social interactions, not displaying social competence?

I argue that social competence should not just be defined in culturally specific forms related to generally shared standards within that culture. It is success at attaining individual goals, or even "effectiveness in interaction" (Rose-

Krasnor, 1997), although the individual must often take into account the social context he or she is in, in order to achieve this. This debate is not just about semantics. It may be time to ask what view of social competence children themselves take, as this is likely to be of more practical use in intervention. If you consider the school or playground as a self-contained culture (Sluckin, 1981), that culture might have quite different definitions of what is socially competent or "effective" interaction, and bullying may be considered more socially competent than "being a weakling." It is questionable whether, as Arsenio and Lemerise (2001) stated, "Most other adults and children view [bullying] as distinctly incompetent" (p. 71). In fact, a significant number of adults despise victims and have probully attitudes (Eslea & Smith, 2000), and many children admire some bullies and aggressive children (Cairns & Cairns, 1991). Most adults and children no doubt see bullying as socially undesirable, but this is *not* the same as considering it incompetent.

It appears best to consider social cognition skills like ToM to be "neutral social tools" (Kaukiainen et al., 1999; see also Repacholi et al., this volume). There are two main implications of this assumption. First, wherever possible ToM should be investigated in relation to bullying or aggression using "value-free" tests of ToM in socially relevant contexts. If a child selects an aggressive behavioral response to a situation with ambiguous beliefs and desires, this should never be taken as a deficiency or bias. Ideally, tests of ToM that do not involve potentially aggressive situations should be used to assess any link between ToM and bullying before going on to examine particular differences between subgroups in, for example, understanding of negative and moral emotions, Machiavellianism, and empathy. Such "value-free" tests could include frequency of reference to mental states and emotions in everyday speech, ToM in the Baron-Cohen et al. (1997) "eyes task" (although some feel this simply measures emotion recognition), or assessing how the child thinks their parents view the family in relation to how his or her parents actually do (see Smith, Myron-Wilson, & Sutton, 2001).

Second, limiting the scope of investigation to ToM or any other single component of social cognition is unlikely to advance our knowledge of either part of the aggression/social cognition question. Instead, we need to consider ToM in relation to a host of other factors and motivations, and ask what influences how the skills are put to use. And when we search the schoolyard or the workplace for such factors, they are not difficult to find. Bullying is rife because, often, "it's easy, it works, and it makes me feel good."

CONCLUSIONS

Research into the link between ToM and bullying is in its infancy, and no doubt I have raised more questions than answers. But I hope to have shown in this chapter that this is a promising avenue for the future in terms of understanding and tackling the problem. And in learning more about bullying, we may also learn more about ToM: how it develops and how the fit between the individual and their environment determines how it is put to use. In these investigations we must ensure that we do not allow our own social values to taint our scientific investigation. The fact that many children and adults, including both bullies and their victims, consider this use of ToM to be socially competent—even superior—is important for researchers in both bullying and ToM.

REFERENCES

Arsenio, W. F., & Lemerise, E. A. (2001). Varieties of childhood bullying: Values, emotion processes and social competence. *Social Development, 10*, 59–73.

Askew, S. (1989). Aggressive behaviour in boys: to what extent is it institutionalized? In D. P. Tattum & D. A. Lane (Eds.), *Bullying in schools* (pp. 59–72). Stoke-on-Trent, UK: Trentham Books.

Baron-Cohen, S., & Hammer, J. (1996). Is autism an extreme form of the male brain? *Advances in Infancy Research, 11*, 193–217.

Baron-Cohen, S., Jolliffe, T., Mortimore, C., & Robertson, M. (1997). Another advanced test of theory of mind: Evidence from very high functioning adults with autism or asperger syndrome. *Journal of Child Psychology and Psychiatry, 38*, 813–822.

Baumeister, R. (1997). *Evil: Inside human cruelty and violence.* New York: W. H. Freeman.

Baumeister, R., Smart, L., & Boden, J. (1996). Relation of threatened egotism to violence and aggression: The dark side of high self-esteem. *Psychological Review, 103*, 5–33.

Besag, V. (1989). *Bullies and victims in schools.* Milton Keynes, UK: Open University Press.

Bjorkqvist, K., Österman, K., & Kaukiainen, A. (1992). The development of direct and indirect aggressive strategies in males and females. In K. Bjorkqvist & P. Niemela (Eds.), *Of mice and women: Aspects of female aggression* (pp. 51–64). San Diego: Academic Press.

Bjorkqvist, K., Österman, K., & Kaukiainen, A. (2000). Social intelligence minus empathy = aggression? *Aggression and Violent Behaviour, 5*, 191–200.

Blair, J., Sellars, C., Strickland, I., Clark, F., et al. (1996). Theory of mind in the psychopath. *Journal of Forensic Psychiatry, 7*, 15–25.

Boldizar, J. P., Perry, D. G., & Perry, L. C. (1989). Outcome values and aggression. *Child Development, 60*, 571–579.

Boulton, M. J., & Smith, P. K. (1994). Bully/victim problems in middle-school children: Stability, self-perceived competence, peer perceptions and peer acceptance. *British Journal of Developmental Psychology, 12*, 315–329.

Bowers, L., Smith, P. K., & Binney, V. (1992). Cohesion and power in the families of children involved in bully/victim problems at school. *Journal of Family Therapy, 14*, 371–387.

Bowers, L., Smith, P. K., & Binney, V. (1994). Perceived family relationships of bullies, victims and bully/victims in middle childhood. *Journal of Social & Personal Relationships, 11*, 215–232.

Bowlby, J. (1988). *A secure base: Clinical applications of attachment theory.* London: Routledge.

Bryant, B. K. (1982). An index of empathy for children and adolescents. *Child Development, 53*, 413–425.

Bushman, B., & Baumeister, R. (1998). Threatened egotism, narcissism, self-esteem, and direct and displaced aggression: Does self-love or self-hate lead to violence? *Journal of Personality and Social Psychology, 75*, 219–229.

Cairns, R. B., & Cairns, B. D. (1991). Social cognition and social networks: A developmental perspective. In D. J. Pepler & K. H. Rubin (Eds.), *The development and treat-*

ment of childhood aggression (pp. 249–278). Mahwah, NJ: Lawrence Erlbaum.

Christie, R., & Geis, F. L. (1970, November). The Machiavellis among us. *Psychology Today*, 82–86.

Cowie, H., & Sharp S. (1996). *Peer counselling in school: A time to listen*. London: David Fulton.

Crick, N. R. (1996). The role of overt aggression, relational aggression, and prosocial behaviour in the prediction of children's future social adjustment. *Child Development, 67,* 2317–2327.

Crick, N. R., & Dodge, K. A. (1994). A review and reformulation of social information-processing mechanisms in children's social adjustment. *Psychological Bulletin*, 115, 74–101.

Crick, N. R., & Dodge, K. A. (1996). Social information processing mechanisms in reactive and proactive aggression. *Child Development, 67,* 993–1002.

Crick, N. R., & Dodge, K. A. (1999). "Superiority" is in the eye of the beholder: A comment on Sutton, Smith and Swettenham. *Social Development, 8,* 128–131.

Crick, N. R., & Grotpeter, J. K. (1995). Relational aggression, gender, and socio-psychological adjustment. *Child Development, 66,* 710–722.

Dodge, K. A. (1991). The structure and function of reactive and proactive aggression. In D. J. Pepler & K. H. Rubin (Eds), *The development and treatment of childhood aggression* (pp. 201–218). Hillsdale, NJ: Lawrence Erlbaum.

Dodge, K. A., Lochman, J. E., Harnish, J. D., Bates, J. E., & Pettit, G. S. (1997). Reactive and proactive aggression in schoolchildren and psychiatrically impaired chronically assaultive youth. *Journal of Abnormal Psychology, 106,* 37–51.

Dodge, K. A., Pettit, G. S., Bates, J. E., & Valente, E. (1995). Social information processing patterns partially mediate the effects of earlier physical abuse on later conduct problems. *Journal of Abnormal Psychology, 104,* 632–643.

Dodge, K. A., Pettit, G. S., McClaskey, C. L., & Brown, M. M. (1986). Social competence in children. *Monographs of the Society for Research in Child Development, 51*(2).

Dodge, K. A., Price, J. M., Coie, J. D., & Christopoulous, C. (1990). On the development of aggressive dyadic relationships in boys' peer groups. *Human Development, 33,* 260–270.

Dunn, J., Brown, J., Slomkowski, C., Tesla, C., & Youngblade, L. M. (1991). Young children's understanding of other people's feelings and beliefs: Individual differences and their antecedents. *Child Development*, 62, 1352–1366.

Eslea, M. J., & Smith, P. K. (1998). The long-term effectiveness of anti-bullying work in primary schools. *Educational Research, 40,* 203–218.

Eslea, M., & Smith, P. K. (2000). Pupil and parent attitudes towards bullying in primary schools. *European Journal of Psychology of Education, 15,* 207–219.

Farrington, D. (1993). Understanding and preventing bullying. In M. Tonry (Ed.), *Crime and justice: A review of research* (Vol. 17, pp. 381–458). Chicago: University of Chicago Press.

Feldman, E., & Dodge, K. A. (1987). Social information processing and sociometric status: Sex, age, and situational effects. *Journal of Abnormal Child Psychology, 15,* 211–277.

Frick, P .J., O'Brien, B. S., Wootton, J. M., & McBurnett, K. (1994). Psychopathy and conduct problems in children. *Journal of Abnormal Psychology, 15,* 211–277.

Gibbins, C., & Craig, W. (1997, April). *Mapping the path to aggression: Validation of a social cognitive model of childhood.* Presented at the Biennial meeting of the Society for Research in Child Development, Washington, DC.

Guerra, N. G., & Slaby, R. G. (1989). Evaluative factors in social problem solving by aggressive boys. *Journal of Abnormal Child Psychology, 17,* 177–289.

Hala, S., & Chandler, M. (1996). The role of strategic planning in accessing false-belief understanding. *Child Development, 67,* 2948–2966.

Halberstadt, A. G., Denham, S. A., & Dunsmore, J. C. (2001). Affective social competence. *Social Development, 10*, 79–119.

Happé, F., & Frith, U. (1996). Theory of mind

and social impairment in children with conduct disorder. *British Journal of Developmental Psychology*, 14, 385–398.

Hare, R. D. (1993). *Without conscience: The disturbing world of the psychopaths among us*. New York: Simon and Schuster.

Hazler, R. J. (1996). *Breaking the cycle of violence: Interventions for bullying and victimization*. Washington, DC: Accelerated Development.

Hewstone, M. (Ed.). (1983). *Attribution theory: Social and functional extensions*. Oxford, UK: Blackwell.

Hinshaw, S. P., Lahey, B. B., & Hart, E. L. (1993). Issues of taxonomy and comorbidity in the development of conduct disorder. *Development and Psychopathology*, 5, 31–49.

Hoffman, M. L. (1975). Developmental synthesis of affect and cognition and its implication for altruistic motivation. *Developmental Psychology*, 11, 607–622.

Hughes, C., Dunn, J., & White, A. (1998). Trick or treat? Uneven understanding of mind and emotion and executive dysfunction in "hard-to-manage" preschoolers. *Journal of Child Psychology & Psychiatry & Allied Disciplines*, 39, 981–994.

Jacobson, N. S. (1992). Behavioural couple therapy: A new beginning. *Behaviour Therapy*, 23, 493–506.

Jenkins, J. M., & Astington, J. W. (1996). Cognitive factors and family structure associated with theory of mind development in young children. *Developmental Psychology*, 32, 70–78.

Kaukiainen, A., Bjorkqvist, K., Lagerspetz, K., Österman, K., Salmivalli, C., Forsblom, S., & Ahlbom, A. (1999). The relationships between social intelligence, empathy, and three types of aggression. *Aggressive Behaviour*, 25, 81–89.

Kaukiainen, A., Peltonen, M., & Sippola, P. (2002). *Bullies can also be "socially smart." Social intelligence and empathy among bullies, victims, and children not involved in bullying*. Unpublished manuscript.

Kaukiainen, A., Salmivalli, C., Lagerspetz, K., Tamminen, M., Vauras, M., Maki, H., & Poskiparta, E. (2002). Learning difficulties, social intelligence, and self-concept: Connections to bully–victim problems. *Scandi-*

navian Journal of Psychology, 43, 269–278.

Keating, C. F., & Heltman, K. R. (1994). Dominance and deception in children and adults: are leaders the best misleaders? *Personality and Social Psychology Bulletin*, 20, 312–321.

Kikkawa, M. (1987). Teachers' opinions and treatments for bully/victim problems among students in junior and senior high schools: Results of a fact-finding survey. *Human Development*, 23, 25–30.

Lagerspetz, K. M. J., Bjorkqvist, K., Berts, M., & King, E. (1982). Group aggression among schoolchildren in three schools. *Scandinavian Journal of Psychology*, 23, 45–52.

Lazarus, A. A. (1973). On assertive behaviour: A brief note. *Behaviour Therapy*, 4, 697–699.

Mealey, L. (1995). The sociobiology of sociopathy: An integrated evolutionary model. *Behavioural and Brain Sciences*, 18, 523–599.

Monks, C., Smith, P. K., & Swettenham, J. (submitted). The psychological correlates of bullying, victimisation and defending in early childhood: Cognitive profiles and family factors.

Myron-Wilson, R., Sutton, J., & Smith, P. K. (submitted). The association between bully/victim role in school and the nature of attachment in middle childhood.

Olweus, D. (1978). *Aggression in the schools: Bullies and whipping boys*. Washington, DC: Hemisphere.

Olweus, D. (1991). Bully/victim problems among schoolchildren: Basic facts and effects of a school based intervention program. In D. Pepler & K. Rubin (Eds.), *The development and treatment of childhood aggression* (pp. 411–448). Hillsdale, NJ: Lawrence Erlbaum.

Olweus, D. (1993). *Bullying—What we know and what we can do*. Oxford, UK: Blackwell.

Olweus, D. (1994). Bullying: Long term outcomes for victims and an effective school based intervention program. In L.R. Huesmann (Ed.), *Aggressive behavior—Current perspectives* (pp. 97–130). New York: Plenum Press.

O'Reilly, C. A., & Chatman, J. A. (1996). Culture as social control: Corporations, cults and commitment. *Research in Organizational Behaviour*, 18, 157–200.

Patterson, G. R., DeBaryshe, B. D., & Ramsey,

E. (1989). A developmental perspective on antisocial behavior. *American Psychologist, 44,* 329–335.

Pepler, D. J., Craig, W., Zeigler, S., & Charach, A. (1993). A school based anti-bullying intervention: Preliminary evaluation. In D. Tattum (Ed.), *Understanding and managing bullying* (pp. 76–91). Oxford, UK: Heinemann Educational.

Pepler, D. J., & Craig, W. M. (1995). A peek behind the fence: Naturalistic observations of aggressive children with remote audiovisual recording. *Developmental Psychology, 31*(4), 548–553.

Pikas, A. (1975). *Sa stoppar vi mobbning.* Stockholm: Prisma.

Premack, D. & Woodruff, G. (1978). Does the chimpanzee have a theory of mind? *Behavioural and Brain Sciences, 1,* 515-526.

Randall, P. (1996). *A community approach to bullying.* Stoke-on-Trent, UK: Trentham Books.

Randall, P. (1997a). *Adult bullying: Perpetrators and victims.* London: Routledge.

Randall, P. (1997b). Pre-school routes to bullying. In D. Tattum & G. Herbert (Eds.), *Bullying: Home, school and community* (pp. 5–16). London: David Fulton.

Randall, P. (2001). *Bullying in adulthood.* Hove, UK: Brunner-Routledge.

Rayner, C. (1997). Incidence of workplace bullying. *Journal of Community and Applied Social Psychology, 7,* 199–208.

Rigby, K., & Slee, P. T. (1991). Bullying among Australian school children: Reported behaviour and attitudes towards victims. *Journal of Social Psychology, 131,* 615–627.

Rivers, I., & Smith, P. K. (1994). Types of bullying behaviour and their correlates. *Aggressive Behaviour, 20,* 359–368.

Robinson, G., & Maines, B. (1997). *Crying for help: The No Blame Approach to bullying.* Bristol, UK: Lucky Duck.

Rose-Krasnor, L. (1997). The nature of social competence: A theoretical review. *Social Development, 6,* 111–135.

Ross, D. M. (1996). *Childhood bullying and teasing.* Alexandria, VA: American Counselling Association.

Ruffman, T., Perner, J., Naito, M., Parkin, L., & Clements, W. A. (1998). Older (but not younger) siblings facilitate false belief understanding. *Developmental Psychology, 34,* 161–174.

Salmivalli, C. (2001). Feeling good about oneself, being bad to others? Remarks on self-esteem, hostility and aggressive behaviour. *Aggression and Violent Behaviour, 6,* 375–393.

Salmivalli, C., Huttenen, A., & Lagerspetz, K. (1997). Peer networks and bullying in schools. *Scandinavian Journal of Psychology, 38,* 305–312.

Salmivalli, C., Lagerspetz, K., Bjorkqvist, K., Österman, K., & Kaukiainen, A. (1996). Bullying as a group process: Participant roles and their relations to social status within the group. *Aggressive Behaviour, 22,* 1–15.

Sharp, S., & Thompson, D. (1992). Sources of stress: A contrast between pupil perspective and pastoral teachers' perception. *School Psychology International, 13,* 229–242.

Sluckin, A. (1981). *Growing up in the playground: The social development of children.* London: Routledge and Kegan Paul.

Smith, P. K., & Brain, P. F. (2000). Bullying in schools: Lessons from two decades of research. *Aggressive Behaviour, 26,* 1–9.

Smith, P. K., Myron-Wilson, R., & Sutton, J. (2001). Comparing parents' and children's perceptions of the family: Can the FAST be used as a measure of social cognition and theory of mind ability? In T. M. Gehring, M. Debry, & P. K. Smith (Eds.), *The Family System Test FAST: Theory and application* (pp. 118–132). Hove, UK: Brunner-Routledge.

Smith, P. K., & Sharp, S. (1994). *School bullying: Insights and perspectives.* London: Routledge.

Smith, P. K., & Shu, S. (2000). What good schools can do about bullying: Findings from a survey in English schools after a decade of research and action. *Childhood, 7,* 193–212.

Smith, P. K., & Thompson, D. (Eds.) (1991). *Practical approaches to bullying.* London: David Fulton.

Sparrow, S., Balla, D., & Cicchetti, D. (1984). *Vineland Adaptive Behavior Scales* [survey form]. Circle Pines, MN: American Guidance Services.

Staub, E. (1979). *Positive social behavior and morality: Socialization and development* (Vol. 2). New York: Academic Press.

Steinberg, M. D., & Dodge, K. A. (1983).

Attributional bias in aggressive adolescent boys and girls. *Journal of Social and Clinical Psychology, 1,* 312–321.

Sutton, J. (1998). *Bullying: Social inadequacy or skilled manipulation?* Doctoral thesis, University of London.

Sutton, J. (2001). Bullies: Thugs or thinkers? *Psychologist, 14*(10), 530–534.

Sutton, J., & Keogh, E. (2000). Social competition in school: Relationships with bullying, Machiavellianism and personality. *British Journal of Educational Psychology, 70,* 443–457.

Sutton, J., & Keogh, E. (2001). Components of Machiavellian beliefs in children: Relationships with personality. *Personality and Individual Differences, 30,* 137–148.

Sutton, J., Reeves, M., & Keogh, E. (2000). Disruptive behaviour, avoidance of responsibility and theory of mind. *British Journal of Developmental Psychology, 18,* 1–11.

Sutton, J., & Smith, P. K. (1999). Bullying as a group process: An adaptation of the Participant Role Scale approach. *Aggressive Behaviour, 25,* 97–111.

Sutton, J., Smith, P. K., & Swettenham, J. (1999a). Bullying and "theory of mind": A critique of the 'social skills deficit' approach to anti-social behaviour. *Social Development, 8,* 117–127.

Sutton, J., Smith, P. K., & Swettenham, J. (1999b). Social cognition and bullying: Social inadequacy or skilled manipulation? *British Journal of Developmental Psychology, 17,* 435–450.

Sutton, J., Smith, P. K., & Swettenham, J. (1999c). Socially undesirable need not be incompetent: A response to Crick and Dodge. *Social Development, 8,* 132–134.

Sutton, J., Smith, P. K., & Swettenham, J. (2001). "It's easy, it works, and it makes me feel good"—A response to Arsenio and Lemerise. *Social Development, 10,* 74–78.

Thomas-Peter, B. A. (1997). Personal standards in professional relationships: Limiting interpersonal harassment. *Journal of Community and Applied Social Psychology, 7,* 233–239.

6

Individual Differences in Theory of Mind
The Preschool Years and Beyond

THOMAS KEENAN
University of Canterbury

Given increasing evidence of a link between children's understanding of false beliefs and their social functioning (e.g., Lalonde & Chandler, 1995; Peterson & Siegal, 2002; Slaughter, Dennis, & Pritchard, 2002; Watson, Nixon, Wilson, & Capage, 1999), it is important to reexamine the notion of individual differences in theory of mind. It is likely that delays or deficits in the formation and/or deployment of a theory of mind may have important consequences for social development. In this chapter, some of the possibilities are outlined. The first thing to be considered is the form that individual differences in theory of mind might take. This is followed by a consideration of the some of the empirical evidence that connects theory of mind to social development. Specifically, this is illustrated by examining the link between children's performance on theory of mind tasks and their status within the peer group. Finally, theory of mind development beyond the preschool years is discussed in terms of individual differences and the implications for later social functioning.

INDIVIDUAL DIFFERENCES IN THEORY OF MIND

In the course of normal development, we all develop a facility for attributing mental states such as *beliefs*, *desires*, *intentions*, and *emotions* to ourselves and other people. We do this in order to understand our own and others' behavior and so that we might better predict and control that behavior. Although many children come to acquire an understanding of key aspects of theory of mind— such as the possibility of possessing a *false belief*—at around age 4 (e.g., Perner, Leekam, & Wimmer, 1987), there is widespread variation in children's performance on these tasks. This variation is typically masked when we simply look at group means. For example, Jenkins and Astington (1996) gave 4 false-belief tasks to a group of children ranging in age from 3 to 5½ years. They found that children's performances across these tasks varied substantially: 37% of children passed all 4 tasks; 10% passed 3 of the tasks; 16% passed 2 of the tasks; 10% passed 1 of the tasks; and 27% failed all 4 of the tasks. As Jenkins and Astington stated, performance on their battery of false-belief tasks was not in the "all or none" category, but rather reflected considerable individual variation.

A useful framework for thinking about the question of individual differences in children's theory of mind has been proposed by Bartsch and Estes (1996). They argued that much of the early research in theory of mind was concerned with establishing a picture of the "typical" development of mental state understanding. They cite a list of issues on which a reasonable amount of consensus has been achieved, for example, when children first engage in pretend play, when they first use mental state terms such as "want" and "know," and when children can take into account false beliefs. Bartsch and Estes suggested that the fact that such a research agenda has dominated work on theory of mind is not surprising, but the authors also illustrated how research on individual differences in mental state understanding is becoming an increasingly important aspect of the theory of mind research agenda. They developed a useful framework or classification for thinking about the nature of individual differences in theory of mind, suggesting that such differences fall into three categories: individual differences in antecedent causes; individual differences in the consequences of arriving early or late to a theory of mind; and the possibility of qualitative differences in theory of mind across individuals. In what follows, each of these categories of individual differences is explored and illustrated with reference to the empirical literature. In addition, I consider an expansion to this framework, looking at another source of individual differences that has recently been identified in the literature, namely, intraindividual differences.

ANTECEDENTS

According to Bartsch and Estes, individual differences might be found in the *antecedents* of a theory of mind. Such research examines how variation in contexts (e.g., a child with no siblings or multiple siblings; the quality of the parent–child attachment relationship) or mechanisms (e.g., individual differences in working memory or inhibitory control processes) may facilitate or delay an understanding of mental states. Studies such as that conducted by Ruffman, Perner, and Parkin (1999) on the effects of maternal talk about mental states on children's later understanding of false belief fall into this category, as does the research demonstrating connections with inhibitory control (Carlson & Moses, 2001; Carlson, Moses & Breton, 2002; Hughes, 1998a, 1998b) and working memory (Keenan, 1998; Keenan, Olson, & Marini, 1998). Examples of some possible antecedents to theory of mind are considered below.

Carlson and Moses (2001) recently showed a strong correlation ($r = .66$) between children's performance on a battery of inhibitory control tasks (tasks that assess the child's ability to suppress inappropriate, prepotent responses) and their performance on a battery of theory-of-mind tasks (including deception, appearance–reality, and false-belief tasks), a finding that remained significant even when controlling for age, sex, and verbal ability. Similarly, Hughes (1998a) found a significant relationship between inhibitory control and performance on a deception task when controlling for age and verbal ability. The intuitively appealing explanation for these findings is that inhibitory control is an antecedent to the development of a mature theory of mind, acting as a precursor for the growth of a more mature theory of mind. Further empirical support for this idea comes from another study by Hughes (1998b), who examined the executive function—theory-of-mind connection using a longitudinal framework. Hughes found that early executive functioning predicted later theory-of-mind ability; in contrast, early theory-of-mind ability did not predict later executive functioning. However, such results are in need of further replication using longitudinal designs before one can conclude, as Perner and Lang (1999) pointed out, that such commonsense viewpoints about the foundational nature of executive functions for theory-of-mind development are in fact reflected in reality.

A number of researchers recently examined the idea that the child's acquisition of a theory of mind might have its roots in the attachment relationship formed between the infant and the primary caregiver (Fonagy, Redfern, & Charman, 1997; Meins, Fernyhough, Russell, & Clark-Carter, 1998). These authors argued that the processes that are responsible for the formation of a secure attachment relationship also lead to differences in the age of acquisition of an understanding of mental states. For example, in the Meins et al. account, the parents of securely attached infants are *mind minded*. That is, they treat their children as individuals with goals and desires that may differ from their own and they verbally communicate this understanding to their infant. Meins et al. argued that this pattern of parent–child interaction leads to an earlier understanding of mental states and the earlier acquisition of a representational theory of mind.

The relationship between attachment and theory of mind development has empirical support derived from a number of studies. Central to this association are findings that indicate the potential role of attachment security in the development and/or expression of behaviors that are conceptually related to, or seen as precursors of, a mature theory of mind. For example, research by Slade (1987) showed that securely attached children were more able to recognize and act on another's perspective in a pretend play scenario than were insecurely attached children. Mothers of securely attached children are more likely to invoke mental states in describing the behavior of others (Fonagy, Steele, Steele, Higgitt, & Target, 1994), thereby teaching their children the appropriate use of such terms. Finally, Laible and Thompson (1998) showed that securely attached children performed better on tests of emotional awareness. Each of these findings suggests a relationship between attachment security and an emerging theory of mind.

Attempts to directly address the impact of attachment security on theory of mind development have been relatively few. What research has been done, however, has provided tentative support for a link between these two factors. Meins et al. (1998) investigated the relationship between an infant measure of attachment security and a preschool measure of theory of mind. Infants aged 11 to 13 months were given the strange situation procedure and classified as securely or insecurely attached. The performance of each group was compared on a number of different mental state tasks over the next 4 years. In general it was found that, compared to their insecurely attached peers, securely attached children: (1) were more able to incorporate an experimenter's suggestions into their sequence of play at 31 months; (2) performed better on a single false-belief task at age 4; and (3) performed better on a test of informational access at age 5. Secure children also had mothers who displayed more sensitive tutoring strategies when working with their children on a task. However, at age 5 there was no difference between the abilities of secure and insecure children on a variant of the false-belief task. Fonagy et al. (1997) also demonstrated a significant positive correlation between attachment security and theory of mind performance in a sample of 3- to 6-year-old children, even when controlling for the contributions of age, social maturity, and verbal mental age. Taken together with the findings of Meins et al. (1998), there would seem to be reasonable evidence for an association between attachment security and the child's developing theory of mind.

CONSEQUENCES

A second area in which individual differences in theory of mind might be found is in the *consequences* surrounding the timing of the child's acquisition of an understanding of mind; that is, whether the child arrives early or late to an understanding of mental states. For example, children who scored higher on a composite measure of theory-of-mind ability were significantly more likely to engage in fantasy play and pretense (Taylor & Carlson, 1997). In another vein, research on children's acquisition of nonliteral language demonstrated that the ability to understand speech acts such as sarcasm and irony depends critically on the understanding of theory of mind concepts such as ignorance, intentions, and second-order belief states. Olson (1988) suggested that the child's ability to comprehend sarcasm requires the ability to recognize that a sarcastic speaker's communicative intention is to be taken as meaning the opposite of what they say. That is, sarcastic speakers say the opposite of what they mean but they intend to be taken by their listener as rejecting the proposition expressed in their utterance. For example, the sarcastic speaker who says "nice day" when it's raining outside does not want the listener to think that he or she thinks it is a nice day; rather, the speaker means to be taken as meaning the opposite, that it is "not a very nice day." Clearly, nonliteral speech acts such as sarcasm and irony depend heavily on the prior acquisition of a theory of mind. Indeed, this conclusion has been reinforced by a number of studies demonstrating that children need to be able to identify critical aspects of the listener's beliefs and the speaker's intentions in order to comprehend sarcastic speech and to distinguish various types of nonliteral speech acts from one another (deGroot, Kaplan, Rosenblatt, Dews, & Winner, 1995; Sullivan, Winner, & Hopfield, 1995; Winner & Leekam, 1991).

Another example of individual differences in the consequences associated with acquiring a theory of mind is the increasingly large body of research linking children's *sociometric status* (e.g., Dockett, 1997; Slaughter et al., 2002), *social skills* (Watson et al., 1999), and *social competence* (Lalonde & Chandler, 1995) to the development of theory of mind. A sampling of this work is summarized in a later section of this chapter. However, a point that needs to be kept in mind when evaluating this research literature is that each of these studies involved a series of concurrent measures of theory of mind understanding and social behavior. In short, we don't know for certain whether the child's acquisition of a theory of mind leads to social skills or socially competent behavior or whether the child's tendency to engage in social behaviors might drive the development of their understanding of mind. What is needed to resolve this issue is more longitudinal studies of the sort conducted by Jenkins and Astington (2000), where measures of theory of mind and social behavior are taken at more than one point in time, allowing the researcher to examine whether early theory of mind predicts later social behavior and vice versa. This issue will be covered in greater detail in a subsequent section of the chapter.

QUALITATIVE DIFFERENCES IN THEORY OF MIND

A third area in which individual differences may be observed is in terms of the *quality* of the child's theory of mind. In essence, the question here is: How might conceptions of mind vary across individuals? Cross-cultural differences in the understanding of mental states is one possibility (Lillard, 1998; Vinden & Astington, 2000), but even within a culture there may be qualitative differences in the implicit theories held by specific individuals as a function of their experiences or other factors (see Blair, this volume; Happé & Frith, 1996; Keenan & Ward, 2000; Ward, 2000; Ward, Keenan, & Hudson, 2000). First I consider qualitative differences across cultures before describing research that suggests that qualitatively different theories of mind may emerge within a given culture.

There is little work examining qualitative differences in theory of mind across cultures, although much of what we know is summarized in Lillard (1998). One possibility of qualitative differences in theory of mind can be found in the work of Lutz (1985). Lutz described the Ifaluk, a people living in Micronesia. According to Lutz, the Ifaluk make basic distinctions between the inner psychological realm and the outer physical realm; however, their conception of "inner" refers to both bodily and psychological functions, making little distinction between the two. As Lutz pointed out, the Ifaluk also draw little distinction between thoughts and emotions, and many of their terms for inner states indicate a high degree of overlap between these domains. Moreover, the Ifaluk often invoke factors other than inner psychological states to explain a person's behavior, preferring to see the causes of behavior as lying in environmental or situational causes. In short, the Ifaluk as described by Lutz seem to have a theory of mind qualitatively different from that ascribed to by most Western psychologists.

How might the quest for further examining qualitative differences in theory of mind across cultures proceed? Vinden and Astington (2000) made the intriguing suggestion that a starting point for investigations on this topic lies in Hobson's (1993) proposal that psychologists give greater attention to the concept of "personhood." Understanding how a given culture views persons (e.g., the person as consisting of mind, body and soul, as seen in the view of many early Western thinkers) might allow us to gain insight into how that culture explains behavior and, ultimately, into the role they give concepts of mind in a theory of human nature.

Regarding the possibility of qualitative differences in theory of mind existing within a given culture as a function of early experience, one intriguing possibility that deserves further investigation is Happé and Frith's (1996) suggestion that some children may have a "theory of nasty minds." There is some evidence (e.g., Dodge & Feldman, 1990; Dodge & Frame, 1982; Steinberg & Dodge, 1983) to suggest that aggressive children may show a bias in their social-information processing that leads them to make specific attributions about the hostility of another's intentions when the act in question seems to be directed specifically at the aggressive child (also see chapters by Repacholi et al., this volume, and Blair, this volume). Under conditions where the act is directed at another, the child makes appropriate, nonbiased attributions about the actor's intent. That is, if the actor in the vignette accidentally hit another actor, the aggressive child viewing the story interprets the action as an accident and not as an intentional act directed at the victim. When the stories are modified such that the aggressive child plays a role in the story as the victim of the accident, their interpretations of the meaning of the act change, with the aggressive child viewing the act as intentional and aggressive. In short, the aggressive child has a hostile bias that leads to the misattribution of hostile intentions and a resultant tendency to misinterpret many acts as aggressive in nature.

For a child growing up in an abusive or hostile environment, such a modification to one's theory of mind might prove quite adaptive in the short term, helping to protect the child from aggressive acts. For example, a hypersensitivity to aggressive intents may prove to be a useful adaptation to their social environment, helping an abused child to avoid acts of aggression and abuse. However, in the long term, it is likely that a hostile attributional bias could negatively impact on many facets of the child's social development, from forming and maintaining close relationships to resolving conflicts with friends, peers, or adults such as teachers.

INTRAINDIVIDUAL DIFFERENCES

A fourth category of individual differences not considered by Bartsch and Estes (1996) is the possibility of *intraindividual differences* in children's application of their theory of mind. Research demonstrating the existence of intraindividual differences in how children use their theory of mind is less than plentiful; however, a recent study by O'Connor and Hirsch (1999) suggests that this might be a fruitful avenue for future research. They tested whether mind reading was more likely to be manifested in positive than negative relationships or whether this social-cognitive ability was a more general characteristic of the child that would be expressed in a similar way across all of their relationships. Using a sample of young adolescents and a methodology based on vignettes and a structured interview, O'Connor and Hirsch looked at adolescents' mind reading in the context of their relationships with teachers who they "most liked" and "least liked." They found that the psychological sophistication with which their early adolescent sample understood and described another's behavior was indeed a function of the affective quality of the relationship under consideration. That is, adolescents were more likely to reason in a sophisticated way about teachers that they most liked than teachers that they least liked. In addition, the adolescents showed significantly less incongruity and distortion in their mentalizing about their most-liked teacher compared with their least-liked teacher. This highlights the possibility that adolescent's mentalizing might depend strongly on the nature of the relationship they have with a target individual. O'Connor and Hirsch argued that the results not only stress the need to consider whether an adolescent engages in mentalizing activity but that researchers should also consider the "accuracy" of their mentalizing, a point that is discussed again later in this chapter.

As Bartsch and Estes (1996) suggested, each of these streams of research is important to generating a better understanding of the nature of individual differences in theory of mind. It follows, then, that the explicit recognition of this framework could also prove very important to the developing research literature examining the relationship between theory of mind and social development. Thinking about the nature of individual differences in these ways helps to identify what is known about the nature of individual differences in social functioning as a consequence of theory of mind, how antecedents such as individual differences in language ability might affect later relationships between theory of mind and social development and whether there are qualitative differences in the concepts and theories that individual children hold about the mind and how this might be related to their social functioning. In addition, thinking about individual differences in this way helps us to better assess the state of knowledge in the field and where research needs to be concentrated.

In short, research into each of the types of individual differences identified by Bartsch and Estes is important to increasing our understanding of the relationships between social development and theory of mind. A key issue for work in this area will be to explore whether there are other measures of the child's theory of mind that may better reflect individual differences in children's functioning: measures that go beyond simply tapping "all-or-none" conceptual knowledge and, instead, begin to assess how they actually apply their knowledge within a variety of social contexts that require everyday mind reading.

THEORY OF MIND AND CHILDREN'S SOCIAL DEVELOPMENT

Early theorizing in the area of children's theory of mind stressed the importance of acquiring a representational theory of mind for social development. For example, Perner (1988) argued that the nature of the theory that a child had acquired was an important determinant of how they understood the social world. In other words, there are important consequences for social development that flow on from the child's acquisition of a theory of mind. However, empirical demonstrations of this insight are conspicuously absent from the early theory of mind research. It is only more recently that the linkage between theory of mind and children's social development has received much attention. In fact, there is now a growing body of evidence for a linkage between specific aspects of theory of mind and social functioning.

Lalonde and Chandler (1995) predicted a relationship between scores on a battery of six false-belief measures and teacher-assessed social competence. Forty questionnaire items were developed to tap either conventional social skills (based on social convention and self-control) or intentional social skills (skills that require an understanding of others' intentions and desires). Their results indicated that an understanding of false belief was associated with intentional, but not conventional, social competence as rated by teachers. Astington and Jenkins (1995) assessed the relationship between theory of mind and pretend play in a sample of children aged 37 to 65 months. Performance on various false-belief tasks was significantly correlated with a greater tendency to generate joint proposals and to assign roles in the context of pretend play, but was not associated with the tendency to engage in pretend play or with peer-nominated empathic concern. The authors concluded that theory-of-mind skills may operate by alerting children to the possibility that others potentially have different beliefs and desires regarding play, resulting in the use of clarification techniques to ensure that all are agreed as to the play situation. They suggest that it is the *quality*, rather than the *quantity*, of pretend play that is influenced by the theory of mind acquisition of its participants; however, it must be borne in mind that there may be differential consequences for social development of poor social interaction in terms of its quality, quantity, or both.

Schwebel, Rosen, and Singer (1999) sought to differentiate between solitary and joint pretend play in assessing the relationship between theory of mind and play in young children. Observation of naturalistic, spontaneous play yielded ratings of imaginativeness within play. Play was also categorized as jointly constructed (i.e., instances in which the target child jointly defined roles with a peer or expanded on another child's pretend suggestions) or solitary play (any other type of pretend play, including solitary symbolic play and noninteractive role play). They reported that children who performed better on a test of false belief were more likely to engage in jointly constructed pretend play, further supporting Astington and Jenkins's (1995) suggestion that it is the joint element of pretend play that is most strongly related to an understanding of others' minds.

Theory of mind has also been associated with teacher-rated social skills. Watson et al. (1999) reported that the false-belief understanding of twenty-six 3- to 6-year-old children was a significant predictor of teacher ratings of positive social skills after age, language, and talkativeness with peers were controlled for. However, the findings of a second study replicated the association of false-belief understanding with teacher-assessed social skills but revealed that peer acceptance was not related to false-belief understanding, once age and language ability were controlled. In contrast, Hughes, White, Sharpen, and Dunn (2000) reported no significant relationships between theory of mind or emotion understanding, and researcher-observed prosocial or antisocial behavior in a sample of 40 children with antisocial behavior problems. Finally, Badenes, Estevan, and Bacete (2000) examined the relations between theory of mind and peer acceptance in a sample of 4- to 6-year-olds. Peer-rejected children showed little difference when compared to average children on a variety of theory of mind tasks, although there was some evidence of an aggressive bias in their social cognition. Specifically, peer-rejected children performed more poorly on figurative language tasks (e.g., understanding white lies) than average or popular children. These same children also showed aggressive sociocognitive biases, with peer-rejected boys transforming positive motivations into negative, hostile intentions.

Slaughter et al. (2002) investigated the relationships between theory of mind, peer acceptance, age, and verbal intelligence in 4- to 6-year-olds. Their findings revealed that children classified as popular scored higher on a battery of five theory-of-mind tasks than did children classified as rejected. In their second study, Slaughter et al. showed that theory of mind was the strongest predictor of peer acceptance in the older children, whereas for younger children, prosocial and aggressive behaviors were the strongest predictors of peer acceptance. However, once the effect of language ability was controlled for, the association between theory-of-mind peer acceptance was not significant.

Most recently, Peterson and Siegal (2002) assessed the links between peer relations, moral understanding, and theory-of-mind development. Using sociometric methods to identify popular and rejected children, Peterson and Siegal showed that rejected children who had a stable, mutual friendship performed better on the theory-of-mind measures than did rejected children without such a friendship. The same relationship held for popular children as well. Regression analyses indicated that a mutual stable friendship also made a significant contribution as a predictor of theory-of-mind performance. Peterson and Siegal suggested that opportunities for social interaction, particularly for conversational interactions within the context of a friendship, are critical to the development of mentalizing abilities.

In summary, the findings regarding a link between theory-of-mind ability and social development are complex. Although the research clearly shows a link between theory of mind and specific social and interactional skills, the evidence regarding a link to peer acceptance is less compelling. A recent study by McNab (2001) was designed to further investigate the association between theory of mind and peer acceptance. Eighty 4- and 5-year-old children were given measures of false-belief understanding and language ability. In addition, children completed a peer rating task to assess peer acceptance. Finally, teachers were asked to rate children's social skills. McNab predicted that children's performance on a test of mental-state understanding would be significantly associated with their performance on a measure of peer status, even when controlling for individual differences in receptive and expressive language skills. Given the findings of Lalonde and Chandler (1995), it was also predicted that there would be an association between theory-of-mind performance and teachers' ratings of children's social skills.

The task chosen to assess children's understanding of the mind was the social false-belief task developed by Nguyen and Frye (1999). The social false-belief task has been shown to be somewhat more difficult than the standard false-belief task. In traditional false-belief tasks, the stories deal with changes in the physical state of the world, such as the location of a hidden object, and tap children's understanding of mental states as they apply to these changes. In contrast, the social false-belief task embeds a representation of a particular state of affairs within a social interaction, that is, two characters who are jointly engaged in an activity.

The task used here closely follows Nguyen and Frye (1999; see this paper for details). The child is introduced to two puppets, Bunny Rabbit and Tiger, who are shown to be reading a book together. Bunny Rabbit has to leave the room and, as he goes, Tiger states to Bunny Rabbit that he will continue to read the book. However, once Bunny Rabbit leaves, Tiger changes his mind and decides to have a nap, and consequently lies down to have a sleep. The child participant is then asked three control questions: a *reality* question (What is Tiger doing now?); a *memory* question (What were Bunny Rabbit and Tiger doing together before Bunny Rabbit left the room?); and a *knowledge* question (Did Bunny Rabbit see Tiger have a nap?). Children were then given the social false-belief test question, *What does Bunny Rabbit think Tiger is doing right now?* If children did not answer this question, they were given a forced-choice prompt: *What does Bunny Rabbit think Tiger is doing right now, reading or sleeping?* The options are presented in a counterbalanced order. Only children who correctly answered all three control questions could be scored as correctly answering the social false-belief test question and received a score of 1.

To assess peer acceptance, McNab used a sociometric rating scale technique, following the methodology developed by Denham, McKinley, Couchoud, and Holt (1990; see also Asher, Singleton, Tinsley, & Hymel, 1979). This measure differs from the peer nominations used by Slaughter et al. (2002) in that children were not asked to nominate specific peers whom they like and dislike. Children were shown a piece of cardboard on which was mounted a Polaroid photograph of every child in the classroom, randomly arranged. Children were then asked to assign the picture of each one of their classmates to one of three boxes having either a happy, a sad, or a neutral face on it. The criterion for sorting was described as whether they liked to play with this peer "a lot," whether they "kind of liked" to play with the peer, or whether they "did not like to play with the peer at all." Scoring of the peer-acceptance measure followed Asher et al. (1979). The *likeability index* was calculated as the mean of a weighted sum of all the participating respondents in each classroom: (3 × the number of *like* ratings) + (2 × the number of *kind of like* ratings) + (1 × the number of *don't like* ratings) divided by the number of raters. Separate scores were also calculated based on the gender of the respondents, one for male respondents and one for female respondents. Thus, for each child there were three measures of peer acceptance: the child when rated by all children in the class, the child when rated only by males, and the child when rated only by females.

In order to assess children's social skills, each child's teacher was given a four-item scale adapted from Harter's (1979) Perceived Competence Scale for Children. Teachers were asked to rate each item using four-point Likert scales anchored by the terms *really true of this child* (4) or *not true of this child* (1). Finally, children's receptive and expressive language ability was measured using the TELD II (Hresko, Reid, & Hammill, 1991). Testing took place over four separate visits to each child's school. The first visit was used to develop a rapport with children and subsequent visits were used to complete the sociometric assessment, the theory-of-mind task, and the TELD II.

Table 6.1 presents the correlations among each of the measures and the partial correlations among these measures controlling for language ability. It is clear from Table 6.1 that the measures of peer acceptance were not uniformly associated with false-belief understanding. Performance on the false-belief task was positively correlated with peer acceptance when rated only by females, $r = .26$, $p < .05$, but was not significantly correlated with peer acceptance as rated by the entire group or when rated only by males. This finding provides some limited support for the suggestion that theory of mind is associated with peer acceptance; however, it also suggests that the story is somewhat more complex than predicted. The pattern of correlations suggests that girls and boys may differentially value an understanding of mind when it comes to judging whether or not someone is likeable. In addition, as found by Watson et al. (1999), there was a significant association between children's social skills and false-belief understanding, $r = .36$, $p < .01$.

Also, as was expected on the basis of previous research, peer acceptance as rated by the group was positively correlated with teacher-nominated social skills, $r = .33$, $p < .05$. Social skills were not correlated with peer acceptance when rated by boys but were positively associated with peer acceptance when rated by girls. Peer acceptance was not significantly correlated with language ability, a finding that echoes the Slaughter et al. study 2, which showed no relation between language ability and measures of social preference and social impact. Language scores were, however, positively correlated with performance on the social false-belief task, a finding that reflects the strong ties between language ability and performance on false-belief tasks more generally (e.g., Jenkins & Astington, 1996).

As suggested by Astington (this volume), it is important to control for the effects of language ability when assessing the relationship between peer acceptance and theory of mind to ensure that the association taps something other than preferences for verbally adept children. In this case, when controlling for language scores, the positive association between peer acceptance as rated by females and performance on the social false belief task remained significant (partial $r = .22$, $p < .05$), as did the relationship between teacher-rated social skills and false belief, partial $r = .32$, $p < .01$.

TABLE 6.1. Zero-Order Correlations Between Sociometric Indices,
Teacher-Rated Social Skills, False-Belief Understanding,
and Language Ability

	1.	2.	3.	4.	5.	6.
1. Sociometric Index: All	1.00					
2. Sociometric Index: Females	.72°°	1.00				
3. Sociometric Index: Males	.60°°	−.01	1.00			
4. Social Skills	.32°°	.26°	.10	1.00		
5. TELD	.15	.14	.05	.18	1.00	
6. False Belief	.11	.24°	−.11	.36°°	.30°°	1.00

Note. Significance: °$p < .05$; °°$p < .01$.

In short, then, we see some evidence for the predicted association between peer acceptance and theory-of-mind understanding. Performance on the
false-belief task was positively correlated with peer acceptance as rated by female subjects. One implication of this finding is that there are multiple pathways to peer acceptance, and that these pathways may differ for boys and girls.
For example, it may be the case that in the preschool years, boys judge whether
or not another person is likable on the basis of qualities such as physical attrac-
tiveness, names, aggressiveness, social status in the group, and so forth, whereas
for girls, the individual's theory of mind also plays a role in their judgments of
likeability. For girls, individuals who do not understand false belief are rated as
less likeable partners, whereas for boys, whether or not an individual child understands false belief is unrelated to their judgments of likeability. Of course,
caution is required in interpreting these results. It is not likely to be the case
that children are assessing each other's theory of mind per se; rather, theory of
mind influences how the child interacts with peers, and those who have a well-
developed theory of mind tend to display certain social behaviors or characteristics that girls find attractive but that boys do not seem to consider. Keenan and

TABLE 6.2. Partial Correlations Between Sociometric Indices,
Teacher-Rated Social Skills, and False-Belief Understanding,
Controlling for Language Ability

	1.	2.	3.	4.	5.
1. Sociometric Index: All	1.00				
2. Sociometric Index: Females	.67°°	1.00			
3. Sociometric Index: Males	.63°°	−.01	1.00		
4. Social Skills	.33°°	.26°	.09	1.00	
5. False Belief	.09	.22°	−.12	.32°°	1.00

Note. Signficance: ° $p < .05$; °°$p < .01$.

Harvey (1998) previously made the suggestion that an individual's theory of mind acted as an organizer of children's social development. That is, that the level and rate of development in theory of mind determine, in part, how an individual fares in the social world. These data suggest that this position may need to be modified somewhat. It may be that theory-of-mind development organizes social development in girls only. Alternatively, theory of mind may organize social development in boys, but at a later point in development. This second point would be consistent with the findings by Slaughter et al. (2001) suggesting that false belief is related to peer acceptance in older but not younger children. In summary, the present study shows that the relationship between theory of mind and social development may be different for boys and and girls, but these differences may also decrease with age.

THEORY OF MIND: A MATTER OF DEGREE?

Astington (this volume) raises an important point regarding the nature of development in the child's theory of mind. Specifically, she argues that for normally developing children, theory of mind as assessed by the false-belief task highlights the fact that children have acquired a conceptual framework, which, as Astington puts it, is not a "matter of degree." That is, although children gradually acquire an understanding of the possibility of false belief between 2 to 5 years of age (Jenkins & Astington, 2000), once they have fully acquired this understanding they can readily apply it in order to predict another's actions or knowledge state, or to solve other sorts of social problems. However, whether or not children choose to apply their newly developed understanding of false belief is almost certainly a matter of degree. As noted earlier, in some contexts or relationships, children are more likely to mentalize in a rich and complex fashion whereas in other contexts they are less prone to do so (O'Connor & Hirsch, 1999). In short, the evidence would seem to suggest that beyond the preschool years where children acquire the foundational concepts of a representational theory of mind, skillful mind reading is also most certainly a matter of degree, being acquired gradually as children age. In other words, there are bound to be individual differences across normal children in their ability to employ their theory of mind in the service of achieving their social goals.

The distinction here is, as Davies and Stone (this volume) suggest, one of competence versus performance. That is, there are differences between the nature of the concepts that children form (i.e., *beliefs* as representations that can accurately or falsely represent the world and *desires* as states that are either fulfilled or unfulfilled by outcomes) and how they employ those concepts when behaving in the real world. In short, although the understanding of concepts like belief, desire, and intention is less a matter of degree than an "all-or-none" acquisition, the ability to employ these constructs in the service of everyday mind reading is likely to vary widely across individuals. Furthermore, it seems highly likely that important aspects of real-world social behavior are associated with individual differences in mind reading. That is, differences in the way in which one's theory of mind is deployed will have important consequences for social behavior. An example is the selection process for entrance into postgraduate clinical psychology programs: In many programs, potential students are given case studies or vignettes and are asked to think through what the individual is thinking and feeling and how one might deal with the problem presented. Entrance is more likely to be granted if candidates show a good facility for mind reading or "getting inside the client's head" and reasoning about their thoughts and feelings. In this case, differences in mind reading have clear effects: gaining or failing to gain entrance to a program. Extending the evidence from the preschool studies of peer acceptance (e.g., Slaughter at al., 2002) suggests that real-world social consequences are the case for children as well.

DEVELOPMENTS BEYOND THE PRESCHOOL YEARS: EMPATHIC ACCURACY AND MORE

Which, if any, aspects of the child's theory of mind continue to develop beyond early childhood? This is an important question, given the idea that individual differences in social intelligence (Cantor & Khilstrom, 1987; Goody, 1995) are related to functioning in the increasingly complex social environments that children experience after the preschool years. One important development that social cognition researchers have identified as developing beyond early childhood is *empathic accuracy* (Eisenberg, Murphy, & Shepard, 1997). Empathic accuracy is an aspect of everyday mind reading that continues to develop into adulthood, particularly in the context of close personal relationships (Ickes, 1997).

Empathic accuracy is a measure of one's skill at empathic inference. According to Ickes (1997), it is a form of "complex psychological inference in which observation, memory, knowledge, and reasoning are combined to yield insights into the thoughts and feelings of others" (p. 2). In other words, empathic accuracy refers to the growing ability to accurately infer mental states in other people: putting one's theory of mind to use and employing it in the service of achieving one's social goals. One of the major issues for researchers in interpersonal perception (see Funder, 1987) is that of *accuracy*, the degree to which an observer's inferences are accurate or "on target" (the other being the question of *bias* or *error* in person perception). Individuals differ in their facility for making accurate inferences about others' thoughts and feelings, and empathic accuracy researchers strive to understand the factors that support or challenge individuals' efforts. Researchers have identified a number of factors that play a role in empathic accuracy, ranging from physiological synchrony between the perceiver and the target (Levenson & Ruef, 1997) to the kinds of theories an individual holds about the target of the inference (e.g., the person's partner) or romantic relationships in general (Thomas & Fletcher, 1997).

Studies that examine the development of empathic accuracy beyond the preschool years are likely to tell us much about how mind-reading skills are put to use and what sorts of factors lead to increased success in one's deployment of these skills. Eisenberg et al. (1997) identified three areas of development—areas beyond the child's acquisition of the rudiments of theory of mind—that show clear progression beyond early childhood. Children's ability to label and to decode emotional states and to use behavioral cues to facilitate this process is one important aspect of developing empathic accuracy. A second dimension in which children's abilities continue to show growth is in refining their inferences on the basis of relevant contextual information. Finally, Eisenberg et al. (1997) suggested that children's perspective-taking ability continues to develop beyond the preschool years as a function of both the maturation of cognitive abilities and the accumulation of relevant social experiences. For example, Perner and Wimmer's (1985) work on the development of second-order mental states (e.g., John thinks that Mary knows that . . .) is a good example of how developments such as the ability to embed mental state expressions within other expressions can increase the complexity of social reasoning.

A challenge for researchers interested in exploring individual differences in empathic accuracy and, specifically, how these differences might be related to later social and emotional development is the design of methods appropriate for testing empathic accuracy with young children. One aspect of the various empathic accuracy paradigms in use is that these tasks involve the assessment of empathic accuracy "online," usually using videotapes of the target in a naturalistic, interpersonal context (Ickes, 1997). Another important aspect is the establishment of a matching criterion; that is, the standard against which an observer's inferences are matched to determine accuracy. Various empathic accuracy tasks have been developed for use with friends, married couples, and even strangers. It seems highly probable that these tasks could be modified for use with younger children, for example, by using standardized targets (e.g., known characters involved in a naturalistic social interaction) for which children are asked to infer thoughts and feelings. The empathic accuracy paradigm should prove sensitive, particularly to individual differences in mind-reading skill, and should positively correlate with children's abilities in related areas such as conflict resolution, friendship formation, and friendship quality (e.g., Parker & Asher, 1993). In short, the adaptation of an empathic accuracy paradigm for young children might provide a way of assessing developments in theory of mind or mind reading after children have acquired foundational knowledge about the mind.

What other tasks might also illustrate the development of mind-reading skills beyond early childhood? One vital task that we engage in every day is the attribution of communicative intentions to speakers. Understanding a speech act requires the listener to grasp what it is that the speaker intends to communicate. With literal messages this process is straightforward; speakers mean to communicate that which they say. However, with nonliteral speech acts such as *sarcasm* and *irony*, listeners must recognize that the speaker intends to convey something other than what he or she says, in most cases the opposite of what the speaker says. Olson (1988) argued that it is not until children appreciate the sarcastic speaker's communicative intention that they can be said to truly understand sarcasm as sarcasm. A great deal of research shows that the ability to correctly attribute a communicative intention to a speaker under conditions of uncertainty develops with age (Ackerman, 1981, 1982; Keenan & Quigley, 2002). Recently, Keenan and Quigley (2002) showed that children's ability to correctly grasp the communicative intentions of literal and sarcastic speakers— operationalized as the child's ability to paraphrase what it is that the speaker in a story intended to make the listener think—increased significantly from 6 to 10 years of age. Interestingly, this study also highlighted the existence of sex differences in children's performance on the task. Although 6- and 8-year-old boys and girls did not differ, at age 10 girls began to significantly outperform boys on this task, suggesting that differences in social intelligence, as it relates to verbal communication, develop as children mature and engage more and more with a socializing environment. This finding fits well with other research suggesting the possibility of sex differences in specific aspects of theory-of-mind development.

An intriguing question that emerges from the work on sarcasm is whether early differences in children's performance on the Keenan and Quigley task would be associated with later differences in social adaptation. That is, might it be the case that children who are more able to glean a sarcastic speaker's communicative intent find it easier to navigate, and perhaps manipulate and control, the complexities of the social world? Longitudinal studies using various measures such as sarcasm and irony comprehension tasks may provide a way to answer these questions. The findings of emerging sex differences in the attribution of communicative intentions fit well with those of Bosacki (2000), who found that for girls, language ability was linked to social understanding but not self-understanding. Bosacki argued that language ability may provide girls with a vehicle for developing increased insight into others' minds.

Given that there are aspects of theory of mind that develop beyond the preschool years, it is also likely that there exists the potential for such developments to proceed atypically, or to "go off the rails." Ward and Keenan (1999) recently suggested that sexual offenders may suffer from theory-of-mind deficits that develop from the early childhood years and beyond. Sex offenders are not likely to suffer from major deficits in their ability to understand and infer mental states. Indeed, many child sex offenders are especially adept at "grooming" children so that they can commit offenses with them. Rather, it is more likely to be the case that sex offenders have distorted theories that arise as a function of their early experiences, much like Happé and Frith's (1996) suggestions regarding the development of a theory of nasty minds.

Keenan and Ward (2000) argued that deficits in the sex offender's implicit theories present an intriguing possibility for understanding both how an offender might sexually offend and, importantly, how this pattern of behavior might develop. They describe a number of possibilities regarding the associations between theory of mind deficits and the etiology of sexual offending. These authors (Ward, 2000; Ward & Keenan, 1999) further argued that the cognitive distortions held by many sexual offenders are best described as *implicit theories*, which guide the mental state inferences that offenders make about their victims. Many offenders hold elaborate theories about their victims that serve to justify their aggressive sexual behavior. For example, many offenders hold a theory that *children are sexual beings*. Children are seen by the offender as possessing sexual needs, desires, and preferences; are viewed as being able to develop their own plans to achieve these goals; and are thought to be capable of making their own choices about how to seek and achieve sexual experiences. One important consequence of understanding the implicit theories that a child molester holds is the ability of clinicians to specifically treat the offender by presenting evidence that directly counters their beliefs.

CONCLUSIONS

A now-substantial body of research has linked the child's acquisition of a representational theory of mind to social development. As the child develops an understanding of the possibility of the mind as a representational medium, there is a cascade of related changes in the child's social functioning. Children begin to appreciate the social world in a different way as they begin to take into account other people's perspectives, thoughts, and feelings. Children can form joint plans with others and negotiate their way through a shared imaginative world as well as through the real world of social relationships. Children's appreciation of communication between others changes as they begin to take into account the communicative intention of a speaker and learn to look behind the surface meaning of an utterance to what it is that the speaker intended to convey. Finally, children begin to employ their skills to achieve social goals such as gaining the acceptance of their peers. Each of these developments is, at least in part, dependent on developments in the child's theory of mind and the child's ability to employ this knowledge in everyday mind reading.

The possibility that individual differences in social functioning are related to issues such as the timing of the acquisition of an adultlike theory of mind, or in children's facility for employing their knowledge for everyday mind reading, should not be surprising. It has been clear for some time that individual differences in a variety of antecedents to the acquisition of a theory of mind influence the timing of children's acquisition of this knowledge. Now evidence is accumulating that there are important consequences that follow from this achievement, related to both the timing and the nature of children's knowledge. In regard to the consequences of developing a theory of mind, the evidence to date suggests that the development of a theory of mind is associated with important aspects of children's social functioning. For example, it appears to be associated with important aspects of social functioning like social skills and peer acceptance. However, given the correlational nature of our work, we cannot definitively say whether changes in children's theory of mind cause changes in peer acceptance or vice versa. Moreover, the research by McNab (2001) and Keenan and Quigley (2002) suggests that the developmental consequences of theory of mind may differ for boys and girls. Further work using longitudinal methods is required in order to make further progress in understanding the relationship between theory of mind and social development.

This chapter also highlights a number of methodological issues that need to be addressed in future work on theory of mind and social development. How we should go about measuring theory-of-mind development and mind reading beyond the preschool years is one such issue that needs to be addressed. As noted, there are a number of promising developments in the literature. A particularly difficult problem will be to find ways of capturing individual differences in the facility for mind reading in school-aged children. Variations on the empathic accuracy paradigms employed by social cognition researchers might provide one solution, but there are likely to be other useful avenues to explore as well. Although there remains much work to be done, the fact that researchers are exploring the variety of ways in which theory of mind and social development may be associated is exciting and should yield new insights into both domains.

REFERENCES

Ackerman, B. (1981). Young children's understanding of a speaker's intentional use of a false utterance. *Developmental Psychology*, 17, 472–480.

Ackerman, B. P. (1982). Contextual integration and utterance interpretation: The ability of children and adults to interpret sarcastic utterances. *Child Development*, 53, 1075–1083.

Asher, S. R., Singleton, L. C., Tinsley, B. R., & Hymel, S. (1979). A reliable sociometric measure for preschool children. *Developmental Psychology*, 15, 443–444.

Astington, J. W., & Jenkins, J. M. (1995). Theory of mind development and social understanding. *Cognition and Emotion*, 9, 151–165.

Badenes, L. V., Estevan, R. A. C., & Bacete, F. J. G. (2000). Theory of mind and peer rejection at school. *Social Development*, 9, 271–283.

Bartsch, K., & Estes, D. (1996). Individual differences in children's developing theory of mind and implications for metacognition. *Learning and Individual Differences*, 8, 281–304.

Bosacki, S. L. (2000). Theory of mind and self-concept in preadolescents: Links with gender and language. *Journal of Educational Psychology, 92,* 707–717.

Cantor, N., & Khilstrom, J. (1987). *Personality and social intelligence.* Englewood Cliffs, NJ: Prentice Hall.

Carlson, S., & Moses, L. J. (2001). Individual differences in inhibitory control and children's theory of mind. *Child Development, 72,* 1032–1053.

Carlson, S., Moses, L. J., & Breton, C. (2002). How specific is the relation between executive function and theory of mind? Contributions of inhibitory control and working memory. *Infant and Child Development, 11,* 73–92.

deGroot, A., Kaplan, J., Rosenblatt, E., Dews, S., & Winner, E. (1995). Understanding versus discriminating nonliteral utterances: Evidence for a dissociation. *Metaphor and Symbol, 10,* 255–273.

Denham, S. A., McKinley, M., Couchoud, E., & Holt, R. (1990). Emotional and behavioral predictors of preschool peer ratings. *Child Development, 61,* 1145–1152.

Dockett, S. (1997, April). *Young children's peer popularity and theories of mind.* Poster presentation at the biennial meeting of the Society for Research in Child Development, Washington, DC.

Dodge, K. A., & Feldman, E. (1990). Issues in social cognition and sociometric status. In S. R. Asher & J. D. Coie (Eds.), *Peer rejection in childhood* (pp. 119–155). New York: Cambridge University Press.

Dodge, K. A., & Frame, C. L. (1982). Social cognition and children's aggressive behavior. *Child Development, 51,* 162–170.

Eisenberg, N., Murphy, B. C., & Shepard, S. (1997). The development of empathic accuracy. In W. Ickes (Ed.), *Empathic accuracy* (pp. 73–116). New York: Guilford Press.

Fonagy, P., Redfern, S., & Charman, T. (1997). The relationship between belief-desire reasoning and a projective measure of attachment security (SAT). *British Journal of Developmental Psychology, 15,* 51–61.

Fonagy, P., Steele, M., Steele, H., Higgitt, A., & Target, M. (1994). The Emmanuel Miller Memorial Lecture 1992: The theory and practice of resilience. *Journal of Child Psychology and Psychiatry and Allied Disciplines, 35,* 231–257.

Funder, D. C. (1987). Errors and mistakes: Evaluating the accuracy of social judgment. *Psychological Bulletin, 102,* 652–670.

Goody, E. E. (1995). *Social intelligence and interaction: Expressions and implications of the social bias in human intelligence.* New York: Cambridge University Press.

Happé, F., & Frith, U. (1996). Theory of mind and social impairment in children with conduct disorder. *British Journal of Developmental Psychology, 14,* 385–398.

Harter, S. (1979). *Perceived competence scale for children.* Boulder, CO: University of Denver Press.

Hobson, R. P. (1993). The emotional origins of social understanding. *Philosophical Psychology, 6,* 227–249.

Hresko, W. P., Reid, D. K., & Hammill, D. (1991). *The Test of Early Language Development–Second edition (TELD–2).* Austin, TX: Pro-Ed.

Hughes, C. (1998a). Executive function in preschoolers: Links with theory of mind and verbal ability. *British Journal of Developmental Psychology, 6,* 233–253.

Hughes, C. (1998b). Finding your marbles: Does preschoolers' strategic behavior predict later understanding of mind? *Developmental Psychology, 34,* 1326–1339.

Hughes, C., White, A., Sharpen, J., & Dunn, J. (2000). Antisocial, angry, and unsympathetic: "Hard to manage" preschoolers' peer problems and possible cognitive influences. *Journal of Child Psychology and Psychiatry and Allied Disciplines, 41,* 169–176.

Ickes, W. (1997). *Empathic accuracy.* New York: Guilford Press.

Jenkins, J. M., & Astington, J. W. (1996). Cognitive factors and family structure associated with theory of mind development in young children. *Developmental Psychology, 32,* 70–78.

Jenkins, J. M., & Astington, J. W. (2000). Theory of mind and social behavior: Causal models tested in a longitudinal study. *Merrill-Palmer Quarterly, 46,* 203–220.

Keenan, T. (1998). Memory span as a predictor of false belief understanding. *New Zealand Journal of Psychology, 27,* 36–43.

Keenan, T., & Harvey, M. (1998). Understanding the development of the child's theory of mind. *New Zealand Science Monthly*, 9, 6–8.

Keenan, T., Olson, D. R., & Marini, Z. (1998). Working memory and children's developing understanding of mind. *Australian Journal of Psychology*, 50, 76–82.

Keenan, T., & Quigley (2002). *Children's attributions of communicative intent to an (apparently) sarcastic speaker*. Manuscript under review.

Keenan, T., & Ward, T. (2000). A theory of mind perspective on cognitive, affective, and intimacy deficits in sex offenders. *Sexual Abuse: A Journal of Research and Treatment, 12*, 49–60.

Laible, D. J., & Thompson, R. A. (1998). Attachment and emotional understanding in preschool children. *Developmental Psychology, 5*, 1038–1045.

Lalonde, C.E., & Chandler, M.J. (1995). False belief understanding goes to school: On the social-emotional consequences of coming early or late to a first theory of mind. *Cognition and Emotion*, 9, 167–185.

Levenson, R. W., & Ruef, A. M. (1997). Physiological aspects of emotional knowledge and rapport. In W. Ickes (Ed.), *Empathic accuracy* (pp. 44–72). New York: Guilford Press.

Lillard, A. S. (1998). Ethnopsychologies: Cultural variations in theories of mind. *Psychological Bulletin, 123*, 3–32.

Lutz, C. (1985). Ethnopsychology compared to what? Explaining behavior and consciousness among the Ifaluk. In G. M. White & J. Kirkpatrick (Eds.), *Person, self, and experience: Exploring Pacific ethnopsychologies* (pp. 35–79). Berkeley: University of California Press.

McNab, C. (2001). *Peer acceptance and theory of mind*. Unpublished MA thesis, University of Canterbury.

Meins, E., Fernyhough, C., Russell, J., & Clark-Carter, D. (1998). Security of attachment as a predictor of symbolic and mentalising abilities: A longitudinal study. *Social Development*, 7, 1–24.

Nguyen, L., & Frye, D. (1999). Children's theory of mind: Understanding of desire, belief and emotion with social referents. *Social Development*, 8, 70–92.

O'Connor, T. G., & Hirsch, N. (1999). Intra-

individual differences and relationship-specificity of mentalizing in early adolescence. *Social Development*, 8, 256–274.

Olson, D. R. (1988). Or what's a metaphor for? *Metaphor and Symbolic Activity*, 3, 215–222.

Parker, J. G., & Asher, S. R. (1993). Friendship and friendship quality in middle childhood: Links with peer group acceptance and feelings of loneliness and social dissatisfaction. *Developmental Psychology*, 29, 611–621.

Perner, J. (1988). Higher-order beliefs and intentions in children's understanding of social interaction. In J. W. Astington, P. L. Harris, & D. R. Olson (Eds.), *Developing theories of mind* (pp. 271–294). Cambridge: Cambridge University Press.

Perner, J., Leekam, S., & Wimmer, H. (1987). Three-year-olds' difficulty with false belief: The case for a conceptual deficit. *British Journal of Developmental Psychology*, 5, 125–137.

Perner, J., & Wimmer, H. (1985). "John thinks that Mary thinks that . . .": Attribution of second-order beliefs by 5- to 10-year-old children. *Journal of Experimental Child Psychology*, 39, 437–471.

Peterson, C., & Siegal, M. (2002). Mindreading and moral awareness in popular and rejected preschoolers. *British Journal of Developmental Psychology*, 20, 205–224.

Ruffman, T., Perner, J., & Parkin, L. (1999). How parenting style affects false belief understanding. *Social Development*, 8, 395–411.

Schwebel, D. C., Rosen, C. S., & Singer, J.L. (1999). Preschoolers' pretend play and theory of mind: The role of jointly constructed pretence. *British Journal of Developmental Psychology*, 17, 333–348.

Slade, A. (1987). Quality of attachment and early symbolic play. *Developmental Psychology, 23*, 78–85.

Slaughter, V., Dennis, M. J., & Pritchard, M. (2002). Theory of mind and peer acceptance in preschool children. *British Journal of Developmental Psychology*, 20, 545–564.

Steinberg, M. S., & Dodge, K. A. (1983). Attributional bias in aggressive adolescent boys and girls. *Journal of Social and Clinical Psychology, 1*, 312–321.

Sullivan, K., Winner, E., & Hopfield, N. (1995). How children tell a lie from a joke: The role of second-order mental state attributions. *British Journal of Developmental Psychology, 13,* 191–204.

Taylor, M., & Carlson, S. M. (1997). The relation between individual differences in fantasy and theory of mind. *Child Development, 68,* 436–455.

Thomas, G., & Fletcher, G. J. (1997). Empathic accuracy in close relationships. In W. Ickes (Ed.), *Empathic accuracy* (pp. 194–217). New York: Guilford Press.

Vinden, P., & Astington, J. (2000). Culture and understanding other minds. In S. Baron-Cohen, Tager-Flusberg, H., & Cohen, D. (Eds.), *Understanding other minds: Perspectives from developmental cognitive neuroscience,* 2nd ed. (pp. 503–519). Oxford: Oxford University Press.

Ward, T. (2000). Sexual offenders' cognitive distortions as implicit theories. *Aggression and Violent Behavior, 5,* 491–507.

Ward, T., & Keenan, T. (1999). Child molesters' implicit theories. *Journal of Interpersonal Violence, 14,* 821–838.

Ward, T., Keenan, T., & Hudson, S. M. (2000). Understanding affective, intimacy, and cognitive deficits in sex offenders. A developmental perspective. *Aggression and Violent Behavior, 5,* 41–62.

Watson, A. C., Nixon, C. L., Wilson, A., & Capage, L. (1999). Social interaction skills and theory of mind in young children. *Developmental Psychology, 35,* 386–391.

Winner, E., & Leekman, S. (1991). Distinguishing irony from deception: Understanding the speaker's second-order intention. *British Journal of Developmental Psychology, 9,* 257–270.

7

Did Cain Fail to Represent the Thoughts of Abel Before He Killed Him?

The Relationship Between Theory of Mind and Aggression

ROBERT JAMES RICHARD BLAIR

Mood and Anxiety Program, National Institute of Mental Health

*T*he goal of this chapter is to consider the relationship between theory of mind and antisocial behavior. Specifically, it questions whether representations of the mental states of others are involved in the inhibition of aggression. In short, this chapter considers whether killers, such as Cain, fail to represent the mental states of their victims and whether it is this failure that allows them to harm others. Toward this goal, I first provide a brief description of theory of mind, distinguishing between the neurocognitive architecture that allows the representation of the mental states of others and connected systems that represent the individuals' theorylike concepts of other individuals' probable mental states. Second, I briefly describe antisocial behavior and draw a distinction between instrumental and reactive aggression. Third, I consider whether theory of mind, specifically the neurocognitive architecture that allows the representation of other individuals' mental states, is involved in the inhibition of either instrumental or reactive aggression. Fourth, I consider whether hostile attribution biases in an individual's theorylike concepts of others' probable mental states might motivate reactive aggression.

WHAT IS THEORY OF MIND?

Theory of mind refers to the ability to represent the mental states of others, that is, their thoughts, desires, beliefs, intentions, and knowledge (Frith, 1989; Leslie, 1987; Premack & Woodruff, 1978). Theory of mind allows the attribution of mental states to self and others in order to explain and predict behavior. As a hypothesis, theory of mind has considerable similarity to earlier ideas of role and perspective taking (Chandler, Greenspan, & Barenboim, 1974; Selman, 1980). Role taking was defined as the ability to recognize another person's expectations and desires, predicting how they might react, and understanding what they mean to communicate. The main difference between the current conceptualization of theory of mind and earlier ideas about role and perspective taking is that theory of mind is a more tightly specified construct. Activities that were grouped together as forms of role or perspective taking, for example, cognitive and visual perspective taking, have been shown to be computationally distinct and mediated by different neurocognitive systems (Baron-Cohen, 1989; Reed & Peterson, 1990).

The classic measure of theory of mind is the Sally–Ann task (Wimmer & Perner, 1983). In this task, the participant is shown two dolls (Sally and Ann), a basket, and a box. The child watches as Sally places her marble in the basket and then leaves the room. While Sally is out, naughty Ann moves Sally's marble from the basket to the box. Then she, too, leaves the room. Now Sally comes back into the room. The child is asked the test question: "Where will Sally look for her marble?" In order to pass this task, the child must represent Sally's mental state—her belief that the marble is in the basket. Without this representation, the child will answer on the basis of the marble's real location, the box. Most typically developing children from the age of 4 years pass this task (Wimmer & Perner, 1983).

There are two main positions on theory of mind: the theory–theory view (e.g., Gopnik & Meltzoff, 1997; Perner, 1991) and the modular view (Leslie, 1987). According to the theory–theory view, children construct mental state concepts (e.g., *belief, misrepresentation*) through the use of domain-general mechanisms for the formation of theories. Effectively, these mechanisms allow the formation of theories about other individuals. The child tests these theories against his or her experience and changes them if they prove unable to predict the behavior of other individuals. In contrast, according to the modular view, the theory-of-mind module (ToMM) is a mechanism that allows the representation of mental states. ToMM is conceptualized as an innately specified system that allows the representation of the mental states of others. The important distinction between these two main positions is that according to the theory–theory view, the capacity to represent the mental states of others is a consequence of having a theory about them. In contrast, the ToMM position stipulates that there must be a dedicated neural substrate for representing the mental states of others. According to the ToMM view, experience only plays a role in determining the type of mental states that are represented at any given time (i.e., I experience Sally placing the marble in the basket that is where she will think that it is). However, it does not lead to the formation of a specific architecture for the representation of the mental states of others.

The theory–theory view faces several major difficulties. These are not detailed here, but one noteworthy example is that manipulating the false-belief paradigm to either decrease the strength of representations of the current state of the object or increase the strength of representations of the false belief massively influence task performance (see Leslie, 2000, for a review). Such data can be elegantly explained by the ToMM model but are incompatible with theory–theory views. Moreover, it is difficult to understand from the perspective of modern cognitive neuroscience how a system allowing the representation of the mental states of others is likely to develop as a consequence of the child forming a theory that this is the case.

However, it is worth considering that some of the debate between the theory–theory and modular camps probably occurs because, in some respects, the positions are models of different phenomena. The theory–theory authors are attempting to describe the child's and the adult's semantic knowledge about other individuals' internal states. In contrast, Leslie (1987), in particular, is attempting to detail a model of the computational architecture that is necessary for the representation of the mental states of others.

From a cognitive neuroscience perspective, it is interesting to note that recent animal work has identified medial frontal cortex involvement in the representation of the animal's goals during instrumental learning paradigms (see Balleine & Dickinson, 1998, for a review). This is intriguing because a series of neuroimaging studies in humans has consistently implicated comparable regions of the medial prefrontal cortex, as well as the temporo-parietal junction and the temporal poles, in the representation of the mental states of others (Baron-Cohen, Ring, Wheelwright, et al., 1999; Brunet, Sarfati, Hardy-Bayle, & Decety, 2000; Castelli, Happe, Frith, & Frith, 2000; Fletcher et al., 1995; Gallagher et al., 2000; Goel, Grafman, Sadato, & Hallett, 1995; Vogeley et al., 2001; see also Frith & Frith, 1999, for a review). Although there is very little work suggesting that animals can represent the mental states of others, the work of Balleine and Dickinson (1998) raises the interesting possibility that the capacity to represent the mental states of others in humans may incorporate older neurocognitive systems that allow the representation of the mental states (in particular, the goals) of the self. This has led to the suggestion of a neurocognitive architecture whereby a mechanism sensitive to biological motion (potentially involving neurons within the temporo-parietal junction) serves to activate systems required for the representation of mental states (Blair, Frith, Smith, Abell, & Cipolotti, 2002; Cipolotti, Robinson, Blair, & Frith, 1999). These systems include the temporal poles and medial frontal cortex. The suggestion would follow recent computational accounts of executive functioning where "Task Demand" units represent the task to be achieved and modulate the functioning of posterior systems (Cohen, Braver, & O'Reilly, 1996; Cohen & Servan-Schreiber, 1992; Liss et al., 2001). The idea would be that theory of mind involves a system of neurons that allow the representation of another individuals' intention and that this neural activity modulates more posterior representations, perhaps requiring the temporal poles, allowing potential predictions of the other individual's behavior. This is not to suggest that theory of mind can be equated with executive functioning. Although correlations between false belief and "inhibitory" tasks are high in children (Carlson & Moses, 2001), perhaps reflecting maturation of spatially proximal systems, there are now data that indicate that theory of mind is dissociable from executive functioning (Blair & Cipolotti, 2000; Fine, Lumsden, & Blair, 2001; Lough, Gregory, & Hodges, 2001). Thus, patients may present with profound impairments of theory of mind in the absence of executive impairment (Fine et al., 2001; Lough et al., 2001) or pronounced impairment in a wide variety of executive functions with no theory-of-mind impairment (Blair & Cipolotti, 2000). The suggestion is thus only that theory of mind may share computational similarities with other executive systems.

According to the perspective briefly described earlier, the theory–theory positions are concerned with the nature of the posterior representations, the concepts of other individuals, whereas the modular position relates to the way in which neurons in the medial frontal cortex interact with posterior systems. I stress this difference here because any discussion of the relationship between antisocial behavior and theory of mind could be between antisocial behavior and the ability to represent the mental states of others or antisocial behavior and peoples' theories about other individuals' internal states. In this chapter, I primarily focus on the relationship between antisocial behavior and the ability to represent the mental states of others. However, the relationship between antisocial behavior and people's theories about other individuals' internal states is considered during the discussion of hostile attribution biases (e.g., Crick & Dodge, 1996).

WHAT IS ANTISOCIAL BEHAVIOR?

For the purposes of the present chapter, antisocial behavior will be defined as any action that impinges on the rights and welfare of others. However, I wish to distinguish between instrumental and reactive antisocial behavior. A considerable amount of theoretical and empirical research has made this distinction (e.g., Barratt, Stanford, Dowdy, Liebman, & Kent, 1999; Berkowitz, 1993; Crick & Dodge, 1996; Linnoila et al., 1983). Instrumental/nonimpulsive aggression is purposeful and goal directed and can be described as "cold-blooded." Reactive/impulsive aggression generally refers to unplanned aggressive acts that are spontaneous in nature, are either unprovoked or out of proportion to the provocation, and occur among persons who are often characterized as "having a short fuse." Reactive aggression is frequently elicited in response to frustration or threat. Interviews and laboratory tasks have shown that instrumental and reactive aggression are independent constructs in both children and adults (Barratt, Stanford, Kent, & Felthous, 1997; Barratt et al., 1999; Dodge & Coie, 1987; Linnoila, DeJong, & Virkkunen, 1989; Vitiello, Behar, Hunt, Stoff, & Ricciuti, 1990).

It is likely that instrumental and reactive aggression are mediated by different neural architectures. Instrumental aggression is goal-directed motor behavior and is likely to recruit the same cortical neural systems as any other goal-directed motor program, such as reaching for an object. In brief, these neural systems will include the temporal cortex, involved in representing the objects to be responded to, and striatal and premotor cortical neurons, involved in implementing the actual behavior. The amygdala and ventral orbitofrontal cortex are involved in the associative learning process that allows the selection of the appropriate behavior to the object to achieve the goal (Killcross, Robbins, & Everitt, 1997; Murray, Bussey, & Wise, 2000; Passingham & Toni, 2001; Passingham, Toni, & Rushworth, 2000). In contrast, reactive aggression in humans can be plausibly related to the eventual fight response of an animal approached by a threat. Most animals show a graded response to an approaching threat: They will freeze, then attempt to escape and, if this is impossible, attack the threat (Blanchard, Blanchard, & Takahashi, 1977). This graded response to an approaching threat is primarily mediated by subcortical systems (Panksepp, 1989; Siegel, Roeling, Gregg, & Kruk, 1999). It is possible that the disorganized aggression shown by individuals displaying reactive aggression is mediated by these subcortical systems.

In this chapter, I consider in turn whether theory-of-mind dysfunction might be related to increased risk of both instrumental and reactive aggression. There are two main ways in which the relationship between theory of mind and antisocial behavior, including instrumental aggression, could be explored. The first is by establishing the degree of association between performance on theory-of-mind measures and antisocial behavior in normally developing individuals. This approach typically involves correlational analyses of performances on tests designed to assess different cognitive functions. The major problem with this approach is that observed correlations may not indicate functional equivalence of core systems but only similar developmental trajectories or the functioning of systems that are commonly required for successful performance on both types of task but not part of the core systems themselves. This problem is particularly severe for exploring the relationship of other variables with theory of mind, as it is highly plausible that much of the variance in theory-of-mind scores, at least if they are obtained through false-belief tests, is due to variance in executive, "inhibitory" systems rather than variance in the ability to represent the mental states of others (Leslie, 2000).

The second approach is neuropsychological. The neuropsychological approach does not face the major problem outlined earlier. Within this approach, populations are identified who present with impairment in a specific neurocognitive system and the implications of this impairment are investigated. Individuals with autism are a population who present with severe theory-of-mind impairment. So, by studying these individuals, we should be able to ascertain the relationship between theory of mind and antisocial behavior.

AUTISM

Autism is a severe developmental disorder described by the American Psychiatric Association's *Diagnostic and Statistical Manual* (DSM–IV; APA, 1994) as "the presence of markedly abnormal or impaired development in social interaction and communication and a markedly restricted repertoire of activities and interests" (p. 66). The main criteria for the diagnosis in *DSM–IV* can be summarized as qualitative impairment in social communication and restricted and repetitive patterns of behavior and interests. These criteria must be evident before 3 years of age. The incidence rate has been estimated as approximately 4 in 10,000 (Lotter, 1966).

Children with autism have been consistently reported to show theory-of-mind impairment. This was originally observed by Baron-Cohen, Leslie, and Frith (1985). Children with autism and two comparison groups, a mildly retarded population to match for mental age and a chronologically (to mental age) matched population of normally developing children, were presented with the Sally–Ann task described earlier. Although most of the members of both comparison groups passed this test, 80% of the children with autism failed it. This finding has now been replicated in a number of studies, using real people instead of toys, a "think" question rather than a "look" question, and a control group of specifically language-impaired children to rule out a language deficit explanation (Leslie & Frith, 1988; Perner, Frith, Leslie, & Leekam, 1989; see Baron-Cohen, 1995, for a review).

It is worth noting that the disorder of autism has also been linked with other impairments such as executive dysfunction (Hughes, Russell, & Robbins, 1994; Liss et al., 2001; see Pennington & Ozonoff, 1996, for a review) and face-processing deficits (Blair et al., 2002; Klin et al., 1999). This could be considered a potential problem, as executive dysfunction has been linked to antisocial behavior (see Morgan & Lilienfeld, 2000, for a review). However, it is interesting to note that the regions of the dorsolateral prefrontal cortex that have been linked to the forms of executive dysfunction that children with autism typically show (Pennington & Ozonoff, 1996) are not regions of the brain that, when lesioned in human patients, lead to heightened levels of antisocial behavior. Acquired lesions of the orbitofrontal cortex, rather than the dorsolateral prefrontal cortex, are associated with increased risk of aggression (Grafman, Schwab, Warden, Pridgen, & Brown, 1996). Thus, it would not be necessary to attribute any demonstrations of antisocial behavior or empathy impairment in individuals with autism to executive dysfunction.

THEORY OF MIND AND
INSTRUMENTAL ANTISOCIAL BEHAVIOR

As stated earlier, instrumental aggression/antisocial behavior is goal-directed motor behavior. In other words, it is behavior that is initiated either because it has been associated with reward or is expected to result in reward. There are clear rewards associated with antisocial behavior. These may include financial gain or increases in prestige as a function of "perceived toughness" within the group. However, most people do not engage in antisocial behavior, certainly not antisocial behavior that results in clear victims. This is thought to be because the distress of others is highly aversive (Blair, 1995). The suggestion is that healthy individuals are punished when they see another in distress and thus learn not to activate/never learn motor programs that will result in another individual's distress (see also Hoffman, 1987). The individual's learning to avoid actions that cause other individuals' distress is the basis of moral socialization (Blair, 1995).

There have been suggestions that theory of mind, or the related concepts of role and perspective taking, are involved in the socialization process (Eisenberg, Murphy, & Shepard, 1997; Feshbach, 1987; Gibbs, 1987). It is argued either that representations of the inner states of others allow the suppression of aggression directly or that these representations are necessary for empathic responding, which inhibits aggression (Batson, Fultz, & Schoenrade, 1987; Eisenberg et al., 1996; Feshbach, 1987). In line with the idea that theory of mind is involved in moral socialization, it, or at least role and perspective taking, has also been considered crucial for the development of morality (Kohlberg, 1981; Turiel, 1983a). For example, Kohlberg (1981) argued that the capacities for more complex perspective taking allow developmental "'advances" in the child's stage of moral reasoning (see also Colby, Kohlberg, Gibbs, & Lieberman, 1983; Eisenberg, 1986; Eisenberg et al., 1997; Keller & Edelstein, 1991).

Thus, if theory of mind is involved in moral socialization it can be predicted that individuals with autism should present with instrumental antisocial behavior, perhaps reduced empathy, and impaired moral reasoning. The first prediction is difficult to address. However, although there are reports of individuals with autism presenting with aggressive episodes, there are no reports of such individuals being involved in instrumental aggression/antisocial behavior (Scragg & Shah, 1994). However, given that the social interactions of individuals with autism are so dysfunctional, their relative lack of instrumental aggression cannot really be considered to be conclusive data.

Is there any indication that theory of mind is involved in empathy? For example, do individuals with autism, individuals who lack the ability to represent the mental states of others, lack empathy? The suggestion that children with autism do lack empathy is certainly an old and widespread idea (APA, 1994; Frith, 1989; Gillberg, 1992; Kanner, 1943). According to Kanner's (1943) description, people "figured in about the same manner as did the desk, the bookshelf, or the filing cabinet" (p. 38). But the empirical data are rather more equivocal.

There are various ways in which empathic reactions to others can be indexed. The most direct and precise of these include (1) autonomic and behavioral reactions to the emotional responses of others and (2) recognition of the expressions of others. These are next considered in turn.

THEORY OF MIND AND AUTONOMIC AND BEHAVIORAL REACTIONS TO THE EMOTIONAL RESPONSES OF OTHERS

Several studies have explored the autonomic and behavioral reactions of individuals with autism to the emotional responses of others (Bacon, Fein, Morris, Waterhouse, & Allen, 1998; Blair, 1999a; Corona, Dissanayake, Arbelle, Wellington, & Sigman, 1998; Dissanayake, Sigman, & Kasari, 1996; Sigman, Kasari, Kwon, & Yirmiya, 1992). In four of these studies, the child with autism has been playing with the experimenter when the experimenter feigns an emotional reaction, usually distress (Bacon et al., 1998; Corona et al., 1998; Dissanayake et al., 1996; Sigman et al., 1992). Three of these four studies have reported reduced empathic responding in the children with autism (Corona et al., 1998; Dissanayake et al., 1996; Sigman et al., 1992). All three of these studies reported that when adults displayed emotional reactions, children with autism looked far less at the adults than was true for mentally retarded and normally developing children of equivalent mental age. Moreover, Corona et al. (1998) found that the children with autism did not show the reduced heart rate observed among the mentally retarded comparison population when the adult feigned distress. However, these studies have relied on the participant switching their attention to the individual feigning distress. This is potentially a problem as in many of these studies, the child, particularly if the child is of more limited intellectual ability, has shown limited attention to the face of the experimenter (Bacon et al., 1998; Corona et al., 1998; Dissanayake et al., 1996; Sigman et al., 1992). Indeed, Dissanayake et al. (1996) found that the emotional responsiveness of the children with autism was related to their intellectual ability. Moreover, Bacon et al. (1998) only found group differences in empathic responsiveness for the low-functioning children with autism. The high-functioning children with autism were as likely as the comparison groups to show empathic concern when the adult simulated distress. The Bacon et al. (1998) results are of particular interest because the same participants, both high and low functioning, showed reduced social referencing relative to the comparison groups following the sound of a loud, unfamiliar, and ambiguous noise. That is, the children with autism were less likely to look toward an adult to elicit clarification in the presence of an ambiguous noise. Attempting to gain additional information from another in an ambiguous situation implies calculation of mental states; it is necessary to calculate that the other may have a different knowledge base from your own. These results indicated that although children with autism did not look toward adults as a source of information in an ambiguous context (i.e., the loud unfamiliar noise), they automatically oriented to adults when presented with a basic emotional stimulus, the sound and display of distress.

Interestingly, the Blair (1999a) study also indicated that children with autism did show autonomic responses to the distress of others if the emotion was unambiguous and occurred under conditions of low distractibility. Blair (1999a) investigated the psycho-physiological responsiveness of children with autism and comparison groups to distress cues (sad faces) and to threatening (angry faces and threatening animals) and neutral stimuli (neutral faces and objects). Twenty children with autism and two mental age-matched comparison groups consisting of 20 children with moderate learning difficulty and 20 normally developing children were shown slides of these three types of stimuli and their electrodermal responses were recorded. The children with autism, like the two comparison groups, showed significantly greater autonomic responses to the distress cues than to the neutral stimuli. These results suggest that theory of mind is not a prerequisite for generating autonomic responses to the distress of others.

THEORY OF MIND AND THE RECOGNITION OF THE EMOTIONAL EXPRESSIONS OF OTHERS

There have been a considerable number of investigations into the ability of individuals with autism to recognize the emotional expressions of others. Many have reported that children with autism have difficulty recognizing the emotional expressions of others (e.g., Bormann-Kischkel, Vilsmeier, & Baude, 1995; Hobson, 1986; Howard et al., 2000). A recent claim has been that this is specific for fearful expressions (Howard et al., 2000). In addition, children with autism have been found to show difficulties in detecting the intermodal correspondence between facial and vocal/linguistic affect (Hobson, Ouston, & Lee, 1989; Loveland et al., 1995).

However, children with autism have usually been found to be unimpaired in facial affect recognition for any emotion when the control group was matched on verbal mental age (e.g., Adolphs, Sears, & Piven, 2001; Baron-Cohen, Wheelwright, & Joliffe, 1997; Ozonoff, Pennington, & Rogers, 1990; Prior, Dahlstrom, & Squires, 1990). In addition, several studies have found the emotion processing impairment to be pronounced only when the emotion is a complex "cognitive" emotion such as surprise or embarrassment (Baron-Cohen, Spitz, & Cross, 1993; Bormann-Kischkel et al., 1995; Capps, Yirmiya, & Sigman, 1992). Finally, although Davies and colleagues found that high-ability children with autism did show difficulties in facial-affect matching tasks relative to controls, they also showed difficulties on matching tasks that involved nonfacial stimuli (Davies, Bishop, Manstead, & Tantam, 1994). Davies et al. (1994) suggested that this indicates that there may be a general perceptual deficit in children with autism that is not specific to faces or emotions. Thus, the bulk of the evidence strongly suggests that theory of mind is not related to the identification of the emotional expressions of others.

DO INDIVIDUALS WITH AUTISM SHOW IMPAIRMENT IN MORAL DEVELOPMENT?

But perhaps theory of mind is crucial for generating a sense of aversion to the distress of others? One of the markers demonstrating moral socialization in the normally developing child is the emergence of the moral/conventional distinction (Blair, 1995; Smetana, 1993; Turiel & Wainryb, 1998). The moral/conventional distinction is the distinction that children and adults make in their judgments between moral and conventional transgressions. This distinction is made from the age of 39 months (Smetana & Braeges, 1990) and is found across cultures (Nucci, Turiel, & Encarnacion-Gawrych, 1983; Song, Smetana, & Kim, 1987). Within the research literature, moral transgressions (e.g., hitting another, damaging another's property) are defined by their consequences for the rights and welfare of others. Conventional transgressions (e.g., talking in class, dressing in opposite-sex clothes) are defined by their consequences for social order. Children and adults generally judge moral transgressions to be more serious than conventional transgressions (Smetana & Braeges, 1990). In addition, and more importantly, modifying the rule conditions (e.g., an authority figure removing the prohibition against the act) only affects the permissibility of conventional transgressions. Even if there is no rule prohibiting the action, individuals generally judge moral transgressions as nonpermissible. In contrast, if there is no rule prohibiting a conventional transgression, they generally judge the act as permissible. Although participants do not always make the moral/conventional distinction in their seriousness judgments, they always make the moral/conventional distinction in their modifiability judgments. Thus, children have been found to judge some conventional transgressions to be as serious as some moral transgressions at some ages (Stoddart & Turiel, 1985; Turiel, 1983a, 1983b). However, even those children who viewed the conventional transgressions to be as serious as the moral transgressions judged the moral transgressions as less rule contingent and less under authority jurisdiction than the conventional transgressions.

It is crucial to note that it is the presence of victims that distinguishes moral and conventional transgressions. If a person considers that a transgression will result in a victim, she will process that transgression as moral. If one considers that a transgression does not result in a victim, she will process that transgression as conventional. Thus, Smetana (1982) showed that whether an individual treats abortion as a moral transgression or conventional transgression is determined by whether he or she judges the act to involve a victim. Similarly, Smetana (1985) found that unknown transgressions (i.e., specified by a nonsense word) were processed as moral or conventional according to the specified consequences of the act. Thus, "X has done dool and made Y cry" would be processed as moral whereas "'X has done dool and the teacher told him off" would be processed as conventional. Thus, if an individual is responsive to the presence of victims, he or she should make the moral/conventional distinction. On the other hand, if an individual is not sensitive to the distress of victims, he or she should not make the moral/conventional distinction.

So, do children with autism make the moral/conventional distinction? I investigated the ability to make the moral/conventional distinction in two groups of 10 children with autism (one group that failed all false-belief tasks and one group that passed first-order tasks) and two comparison groups (10 children with moderate learning difficulty and 10 typically developing children). All four groups of children, even the least able group of children with autism, made the moral/conventional distinction. That is, they were less likely to permit the moral transgressions than the conventional transgressions under normal and, crucially, under modified rule conditions. The children with autism, even those who, according to their false-belief test results, showed no ability to represent the mental states of others, still prohibited the moral, but not the conventional, transgressions in the absence of prohibitory rules (Blair, 1996). Thus, not only do children with autism generate appropriate autonomic responses to the distress of others, but they also appear to generate appropriate aversion to acts that typically result in harm to others.

SUMMARY OF THEORY OF MIND AND INSTRUMENTAL ANTISOCIAL BEHAVIOR

If moral socialization required the developmental integrity of the ability to represent the mental states of others, then individuals with autism, who present with profound theory of mind dysfunction, should present with increased risk of instrumental aggression, reduced empathy, and impaired moral reasoning. In the evidence just reviewed, it was concluded that such individuals show no heightened risk of instrumental aggression, no impairment in empathy (i.e., no impairment in the basic emotional response to another's distress—although they may show reduced prosocial behavior in response to the other's distress), and no impairment in moral reasoning (at least, in their reasoning in the fundamental index of basic moral socialization, the moral/conventional distinction task). Thus, it must be concluded that there is no data to indicate that theory of mind is involved in the control of instrumental antisocial behavior.

Of course, there is another way to consider the relationship between theory of mind and instrumental antisocial behavior. This would involve exploring a population whose members present with severe levels of instrumental antisocial behavior and determining whether this population also presents with theory-of-mind dysfunction. Individuals with psychopathy show significantly higher levels of aggressive and antisocial behavior in prison than nonpsychopathic inmates (Hare & Jutai, 1983). Moreover, they present with a marked preponderance for instrumental, rather than reactive, antisocial behavior (Cornell et al., 1996; Williamson, Hare, & Wong, 1987). In the following sections, I describe the disorder of psychopathy and then consider whether this population presents with any theory-of-mind dysfunction.

PSYCHOPATHY AND THEORY OF MIND

Psychopathy is a disorder characterized in part by callousness, a diminished capacity for remorse, impulsivity, and poor behavioral control (Hare, 1991). Psychopathy is identified in children with the Antisocial Process Screening Device (Frick & Hare, 2002) and in adults with the Revised Psychopathy Checklist (Hare, 1991). Importantly, this disorder is not equivalent to the psychiatric diagnoses of conduct disorder or antisocial personality disorder (APA, 1994). These psychiatric diagnoses are relatively poorly specified and concentrate almost entirely on the antisocial behavior shown by the individual rather than on any form of functional impairment. Because of this lack of specification, rates of diagnosis of conduct disorder reach up to 16% of boys in mainstream education (APA, 1994), and rates of diagnosis of antisocial personality disorder are over 80% in forensic institutions (Hart & Hare, 1996). Because of these high rates of diagnosis, populations identified with these diagnostic tools are highly heterogeneous and include many individuals with other disorders. Psychopathy, in contrast, is shown by less than 1% of individuals in mainstream education (Blair & Coles, 2000) and less than 30% of individuals incarcerated in forensic institutions (Hart & Hare, 1996).

Psychopathic individuals do not present with theory-of-mind impairment. Four out of five studies on psychopathic individuals found no indications of theory-of-mind impairment (Blair et al., 1996; Blair, Mitchell, & Colledge, submitted; Richell et al., 2003; Widom, 1978—did not; Widom, 1976—did). Moreover, even in the broader spectrum of antisocial individuals, there is little data suggesting any link between theory-of-mind impairment and antisocial behavior. Hughes, Dunn, and White (1998) did find some indication of theory-of-mind impairment in their "hard-to-manage" preschoolers relative to the comparison group. However, Happé and Frith (1996) found no impairment in their children with emotional and behavioral difficulties. Similarly, a study of school bullies found no indications of theory-of-mind impairment (Sutton, Smith, & Swettenham, 1999). Sutton and colleagues also found no relationship between theory-of-mind performance on the advanced Eyes task (Baron-Cohen et al., 1997) and "disruptive behavior disorder" symptoms in children aged 11–13 years (Sutton, Reeves, & Keogh, 2000). Thus, the current data clearly suggest that high levels of antisocial behavior are not associated with any impairment in the ability to represent the mental states of others (see Sutton, this volume).

EMPATHY IMPAIRMENT AND INSTRUMENTAL ANTISOCIAL BEHAVIOR

In the preceding sections, I considered whether theory of mind might play a role in socialization either directly or through a potential role in mediating empathy. Theory-of-mind dysfunction was not associated with either disturbance in socialization, at least as indexed by the moral/conventional distinction, or even empathy. Psychopathic individuals certainly show indications of disturbed socialization in their high levels of instrumental antisocial behavior (Cornell et al., 1996; Williamson et al., 1987). Moreover, psychopathic individuals, both in child- and adulthood, show severe impairment on the moral/conventional distinction task (Blair, 1995, 1997; Blair, Jones, Clark, & Smith, 1995; Blair, Monson, & Frederickson, 2001; for similar work with nonpsychopathic but behaviorally disturbed populations see Arsenio & Fleiss, 1996; Hughes & Dunn, 2000; Nucci & Herman, 1982).

The disturbed socialization of psychopathic individuals has long been linked to empathy dysfunction (Blair, 1995; Cleckley, 1967; Gibbs, 1987; Hare, 1980; Schalling, 1978). A model of this empathy dysfunction has been most clearly specified, at both the anatomical and cognitive levels, in Blair's violence inhibition mechanism model. Detailed descriptions of this model are available elsewhere (Blair, 1995, 2001); however, the important details of the model are that sad and fearful facial and vocal expressions act as punishing stimuli that, when experienced, reduce the probability that a healthy individual will engage in any action associated with the display of these expressions. In other words, the healthy individual is punished for engaging in antisocial activity by the distress of the victims. The suggestion is that the sadness or fear of another is a basic aversive unconditioned stimulus that is computationally equivalent to a loud noise or an electric shock; individuals learn to avoid behaviors that are associated with these unconditioned stimuli. It is thought that the response to sad and fearful expressions is muted in psychopathic individuals, so they are less punished by the victim's distress. If the psychopathic individual is brought up in a social environment where there are significant relative rewards for antisocial behavior, these individuals will be more likely to engage in instrumental antisocial behavior. At the biological level, the impairment is thought to be due to amygdala dysfunction.

The model makes a variety of predictions at both the cognitive and anatomical levels. Importantly, the model predicts that psychopathic individuals will show selective impairment in the processing of the sad and fearful facial and vocal affect of others. Five studies have examined the responsiveness of psychopathic individuals to distress cues (Aniskiewicz, 1979; Blair, 1999b; Blair, Jones, Clark, & Smith, 1997; House & Milligan, 1976; Sutker, 1970). Three of these studies involved a similar design where participants had to observe confederates who they thought were being given electric shocks. Skin conductance responses to the sight of the apparently shocked confederates were recorded. Of these three studies, two reported less responsiveness in the psychopath relative to controls (Aniskiewicz, 1979; House & Milligan, 1976) whereas one did not (Sutker, 1970). In the fourth study, 18 adult psychopaths and 18 incarcerated controls were shown slides of distress cues and of threatening and neutral stimuli and their electrodermal responses were recorded (Blair et al., 1997). The threatening stimuli included images of angry expressions. This study found that the psychopaths showed, relative to the controls, reduced electrodermal responses to the distress cues. In contrast, the two groups did not differ in their electrodermal responses to the threatening stimuli, including the angry face, or to the neutral stimuli. A fifth study utilized an identical design to the fourth but examined the responses of three groups of 16 children (Blair, 1999b). Two of these groups were children with emotional and behavioral difficulties, divided according to their Psychopathy Screening Device scores (Frick & Hare, 2002). A further 16 normally developing children in mainstream education were also presented with these stimuli. The children with high scores on the Psychopathy Screening Device showed, relative to the controls, and like the adult psychopathic individuals, reduced electrodermal responses to the distress cues. Importantly, these results indicate that the psychopathic individual does not have a global empathy impairment—they respond appropriately to angry expressions (Blair et al., 1997) but show a specific impairment in their response to distress cues.

Four studies have examined the ability of children with psychopathic tendencies and psychopathic adults to recognize the facial expressions of other individuals. In three of these, children with psychopathic tendencies were found to show selective impairment for the recognition of sad and fearful expressions

(Blair & Coles, 2000; Blair, Colledge, Murray, & Mitchell, 2001; Stevens, Charman, & Blair, 2001). The fourth observed a selective impairment for only fearful expressions in adult psychopathic individuals (Blair et al., submitted).

Thus, to summarize, the research just described on individuals who present with high levels of instrumental antisocial behavior suggests two main conclusions. First, these individuals do not present with theory-of-mind impairment. Second, these individuals, particularly psychopathic individuals, do present with an impairment in empathy and this impairment is independent of theory-of-mind functioning. In short, these individuals can even use their theory of mind to achieve their antisocial goals, particularly in fraud or con cases. They will even know that they have caused distress to their victims; they will just be indifferent to this distress (see Repacholi et al., this volume).

REACTIVE AGGRESSION AND THEORY OF MIND

Reactive or impulsive aggression is elicited in response to frustration or perceived threat and can be related to the eventual fight response of an animal confronted with a threat (Blair, 2001). This fight response is mediated by subcortical systems (Panksepp, 1989; Siegel et al., 1999). The orbitofrontal cortex is thought to be involved in controlling the activity of these subcortical regions (Davidson, Putnam, & Larson, 2000; LeDoux, 1998). Patients with lesions to the orbitofrontal cortex present with heightened levels of reactive aggression, whether they occur in childhood (Anderson, Bechara, Damasio, Tranel, & Damasio, 1999; Pennington & Bennetto, 1993) or adulthood (Blair & Cipolotti, 2000; Grafman et al., 1996). Indeed, such patients have been described as presenting with pseudo-psychopathy (Blumer & Benson, 1975) or "acquired sociopathy" (Damasio, 1994).

The orbitofrontal cortex has been activated in two neuroimaging studies of theory of mind (Baron-Cohen et al., 1994; Baron-Cohen, Ring, et al., 1999). The fact that representing the mental states of others may recruit regions of the cortex that are involved in the control of aggression and socially inappropriate behavior could prompt the suggestion that theory of mind plays a role in the control of this behavior. Certainly, the few instances of aggression reported in individuals with autism have been of a reactive, rather than instrumental, nature (Baron-Cohen, 1988; Scragg & Shah, 1994). Baron-Cohen (1995) interpreted the impairment of patients with orbito- and medial frontal cortex damage in terms of damage to the neural circuit mediating theory of mind. He suggested that individuals who, because of orbitofrontal damage, cannot represent the mental states of others are unable to modulate their emotional and social behavior.

In line with Baron-Cohen's suggestion, Price, Daffner, Stowe, and Mesulam (1990) reported on two patients with frontal-lobe lesions who performed poorly on a test of visual perspective taking. In addition, Stone, Baron-Cohen, and Knight (1998) reported impairment on a task involving the recognition of faux pas in five patients with acquired lesions of the orbitofrontal cortex (Baron-Cohen, O'Riordan, Stone, Jones, & Plaisted, 1999). However, although two neuroimaging studies of theory of mind have observed orbitofrontal cortex activation, most have not (Brunet et al., 2000; Castelli et al., 2000; Fletcher et al., 1995; Gallagher et al., 2000; Goel et al., 1995; Vogeley et al., 2001). Moreover, as regards the Price et al. (1990) study, it is unclear whether visual perspective taking requires the representation of mental states (Leslie & Frith, 1988). In addition, the patients in the Stone et al. (1998) study were intact on several measures designed to purely assess the representation of mental states rather than the emotionally driven recognition of faux pas. Finally, there are several reports of patients with lesions to the orbitofrontal cortex presenting with no theory-of-mind impairment. Thus, Saver and Damasio (1991) found that patient EVR was unimpaired in a test that required representing potential mental states. Similarly, although patient JS presented with severe behavioral disturbance, this was not accompanied by any dysfunction in theory of mind (Blair & Cipolotti, 2000).

The data just described therefore suggest that the orbitofrontal cortex is not involved in the representation of the mental states of others and that patients with "acquired sociopathy" need not present with theory-of-mind impairment. But such patients may still have suffered disruption to systems involved in social cognition. Blair suggested that there is a system, the social response reversal system, involving the orbitofrontal cortex but independent of theory of mind. Blair's position makes reference to the role of the orbitofrontal cortex in response reversal. Response reversal occurs in situations when the individual has been previously rewarded for doing a particular act and is now being punished; the individual learns to reverse the previous response. Lesions to the orbital frontal cortex interfere with response reversal; the individual continues to do the previously rewarded response even though it is now being punished (Dias, Robbins, & Roberts, 1996; Rolls, 2000). However, this position stresses the role of social cues in modulating social behavior (Blair, 2001; Blair & Cipolotti, 2000). Angry expressions are known to curtail the behavior of others in situations where social rules or expectations have been violated (Averill, 1982). It is suggested that there is a system that is activated by another individual's angry expressions or, possibly, other negative affective expressions (e.g., the staring expressions of others that can precede a sense of embarrassment and perhaps others' disgusted expressions) or the expectations of another's anger. The suggestion is that activation of this system results in the modulation of current behavioral responding preventing the individual from engaging in inappropriate behavior, including reactive aggression.

Blair's position has drawn support from findings that the ventrolateral orbitofrontal cortex (BA47) is activated by negative emotional expressions, in particular anger but also fear and disgust (Blair, Morris, Frith, Perrett, & Dolan, 1999; Kesler-West et al., 2001; Sprengelmeyer, Rausch, Eysel, & Przuntek, 1998). Moreover, patients who present with reactive aggression following lesions of the frontal, particularly orbitofrontal, cortex present with impairment in expression recognition, particularly for the expression of anger (Blair & Cipolotti, 2000; Hornak, Rolls, & Wade, 1996). Such patients have also been found to show impairment in appropriately attributing anger and embarrassment, but not other emotions, to story protagonists (Blair & Cipolotti, 2000). In addition, they have been found to show impairment in identifying violations of social norms (Blair & Cipolotti, 2000; Stone et al., 1998).

Interestingly, in the current context, it is highly likely that the social response reversal system may function in synchrony with theory of mind when determining whether particular behaviors are appropriate. In order to determine whether another individual has violated social norms, it is necessary to calculate whether the action could be construed as a violation and, crucially, whether the action was conducted intentionally. Actions that could be construed as violations but that are initiated unintentionally are generally considered embarrassing rather than social violations (Garland & Brown, 1972; Semin & Manstead, 1982). To illustrate, hitting another individual with a baseball bat is a norm violation if you do it intentionally but embarrassing if you did not notice that the individual was behind you.

Following this analysis, we might consider that both the capacity to represent the intentions of others (theory of mind) and the capacity to respond to expectancies of another's negative affect will be related to the ability to identify social norm violations and to the presentation of reactive aggression. This is indeed the case. Patients with theory-of-mind impairment as well as impairment in a system for responding to another's anger or other negative affect, or expectancies of that affect, have been found to show impairment in the ability to identify norm violations (Baron-Cohen, Ring, et al., 1999; Blair & Cipolotti, 2000; Dewey, 1991; Stone et al., 1998). Moreover, such patients present with increased risk for reactive aggression (Blair & Cipolotti, 2000; Grafman et al., 1996) In addition, a recent neuroimaging study has demonstrated that the neural response to violations of social norms as well as embarrassing situations recruits regions of the medial frontal cortex, temporo-parietal junction, and temporal pole associated with theory of mind as well as regions of the orbitofrontal cortex associated with social response reversal (Berthoz, Blair, Armony, & Dolan, 2002).

Thus, in conclusion, although dysfunction in theory of mind has not been found in any individual with acquired sociopathy, it appears that theory of mind could play a role in the inhibition of reactive aggression. It may be disruption in the synchronized functioning of the social response reversal system and theory of mind that leads to the reactive aggression shown by a minority of individuals with autism (Baron-Cohen, 1988; Scragg & Shah, 1994).

HOSTILE ATTRIBUTION BIASES AND THEORY OF MIND

In this chapter, I have considered the possibility that theory-of-mind dysfunction might result in antisocial behavior. I have investigated whether theory-of-mind dysfunction might put the individual at risk of presenting with high levels of instrumental aggression because theory of mind is involved in moral socialization either directly or through its potential necessary role in the empathic process. In addition, I have investigated whether theory-of-mind dysfunction may reduce the individual's control over aggression and other forms of antisocial behavior. However, we need not suggest that it is only dysfunction in the neurocognitive architecture allowing the representation of mental states that might give rise to antisocial behavior. It is possible that an individual might have no impairment in the ability to represent the mental states of others but might rather show hostile attribution biases in his or her theorylike concepts of others' probable mental states (cf. Crick & Dodge, 1994). In short, they might present with a theory of nasty minds (Happé & Frith, 1996; see also Repacholi et al. and McIlwain, this volume).

Unlike the suggestion that antisocial behavior is associated with theory-of-mind dysfunction discussed earlier, there are considerable data that support the idea that antisocial individuals present with hostile attribution biases. Dodge (1980) exposed aggressive and nonaggressive boys to a frustrating outcome instigated by an ambiguously intentioned peer. In response to the ambiguous provocation, aggressive boys demonstrated a bias toward attributing a hostile intention to the peer. Also, this attributional bias directly mediated the retaliatory aggressive behavior of these boys. As a result, they displayed retaliatory aggressive behavior more frequently than did nonaggressive boys. Hostile attribution biases in aggressive boys have been found in response to photographs of peers and in response to actual ambiguous situations (Feldman & Dodge, 1987; Steinberg & Dodge, 1983).

There are two important points to note about the relationship between hostile attribution biases and antisocial behavior. First, hostile attribution biases are more typically found in individuals presenting with reactive rather than proactive aggression (Hubbard, Dodge, Cillessen, Coie, & Schwartz, 2001; see Crick & Dodge, 1996, for a review). In other words, they are associated with unplanned bursts of aggression rather than the goal-directed antisocial behavior discussed earlier. Second, aggressive children are not globally impaired in their attributions of intent. Although they are more likely to attribute hostile intent to another's ambiguous behavior that is directed at themselves, they show no such bias if the ambiguous behavior is directed at a third individual (Dodge & Frame, 1982). The data imply that there is no dysfunction in the ability to represent the mental states of others; the children only show impairment if the ambiguous behavior is directed at the self. Moreover, the data also imply that the "bias" in these children's theory of mind is specific to the self. These children do not have theory-of-mind concepts such as, "In this ambiguous situation, people want to do others harm." Rather, the biased concepts are of the form, "If I am in this ambiguous situation, then people want to do me harm."

At present, the developmental origins of this bias are unclear. There has been some suggestion that it may be associated with early physical abuse (Dodge, Pettit, Bates, & Valente, 1995) or is a product of an earlier propensity to be aggressive in these individuals (Dodge & Frame, 1982). However, a hostile attribution bias is seen in not only aggressive children but also children with depression (Quiggle, Garber, Panak, & Dodge, 1992). Thus, hostile attribution biases may be a consequence of development in an environment appreciated to be hostile.

From a cognitive neuroscience perspective, hostile attribution biases may be related to reactive aggression because some individuals have a heightened responsiveness to threat. As stated earlier, the mammalian response to threat is measured according to the intensity of that threat, with freezing being the initial response to a distant threat and aggression being the ultimate response to an inescapable threat (Blanchard et al., 1977). The individual presenting with elevated levels of reactive aggression may be an individual whose basic threat response system is already highly active. Thus, when threatened, this individual will not freeze or attempt to run away but attack instead. Individuals whose basic threat response system is already highly active do show heightened attention to threatening stimuli in the environment (e.g., Matthews & Wells, 1999). This heightened attention to threatening stimuli may give rise to the verbal hostile attribution biases measured in the tasks developed by Dodge and colleagues (Crick & Dodge, 1996). This perspective would explain why hostile attribution biases are associated with early physical abuse and depression (Dodge et al., 1995; Quiggle et al., 1992). Neuroimaging research has demonstrated that threats such as physical abuse and depression activate similar neural systems including the amygdala (Drevets, 2001; Morris et al., 1998). The suggestion would be that these similar neural responses imply similar processing sequelae; that is, heightened attention for threatening stimuli. The implication of this position is that the verbal statements of hostile attribution (i.e., the individual's theories about the probability of another person's malevolent intent) would have no causal role in the production of the reactive aggression.

Alternatively, and less affectively driven, the reactively aggressive individual, presented with an ambiguous situation, may represent the mental state of the other person and because of a hostile attribution bias perceive this person's intention to be hostile, precipitating violence. From this perspective, the individual's theories about other minds would have a direct causal role in the production of the reactive aggression. Currently, there are no data to distinguish between these two perspectives on the importance of hostile attribution biases.

CONCLUSION

In this chapter, I considered potential links between theory of mind and antisocial personality disorder. The chapter began with a discussion of the nature of theory of mind. I distinguished between the neurocognitive architecture that allows the representation of the mental states of others and connected systems that represent the individual's theorylike concepts of other individuals' probable mental states. I then used this distinction to examine whether impairment in the basic ability to represent mental states might be linked to either instrumental or reactive aggression. On the basis of the available data, it can be concluded that the ability to represent the mental states of others is not related to instrumental aggression. Theory of mind appears to doubly dissociate from the empathic response to the distress of others. The empathic response to the distress of others is crucial for moral socialization and the inhibition of instrumental aggression. Individuals with empathy impairment, such as psychopathic individuals, have difficulties with moral socialization and present with highly elevated levels of instrumental aggression. However, they present with no theory-of-mind impairment. Individuals with autism, who have profound impairment in the ability to represent the mental states of others, show emotional, empathic responses to the distress of others (even though their knowledge of how to respond to another's distress may be deficient) and moral socialization (at least as measured by the moral/ conventional distinction task) and do not present with instrumental aggression.

The ability to represent mental states may be linked to reactive aggression. Although most patients who present with elevated levels of reactive aggression following frontal-lobe lesions do not present with theory-of-mind impairment, such an impairment may be associated with increased risk of reactive aggression. This may be because, under specific stimulus conditions, theory of mind functions in synchrony with what I have termed the social response reversal system. Under confrontational conditions, the healthy individual may represent expectations of the other individual's affective response (will they be angry if I react in this way?), their authority position (are they my boss?), and their intention (why did they just behave in this provocative way?). Dysfunction in either theory of mind or the social response reversal system may disrupt this computational process, giving rise to increased risk of reactive aggression.

Not only may dysfunction in the ability to represent mental states increase risk of reactive aggression, but hostile attribution biases in an individual's theorylike concepts of other individuals' probable mental states may also be linked to reactive aggression. There is no doubt that individuals presenting with reactive aggression are more likely to also present with hostile attribution biases (Crick & Dodge, 1996). What is less clear is whether these hostile attribution biases are causally linked to the aggression. I presented two non-mutually exclusive suggestions that would link hostile attribution biases in an individual's theories of theory of mind to reactive aggression, one where the connection was epiphenomenal and the other where it was causal.

ACKNOWLEDGMENTS

This work was supported by a Medical Research Council grant (G9716841) and the Department of Health (VISPED initiative).

REFERENCES

Adolphs, R., Sears, L., & Piven, J. (2001). Abnormal processing of social information from faces in autism. *Journal of Cognitive Neuroscience, 13*(2), 232–240.

American Psychiatric Association. (1994). *Diagnostic and statistical manual of mental disorders* (4th ed.). Washington, DC: American Psychiatric Association.

Anderson, S. W., Bechara, A., Damasio, H., Tranel, D., & Damasio, A. R. (1999). Impairment of social and moral behavior related to early damage in human prefrontal cortex. *Nature Neuroscience, 2*, 1032–1037.

Aniskiewicz, A. S. (1979). Autonomic components of vicarious conditioning and psychopathy. *Journal of Clinical Psychology, 35*, 60–67.

Arsenio, W. F., & Fleiss, K. (1996). Typical and behaviourally disruptive children's understanding of the emotion consequences of socio-moral events. *British Journal of Developmental Psychology, 14*, 173–186.

Averill, J. R. (1982). *Anger and aggression: An essay on emotion*. New York: Springer-Verlag.

Bacon, A. L., Fein, D., Morris, R., Waterhouse, L., & Allen, D. (1998). The responses of autistic children to the distress of others. *Journal of Autism and Developmental Disorders, 28*(2), 129–142.

Balleine, B. W., & Dickinson, A. (1998). Goal-directed instrumental action: Contingency and incentive learning and their cortical substrates. *Neuropharmacology, 37*(4–5), 407–419.

Baron-Cohen, S. (1988). An assessment of violence in a young man with Asperger's syndrome. *Journal of Child Psychology and Psychiatry, 29*, 351–360.

Baron-Cohen, S. (1989). Perceptual role taking and protodeclarative pointing in autism. *British Journal of Developmental Psychology, 7*(2), 113–127.

Baron-Cohen, S. (1995). *Mindblindness: An essay on autism and theory of mind*. Cambridge, MA: MIT Press.

Baron-Cohen, S., Leslie, A. M., & Frith, U. (1985). Does the autistic child have a "theory of mind"? *Cognition, 21*, 37–46.

Baron-Cohen, S., O'Riordan, M., Stone, V., Jones, R., & Plaisted, K. (1999). Recognition of faux pas by normally developing children and children with Asperger's syndrome or high-functioning autism. *Journal of Autism and Developmental Disorders, 29*(5), 407–418.

Baron-Cohen, S., Ring, H., Moriarty, J., Schmits, B., Costa, D., & Ell, P. (1994). Recognition of mental state terms. Clinical findings in children with autism and a functional neuroimaging study of normal adults. *British Journal of Psychiatry, 165*, 640–649.

Baron-Cohen, S., Ring, H. A., Wheelwright, S., Bullmore, E. T., Brammer, M. J., Simmons, A., & Williams, S. C. (1999). Social intelligence in the normal and autistic brain: An fMRI study. *European Journal of Neuroscience, 11*(6), 1891–1898.

Baron-Cohen, S., Spitz, A., & Cross, P. (1993). Do children with autism recognize surprise? A research note. *Cognition and Emotion, 7*, 507–516.

Baron-Cohen, S., Wheelwright, S., & Joliffe, T. (1997). Is there a "language of the eyes"? Evidence from normal adults, and adults with autism or Asperger's syndrome. *Visual Cognition, 4*(3), 311.

Barratt, E. S., Stanford, M. S., Dowdy, L.,

Liebman, M. J., & Kent, T. A. (1999). Impulsive and premeditated aggression: A factor analysis of self-reported acts. *Psychiatry Research, 86*(2), 163–173.

Barratt, E. S., Stanford, M. S., Kent, T. A., & Felthous, A. (1997). Neuropsychological and cognitive psychophysiological substrates of impulsive aggression. *Biological Psychiatry, 41*(10), 1045–1061.

Batson, C. D., Fultz, J., & Schoenrade, P. A. (1987). Adults' emotional reactions to the distress of others. In N. Eisenberg & J. Strayer (Eds.), *Empathy and its development* (pp. 163–185). Cambridge: Cambridge University Press.

Berkowitz, L. (1993). *Aggression: Its causes, consequences, and control.* Philadelphia: Temple University Press.

Berthoz, S., Armony, J., Blair, R. J. R., & Dolan, R. (2002). Neural correlates of violation of social norms and embarrassment. *Brain, 125*(8), 1696–1708.

Blair, R. J. R. (1995). A cognitive developmental approach to morality: Investigating the psychopath. *Cognition, 57*, 1–29.

Blair, R. J. R. (1996). Brief report: Morality in the autistic child. *Journal of Autism and Developmental Disorders, 26*, 571–579.

Blair, R. J. R. (1997). Moral reasoning in the child with psychopathic tendencies. *Personality and Individual Differences, 22*, 731–739.

Blair, R. J. R. (1999a). Psycho-physiological responsiveness to the distress of others in children with autism. *Personality and Individual Differences, 26*, 477–485.

Blair, R. J. R. (1999b). Responsiveness to distress cues in the child with psychopathic tendencies. *Personality and Individual Differences, 27*, 135–145.

Blair, R. J. R. (2001). Neuro-cognitive models of aggression, the antisocial personality disorders and psychopathy. *Journal of Neurology, Neurosurgery & Psychiatry, 71*, 1–4.

Blair, R. J. R., & Cipolotti, L. (2000). Impaired social response reversal: A case of "acquired sociopathy." *Brain, 123*, 1122–1141.

Blair, R. J. R., & Coles, M. (2000). Expression recognition and behavioral problems in early adolescence. *Cognitive Development, 15*, 421–434.

Blair, R. J. R., Colledge, E., Murray, L., &

Mitchell, D. (2001). A selective impairment in the processing of sad and fearful expressions in boys with psychopathic tendencies. *Journal of Abnormal Child Psychology.*

Blair, R. J. R., Frith, U., Smith, N., Abell, F., & Cipolotti, L. (2002). Fractionation of visual memory: Agency detection and its impairment in autism. *Neuropsychologia, 40*, 108–118.

Blair, R. J. R., Jones, L., Clark, F., & Smith, M. (1995). Is the psychopath "morally insane"? *Personality and Individual Differences, 19*, 741–752.

Blair, R. J. R., Jones, L., Clark, F., & Smith, M. (1997). The psychopathic individual: A lack of responsiveness to distress cues? *Psychophysiology, 34*, 192–198.

Blair, R. J. R., Mitchell, D. G. V., & Colledge, E. (submitted). *Reduced sensitivity to others' fearful expressions in psychopathic individuals.*

Blair, R. J. R., Monson, J., & Frederickson, N. (2001). Moral reasoning and conduct problems in children with emotional and behavioral difficulties. *Personality and Individual Differences, 31*, 799–811.

Blair, R. J. R., Morris, J. S., Frith, C. D., Perrett, D. I., & Dolan, R. (1999). Dissociable neural responses to facial expressions of sadness and anger. *Brain, 122*, 883–893.

Blair, R. J. R., Sellars, C., Strickland, I., Clark, F., Williams, A., Smith, M., & Jones, L. (1996). Theory of Mind in the psychopath. *Journal of Forensic Psychiatry, 7*, 15–25.

Blanchard, R. J., Blanchard, D. C., & Takahashi, L. K. (1977). Attack and defensive behavior in the albino rat. *Animal Behavior, 25*, 197–224.

Blumer, D., & Benson, D. F. (1975). Personality changes with frontal and temporal lobe lesions. In D. F. Benson & D. Blumer (Eds.), *Psychiatric aspects of neurological disease* (pp. 151–170). New York: Grune & Stratton.

Bormann-Kischkel, C., Vilsmeier, M., & Baude, B. (1995). The development of emotional concepts in autism. *Journal of Child Psychology and Psychiatry, 36*(7), 1243–1259.

Brunet, E., Sarfati, Y., Hardy-Bayle, M. C., & Decety, J. (2000). A PET investigation of the attribution of intentions with a nonverbal task. *Neuroimage, 11*(2), 157–166.

Capps, L., Yirmiya, N., & Sigman, M. (1992). Understanding of simple and complex emotions in non-retarded children with autism. *Journal of Child Psychology and Psychiatry,* 33(7), 1169–1182.

Carlson, S. M., & Moses, L. J. (2001). Individual differences in inhibitory control and children's theory of mind. *Child Development,* 72(4), 1032–1053.

Castelli, F. , Happe, F., Frith, U., & Frith, C. (2000). Movement and mind: A functional imaging study of perception and interpretation of complex intentional movement patterns. *Neuroimage, 12,* 314–325.

Chandler, M. J., Greenspan, S., & Barenboim, C. (1974). Assessment and training of role-taking and referential communication skills in institutionalized, emotionally disturbed children. *Developmental Psychology, 10,* 546–553.

Cipolotti, L., Robinson, G., Blair, R. J. R., & Frith, U. (1999). Fractionation of visual memory: Evidence from a case with multiple neurodevelopmental impairments. *Neuropsychologia, 37,* 455–465.

Cleckley, H. (1967). *The mask of sanity* (4th ed.). St Louis, MO: C. V. Mosby.

Cohen, J. D. , Braver, T. S., & O'Reilly, R. C. (1996). A computational approach to prefrontal cortex, cognitive control and schizophrenia: Recent developments and current challenges. *Philosophical Transactions of the Royal Society B, 351,* 1515–1527.

Cohen, J. D., & Servan-Schreiber, D. (1992). Context, cortex, and dopamine: A connectionist approach to behavior and biology in schizophrenia. *Psychological Review, 99,* 45–77.

Colby, A., Kohlberg, L., Gibbs, J., & Lieberman, M. (1983). A longitudinal study of moral judgment. *Monographs of the Society for Research in Child Development, 48,* 124.

Cornell, D. G., Warren, J., Hawk, G., Stafford, E., Oram, G., & Pine, D. (1996). Psychopathy in instrumental and reactive violent offenders. *Journal of Consulting and Clinical Psychology, 64,* 783–790.

Corona, C., Dissanayake, C., Arbelle, A., Wellington, P., & Sigman, M. (1998). Is affect aversive to young children with autism? Behavioral and cardiac responses to experimenter distress. *Child Development, 69*(6), 1494–1502.

Crick, N. R., & Dodge, K. A. (1994). A review and reformulation of social information-processing mechanisms in children's social adjustment. *Psychological Bulletin, 115,* 74–101.

Crick, N. R. , & Dodge, K. A. (1996). Social information-processing mechanisms on reactive and proactive aggression. *Child Development, 67*(3), 993–1002.

Damasio, A. R. (1994). *Descartes' error: Emotion, rationality and the human brain.* New York: Putnam (Grosset Books).

Davidson, R. J., Putnam, K. M., & Larson, C. L. (2000). Dysfunction in the neural circuitry of emotion regulation—A possible prelude to violence. *Science, 289*(5479), 591–594.

Davies, S., Bishop, D., Manstead, A. S. R., & Tantam, D. (1994). Face perception in children with autism and Asperger's syndrome. *Journal of Child Psychology and Psychiatry and Allied Disciplines, 35*(6), 1033–1057.

Dewey, M. (1991). Living with Asperger's syndrome. In U. Frith (Ed.), *Autism and Asperger's syndrome* (pp. 184–206). Cambridge: Cambridge University Press.

Dias, R., Robbins, T. W., & Roberts, A. C. (1996). Dissociation in prefrontal cortex of affective and attentional shifts. *Nature, 380,* 69–72.

Dissanayake, C., Sigman, M., & Kasari, C. (1996). Long-term stability of individual differences in the emotional responsiveness of children with autism. *Journal of Child Psychology and Psychiatry and Allied Disciplines, 37*(4), 461–467.

Dodge, K. A. (1980). Social cognition and children's aggressive behavior. *Child Development, 51,* 162–170.

Dodge, K. A., & Coie, J. D. (1987). Social information processing factors in reactive and proactive aggression in children's peer groups. *Journal of Personality and Social Psychology, 53,* 1146–1158.

Dodge, K. A. , & Frame, C. L. (1982). Social cognitive biases and deficits in aggressive boys. *Child Development, 53,* 620–635.

Dodge, K. A., Pettit, G. S., Bates, J. E., & Valente, E. (1995). Social information-processing patterns partially mediate the effect of early physical abuse on later conduct

problems. *Journal of Abnormal Psychology,*
104, 632–643.

Drevets, W. C. (2001). Neuroimaging and neu-
ropathological studies of depression: Implications for the cognitive-emotional features
of mood disorders. *Current Opinions in*
Neurobiology, 11(2), 240–249.

Eisenberg, N. (1986). *Altruistic cognition,*
emotion, and behavior. Hillsdale, NJ:
Lawrence Erlbaum.

Eisenberg, N., Fabes, R. A., Guthrie, I. K.,
Murphy, B. C., Maszk, P., Holmgren, R., &
Suh, K. (1996). The relations of regulation
and emotionality to problem behavior in el-
ementary school children. *Development and*
Psychopathology, 8, 141–162.

Eisenberg, N., Murphy, B. C., & Shepard, S.
(1997). The development of empathic accuracy. In W. J. Ickes (Ed.), *Empathic accu-*
racy (pp. 73–116). New York: Guilford
Press.

Feldman, E., & Dodge, K. A. (1987). Social
information processing and sociometric status: Sex, age, and situational effects. *Jour-*
nal of Abnormal Child Psychology, 15(2),
211–227.

Feshbach, N. D. (1987). Parental empathy and
child adjustment/maladjustment. In N.
Eisenberg & J. Strayer (Eds.), *Empathy and*
its development (pp. 271–291). New York:
Cambridge University Press.

Fine, C., Lumsden, J., & Blair, R. J. (2001).
Dissociation between "theory of mind" and
executive functions in a patient with early
left amygdala damage. *Brain, 124*(Pt. 2),
287–298.

Fletcher, P. C., Happé, F., Frith, U., Baker, S.
C., Dolan, R. J., Frackowiak, R. S., & Frith,
C. D. (1995). Other minds in the brain: A
functional imaging study of "theory of mind"
in story comprehension. *Cognition, 57,* 109–
128.

Frick, P. J., & Hare, R. D. (2002). *The antiso-*
cial process screening device. Toronto, ON:
Multi-Health Systems.

Frith, C. D., & Frith, U. (1999). Interacting
minds—A biological basis. *Science, 286,*
1692–1695.

Frith, U. (1989). *Autism: Explaining the*
enigma. Oxford: Blackwell.

Gallagher, H. L., Happé, F., Brunswick, N.,
Fletcher, P. C., Frith, U., & Frith, C. D.

(2000). Reading the mind in cartoons and
stories: an fMRI study of "theory of mind"
in verbal and nonverbal tasks. *Neuro-*
psychologia, 38(1), 11–21.

Garland, H., & Brown, B. R. (1972). Face-sav-
ing as affected by subjects' sex, audiences'
sex and audience expertise. *Sociometry,*
35(2), 280–289.

Gibbs, J. C. (1987). Social processes in delinquency: The need to facilitate empathy as
well as sociomoral reasoning. In W. M.
Kurtines & J. L. Gewirtz (Eds.), *Moral de-*
velopment through social interaction (pp.
301–321). New York: Wiley.

Gillberg, C. (1992). The Emmanuel Miller
Lecture, 1991. Autism and autistic-like conditions: Subclasses among disorders of empathy. *Journal of Child Psychology and Psy-*
chiatry, 33, 813–842.

Goel, V., Grafman, J., Sadato, N., & Hallett,
M. (1995). Modeling other minds. *Neuro-*
report, 11 , 1741–1746.

Gopnik, A., & Meltzoff, A. N. (1997). *Words,*
thoughts, and theories. Cambridge, MA:
MIT Press.

Grafman, J., Schwab, K., Warden, D., Pridgen,
B. S., & Brown, H. R. (1996). Frontal lobe
injuries, violence, and aggression: A report
of the Vietnam head injury study. *Neurol-*
ogy, 46, 1231–1238.

Happé, F. G. E., & Frith, U. (1996). Theory of
mind and social impairment in children with
conduct disorder. *British Journal of Devel-*
opmental Psychology, 14(4), 385–398.

Hare, R. D. (1980). A research scale for the
assessment of psychopathy in criminal populations. *Personality and Individual Differ-*
ences, 1, 111–119.

Hare, R. D. (1991). *The Hare Psychopathy*
Checklist-Revised. Toronto, ON: Multi-
Health Systems.

Hare, R. D., & Jutai, J. W. (1983). Criminal
history of the male psychopath: Some preliminary data. In K. T. Van Dusen & S. A.
Mednick (Eds.), *Prospective studies of crime*
and delinquency (pp. 225–236). Boston:
Kluwer-Nijhoff.

Hart, S. D., & Hare, R. D. (1996). Psychopathy and antisocial personality disorder.
Current Opinion in Psychiatry, 9, 129–132.

Hobson, P. (1986). The autistic child's appraisal
of expressions of emotion. *Journal of Child*

Psychology and Psychiatry, 27, 321–342.

Hobson, R. P., Ouston, J., & Lee, A. (1989). Naming emotion in faces and voices: Abilities and disabilities in autism and mental retardation. *British Journal of Developmental Psychology, 7*(3), 237–250.

Hoffman, M. L. (1987). The contribution of empathy to justice and moral judgment. In N. Eisenberg & J. Strayer (Eds.), *Empathy and its development* (pp. 47–80). Cambridge: Cambridge University Press.

Hornak, J., Rolls, E. T., & Wade, D. (1996). Face and voice expression identification in patients with emotional and behavioral changes following ventral frontal damage. *Neuropsychologia, 34,* 247–261.

House, T. H., & Milligan, W. L. (1976). Autonomic responses to modeled distress in prison psychopaths. *Journal of Personality and Social Psychology, 34,* 556–560.

Howard, M. A., Cowell, P. E., Boucher, J., Broks, P., Mayes, A., Farrant, A., & Roberts, N. (2000). Convergent neuroanatomical and behavioral evidence of an amygdala hypothesis of autism. *Neuroreport, 11*(13), 1931–1935.

Hubbard, J. A., Dodge, K. A., Cillessen, A. H. N., Coie, J. D., & Schwartz, D. (2001). The dyadic nature of social information processing in boys' reactive and proactive aggression. *Journal of Personality and Social Psychology, 80*(2), 268–280.

Hughes, C., & Dunn, J. (2000). Hedonism or empathy? Hard-to-manage children's moral awareness and links with cognitive and maternal characteristics. *British Journal of Developmental Psychology, 18,* 227–245.

Hughes, C., Dunn, J., & White, A. (1998). Trick or treat?: Uneven understanding of mind and emotion and executive dysfunction in "hard-to-manage" preschoolers. *Journal of Child Psychology and Psychiatry, 39*(7), 981–994.

Hughes, C., Russell, J., & Robbins, T. W. (1994). Evidence for executive dysfunction in autism. *Neuropsychologia, 32,* 477–492.

Kanner, L. (1943). Autistic disturbances of affective contact. *Nervous Child, 2,* 217–250.

Keller, M., & Edelstein, W. (1991). The development of socio-moral meaning making: Domains, categories, and perspective-taking. In W. M. Kurtinez & J. L. Gewirtz (Eds.), *Handbook of moral behavior and development, Vol. 1: Theory, Vol. 2: Research, Vol. 3: Application* (pp. 89–114). Hillsdale, NJ: Lawrence Erlbaum.

Kesler-West, M. L., Andersen, A. H., Smith, C. D., Avison, M. J., Davis, C. E., Kryscio, R. J., & Blonder, L. X. (2001). Neural substrates of facial emotion processing using fMRI. *Cognitive Brain Research, 11* (2), 213–226.

Killcross, S., Robbins, T. W., & Everitt, B. J. (1997). Different types of fear-conditioned behavior mediated by separate nuclei within the amygdala. *Nature, 388,* 377–380.

Klin, A., Sparrow, S. S., de Bildt, A., Cicchetti, D. V., Cohen, D. J., & Volkmar, F. R. (1999). A normed study of face recognition in autism and related disorders. *Journal of Autism and Developmental Disorders, 29*(6), 499–508.

Kohlberg, L. (1981). The philosophy of moral development: Moral stages and the idea of justice. *Vol 1. of Essays on moral development.* San Francisco: Harper and Row.

LeDoux, J. (1998). *The emotional brain.* New York: Weidenfeld & Nicolson.

Leslie, A. (2000). *"Theory of mind" as a mechanism of selective attention.* Cambridge, MA: MIT Press.

Leslie, A. M. (1987). Pretense and representation: The origins of "theory of mind." *Psychological Review, 94,* 412–426.

Leslie, A. M., & Frith, U. (1988). Autistic children's understanding of seeing, knowing and believing. *British Journal of Developmental Psychology, 6,* 315–324.

Linnoila, M., DeJong, J., & Virkkunen, M. (1989). Monoamines, glucose metabolism, and impulse control. *Psychopharmacology Bulletin, 25,* 404–406.

Linnoila, M., Virkkunen, M., Scheinin, M., Nuutila, A., Rimon, R., & Goodwin, F. K. (1983). Low cerebrospinal fluid 5-hydroxy indoleacetic acid concentration differentiates impulsive from nonimpulsive violent behavior. *Life Sciences, 33,* 2609–2614.

Liss, M., Fein, D., Allen, D., Dunn, M., Feinstein, C., Morris, R., Waterhouse, L., & Rapin, I. (2001). Executive functioning in high-functioning children with autism. *Journal of Child Psychology and Psychiatry, 42*(2), 261–270.

Lotter, V. (1966). Epidemiology of autistic conditions in young children: I. Prevalence. *Social Psychiatry, 1,* 124–137.

Lough, S., Gregory, C., & Hodges, J. R. (2001). Dissociation of social cognition and executive function in frontal variant frontotemporal dementia. *Neurocase, 7*(2), 123–130.

Loveland, K. A., Tunali, K. B., Chen, R., Brelsford, K. A., Ortegon, P., & Pearson, A. (1995). Intermodal perception of affect in persons with autism or Down syndrome. *Development and Psychopathology, 7*(3), 409–418.

Matthews, G., & Wells, A. (1999). The cognitive science of attention and emotion. In T. Dalgleish & M. J. Power (Eds.), *Handbook of cognition and emotion* (pp. 171–192). New York: Wiley.

Morgan, A. B., & Lilienfield, S. O. (2000). A meta-analytic review of the relation between antisocial behavior and neuropsychological measures of executive function. *Clinical Psychology Review, 20,* 113–136.

Morris, J., Friston, K. J., Buchel, C., Frith, C. D., Young, A. W., Calder, A. J., & Dolan, R. J. (1998). A neuromodulatory role for the human amygdala in processing emotional facial expressions. *Brain, 121,* 47–57.

Murray, E. A., Bussey, T. J., & Wise, S. P. (2000). Role of prefrontal cortex in a network for arbitrary visuomotor mapping. *Experimental Brain Research, 133*(1), 114–129.

Nucci, L., Turiel, E., & Encarnacion-Gawrych, G. E. (1983). Social interactions and social concepts: Analysis of morality and convention in the Virgin Islands. *Journal of Cross Cultural Psychology, 14,* 469–487.

Nucci, L. P., & Herman, S. (1982). Behavioral disordered children's conceptions of moral, conventional, and personal issues. *Journal of Abnormal Child Psychology, 10,* 411–425.

Ozonoff, S., Pennington, B., & Rogers, S. (1990). Are there emotion perception deficits in young autistic children? *Journal of Child Psychology and Psychiatry, 31,* 343–363.

Panksepp, J. (1989). The neurobiology of emotions: Of animal brains and human feelings. In H. Wagner & A. Manstead (Eds.), *Handbook of social psychophysiology* (pp. 5–26). Chichester: Wiley.

Passingham, R. E., & Toni, I. (2001). Contrasting the dorsal and ventral visual systems: Guidance of movement versus decision making. *Neuroimage, 14*(1 Pt 2), S125–S131.

Passingham, R. E., Toni, I., & Rushworth, M. F. (2000). Specialization within the prefrontal cortex: The ventral prefrontal cortex and associative learning. *Experimental Brain Research, 133*(1), 103–113.

Pennington, B. F., & Bennetto, L. (1993). Main effects or transaction in the neuropsychology of conduct disorder? Commentary on "The neuropsychology of conduct disorder." *Development and Psychopathology, 5,* 153–164.

Pennington, B. F., & Ozonoff, S. (1996). Executive functions and developmental psychopathology. *Journal of Child Psychology and Psychiatry, 37,* 51–87.

Perner, J. (1991). *Understanding the representational mind.* Cambridge, MA: MIT Press.

Perner, J., Frith, U., Leslie, A. M., & Leekam, S. R. (1989). Exploration of the autistic child's theory of mind: Knowledge, belief and communication. *Child Development, 60,* 689–700.

Premack, D., & Woodruff, G. (1978). Does the chimpanzee have a theory of mind? *Behavioral and Brain Sciences, 1*(4), 515–526.

Price, B. H., Daffner, K. R., Stowe, R. M., & Mesulam, M. M. (1990). The compartmental learning disabilities of early frontal lobe damage. *Brain, 113,* 1383–1393.

Prior, M., Dahlstrom, B., & Squires, T. (1990). Autistic children's knowledge of thinking and feeling states in other people. *Journal of Autism and Developmental Disorders, 31,* 587–602.

Quiggle, N. L., Garber, J., Panak, W. F., & Dodge, K. A. (1992). Social information processing in aggressive and depressed children. *Child Development, 63*(6), 1305–1320.

Reed, T., & Peterson, C. (1990). A comparative study of autistic subjects' performance at two levels of visual and cognitive perspective taking. *Journal of Autism and Developmental Disorders, 20,* 555–568.

Richell, R. A., Mitchell, D. G. V., Newman, C., Leonard, A., Baron-Cohen, S., & Blair, R. J. R. (2003). Theory of mind and psychopathy: Can psychopathic individuals read the "Language of the Eyes"? *Neuropsychologia, 41,* 523–643.

Rolls, E. T. (2000). The orbitofrontal cortex and reward. *Cerebral Cortex, 10*, 284–294.

Saver, J. L., & Damasio, A. R. (1991). Preserved access and processing of social knowledge in a patient with acquired sociopathy due to ventromedial frontal damage. *Neuropsychologia, 29*, 1241–1249.

Schalling, D. (1978). Psychopathy-related personality variables and the psychophysiology of socialization. In R. D. Hare & D. Schalling (Eds.), *Psychopathic behavior: Approaches to research* (pp. 85–106). Chichester, England: Wiley.

Scragg, P., & Shah, A. (1994). Prevalence of Asperger's syndrome in a secure hospital. *British Journal of Psychiatry, 165*(5), 679–682.

Selman, R. L. (1980). *The growth of interpersonal understanding*. New York: Academic Press.

Semin, G. R., & Manstead, A. S. (1982). The social implications of embarrassment displays and restitution behavior. *European Journal of Social Psychology, 12*(4), 367–377.

Siegel, A., Roeling, T. A., Gregg, T. R., & Kruk, M. R. (1999). Neuropharmacology of brain-stimulation-evoked aggression. *Neuroscience Biobehavioral Review, 23*, 359–389.

Sigman, M. D., Kasari, C., Kwon, J., & Yirmiya, N. (1992). Responses to the negative emotions of others by autistic, mentally retarded, and normal children. *Child Development, 63*, 796–807.

Smetana, J. G. (1982). *Concepts of self and morality: Women's reasoning about abortion*. New York: Praeger.

Smetana, J. G. (1985). Preschool children's conceptions of transgressions: The effects of varying moral and conventional domain-related attributes. *Developmental Psychology, 21*, 18–29.

Smetana, J. G. (1993). Understanding of social rules. In M. Bennett (Ed.), *The child as psychologist: An introduction to the development of social cognition* (pp. 111–141). New York: Harvester Wheatsheaf.

Smetana, J. G., & Braeges, J. L. (1990). The development of toddlers' moral and conventional judgments. *Merrill-Palmer-Quarterly, 36*, 329–346.

Song, M., Smetana, J. G., & Kim, S. Y. (1987). Korean children's conceptions of moral and conventional transgressions. *Developmental Psychology, 23*, 577–582.

Sprengelmeyer, R., Rausch, M., Eysel, U. T., & Przuntek, H. (1998). Neural structures associated with the recognition of facial basic emotions. *Proceedings of the Royal Society of London, B, 265*, 1927–1931.

Steinberg, M. S., & Dodge, K. A. (1983). Attributional bias in aggressive adolescent boys and girls. *Journal of Social and Clinical Psychology, 1*(4), 312–321.

Stevens, D., Charman, T., & Blair, R. J. R. (2001). Recognition of emotion in facial expressions and vocal tones in children with psychopathic tendencies. *Journal of Genetic Psychology, 162*(2), 201–211.

Stoddart, T., & Turiel, E. (1985). Children's concepts of cross-gender activities. *Child Development, 56*, 1241–1252.

Stone, V. E., Baron-Cohen, S., & Knight, R. T. (1998). Frontal lobe contributions to theory of mind. *Journal of Cognitive Neuroscience, 10*(5), 640–656.

Sutker, P. B. (1970). Vicarious conditioning and sociopathy. *Journal of Abnormal Psychology, 76*, 380–386.

Sutton, J., Reeves, M., & Keogh, E. (2000). Disruptive behaviour, avoidance of responsibility and theory of mind. *British Journal of Developmental Psychology, 18*(1), 1–11.

Sutton, J., Smith, P. K., & Swettenham, J. (1999). Social cognition and bullying: Social inadequacy or skilled manipulation? *British Journal of Developmental Psychology, 17*(3), 435–450.

Turiel, E. (1983a). *The development of social knowledge: Morality and Convention*. Cambridge: Cambridge University Press.

Turiel, E. (1983b). Domains and categories in social cognitive development. In W. Overton (Ed.), *The relationship between social and cognitive development* (pp. 63–89). Hillside, NJ: Lawrence Erlbaum.

Turiel, E., & Wainryb, C. (1998). Concept of freedoms and rights in a traditional, hierarchical organized society. *British Journal of Developmental Psychology, 16*, 375–395.

Vitiello, B., Behar, D., Hunt, J., Stoff, D., & Ricciuti, A. (1990). Subtyping aggression in children and adolescents. *Journal of Neuropsychiatry and Clinical Neurosciences, 2*, 189–192.

Vogeley, K. , Bussfeld, S. P., Newen, A., Herrmann, S., Happé, F., Falkai, P., Maier, W., Shah, N. J., Fink, G. R., & Zilles, K. (2001). Mind reading: Neural mechanisms of theory of mind and self-perspective. *NeuroImage, 14,* 170–181.

Widom, C. S. (1976). Interpersonal and personal construct systems in psychopaths. *Journal of Consulting and Clinical Psychology, 44,* 614–623.

Widom, C. S. (1978). An empirical classifica-tion of female offenders. *Criminal Justice and Behavior, 5,* 35–52.

Williamson, S., Hare, R. D., & Wong, S. (1987). Violence: Criminal psychopaths and their victims. *Canadian Journal of Behavioural Science, 19,* 454–462.

Wimmer, H., & Perner, J. (1983). Beliefs about beliefs: Representation and the constraining function of wrong beliefs in young children's understanding of deception. *Cognition, 13,* 103–128.

8

The Social Face of Theory of Mind

The Development of Concepts of Emotion, Desire, Visual Perspective, and False Belief in Deaf and Hearing Children

CANDIDA C. PETERSON
University of Queensland

> *"There's no art to find the mind's construction in the face."*
> Shakespeare, Macbeth (I, iv)

The ability to infer mental states like intentions, memories, desires, and beliefs, and to use these for understanding and predicting the behavior of self and others, is "one of the quintessential abilities that makes us human" (Baron-Cohen, 2000, p. 3). Known as a "theory of mind" (ToM), this capacity is frequently equated with success on inferential false-belief tests that require children to predict what a protagonist will do, say, or think when in the grip of a mistaken belief (Flavell, 1999; Wellman, 1993). A large body of research over the past 15 years shows that most typically developing 4- to 5-year-old children consistently pass these tests (Wellman, Cross, & Watson, 2001), whereas failure is routine among normal 3-year-olds and children, adolescents, and adults with autism (Baron-Cohen, Leslie, & Frith, 1985; Baron-Cohen, Tager-Flusberg, & Cohen, 2000; Tager-Flusberg, this volume).

Indeed, from a recent review of 28 separate studies of inferential false-belief performance conducted over a decade in several different countries,

Happé (1995) obtained strong evidence of a severe false-belief deficit associated with autism. Collectively sampling more than 300 autistic individuals (all with mean verbal mental ages of 5 years and over), these studies consistently revealed high failure rates on false-belief tasks that were not echoed among mentally retarded or typically developing children of similar verbal and nonverbal mental ages. For example, pass rates for autistic participants (predominantly adolescents) in 14 studies conducted from 1985 to 1993 ranged from 15 to 60%, with a mean of just 33% passing. In Happé's (1995) own sample, only 20% of autistic 12-year-olds passed a pair of false-belief tests, as compared with 56% of normal 4-year-olds and 59% of 12-year-olds with mental retardation. The use of age- and language-matched children with mental retardation as a control group is important methodologically in order to rule out general cognitive or linguistic deficits as an explanation for the difficulties associated with autism. In fact, children with mental retardation are found to develop concepts of false belief at significantly more advanced mental ages than typically developing children, but at less-advanced mental and chronological ages than children with autism (Yirmiya, Erel, Shaked, & Solomonica-Levi, 1998), prompting the conclusion that "ToM deficits can no longer be conceptualized as a core deficit that is unique to autism" (p. 302).

Similarly, it has been found that children of normal intelligence who have severe sensory disabilities but none of the diagnostically significant social or cognitive markers of autism (Frith, 1989) may be as slow as those with autism to develop a ToM if they are congenitally blind (McAlpine & Moore, 1995; Minter, Hobson, & Bishop, 1998; Peterson, Peterson, & Webb, 2000) or deaf in a hearing–speaking family (Peterson & Siegal, 1995, 1998, 1999).

In fact, when Peterson and Siegal (2000) reviewed results of 11 separate studies of false-belief understanding in signing deaf children published between 1995 and 1999, they found evidence of a ToM deficit that appeared to be as severe and protracted as that seen among high-functioning autistic children (Happé, 1995). The populations of severely and profoundly deaf children sampled in these studies were impressively varied, having been drawn from a wide variety of family backgrounds, preferred communication modalities, sign-language communities, and several different countries (Australia, France, England, Scotland, United States) where sign languages and philosophies of deaf education differ markedly. Yet the results of the studies reviewed were consistent in revealing substantial delays in false-belief understanding among the vast majority of deaf children from hearing families, despite normal intelligence, normal social responsiveness, and freedom from most of the other clinical impairments diagnosed, or highly correlated, with autism.

According to Peterson and Siegal (1999, 2000) however, it is not deafness per se, but rather deafness in conjunction with a hearing family that predicts severe delays in ToM development. Profoundly deaf offspring of signing deaf parents (second-generation deaf signers), along with those who have another native speaker of sign language in their immediate household (e.g., a signing deaf grandparent or an older deaf sibling who has become a fluent signer at school), can be dubbed "native signers" owing to their access, throughout their growing up, to a fluent conversational partner at home with whom they are able to share a common first language, such as ASL (American Sign Language) or Auslan (Australian Sign Language). Native signers are consistently found to perform significantly better on theory of mind tasks than late-signing deaf children from hearing families (Peterson & Siegal, 1999, 2000; Remmel, Bettger, & Weinberg, 1998) and may even acquire an understanding of false belief at a slightly earlier age than preschoolers with normal hearing from hearing families (Courtin & Melot, 1998).

De Villiers and de Villiers (2000) studied oral deaf children who, rather than acquiring sign language either as a native language or belatedly in school, used hearing aids and learned lip-reading and attended an oralist special school where the medium of instruction was amplified speech. Their rate of language development was delayed by their auditory disability. As deVilliers (2000) explained: "On average, oral deaf children in the age range of four to nine years perform on standard tests such as the PPVT (vocabulary) and the CELF (syntax subscale) as being about three to four years delayed compared with hearing children" (p. 107). The 27 moderately to profoundly deaf 5- to 10-year-olds in the deVilliers study were tested on a battery of verbal and nonverbal false-belief tasks, along with language and IQ tests. The findings supported those of earlier studies of deaf signers that were reviewed by Peterson and Siegal (2000) in showing that the oral deaf children's ToM development was "delayed by several years, even with nonverbal tasks" (p. 114). In addition, even after controlling for chronological age, level of hearing loss, and nonverbal IQ, the results of multiple regression analyses indicated that language maturity (especially the syntax of embedded sentence complements like "X thinks that [clause]") significantly predicted these oral deaf children's levels of false-belief understanding. According to de Villiers (2000): "Together these points suggest that it is specifically the linguistic problems that cause the delay for deaf children since in all other respects—intelligence, active sociability, attentiveness—they are not initially impaired" (p. 114). She speculated further that, because "children with autism have problems that extend beyond language" (p. 118), their delays in the ToM domain would be expected to extend quite broadly into concepts like emotion, desire, perception, motivation, intention, social relationships, and morality. One possibility, then, is that the deaf child's only ToM difficulty is quite specifically the syntactic problem of delayed mastery of the language of embedded clause constructions, which provides the means by which false beliefs are represented and communicated. If so, deaf children, unlike their peers with autism, could be expected to develop other kinds of mentalistic concepts in the realm of intentionality, motivation, or emotion at the same age as children with normal hearing.

On the other hand, there are many departures from the normal courses of development for language, conversation, and social interaction when deaf children are reared in hearing homes with no fluent signers and quite a number of these, in addition to a limited syntax for representing belief, could conceivably delay the growth of the child's understanding of mental states. Thus, the deaf child's difficulties might not be confined to false-belief understanding, but could conceivably apply at a broader level as a result of restrictions on the language and social experiences that are jointly needed to nurture and cultivate a ToM (Garfield, Peterson, & Perry, 2001). Indeed, in the absence of a fluently shared common language, it is difficult to converse about ideas that have no immediately present physical referent. Thus, deaf children would find it hard to engage in shared fantasy, imaginative planning, or make-believe play with family members, as well as having difficulty understanding emotions and desires that relate to abstract, absent, past, or future objects and events. Stories and conversational commentary on people's unexpected or problematic behavior arise commonly in hearing–speaking households and are thought to serve as a cultural socialization mechanism to "bring mental states to children's attention" (Astington, 2001, p. 686). But the deaf child's access to any of these avenues of family conversation will be seriously restricted in the absence of a fluently shared common language. Thus, to the extent that these social-interactive and conversational influences are necessary to the growth of a ToM, delays in many aspects of mental state understanding in addition to false belief should also be observed among oral and late-signing deaf children from hearing families, in direct proportion to the extent to which their auditory impairment restricts their opportunity to take part in family dialogue, arguments, pretend play, and other everyday forms of spontaneous conversation.

There has been relatively little systematic investigation of aspects of deaf children's naïve psychological theorizing apart from false belief and, indeed, this a problem for the field of ToM research more generally. As Astington (2001) pointed out: "There is a danger in letting a single task become a marker for complex development. Future work should focus on developing tasks that assess children's understanding of desire and intention that are as clear and compelling as the false belief task" (p. 687).

The major aim of this chapter, then, is to begin to move studies of deaf children in this broader direction. As a starting point, the very limited amount of previous research that has stretched beyond the radius of the false-belief task to examine how deaf children develop concepts of visual perception, emotion, and desire will be reviewed. The findings from a recent empirical study are then presented. The goal of this research was to more closely investigate deaf children's understanding of these subdomains of naïve psychological understanding, that, like false belief, require an appreciation of mental representation, along with its potential for error and for representational diversity. In addition, a battery of false-belief tests was given to test how difficult these are relative to tasks requiring an understanding of representational diversity in other mental domains. Finally, comparisons were made between deaf elementary school children and 4-year-old children with normal hearing in terms of the levels of mastery and sequences of development for these varied aspects of social understanding.

VISUAL PERSPECTIVE-TAKING

According to Flavell, Everett, Croft, and Flavell (1981), a mature "Level 2" understanding of visual perspectives requires an accurate awareness of other people's distinctive visual images of a scene when viewed from different vantage points (e.g., if the tail of a dog is seen by one observer, the head will be seen by a viewer seated opposite). This nonegocentric awareness of viewers' distinctive visual perspectives can plausibly be compared with successful performance on standard false-belief tests that require a similar awareness, at the mental level, that people's beliefs will differ depending on their access to relevant information. Gopnik, Slaughter, and Meltzoff (1994) proposed that, in normally developing children, Level 2 visual perspective-taking may both precede and facilitate the development of concepts of false belief. They suggested a "bootstrapping" process in which notions about divergent beliefs emerge initially as postulates about what other people see in their "mind's eye." By imagining such views for self and other, skilled visual perspective-takers may gain a preliminary degree of insight into the varied mental states of other people, which need not correspond either to one's own or to objective reality.

However, although possibly necessary, there is evidence that skilled Level 2 visual perspective-taking is not a sufficient precondition for false-belief understanding, at least among certain groups of children with developmental disabilities. For example, Reed and Peterson (1990) found that a group of autistic children and adolescents who performed near ceiling on tests of visual perspective-taking (and at as high a level as chronological and mental-aged matched control groups) were nonetheless seriously impaired on corresponding tests of ToM. For example, even though these young people with autism readily passed Level 1 visual perspective-taking problems (i.e., understanding invisibility when line of sight is blocked), they overwhelmingly failed a belief task in which they similarly had to infer a protagonist's ignorance based on lack of informational access. Furthermore, although the vast majority of these participants passed standard Level 2 perspective-taking tests (i.e., understood the varied visual percepts of viewers seated at different angles around an array), over 80% of them failed the corresponding Sally–Ann false-belief test (Baron-Cohen et al., 1985). This latter task required an understanding of varied beliefs about the location of an object among viewers who had last seen this object in different hiding places.

Even more striking evidence of the disjunction between accurate Level 2 visual perspective-taking and impaired understanding of false belief emerged in a study of blind 6- to 12-year-old children, who were tested on standard measures of each of these abilities (Peterson, Peterson, & Webb, 2000). Even the youngest blind children, regardless of their degree of visual impairment, displayed a highly accurate understanding of the varied views that tactually distinctive arrays would present to observers seated at different angles, yet a majority failed a battery of false-belief tests through the age of 9 years.

Even if an awareness of the diversity of people's varied visual perspectives on the physical world is not, by itself, a sufficient precondition for accurately understanding the diversity of belief states, it may still be helpful in paving the way for the growth of mental state understanding. Consequently, based indirectly on the results of these studies of children with blindness and with autism, as well as more extensive research on typically developing preschoolers, two predictions can be tentatively put forward for empirical testing in the present study: (1) Severely and profoundly deaf children should perform at a higher level on standard Level 2 visual perspective-taking problems than on standard tests of false-belief understanding, and (2) a prerequisite relationship is likely to apply, such that no deaf child who consistently passes false-belief tests should be found to consistently fail Level 2 visual perspective-taking tasks.

In addition to testing deaf children's awareness of visual perspectives using the Flavell et al. (1981) standard turntable tests (derived from Piaget's [1970] three-mountains experiment), a gaze-direction test of visual understanding (Baron-Cohen, 1995) was included to assess children's sensitivity to eye direction alone as an indicator of others' percepts and attentional foci. Again, it was predicted that, given their normal and extensive social experience of looking at people's faces and drawing inferences about inner states from the nonverbal cues a face so often betrays, even those deaf children who failed the false-belief tests would be relatively skilled at reading information about perception and attention from the focus of people's eyes.

EMOTION UNDERSTANDING

A number of simple emotions, such as joy, anger, and fear, can be visually and relatively unambiguously communicated via facial expression (Ekman, 1994). Furthermore, even from birth, humans are highly sensitive to this cue. For instance, 1-day-old infants have been found to discriminate between happy and sad faces (Field, Woodson, Greenberg, & Cohen, 1982) and 1-year-olds routinely use their caregiver's facial expressions of fear or joy in order to determine whether they should approach or avoid an unfamiliar stimulus (Campos & Sternberg, 1981). Furthermore, as Repacholi and Gopnik (1997) persuasively showed, normally developing children from 18 months old onward can, without language, infer the gustatory likes and dislikes of others from their visual and vocal expressions of satisfaction or disgust. Moreover, these young children can make appropriate use of this information, while overcoming a cognitively egocentric focus on their own taste perspectives (such as a dislike for broccoli), in order to offer foods to others on the basis of these people's unconventional emotions, preferences, and desires.

In theory, these kinds of emotional preference cues should be readily accessible to deaf children via the visual channel during everyday social interaction, even if the child has been reared in a family without a fluently shared language. However, there has been relatively little study of how deaf children actually use facial expression cues to infer the emotions, preferences, or desires of others. In addition, provided that deaf children's sensitivity to facial emotion cues can be established, it is important also to discover how capable they are at emotional (or "affective") perspective-taking of the kind studied in infants by Repacholi and Gopnik (1997). Consequently, the present battery of social understanding tasks includes measures of both face reading and emotional perspective-taking. In keeping with Repacholi and Gopnik's (1997) procedure, the former required inferences about likes and dislikes for food, wheras the emotional perspective-taking tests required inferences about the emotions of protagonists who displayed visible preferences that were the diametric opposite of those held by the participating child. In addition to exploring deaf children's capacity to predict emotions nonegocentrically, it is important to determine whether this potentially nonverbal capability (a) develops in advance of and (b) serves as a necessary precursor to, a nonegocentric understanding of others' false beliefs.

Using a narrative method, Rieffe and Meerum Terwogt (2000) explored sensitivity to typical and atypical emotions in a sample of deaf children aged 6 to 10 years from a total communication (signed Dutch) school in the Netherlands. The procedure involved presenting stories with emotive themes ("Petra sees a person whom she cannot identify in a dark living room") and asking children to name and explain the character's likely emotional reaction. Then an atypical emotional reaction was narrated ("Petra is happy to see the stranger in the dark") and the subject was again asked for an explanation. The deaf children were tested by a skilled interpreter in their familiar mode of sign language, whereas those in a hearing control group responded orally.

The results revealed very few references to beliefs by either deaf or hearing children. But even the 6-year-olds in both groups made frequent use of desire as an explanation for the protagonists' typical and atypical emotional reactions, for example, by stating that "she is happy because she wants to play with her friend." Interestingly, the deaf children made more references to desire overall than did their hearing peers, and were also less likely than hearing children to limit their mention of desire to the atypical emotion. Although they did not observe much reference to belief by either deaf or hearing children, the authors drew on previous findings of deaf children's delayed false-belief understanding to speculate that limited exposure to conversation while growing up in a hearing family may have undermined the deaf child's capacity to discuss mental states that had no obvious hedonic significance. As they explained: "Deaf children participate less in daily conversations that concentrate around mental states. Their limited access to everyday conversations might cause deaf children to react more briefly and to the point when they are asked for a prediction of others' emotions. They might head directly for the final outcome of the story—the fulfillment of the protagonist's desire—without regard to the protagonist's beliefs" (p. 605). On the basis of these suggestions, it can be predicted that most of the deaf children in the present sample will be skilled at inferring atypical emotions and at taking the perspectives of protagonists with typical and atypical desires, even if they fail standard false-belief tests.

DESIRE UNDERSTANDING

In a study of late-signing deaf children's sensitivity to the desires and acquisitive intentions of others, Scott, Russell, Gray, Hosie, and Hunter (1999) used a task that had previously been employed by Baron-Cohen, Campbell, Karmiloff-Smith, and Grant (1995) to compare normally developing 4-year-olds with older children and adolescents who had autism. The stimuli were cartoon drawings of faces that were completely neutral in emotional expression (i.e., a straight-line mouth that neither smiled nor frowned, no eyebrows, etc.; see Baron-Cohen, 2000, p. 10, for an example). The eyes on the cartoon pointed, in various conditions of the task, at different packages of candy located in each corner of the larger array. The deaf children, like the children with autism who had been tested previously, were highly accurate in identifying the target of the eye's focus when asked an explicit question about visual perception: "What is Charlie looking at?" Most of the normally developing 4-year-olds in the Baron-Cohen et al. original study also used gaze direction on this emotionally neutral face as evidence of the character's desire for the item he was looking at. This was not the case for either the older autistic children or the deaf children under age 11 who were tested by Scott et al. In fact, deaf children between the ages of 5 and 11 years achieved only chance accuracy when asked "What does Charlie want?" or "What will Charlie take?" in response to these stimuli. On this basis, Scott et al. concluded that "deaf children's ability to infer the desires and intentions of others, on the basis of line of regard, may be subject to a degree of developmental delay" (p. 419).

However, a problem with this task as an ecologically valid measure is that, in the absence of language or other expressive or behavioral cues (e.g., beckoning or reaching), the direction of gaze alone is insufficient to unambiguously convey even that a feeling for the object is being expressed, let alone the valence of such a feeling as positive desire rather than rejection. Indeed, the magnetic fascination with which people's gaze is often drawn to stimuli charged with negative emotion (such as dangerous creatures in zoos, disgusting substances, car accidents, etc.) is well known, suggesting that gaze direction alone is an unreliable discriminator between the extremes of intense attraction and intense aversion. Consequently, the younger deaf children's poor performance on the Scott et al. test may not have been a fully accurate indicator of their ability to read desire from a face under more realistically natural conditions, possibly instead reflecting insensitivity to the subtle conversational demand characteristics of the testing situation (Siegal, 1997).

In order to empirically test this possibility, and at the same time explore deaf children's ability to use both eye direction and facial expressions to draw inferences about desires, a modified version of the task used by Baron-Cohen et al. (1995) and Scott et al. (1999) was incorporated into the present test battery. Success on this new desire perspective-taking task required the integration of gaze direction information with children's readings of the positive or negative expressions of emotion on the faces in order, first of all, to infer cartoon characters' like or dislike for pictured foods, and to then use these inferred preferences to predict the characters' desires from among a range of food items. In addition, success on this desire test provided evidence of the child's capacity to overcome Piagetian egocentrism in order to ascribe to a character a desire that was not their own. As suggested by Harris (1996), the task was constructed in such a way that the item the character was pictured as liking was always one that the child had previously rejected in favor of a more highly desired item.

Under these conditions, it was predicted that deaf children would display a greater awareness of facially expressed desire than had been evident in the Scott et al. study. Furthermore, based on Wellman's (1993) suggestion that desire understanding precedes belief understanding in normal hearing children, it was predicted that deaf children's success on this desire perspective-taking test would both precede and help to predict success on standard tests of false belief.

METHODS AND SAMPLE

The sample consisted of 18 severely and profoundly deaf children from Total Communication schools in Australia, along with a comparison group of 14 Australian preschoolers with normal hearing; no known, or suspected, developmental disabilities; and English as their first language. The deaf children were selected on the basis of the following criteria: (a) the child had been a pupil in the Total Communication school (where signed English was the medium of classroom communication, supplemented by lipreading and amplifying hearing aids) for at least 6 months and was rated by the classroom teacher to be skilled enough in this mode of communication to be capable of understanding task instructions when these were presented bilingually in signed English and speech by a professionally trained sign language interpreter (a prediction that was confirmed by the satisfactory performance on control questions of all children in this sample); (b) the child was severely or profoundly deaf and had become so prior to the acquisition of language; (c) neither parent was deaf or a native speaker of sign language; and (d) the child had no known handicaps apart from deafness (e.g., autism, mental retardation, visual impairment, or cerebral palsy).

The sample of 18 deaf children had a mean age of 9 years 10 months (range: 4 years 6 months to 13 years 8 months) and 10 of them were boys. Their levels of hearing loss (measured in decibels in the better ear while wearing their amplifying aids) ranged from 62 to 120 dB with a mean of 95.5 dB. All but one of the children had amplified losses of 71 dB or more, placing them in categorical ranges of severe (71 dB+) to profound (91 dB+) deafness (Marschark, 1993).

Teachers were asked to rate each child's level of productive and receptive language ability, first in terms of signed English and then in terms of speech. They were also asked which of these modalities the child most often used when communicating with teachers and deaf classmates. No deaf child in this sample was rated by the teacher as being fluent enough in oral–aural communication to be capable of conversing unassisted with strangers in this modality. Consequently, all of the children required an interpreter's signed translations during the experimental testing.

The hearing preschoolers had a mean age of 4 years 10 months (range: 4 years 3 months to 5 years 1 month) and 5 of them were boys. To ensure that no children with language delays or difficulties were inadvertently included in the control group, the PPVT (Peabody Picture Vocabulary Test; Dunn & Dunn, 1981) was administered. All of the preschoolers were found to have a verbal mental age (VMA) of 4 years 6 months or higher, and none of them had a VMA that was more than 4 months below their chronological age.

Each child was tested individually. For the deaf children, two adults were present, one male and one female. The latter was a professionally trained Auslan interpreter who was highly familiar with the style of Total Communication used in each deaf child's classroom, as well as with each child's own particular language preferences (e.g., for signed English vs. Auslan). The interpreter, who was seated beside the male experimenter (E) and directly opposite and in full view of the participant, simultaneously translated E's spoken narrative and questions into the child's preferred mode of sign language, using a style of interpretation that was highly familiar to these children. The narrators both paused while critical bits of stories were acted out (such as hiding the marble during the false-belief task), and both of them also monitored that the child's gaze was directed at the pictures, the props, or the interpreter (as appropriate) before continuing each part of the procedure. Both adults independently recorded the child's pointing responses, and subsequent matching of their records revealed complete agreement. In addition, the interpreter supplied an ongoing oral translation of all the child's signed communication, which was recorded by E on the data sheets.

The ToM tasks were presented in a fixed order (as detailed next) and generally in two sessions.

Visual Perspective-Taking (VPT). This eight-trial Level 2 turntable test followed a procedure that Flavell et al. (1981) adapted from Massangkay et al. (1974). The child was seated directly opposite to E at a high square table with 60-cm sides. Another observer (the interpreter or a large doll introduced as "my friend Jane") was seated 90° to the child's left. After positioning a turntable in the center of the square table and demonstrating its use, a toy dog was positioned side-on to the child at approximately eye level. E said: "See the dog?" (1) "Can you turn it so you can see the dog's eyes?" (control trial), (2) "Okay, now turn it so I can see the dog's nose," (3) "Now, turn it so [Jane] can see the dog's tail," and (4) "Now, turn it so I can see the tail." The procedure was then repeated with a large (25-cm) cube on the turntable. It was painted all over in a solid color, with small, brightly colored pictures of familiar items (a train, a birthday cake, a kitten, a clothesline with washing on it) in the center of each vertical side. After the child had correctly labeled each of these pictures, E repeated the above 4 questions using the new stimulus (e.g., "Turn it so I can see the washing on the line"). Control trials (which all children passed) were omitted from scoring. Children could earn a total VPT score ranging from 0 to 6, reflecting the number of times they correctly constructed the perspective of the target viewer.

False Belief. Baron-Cohen et al.'s (1985) two-trial Sally–Ann task was presented exactly as described by the authors apart from substitution of a boy doll for "Ann" to avoid confusion over girls' names (Peterson & Siegal, 1995, 1998). At the start of each trial, the girl doll placed her marble in a covered basket and left the scene, after which a boy doll shifted the marble to a box (Trial 1) or E's pocket (Trial 2). Control questions establishing memory for the original hiding place (Where did the girl put her marble?) and awareness of the current location (Where is the marble now?) were passed by all subjects on both trials. The test question "Where will the girl look for her marble?" required inference about the protagonist's behavior based on the awareness that she would have a false belief. Children earned 1 point for each correct response to the test questions, resulting in a maximum possible score of 2 across both trials.

The second false-belief test was a standard misleading container task using a familiar Smarties box (Gopnik & Slaughter, 1991). After seeing the closed container and naming the expected contents, children were shown that it actually held pencils. The box was resealed and three questions were presented in the following order: (1) "X [a classmate] is coming next. He (or she) hasn't seen inside this box. When I show it to him (or her) all closed up like this, what will he (or she) say is in it?" A correct answer ("Smarties") earned 1 point. This was summed with the child's score on the Sally task so that across the three test trials combined, children earned a Total False Belief (TFB) score that could range from 0 to 3.

Emotion Recognition (ER). In this simple test of the capacity to distinguish between facial expressions of positive and negative affect children were shown drawings of expressive faces similar to the central portions of the upper and lower parts of Figure 8.1. There were two male and two female faces, with one of each sex showing a positive and the other a negative expression. The order of these faces was randomized across children. As each picture was displayed, E said, "Here is a boy (girl). How does he (she) feel?" In the (infrequent) instances where the child failed to spontaneously name an emotion, E prompted: "Does he (she) feel happy or sad?" Appropriate naming of happiness or a synonym (e.g., "joyful") for the positive faces and either sadness or anger (based on adult judges' most frequent designation) or synonyms (e.g., "unhappy," "cranky," "grumpy") for the negative faces was scored as correct. Children earned 1 point for each correct answer, with total ER scores of up to 4.

Gaze Reading (GR). Four drawings of faces with neutral emotional expressions and eyes directed at objects closely resembling the cartoon stimuli used by Baron-Cohen et al. (1995; see Baron-Cohen, 2000, p. 10, for an example) were used in this four-trial task. Care was taken in producing the stimuli that each face was devoid of emotional expressions of any kind. Indeed, as in Baron-Cohen et al. (1995), the only distinction among the faces used on each trial was the direction in which the pupils of the eyes appeared to glance. Pictures of familiar items surrounded each face at the four quadrants (as in Figure 8.1). Two trials had food items as stimuli and two had familiar nonfoods (e.g., a kitten, sun, leaf). For each drawing, E said: "Here is a boy. What is he looking at?" Naming or touching the object in the eyes' focus earned 1 point and these were summed over the four trials to yield a total possible GR score of 4. There was also a control trial, as in Baron-Cohen et al. (1995). The protagonist's eyes were directed at a yellow sun but E asked: "Which one is green, the same color as grass?" Correct (leaf) responses (which all subjects in this sample produced) established that correct responses to the test questions had been based on eye direction as a unique cue about looking, rather than on a global strategy of using gaze as the basis for answering any question at all that the experimenter might pose, even if totally irrelevant to vision.

Face Reading (FR). This task used a set of gaze stimuli that were richer in nonverbal cues than those employed in the previous task. Gender was evident in the distinctive hairstyles of the characters and the faces were more realistic in

FIGURE 8.1. Examples of stimuli used in the face-reading task.

that they combined positive or negative expressions with eye direction in order to test children's ability to integrate gaze and emotion cues to infer the protagonist's likes and dislikes for food items. There were four stimulus arrays, two of which are shown in Figure 8.1. (The remaining two were similar except that the face was male.) In order to make sure that all children possessed the prerequisite skill of locating the focus of the protagonist's attention, an initial phase of pretraining was given to any child who had made a gaze-reading error on the previous task. For this, E directed children to identify the pupils of the protagonist's eyes. Then, by tracing with their fingers, they were shown how to locate the object of his gaze at each quadrant. Two gaze-reading test trials (not counted in the final scoring) were then given and, upon passing (which all pretrained subjects did), the main face-reading task was immediately undertaken.

On each trial of the main test, a different face picture was shown and E said: "Here is a girl (boy). What is she (he) looking at? Does she (he) like [raisins]? Subjects could earn 1 point per trial for both identifying the correct food and appropriately reporting that the character liked it (if the face smiled) or disliked it (if the face frowned). No points were earned on a trial if either the emotion or the direction of glance was reported incorrectly. Thus, total FR scores could range from 0 to 4.

Emotion Perspective-Taking (EPT). This test followed naturally on from the face-reading task, using the same set of pictorial stimuli. For the first trial, the female frowning and smiling arrays were presented together (as in Figure 8.1) and E said: "Here is the girl again. It is the same girl. Remember her? Remember the snack she likes? Remember the snack that she doesn't like? Now it is time for a little lunch. She is going to eat. Here comes Mum, bringing a snack." A picture was then displayed of a packaged food item being handed to the girl (whose upper face was out of the frame so that, while she was clearly identifiable from her clothing, her facial expression was not visible). E said "Mum gives the girl [some raisins]. How does the girl feel?" If the child failed to name an emotion, E continued: "When she gets [raisins], is the girl happy or sad?" There were three remaining trials so that both the male and the female characters each received their smiled-at food on one trial and their frowned-at food on another. Correct responses (consisting of saying "happy" when the gift had been smiled at, and "sad" or "angry" to gifts of the frowned-upon item) were summed to produce a total EPT score of up to 4.

Desire Perspective-Taking (DPT). This test of children's appreciation of atypical desires (i.e., desires that were nonegocentric in the Piagetian sense) had two trials, one pictorial and the other involving a story. The picture trial used a new set of expressive faces similar to those in Figure 8.1 but drawn in black ink on clear plastic. As a pretest, children had been shown a set of real packaged snacks (e.g., a chocolate bar, a package of bubble gum, and a box of cheese twists) and asked which one they liked best. By placing the clear plastic over photos of snack wrappers, a customized stimulus array was arranged in which this favorite food of the child's was the target of a same-sex cartoon character's frowning gaze. E said: "Here is another boy (girl) named [Bill/Susan]. See? He (she) doesn't like [Mars bars]. But see, he (she) does like oranges." [E displayed an appropriate picture.] "Now he (she) is feeling hungry. Which of these foods does he (she) want most?" Packages of the liked, the disliked, and a novel food were available to enable pointing responses. One point was given for choosing the item the character smiled at, with no credit for choosing either the child's own favorite food (egocentric error) or the novel food item.

The story trial involved a female doll. Having ascertained the child's own preference from a choice of jelly beans vs. carrots, E said: "This is my friend Susan. Her favorite food is carrots [i.e., the subject's nonpreferred food]. Let's give Susan her snack." E produced a carrot and a box of jelly beans, saying: "I am going to let Susan choose one of these. Which one will she want to eat?" One point was given for a choice of the doll's favorite, which, when summed with the child's score on the picture trial, produced a DPT total that could range from 0 to 2.

PRELIMINARY ANALYSES

According to teacher reports, 5 of the deaf children made frequent use of oral communication during classroom interaction whereas the remaining 13 were predominantly or exclusively signing. Preliminary statistical analyses were therefore conducted to examine possible links between language preferences and social understanding. The only significant differences that emerged from these comparisons involved demographic characteristics. Specifically, the exclusively signing deaf children were significantly older (mean age = 10.83 years) than their classmates with an oral preference (mean age = 7.10 years), $t(16) = 3.13$, $p < .01$. With a mean auditory loss in the better ear of 105 dB, the exclusive signers likewise had significantly poorer hearing than the more oral group, whose mean loss was 71 dB in the better ear, $t(16) = 7.62$, $p < .01$. There were no significant differences between the two deaf subgroups, however, for any of the social understanding measures, all $ps > .10$. This, coupled with the fact that even the children with an oral preference required an interpreter, and often interacted with her in signed English, suggested that the deaf subgroups were sufficiently alike, in communication modality and the key experimental variables, to justify collapsing them for the main analyses.

A similar set of preliminary t tests for gender differences on all key variables in the study yielded no statistically significant differences, all $p > .05$. This likewise enabled the collapsing of boys' and girls' data in the interests of having larger groups for the main analyses. Finally, because all children in the deaf and hearing groups received perfect scores on the emotion labeling task, this measure was treated as a comprehension check and was not included in subsequent analyses.

COMPARISONS BETWEEN DEAF AND HEARING CHILDREN

Table 8.1 shows the mean chronological ages of children in the deaf and hearing groups (which differed in the expected direction, $t(30) = 6.24, p < .01$), along with their mean scores on the social understanding measures and the percentages in each group who earned perfect scores on each task. With a mean total false-belief (TFB) score of 2.64, the hearing preschoolers significantly outperformed the deaf children ($M = 1.56$), $t(30) = 3.40, p < .01$. In addition, a larger proportion of the hearing (71%) than the deaf (27%) children received perfect TFB scores by passing all of the false-belief tasks (see Figure 8.2), $\chi^2(1, n = 32) = 6.03, p < .05$. Thus, in line with previous research (Peterson & Siegal, 2000), the late-signing deaf children in this sample were less adept than hearing children some 5 years younger at passing standard false-belief tasks, which

TABLE 8.1. Means, Standard Deviations, and Percentages of Perfect Scores for Deaf and Hearing Children on Social Understanding Measures

Group	Deaf children (n = 18)		Hearing preschoolers (n = 14)		Total sample (N = 32)	
	Mean score	Percent errorless	Mean score	Percent errorless	Mean score	Percent errorless
Age (years)	9.85	N/A	4.86	N/A	7.67	N/A
	(2.75)		(0.25)		(3.23)	
Total false belief	1.56		2.64		2.03	
(TFB)	(1.15)	27%	(0.63)	71%°°	(1.09)	47%
Visual perspective	5.83		6.00		5.91	
taking (VPT)	(0.38)	83%°°	(0)	100%°°	(0.30)	91%°°
Gaze reading	3.94		3.64		3.81	
(GR)	(0.24)	94%°°	(0.84)	79%°°	(0.59)	88%°°
Face reading	3.83		3.71		3.78	
(FR)	(0.51)	88%°°	(0.61)	79%°°	(0.55)	84%°°
Emotion	3.50		3.93		3.69	
perspective	(0.86)	72%°°	(0.27)	93%°°	(0.69)	81%°°
taking (EPT)						
Desire perspective	1.44		1.86		1.63	
taking (DPT)	(0.78)	61%	(0.36)	86%°°	(0.66)	72%°°

Note. Standard deviations are in parenthesis. Significance: °° $p < .01$.

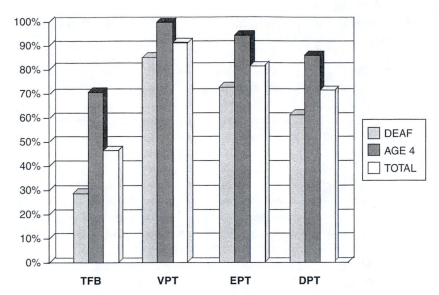

FIGURE 8.2. Percent errorless task performance. TFB, total false-belief score; VPT, visual perspective-taking score; EPT, emotion perspective-taking score; DPT, desire perspective-taking score.

can be deemed "litmus tests" (Baron-Cohen, 1995) for a theory of mind.

There were no significant differences between the deaf and hearing groups on tests of visual perspective-taking or gaze or face reading, all $ps > .10$. Indeed, both groups performed exceptionally well on each of these tasks, with the vast majority of deaf children, like their hearing peers, making no errors at all (see Table 8.1). It would seem that neither the visual perspective-taking challenges of (a) following people's gaze to determine what they are attending to, nor (b) overcoming one's own egocentric viewpoint in order to appreciate how scenes would look from other vantage points, or even the more comprehensive challenges of integrating gaze with affective expression in order to "read" another person's face, were beyond the reach of many of the deaf children in this study.

On the other hand, when it came to the tests of emotion and desire perspective-taking, both of which required children to put aside their own affective states in order to appreciate the unconventional wishes and feelings of others, the deaf group displayed somewhat less competence overall than the hearing control group. In fact, the deaf children's mean EPT and DPT scores were both marginally lower than those of the hearing preschoolers, who were near ceiling on both tests, $t(30) = 1.99$ and 1.98, respectively, $p < .06$. It seemed that deaf children had more difficulty than hearing children in appreciating characters' unconventional desires (e.g., for carrots rather than chocolate) and paradoxical emotions (e.g., anger on being given chewing gum).

HIERARCHICAL MULTIPLE REGRESSION ANALYSIS PREDICTING FALSE BELIEF

Hierarchical multiple regression was used to explore how age and hearing status might combine with indices of perceptual, emotional, and desire understanding to predict children's false-belief performance. Before doing so, simple univariate product-moment correlations were computed to examine discrete relationships among the social understanding variables for the deaf and hearing children combined. TFB scores were significantly and positively correlated with EPT scores, $r(30) = .35$, $p < .05$, and DPT scores, $r(30) = .55$, $p < .01$, but not significantly with any of the remaining indices of social understanding. For the regression analysis, the dependent variable was the child's TFB score. When chronological age and hearing status (deaf vs. hearing) were entered as control predictors in the first step, the resulting regression equation was statistically significant, Adj. $R^2 = .22$, $F(2,29) = 5.26$, $p < .01$. DPT and EPT scores were entered at Step 2 to see if children's affective understanding accounted for a significant proportion of the variance in false-belief scores, once the effects of age and hearing status had been taken into account. When these scores were entered, there was a significant increase in explained variance, $F(\text{change}) = 4.70$, $p < .02$. The overall regression equation likewise remained statistically significant at this step, Adj. $R^2 = .38$, $F(4,27) = 5.65$, $p < .01$. Finally, at Step 3, scores on the remaining social understanding variables (VPT, GR, FR) were entered. As a group, these additional variables failed to enhance the prediction of variability in children's TFB scores, although the overall equation remained significant, Adj. $R^2 = .32$, $F(7,24) = 3.06$, $p < .02$. Table 8.2 shows the beta weights and t values for each of the predictor variables in the full model at Step 3. Inspection of these indicates that only the desire perspective-taking (DPT) scores continued to make a significant and independent contribution to the prediction of unique variance in false-belief understanding at this final step.

In other words, for deaf and hearing children alike, levels of success in understanding concepts of false belief appear to be linked with the somewhat earlier developing ability to pass desire perspective-taking tests in which the children must set aside their own egocentric wants/preferences in order to predict a protagonist's atypical desires.

DISCUSSION

These results support much previous research, as referenced earlier, by showing that yet another sample of signing deaf children from hearing families had serious difficulties with the concepts of false belief that are often deemed to be litmus tests for a theory of mind. The performance of these deaf children on a battery of false-belief tests was significantly lower than that of children with

TABLE 8.2. Results (Full Model at Step 3) of Hierarchical Multiple Regression Equation Predicting False-Belief Understanding

Predictor variables	B	SE(B)	Beta	t	Significance
Hearing status group	−.894	.552	−.413	−1.620	$p = 118$
Age	.006	.085	.183	.726	$p = .475$
Desire (DPT) score	.661	.273	.399	2.420	$p = .023$[a]
Emotion (EPT) score	.325	.284	.206	1.145	$p = .263$
Gaze reading	.001	.350	.004	.023	$p = .982$
Visual (VPT) score	.355	.626	.096	.567	$p = .576$
Face reading	−.266	.429	−.135	−.621	$p = .541$

[a] Significant.

normal hearing who were approximately 5 years younger. Although many explanations for the lag are conceivable, restricted exposure to conversation while growing up in an exclusively hearing family is a plausible contributing factor. Severe hearing impairments in conjunction with the absence of native fluent signers is likely to hamper conversation with hearing family members, especially about inner experiences like emotions, desires, fantasies, and true or false beliefs that may have no immediately obvious physical referent (Marschark, 1993). Thus, the present group of deaf children may have lacked the opportunities often available to hearing preschoolers in hearing–speaking families for querying, commenting on, or justifying seemingly false or deviant beliefs, feelings, and desires.

This could also help to explain why the deaf elementary school children in the present sample, despite having no difficulty reading emotions and preferences from facial expressions, were less skilled than the hearing 4-year-olds at using this information about others' feelings to pass the emotion and desire perspective-taking tests. In order to succeed on these latter tasks, children had to set aside their own points of view and consider the diversity of people's affective states in order to predict how other people's atypical wants and unexpected emotional reactions would direct their behavior. It seems that simply recognizing a preference for something on a person's face goes only part of the way toward enabling their actions to be anticipated. Deaf children who succeeded perfectly at face reading still had difficulty inferring both atypical desires and the behavioral consequences of false beliefs. Possibly something like a "desire psychology" (Wellman, 1993) is also necessary in order for children to make accurate sense of people's atypical behavior. In other words, a child may need a systematically organized conceptual framework of possible reasons *why* a person could have atypical affective reactions (e.g., loving carrots while hating candy), to be able to confidently predict how such unexpected taste preferences will translate themselves into behavior (like rejecting a gift of candy).

If so, then the signing deaf children's more limited understanding could reflect their restricted exposure to family discourse in which causes for emotions, desires, and true or false beliefs are openly commented on, discussed, and explained. Gregory (1976) reported that explanations of actions and emotional reactions were much less frequent and much less competent between deaf offspring and their hearing parents as compared with the case where the parent was also deaf. Consequently, while growing up in a hearing family, deaf children may often miss out on the causal conversations about internal states that Dunn (1991, 1995) identified in hearing families with hearing preschoolers (e.g., "Why is she sad?"; "Why don't you like to eat ice cream before dinner?"; etc.). Indeed, Dunn (1994) found a dramatic increase in the frequency of these kinds of conversations among hearing preschoolers with mothers and siblings over the period from 33 to 40 months, just before the normal age for passing standard ToM tests. As Dunn (1991) explained: "One inference from these findings is that children use their intelligence on what matters most to them emotionally. . . . In real life, the emotional state of the child, the salience of the topic and the mother's articulation of reasons and excuses are closely linked in the children's experience. . . . It could well be that it is this combination of a powerful cognitive and affective experience that contributes to children's developing grasp of the way social rules and others' behavior are linked" (p. 110). But for a deaf child in a hearing family, the lack of a fluently shared language in which to discuss these kinds of inner emotional or mental states may block this important early window into a representational understanding of both desire and belief.

Indeed, although the discrepancy between the deaf and hearing groups in this study was not as great on the desire and emotion perspective-taking tests as on the tests of false belief, the former tasks did nonetheless pose somewhat more difficulty for the deaf elementary school children than for the hearing preschoolers (see Figure 8.2). Possibly the developmental sequence from desire–reasoning to subsequent belief–reasoning is the same for deaf and hearing children. However, both of these social cognitive milestones appear to be somewhat delayed for the deaf group. Thus, although more than two-thirds of the hearing children had already mastered false belief and desire and emotion perspective-taking by age 4, the deaf children were just beginning to succeed on the affective perspective taking tasks at a mean age of 9 years, and most of them had not yet begun to comprehend concepts of false belief. The fact that only about half of these deaf elementary school children managed to pass each of the desire perspective-taking questions (see Figure 8.2) suggests that their sociocognitive delays were more pervasive than simply the problems with the syntax of embedded ("Thinks that . . .") questions that were highlighted by deVilliers (2000).

In fact, there is some empirical evidence to suggest that hearing preschoolers do acquire a representational understanding of desire ahead of a representational understanding of belief. Gopnik and Slaughter (1991) presented 3-year-olds with representational change problems involving either obsolete desires or their own obsolete beliefs that changed circumstances had rendered false. Many of the children who failed the tests of representational change that were based on false belief were able to pass them in relation to changed desires by, for example, correctly recalling which book they had initially wanted to look at even after the satiation of this desire had caused them to want to see a different one. Flavell, Flavell, Green, and Moses (1990) likewise found that 3-year-olds were significantly better at predicting the behavior of an adult who had deviant preferences, or "value beliefs" (such as thinking that a wilted flower was prettier than a fresh one), than they were at predicting her behavior when her factual beliefs were false (e.g., she falsely thought a Band-Aid box contained Band-Aids). However, not all of the evidence from hearing children supports this ordering of relative difficulty. Flavell, Mumme, Green, and Flavell (1992) failed to replicate the value/fact belief discrepancy using an explicit belief test with picture stories. Only 44% of the 3-year-olds they tested passed simple questions requiring them to report the explicitly stated value belief of a story character when this differed from their own ("Sally thinks it is fun to eat grass. Does Sally think it is fun or not fun to eat grass?"). Despite the seeming simplicity of this task, 3-years-olds did no better on it than on standard tests of factual false beliefs. Similarly, Cutting and Dunn (1999) found that hearing preschoolers' skills at identifying the name or facial expression of puppets' feelings in an emotion perspective-taking test portraying typical and atypical emotions (e.g., sadness versus joy, respectively, after having a bad dream), were highly correlated with their age and their scores on tests of language ability and false belief. However, the results of regression analyses indicated that once the influences of age, language, and family background were partialed out, emotion understanding did not contribute uniquely to variance in false-belief understanding, nor vice versa. In other words, as the authors noted: "False-belief and emotion understanding are distinct aspects of social cognition . . . [with] different precursors and sequelae" (p. 863) that happen to develop simultaneously in normal children as they grow older and gain skill in language. This suggestion is consistent with the present finding that, unlike desire perspective-taking, emotion perspective-taking did not contribute uniquely to variability in children's false-belief understanding once effects of age and hearing status were taken into account.

Further research, ideally employing a longitudinal methodology and additional kinds of tests of the understanding of both emotion and desire in deaf and hearing children, is now clearly called for. More information is also needed on deaf children's understanding of representational diversity involving atypical emotions and desires relative to false belief. Such evidence would be needed before firm conclusions could be drawn about their developmental order or timing in children with different kinds and levels of language skill. Yet the finding that many of the deaf children in the present study found it quite hard to take the perspectives of characters with unconventional desires, despite using largely nonverbal measures, is in keeping with Rieffe and Meerum Terwogt's (2000) observations. Using the narrative-justification test described earlier in which children had to explain a story character's atypical emotions, these authors found that those who were deaf, more often than those who were hearing children, simply refused to accept story information involving atypical emotions, perseverating instead on the typical emotional response irrespective of contradictions within the story (e.g., by insisting that a character who was not allowed to go to the zoo would be angry and would desire to go, even though the story had portrayed her as happy not to be going). Rieffe and Meerum Terwogt noted, "They [deaf children] get stuck on Linda's [the protagonist's] initial desire without much consideration of external factors that may have caused this situation" (p. 606), and suggested that this could conceivably explain the acting-out behavior problems and difficulties with peer relationships that older deaf elementary school and high school children sometimes encounter (Gregory, 1976), especially in mainstream school settings where they lack playmates fluent in sign. On the other hand, Marschark (1993) reports that signing deaf children who attend signing residential schools for the deaf develop social skills and social cooperation relatively normally. As Marschark explained: "Within this setting, the normal demands for achievement, prosocial behavior, cooperation, and morality are communicated by a somewhat different means than previously available: via identification and modeling of similar peers" (p. 71). Opportunities to converse and discuss conflicting viewpoints with deaf peers in sign language can also have important benefits for the deaf children's social-cognitive development. Peterson and Peterson (1989, 1990) observed gains in signing deaf children's social understanding of perspective taking and distributive justice as a result of a sociocognitive conflict intervention in which they had to debate the solutions to problems with deaf peers in order to arrive at mutually acceptable solutions.

The present findings suggest that the high levels of skill at gaze reading and discerning emotions in faces that the deaf children in this sample were already displaying might eventually prove to be of assistance in their development of an understanding of the atypical wants and feelings of others, even in the face of restricted opportunities to converse with hearing family members about emotion and desire. To the extent that peer interaction over conflicting desires may arise spontaneously among signing deaf peers on the school playground, these conversational experiences could likewise help to boost desire perspective-taking skills for deaf children in Total Communication schools like the one that we studied. In its turn, the development of desire perspective-taking may promote the growth of false-belief understanding and, ultimately, a full-fledged ToM.

As Dunn's (1991, 1994) research has shown, emotionally charged situations and conversations about the causes for atypical feelings are frequent occurrences in hearing–speaking families and "given the adaptive importance of understanding the emotional state of someone with whom one shares a family world" (p. 112), it is certainly not surprising that preschoolers' frequent participation in these dialogues is linked with their more advanced social understanding. Deaf children may have restricted access to such experiences when they grow up in hearing families. However, social contact with signing peers may eventually provide a substitute, at least among those deaf children who enter a community of native speakers of sign language in elementary school. Indeed, emotions and desires, both typical and atypical, are clearly bound up in much of a child's spontaneous social interaction with other children. Consequently, the provision to deaf children of frequent social interaction opportunities, especially chances to interact with signing deaf classmates who share their native language, may be uniquely beneficial. Given deaf children's active social interest and normal sociability, in contrast to children with autism (deVilliers, 2000), peer interaction holds special promise as compensation for restricted early conversational experience at home. Thus, peers may be especially beneficial for deaf children in stimulating the growth of the kind of social cognitive awareness of others' minds and feelings that is needed both to pass standard false-belief tasks in the laboratory, and to enjoy the rewards of empathy, friendship, and mutuality in daily life.

Moreover, it is likely that for hearing children, as well as those who are deaf, peer relations, with their egalitarian power structures and frequent possibilities for intense positive emotion (as in play and humor) and intense negative feelings (as in conflict and social exclusion), may supply unique insights beyond those available in interaction with teachers and parents, thus explaining findings, for example, that children with many closely spaced siblings do better on false-belief tests than only children (Jenkins & Astington, 1996; Peterson, 2001) and that those who are popular with their peers are more advanced in ToM than those who suffer peer rejection (Peterson & Siegal, 2002; Repacholi, Slaughter, Pritchard, & Gibbs, this volume).

Further studies are now warranted, ideally incorporating observational techniques and longitudinal methodologies, in order to confirm patterns tentatively sketched by the present findings and to more fully clarify the directions of causal influence among hearing impairment, conversational experience, social interaction, and interconnected aspects of cognitions about emotions, desires, and false beliefs. It will also be important in future research to compare and contrast the developmental courses of deaf children's mastery of perspectives on others' emotions, desires, and beliefs with those of children who have blindness, mental retardation, and autism in order to gain a fuller understanding of the ways in which the social and conversational consequences of different disabilities may interact with varying courses of sensory experience and neurocognitive maturation in the development of social cognition.

REFERENCES

Astington, J. W. (2001). The future of theory of mind research: Understanding motivational states, the role of language and real-world consequences. *Child Development, 72,* 685–687.

Baron-Cohen, S. (1995). *Mindblindness.* Cambridge, MA: MIT Press.

Baron-Cohen, S. (2000). Theory of mind and autism. In S. Baron-Cohen, H. Tager-Flusberg, & D. Cohen (Eds.), *Understanding other minds: Perspectives from developmental cognitive neuroscience* (pp. 3–20). Oxford: Oxford University Press.

Baron-Cohen, S., Campbell, R., Karmiloff-Smith, A., & Grant, J. (1995). Are children with autism blind to the mentalistic significance of the eyes? *British Journal of Developmental Psychology, 13,* 379–398.

Baron-Cohen, S., Leslie, A. M., & Frith, U. (1985). Does the autistic child have a theory of mind? *Cognition, 21,* 37–46.

Baron-Cohen, S., Tager-Flusberg, H., & Cohen, D. (2000). *Understanding other minds: Perspectives from developmental cognitive neuroscience.* Oxford: Oxford University Press.

Campos, J., & Sternberg, C. R . (1981). Perception, appraisal and emotions: The onset of social referencing. In M. Lamb & L. Sherrod (Eds.), *Infant social cognition* (pp. 273–314). Hillsdale, NJ: Lawrence Erlbaum.

Courtin, C., & Melot, A. M. (1998). Development of theories of mind in deaf children. In M. Marschark & M. Clark (Eds.), *Psychological perspectives on deafness* (pp. 79–102). Hillsdale, NJ: Lawrence Erlbaum.

Cutting, A. L., & Dunn, J. (1999). Theory of mind, emotion understanding, language, and family background: Individual differences and interrelations. *Child Development, 70,* 853–865.

deVilliers, J. (2000). Language and theory of mind: What are the developmental relationships? In S. Baron-Cohen, H. Tager-Flusberg, & D. Cohen (Eds.), *Understanding other minds: Perspectives from developmental cognitive neuroscience* (2nd ed., pp. 83–122). Oxford: Oxford University Press.

de Villiers, J., & de Villiers, P. (2000). Linguistic determinism and the understanding of false beliefs. In P. Mitchell & K. Riggs (Eds.), *Children's reasoning and the mind* (pp. 191–228). Hove, UK: Psychology Press.

Dunn, J. (1991). Young children's understanding of other people. In D. Frye & C. Moore (Eds.), *Children's theories of mind* (pp. 97–114). Hillsdale, NJ: Lawrence Erlbaum.

Dunn, J. (1994). Changing minds and changing relationships. In C. Lewis & P. Mitchell (Eds.), *Origins of an understanding of mind* (pp. 297–310). Hove, UK: Lawrence Erlbaum.

Dunn, J. (1995). Children as psychologists—The later correlates of individual differences in understanding of emotions and other minds. *Cognition and Emotion, 9,* 187–201.

Dunn, J. (1996). The Emanuel Miller Memorial Lecture: 1995. *Journal of Child Psychology and Psychiatry, 37,* 507–518.

Dunn, L. M., & Dunn, L. M. (1981). *Peabody Picture Vocabulary Test–Revised.* Circle Pines, MN: American Guidance Service.

Ekman, P. (1994). Strong evidence for universals in facial expressions: A reply to Russell's mistaken critique. *Psychological Bulletin, 115,* 268–287.

Field, T., Woodson, R., Greenberg, R., & Cohen, D. (1982). Discrimination and imitation of facial expression by neonates. *Science, 218,* 179–181.

Flavell, J. H. (1999). Cognitive development. *Annual Review of Psychology, 50,* 21–45.

Flavell, J. H., Everett, B., Croft, K., & Flavell, E. (1981). Young children's knowledge about visual perception. *Developmental Psychology, 17,* 99–103.

Flavell, J. H., Flavell, E. R., Green, F. L., & Moses, L. J. (1990). Young children's understanding of fact beliefs versus value beliefs. *Child Development, 61,* 915–928.

Flavell, J. H., Mumme, D. L., Green, F. L., & Flavell, E. R. (1992). Young children's understanding of moral and other beliefs. *Child Development, 63,* 960–977.

Frith, U. (1989). *Autism: Explaining the enigma.* Oxford: Oxford University Press.

Garfield, J. L., Peterson, C. C., & Perry, T. (2001). Social cognition, language acquisition and the development of theory of mind. *Mind & Language, 16,* 494–541.

Gopnik, A., & Slaughter, V. P. (1991). Young children's understanding of changes in their mental states. *Child Development, 62,* 98–110.

Gopnik, A., Slaughter, V. P., & Meltzoff, A. (1994). Changing your views: How understanding visual perception can lead to a theory of mind. In C. Lewis & P. Mitchell (Eds.), *Origins of an understanding of mind* (pp. 157–181). Hove, UK: Lawrence Erlbaum.

Gregory, S. (1976). *The deaf child and his family.* New York: Halsted Press.

Happé, F. (1995). The role of age and verbal ability in ToM performance of children with autism. *Child Development, 66,* 843–855.

Harris, P. L. (1989). *Children and emotion.* Oxford: Blackwell.

Harris, P. L. (1996). Desires, beliefs and language. In P. Carruthers & P. K. Smith (Eds.), *Theories of theories of mind* (pp. 200–220). Cambridge: Cambridge University Press.

Jenkins, J. M., & Astington, J. W. (1996). Cognitive factors and family structure associated with theory of mind development in young children. *Developmental Psychology, 32,* 70–78.

Marschark, M. (1993). *Psychological development of deaf children.* New York: Oxford University Press.

Masangkay, Z. S., McClusky, K. A., McIntyre, C. W., Sims-Knight, J., Vaughn, B. E., & Flavell, J. H. (1974). The early development of inferences about the visual percepts of others. *Child Development, 45,* 237–246.

McAlpine, L. M., & Moore, C. L. (1995). The development of social understanding in children with visual impairments. *Journal of Visual Impairment and Blindness, 89,* 349–358.

Minter, M., Hobson, R. P., & Bishop, M. (1998). Congenital visual impairment and theory of mind. *British Journal of Developmental Psychology, 16,* 183–196.

Peterson, C. C. (2001). Kindred spirits: Influences of siblings' perspectives on the child's development of a theory of mind. *Cognitive Development, 15,* 435–455.

Peterson, C. C., & Peterson, J. L. (1989). Positive justice reasoning in deaf and hearing children before and after exposure to cognitive conflict. *American Annals of the Deaf, 134,* 277–282.

Peterson, C. C., & Peterson, J. L. (1990). Sociocognitive conflict and spatial perspective-taking in deaf children. *Journal of Applied Developmental Psychology, 11,* 267–281.

Peterson, C., Peterson, J., & Webb, J. (2000). Factors influencing the development of a theory of mind in blind children. *British Journal of Developmental Psychology, 18,* 431–447.

Peterson, C. C., & Siegal, M. (1995). Deafness, conversation and theory of mind. *Journal of Child Psychology and Psychiatry, 36,* 459–474.

Peterson, C., & Siegal, M. (1998). Changing focus on the representational mind. *British Journal of Developmental Psychology, 16,* 301–320.

Peterson, C. C., & Siegal, M. (1999). Representing inner worlds: Theory of mind in autistic, deaf and normal hearing children. *Psychological Science, 10,* 126–129.

Peterson, C. C., & Siegal, M. (2000). Insights into a theory of mind from deafness and autism. *Mind and Language, 15,* 123–145.

Peterson, C., & Siegal, M. (2002). Mindreading and moral awareness in popular and rejected preschoolers. *British Journal of Developmental Psychology, 20,* 205–224.

Peterson, C., Webb, J., & Peterson, J. (2000). Factors influencing the development of a theory of mind in blind children. *British Journal of Developmental Psychology, 18,* 431–447.

Piaget, J. (1970). Piaget's theory. In P. H. Mussen (Ed.), *Carmichael's manual of child psychology* (pp. 703–732). New York: Wiley.

Reed, T., & Peterson, C. (1990). A comparative study of autistic subjects' performance at two levels of visual and cognitive perspective-taking. *Journal of Autism and Developmental Disorders, 20,* 555–567.

Remmel, E., Bettger, J., & Weinberg, A. (1998, November). *The impact of ASL on theory of mind.* Paper presented at the meeting of TIRSL 6, Washington D.C.

Repacholi, B. M., & Gopnik, A. (1997). Early reasoning about desires: Evidence from 14- and 18-month-olds. *Developmental Psychology, 33,* 12–21.

Rieffe, C. & Meerum Terwogt, M. (2000). Deaf children's understanding of emotions: Desires take precedence. *Journal of Child Psychology and Psychiatry, 41,* 601–608.

Siegal, M. (1997). *Knowing children: Experiments in conversation and cognition* (2nd ed.). Hove, UK: Psychology Press.

Scott, C., Russell, P., Gray, C., Hosie, J., & Hunter, N. (1999). The interpretation of line of regard by prelingually deaf children. *Social Development, 8,* 4512–425.

Wellman, H. M. (1993). Early understanding of mind: The normal case. In S. Baron-Cohen, H. Tager-Flusberg, & D. Cohen (Eds.), *Understanding other minds* (pp. 10–39). Oxford: Oxford University Press.

Wellman, H. M., Cross, D., & Watson, J. (2000). The truth about false belief. *Child Development, 72,* 655–684.

Yirmiya, N., Erel, O., Shaked, M., & Solomonica-Levi, D. (1998). Meta-analyses comparing theory of mind abilities of individuals with autism, mental retardation and normally developing individuals. *Psychological Bulletin, 124,* 283–307.

9

Exploring the Relationship Between Theory of Mind and Social-Communicative Functioning in Children with Autism

HELEN TAGER-FLUSBERG

Boston University

O ne of the most productive areas in theory-of-mind research has explored the hypothesis that children with autism have fundamental and specific deficits in this domain (Baron-Cohen, Tager-Flusberg, & Cohen, 1993, 2000). This hypothesis has been used to explain the core impairments in both social functioning and communication, which constitute two of the major symptoms of this disorder (Baron-Cohen, 1988; Frith, 1989; Happé, 1994). Since the initial demonstration by Baron-Cohen and his colleagues that the majority of children with autism fail the standard false-belief task (Baron-Cohen, Leslie, & Frith, 1985), many studies have confirmed the finding that children with autism have difficulty with a wide variety of theory-of-mind tasks (Baron-Cohen, 2000). Nevertheless, there has been relatively little research that has explicitly examined the relationship between theory-of-mind deficits and the core symptoms or severity of impairments in autism.

From the earliest reports on the theory-of-mind deficit in autism, the emphasis was on the theoretical significance of this deficit in providing a cognitive explanation for a range of symptoms that characterize the syndrome, especially deficits in social interaction and communication (Baron-Cohen, 1988; Frith, 1989; Happé, 1994). The theory-of-mind hypothesis of autism (cf. Baron-Cohen et al., 1993, 2000) was especially important in that it was able to account not only for the impairments that define the syndrome, but also for aspects of cognitive functioning that were spared. Thus, a single cognitive mechanism could explain the selective and specific impairments that define this neurodevelopmental disorder. Despite the potential significance of the explanatory power of the theory-of-mind hypothesis, surprisingly little research has been conducted with the goal of providing a direct and explicit empirical test of this hypothesis. In our current research, we have been investigating theory of mind in autism, with a view toward testing three important hypotheses that emerge from this theory. Specifically, we predict that in children with autism, performance on theory-of-mind tasks will be directly related to measures of social functioning, pragmatic and communicative behavior, and severity of autistic impairment.

PRIOR RESEARCH ON THE THEORY-OF-MIND HYPOTHESIS OF AUTISM

The most obvious place to search for links between theory of mind and autistic symptoms is in relation to the cardinal feature of social impairment. In everyday life, people with autism have great difficulty in engaging in social interactions and developing peer relationships, and they show severe limitations in social and emotional reciprocity in their relationships with other people. Several studies have investigated whether these real-life social problems are directly related to underlying impairments in theory of mind.

Frith and her colleagues examined the relationship between performance on false-belief tasks and scores on a parent report standardized measure of social functioning, the Socialization subscale on the Vineland Adaptive Behavior Scales, and an unnormed set of "Interactive Sociability" items, which all required "mentalizing" skills, according to the authors (Frith, Happé, & Siddons, 1994). For the 24 children with autism in their study, who ranged in age from 7 to 19 years old, false-belief performance was not significantly related to Socialization scores; however, the Interactive Sociability scale did significantly discriminate between children who passed or failed false-belief tasks. These findings were replicated by Fombonne and colleagues; however, the relationship between false belief and the Interactive Sociability scale was no longer significant after age and verbal ability were factored into the analysis (Fombonne, Siddons, Achard, Frith, & Happé, 1994). More recently, Travis, Sigman, and Ruskin (2001) failed to find a relationship between false-belief understanding and observational measures of social behavior at recess on the playground in a group of 8- to 18-year-old children with autism. Taken together, these studies do not provide compelling evidence for the theory-of-mind hypothesis linking theory of mind to everyday social behavior.

Evidence in the domain of language and communication is also sparse.

Although many researchers have argued that deficits in pragmatics and discourse reflect theory-of-mind impairment in autism (e.g., Baron-Cohen, 1988; Loveland & Tunali, 1993; Tager-Flusberg, 1992, 1996; Tager-Flusberg & Anderson, 1991), only one study has directly examined links between discourse and theory of mind among children with autism. Capps, Kehres, and Sigman (1998) found a significant relationship among 15 children with autism between false-belief performance and the ability to contribute new information in conversation with an examiner, but as in the studies on social functioning, this relationship was no longer significant after the effects of language were partialed out.

Taken together, these studies do *not* provide strong evidence for the theory-of-mind hypothesis of autism, despite more than 15 years of research on this topic. Several methodological limitations can be identified in these earlier studies. First, they included very small numbers of children with autism, suggesting that they may lack the statistical power to detect hypothesized links between theory of mind and core symptoms in autism. Second, these small samples included children of widely varying ages and ability, which may also have obscured the ability to detect significant relationships. This is a particular concern given that language is strongly related to both theory of mind and to autistic social and communicative impairments. In those studies where language was covaried, significant relationships were eliminated (e.g., Capps et al., 1998; Fombonne et al., 1994). Finally, in these studies, theory of mind is defined in a narrow and limited way. All of the studies rely exclusively on first-order false-belief tasks, which are designed to assess developmental changes that take place between 3 and 5 years of age in normally developing children (cf. Wellman, Cross, & Watson, 2001). Although the initial emphasis in studies on theory of mind focused on representational changes that take place during the preschool years, when children become capable of understanding that minds are opaque, the past decade has witnessed a broadening of the developmental perspective on theory of mind. Research has demonstrated that developments in mental state knowledge begin during infancy and continue through middle childhood and early adolescence (e.g., Perner, 1988; Wellman & Lagattuta, 2000); however, this broader perspective on theory of mind has not been incorporated in studies addressing the theory-of-mind hypothesis of autism. Perhaps the measures of social or communicative functioning that are used in the studies summarized here are more closely tied to theory-of-mind developments that occur over a wider developmental span than is captured on false-belief tasks.

CURRENT RESEARCH PROGRAM

We are currently engaged in a large-scale longitudinal study of theory of mind in children with autism. The data I report in this chapter are drawn from the first year of this investigation, during which we collected a wide variety of standardized and experimental measures of diagnostic, social, cognitive, and linguistic functioning. The specific questions that are addressed in this chapter include:

1. Is there a relationship between everyday social functioning, as assessed by the Vineland Adaptive Behavior Scales and theory-of-mind ability in children with autism?
2. Are there specific links between certain aspects of discourse ability and theory of mind in children with autism?
3. Does performance on theory-of-mind tasks predict the severity of symptoms in children with autism?

At the start of the project, we enrolled 69 children with autism, including 60 boys and 9 girls, who were all between the ages of 4 and 14 years old. These children all had some spontaneous language, although they varied widely on standardized measures of vocabulary, syntax, and semantics (cf. Kjelgaard & Tager-Flusberg, 2001). The diagnosis of autism was made objectively on the basis of two instruments: the Autism Diagnostic Interview—Revised (Lord, Rutter, & LeCouteur, 1994) and the Autism Diagnostic Observation Schedule (Lord, Rutter, DiLavore, & Risi, 1999; Lord et al., 2000). The children were also clinically confirmed to meet *DSM–IV* (APA, 1994) criteria for autism by experienced clinicians who observed and interacted with them over the course of their assessments.

The children's IQ was assessed using the Differential Ability Scales (DAS; Elliott, 1990) using either the preschool or school-age version. For children assessed within age level, full-scale, verbal and nonverbal standardized scores were available. A comprehensive language battery was administered to each child. Because vocabulary scores, as assessed by the Peabody Picture Vocabulary Test–III (PPVT; Dunn & Dunn, 1997) and the Expressive Vocabulary Test (EVT; Williams, 1997), correlate highly in this group of children with other language measures including omnibus tests of higher order language such as the Clinical Evaluation of Language Fundamentals (see Kjelgaard & Tager-Flusberg, 2001), we used a combined receptive and expressive vocabulary score based on the PPVT and EVT as a measure of general language ability.

To assess theory-of-mind ability, we assembled a series of 10 tasks designed to be developmentally sensitive across the age range of the children in the study. The tasks were sequenced into three batteries, tapping early, middle, and more advanced aspects of theory of mind, and children were always given all the tasks within each battery. All children were administered the early battery. If children were able to perform well on at least one task in this battery (Tasks 1–2), they were given the middle battery (Tasks 3–6), which included several false-belief tasks. Children who passed at least one false-belief task were also administered the advanced battery (Tasks 7–10). Each task included both control and test questions. Children received points for each task, based on the number of key test questions that were answered correctly. Theory-of-mind scores summed across all tasks could range from 0 to 56.

THEORY-OF-MIND TASKS

1. *Pretend:* This task tested the ability to use a doll as an independent agent in a pretend scenario. The task included four vignettes involving a mother and baby. Children were asked to complete each vignette by using the mother doll to act out the next logical event in a scenario (e.g., bathing the baby) initiated by the experimenter (Kavanaugh, Eizenman, & Harris, 1997).

2. *Desire:* This task tested the ability to predict action based on an agent's stated desire. In the stories, the main character is looking for an object, which could be in one of two named locations. The character fails to find the desired object in the first location. The test questions ask whether the character will continue to search, and why (Wellman & Wooley, 1990).

3. *Perception/Knowledge:* This task tested the ability to infer knowledge from perceptual access. On each trial, children observed one doll who looked in a box and another doll who simply touched the box, and were then asked whether one of the dolls knew what was in the box (Pratt & Bryant, 1990).

4. *Location-Change False Belief:* This task included stories in which an object is moved while the main character is absent. Children were asked knowledge, prediction, and justification questions (Wimmer & Perner, 1983).

5. *Unexpected-Contents False Belief:* Children were shown familiar containers that had unexpected objects inside. Test questions included representational change and false-belief questions (Perner, Leekam & Wimmer, 1987).

6. *Sticker Hiding:* This task required the child to hide a sticker in one hand, while the experimenter guessed its location. The experimenter's wrong answers resulted in the child keeping the sticker. The ability to hide the sticker from the experimenter and to engage in deceptive strategies were scored (Devries, 1970).

7. *Second-Order False Belief:* Children were told stories in which a child character is to receive a surprise gift from a parent. Unbeknownst to the parent, the child inadvertently finds the object. Second-order ignorance, belief, and justification questions tapped children's ability to judge what the parent thinks/knows about what the child thinks/knows (Sullivan, Zaitchik, & Tager-Flusberg, 1994).

8. *Lies and Jokes:* This task tested the ability to distinguish between lies and ironic jokes (or sarcasm). In each story, one character utters a literal falsehood that another character knows to be false. To distinguish a joke from a lie, children had to take into account whether the first character knows that

the second character knows the truth. Test questions included judging the false statement as a lie or joke and justifying the answer (Sullivan, Winner, & Hopfield, 1995).

9. *Traits:* This task tested children's ability to judge intent on the basis of personality traits. Children were told stories in which one of two characters is described in terms of a personality trait. Each story ends with a negative outcome of ambiguous intent. Test questions tapped the ability to use the trait information to judge whether the outcome was intended or accidental (Yuill, 1992).

10. *Moral Commitment:* Children were told stories in which two friends make plans to meet. In each story, the main character fails to come to the planned meeting either as a result of canceling the plans without telling the other character or as a result of an uncontrollable event. At the end of each story, children were asked to make a moral judgment and to justify their response (Mant & Perner, 1988).

THE RELATIONSHIP BETWEEN THEORY OF MIND AND SOCIAL FUNCTIONING IN AUTISM

To address the question about the relationship between theory of mind and everyday social abilities in children with autism, we used the Vineland Adaptive Behavior Scales to provide an objective and standardized assessment of socialization skills (see also Fombonne et al., 1994; Frith et al., 1994). This instrument is designed to assess adaptive skills from birth through 18 years old (Sparrow, Balla, & Cicchetti, 1984), and supplementary norms for individuals with autism are available (Carter et al., 1998), which provide age-referenced scores in three subdomains: Daily Living Skills, Communication, and Socialization. The expanded version of the interview form was administered to one or both parents of each child in the project by a trained examiner.

Complete data on both theory of mind and the Vineland were available for 67 children with autism in the original sample. For this group, standard scores (with a mean of 100 and a standard deviation of 15) on each subdomain of the Vineland were as follows: Daily Living Skills = 63, Communication = 75, and Socialization = 67. We conducted a stepwise regression analysis to explore which variables best predicted the children's scores on each of these subdomains. For this analysis, raw scores on the Vineland were used, and the predictor variables that were entered in the regression analyses were IQ, language (using the combined PPVT and EVT raw scores), and theory of mind. For both Daily Living Skills (R^2 = .45; $F(1,65)$ = 53.1, p < .001) and Communication (R^2 = .33; $F(1,65)$ = 32.7, p < .001), language was the only significant predictor variable; neither IQ nor theory of mind contributed any additional significant variance to these scores. In contrast, theory of mind was the single best predictor of Socialization scores in this group of children with autism, R^2 = .18; $F(1,65)$ = 14.5, p < .001.

These findings provide support for the hypothesis that theory of mind is significantly related to everyday social functioning in children with autism, as assessed by the Vineland Socialization scale. This relationship held even when language ability was included in the analysis, overturning earlier studies, which had failed to support the theory-of-mind hypothesis of autism. The inclusion of a developmental measure of theory of mind and a much larger sample of children with autism probably accounts for the differences in the findings.

THE RELATIONSHIP BETWEEN THEORY OF MIND AND DISCOURSE IN AUTISM

Research on theory of mind in normally developing preschoolers has included investigations of how children talk about the mind. Studies by Bartsch and Wellman (1995), for example, have systematically examined children's use of mental state words such as *think*, *know*, or *believe*, as a measure of their knowledge of the mind. Children with autism make significantly less reference to cognitive mental states than matched control subjects both in conversation with their mothers (Tager-Flusberg, 1992) and in narrative tasks (Baron-Cohen, Leslie, & Frith, 1986). These findings have been taken as evidence that such deficits in discourse about the mind reflect deficits in theory of mind; however, these studies did not directly examine the relationship between discourse and formal theory-of-mind tasks.

As part of our research project, we collected a natural language sample from each child while they played informally with one of their parents for 30 minutes with a standard set of developmentally appropriate toys. The language samples were collected in the laboratory and were both audiotaped and videotaped through a one-way mirror. The language samples were transcribed using the SALT transcription format (Miller & Chapman, 2000) by a team of research assistants trained in transcription procedures. Transcripts were prepared by one person and checked by a second trained transcriber using the audio and video recordings. All transcription disagreements were resolved through consensus. For this investigation we had complete data from the language samples and the theory-of-mind tasks from 58 children in the study.

A corpus of 100 consecutive, complete and intelligible, nonimitative child utterances was selected from each transcript to compute standard measures. These included mean length of utterance in morphemes (MLU; Brown, 1973), a measure of grammatical complexity, and number of different word roots, a measure of lexical diversity. The complete transcripts were used for coding the presence of mental words in the child's speech. The word lists used for this coding scheme were derived from Tager-Flusberg (1992) and the coding rules were based on those used by Shatz and her colleagues (Shatz, Wellman, & Silber, 1983) and elaborated by Bartsch and Wellman (1995). All child utterances that included a mental word drawn from three categories, desire, emotion, and

TABLE 9.1. Use of Mental Words and Reference
to Mental States

| | Frequency per 100 utterances | |
Category	Mean	Standard deviation
Desire		
Total words	6.0	8.5
Mental state reference	1.1	3.8
Emotion		
Total words	3.4	3.3
Mental state reference	0.6	1.4
Cognition		
Total words	9.3	9.8
Mental state reference	1.2	2.0

cognition were identified. Utterances that were full or partial repetitions or imitations, or that were quotes from songs, stories, and so forth, were excluded from further analysis. Two measures of mental word use were computed within each category. The first measure was the total number of utterances that included a mental word from that category. These utterances included idioms, conversational uses of such words, references to mental states, and all unclear uses. The second measure was the number of utterances that referred directly to mental state, a subset of the utterances in the first measure. Table 9.1 shows the frequency per 100 utterances of total mental words and reference to mental states in each category.

We then computed correlations between these measures and other variables, including age, IQ, language measures (including standardized vocabulary scores and measures from the natural language samples), and theory of mind, for the 58 children in the sample. For the use of desire and emotion words and reference to these mental states, none of the correlations were statistically significant. In contrast, most of these variables correlated significantly with the total number of cognition words and reference to cognitive mental states, as shown in Table 9.2.

TABLE 9.2. Correlations for Children's Talk About Cognition

	Total cognition words	Reference to cognitive mental states
Age	.40°°	.52°°
Full-scale IQ	.30°	.25
Nonverbal IQ	.20	.07
Vocabulary (PPVT + EVT)	.21	.29
MLU	.57°°	.53°°
Lexical diversity	.54°°	.52°°
Theory of mind	.51°°	.63°°

Note. Significance: °$p < .05$; °°$p < .01$.

The main hypothesis that was tested in this study concerned the relationship between discourse about cognitive mental states and theory-of-mind ability. Because use of cognition words and reference to cognitive mental states were both significantly correlated with age, IQ, and general language measures derived from the language samples, we used hierarchical regression analyses to address this issue. The first regression analysis looked at the predictors of the total use of cognition words. On the initial step of the regression analysis, age, IQ, MLU, and lexical diversity were entered. Together, these variables accounted for 43% of the variance, and were highly significant, $F(4,52) = 9.7$, $p < .0001$. On the next step, the theory-of-mind score was entered; however, this did not explain any additional variance and was not a statistically significant predictor for the total number of utterances containing a cognition word. The same analysis was conducted for the actual reference to cognitive mental states. On the first step, age, MLU, and lexical diversity were entered, and together accounted for 44% of the variance, $F(3,53) = 13.9$, $p < .0001$. When theory-of-mind score was entered at the second step, it accounted for an additional 8% of the variance, which was statistically significant, $F(1,52) = 8.4$, $p < .006$.

There was considerable variability among the children with autism in their use of different mental state words, as noted in the large standard deviations shown in Table 9.1. Some children used no mental state words at all, whereas others referred to a range of different mental states, especially desire and cognition. Interestingly, references to desires and emotions and the use of these word categories were not related at all to the theory-of-mind scores. One likely explanation for this is that the tasks in the theory-of-mind battery were weighted in favor of cognitive mental state knowledge. Only one task tapped knowledge of desire, and none was related to emotion. On the other hand, significant correlations were obtained between use of cognition words, reference to cognitive mental states and theory-of-mind ability. When age and general language level were partialed out in the regression analyses, the main finding was that reference to cognitive mental states in informal conversation was significantly related to performance on theory-of-mind tasks. This is exactly what would be expected according to the theory-of-mind hypothesis of autism.

A second aspect of discourse that has been related to theory of mind is the ability to maintain an ongoing topic of conversation. Children with autism show significant deficits in responding to their conversational partners by staying on topic; instead, they often respond by introducing irrelevant information on a different topic (Tager-Flusberg & Anderson, 1991). Capps and her colleagues found that the ability to maintain topic, especially adding new information to the conversation, was correlated with theory-of-mind ability, as assessed on false-belief tasks. However, as noted earlier, this relationship did not remain significant when general language level was partialed out (Capps et al., 1998). Given our larger sample of children and the developmentally defined theory of mind measure, we reopened the question of whether conversational skills are related to theory of mind in children with autism, independent of general language skills.

The natural language samples were coded using the guidelines described in Tager-Flusberg and Anderson (1991). At the first level, all child utterances that directly followed an parent utterance were extracted. These utterances were coded as *contingent* (defined as related to the topic of the prior parent utterance), *noncontingent* (defined as unrelated to the topic of the prior utterance), or *imitation* (defined as full or partial repetition of the prior utterance). For each child, the proportion of utterances contingently related to the parent's prior utterance was calculated. Table 9.3 presents the correlations between this contingent discourse variable and other variables, including age, IQ, general language (as measured by the combined vocabulary score), and theory of mind.

We then computed a hierarchical regression analysis similar to the analyses conducted on the cognitive mental state words. On the first step, age, IQ, and vocabulary were entered and together they accounted for 16% of the variance in the contingent discourse score, $F(3,53) = 3.5$, $p < .05$. At the second step, theory of mind was added, and this contributed an additional 8% of the variance, $F(1,52) = 5.57$, $p < .05$. These results suggest that theory of mind and contingent discourse ability are significantly related, even when general language ability is taken into account in the analysis.

These findings provide further support for the theory-of-mind hypothesis of autism, linking deficits in communication to underlying impairments in theory of mind. This study underscores the need to test this hypothesis using a much broader definition of theory of mind, which is developmentally sensitive and has a wider score range than has been used in studies that were limited to false-belief tasks.

THE RELATIONSHIP BETWEEN THEORY OF MIND AND SEVERITY OF AUTISM

The main assumption underlying the theory-of-mind hypothesis of autism is that impairments in this domain account for the major symptoms that define the disorder. If this is the case, then one would predict that there would be links between theory-of-mind impairment and the severity of the autism diagnosis.

TABLE 9.3. Correlations for Contingent
Discourse Skills

Age	.28°
Full-scale IQ	.24
Vocabulary (PPVT + EVT)	.40°°
Theory of mind	.49°°

Note. Significance: °$p < .05$; °°$p < .01$.

To explore this prediction, we used the children's scores on the Autism Diagnostic Observation Schedule (ADOS) as a measure of symptom severity and scores on our theory-of-mind battery. We had complete data for this study from 68 children enrolled in the project.

The ADOS is a semistructured, interactive observation schedule designed to assess social and communicative functioning in individuals suspected of having autism. The assessment involves a variety of social occasions and "presses" designed to elicit behaviors relevant to a diagnosis of autism. The schedule consists of four developmentally sequenced modules, each approximately 30 minutes in duration. Only one module is administered, depending on the child's age and language level. Each module includes a standardized diagnostic algorithm composed of a subset of the social and communicative behaviors rated. Although there are several ratings for repetitive behaviors, they are not included in the diagnostic algorithms because they cannot be observed reliably during a brief assessment. Ratings (e.g., *facial expressions directed to others*) are based on a hierarchy of mutually exclusive operational definitions corresponding to the following codes: 0 = not autistic; 1 = atypical, but not clearly autistic; 2 = autistic. Thus, higher scores on the ADOS reflect greater impairment. Scores for Communication may vary from 0 to 10 (depending on which module is administered) and for Social behavior they vary from 0 to 14.

Table 9.4 presents the correlations between theory of mind, ADOS scores, and other control variables. To test the hypothesis that theory of mind will predict ADOS severity scores, we computed hierarchical regression analyses. For the ADOS total score, the control variables (age, IQ, and language) were entered in the first step, accounting for 24% of the variance, $F(3,64) = 6.86$, $p < .0001$. Theory of mind was then entered, accounting for an additional 16.8% of the variance, $F(1,63) = 18.02$, $p < .05$. For ADOS Social, the control variables explained 15.6% of the variance, $F(3,64) = 3.96$, $p < .02$, and theory of mind an additional 10.5%, $F(1,63) = 8.95$, $p < .004$. Finally, for ADOS communication the control variables accounted for 30.7% of variance, $F(3,64) = 9.45$, $p < .0001$, and theory of mind an additional 18.2%, $F(1,63) = 22.41$, $p < .0001$.

TABLE 9.4. Correlations for Theory of Mind
and ADOS Scores

Age	.53°°
Full-scale IQ	.38°°
Vocabulary (PPVT + EVT)	.59°°
ADOS Social	−.46°°
ADOS Communication	−.69°°
ADOS Total	−.63°°

Note. Significance: °°$p < .01$.

Taken together, these analyses provide strong evidence that theory of mind is a significant predictor of the severity of autism diagnosis, independent of IQ and language level. It is interesting to note that theory of mind explains significantly more of the variance for ADOS Communication than for ADOS Social scores, even after partialing out the variance contributed by language. This suggests that performance on theory-of-mind tasks depends quite heavily on communicative and language competence, especially among children with autism (cf. Garfield, Peterson, & Perry, 2001; Tager-Flusberg, 2000).

These analyses focused on linking theory of mind to two of the three criteria for autism: deficits in the social and communication domains. The diagnosis of autism also includes restricted repetitive and stereotyped behaviors, interests, or activities. To what extent can these aspects of autism be explained by the theory-of-mind hypothesis? Although some have argued that these deficits might also be related to theory-of-mind impairments (e.g., Baron-Cohen, 1989), others claim that they are independent of theory of mind, but more closely linked to executive dysfunction (e.g., Turner, 1997, 1999).

We investigated whether theory of mind was related to deficits in repetitive behaviors and interests using information available from the Autism Diagnostic Interview (ADI) because the ADOS does not provide a reliable score for this domain of autism. The ADI is a lengthy semistructured interview that we conducted with one or both parents of the children in the project. Questions address key areas of the child's development and the presence of autism symptoms during early childhood (between ages 4 and 5) as well as currently. As with the ADOS, scores ranging from 0 to 2 are given to the parent's responses that reflect whether the child shows definite presence of abnormal behavior that are found in autism. We took all the questions that focused on current behavior in the repetitive behaviors and interests domain to compute a summary score. The correlation between this score and theory of mind was 0.16, which was not statistically significant. Thus, our data suggest that theory of mind is not related to these aspects of autism impairment.

SUMMARY AND CONCLUSIONS

Over the past two decades, research on theory of mind in autism has radically altered our understanding of this enigmatic syndrome. More than 200 publications have addressed the hypothesis that autism involves specific impairments in theory of mind, yet only a handful of studies have systematically investigated whether deficits in theory of mind are directly related to the defining symptoms. The findings from the our project provide the best evidence to date that theory of mind is closely related to core deficits in social functioning and communicative behavior, but not to repetitive behaviors and interests.

In contrast to earlier work addressing this question, our study was able to demonstrate links between theory of mind and social and communicative impairments in autism that were independent of IQ or language level. We had the advantage of being able to test the theory-of-mind hypothesis on a very large and well-characterized group of children with autism, which provided sufficient statistical power to detect potential relationships. Given the enormous variability within the autism population, even when the age range is limited and only verbal children are included, it is clear that large samples are needed for these kinds of studies. Thus earlier studies that failed to find significant links between theory of mind and social behavior (e.g., Fombonne et al., 1994), for example, may have suffered from Type II statistical error. Another important contribution of our project was the use of a much broader and more sensitive measure of theory-of-mind ability. The battery of tasks that we included covered the developmental span from 18 months (understanding pretense) to early adolescence (understanding moral commitment). This contrasts with the more limited assessment of theory-of-mind ability in other studies, which relied exclusively on first-order false-belief tasks. In creating this developmental assessment of theory of mind, we ensured that most children did not have scores that were at the floor, and none were at ceiling levels. With the wide range of scores possible on this battery, our measure of theory-of-mind ability was more sensitive than those typically used in this research.

It remains to be seen whether theory of mind is closely related to other ways of assessing an autistic child's social functioning or communicative competence. For example, does theory-of-mind performance predict how well children with autism interact with others, using direct observational measures? Will theory of mind predict conversational competence using different measures, or with different conversational partners such as peers? Using the kinds of methods that we have introduced in this project, future studies may help to define exactly which aspects of social engagement and communicative ability depend on understanding mental states in other people. This will pave the way to developing more finely tuned and appropriate intervention programs to foster developments in all these domains in children with autism.

ACKNOWLEDGMENTS

Preparation of this chapter was supported by a grant from the National Institute on Deafness and Communication Disorders (PO1 DC 03610), which is part of the NICHD/NIDCD funded Collaborative Programs of Excellence in Autism. I thank the following people for their particular help with this project: Susan Bacalman, Karen Condouris, Milana Flusberg, Susan Folstein, Courtney Hale, Robert Joseph, Echo Meyer, Lauren McGrath, Naomi Ornstein, and Shelly Steele. I am especially grateful to the children and families who participated in the research project described in this chapter.

REFERENCES

American Psychiatric Association. (1994). *DSM–IV: Diagnostic and statistic manual of mental disorders* (4th ed.). Washington, DC: Author.

Baron-Cohen, S. (1988). Social and pragmatic deficits in autism: Cognitive or affective? *Journal of Autism and Developmental Disorders, 18*, 379–402.

Baron-Cohen, S. (1989). Do autistic children have obsessions and compulsions? *British Journal of Clinical Psychology, 28*, 193–200.

Baron-Cohen, S. (2000). Theory of mind and autism: A fifteen year review. In S. Baron-Cohen, H. Tager-Flusberg, & D. J. Cohen (Eds.), *Understanding other minds: Perspectives from developmental cognitive neuroscience* (pp. 3–20). Oxford: Oxford University Press.

Baron-Cohen, S., Leslie, A. M., & Frith, U. (1985). Does the autistic child have a "theory of mind"? *Cognition, 21*, 37–46.

Baron-Cohen, S., Leslie, A. M., & Frith, U. (1986). Mechanical, behavioral and intentional understanding of picture stories in autistic children. *British Journal of Developmental Psychology, 4*, 113–125.

Baron-Cohen, S., Tager-Flusberg, H., & Cohen, D. J. (Eds.). (1993). *Understanding other minds: Perspectives from autism.* Oxford: Oxford University Press.

Baron-Cohen, S., Tager-Flusberg, H., & Cohen, D. J. (Eds.). (2000). *Understanding other minds: Perspectives from developmental cognitive neuroscience.* Oxford: Oxford University Press.

Bartsch, K., & Wellman, H. (1995). *Children talk about the mind.* New York: Oxford University Press.

Brown, R. (1973). *A first language: The early stages.* Oxford, England: Harvard University Press.

Capps, L., Kehres, J., & Sigman, M. (1998). Conversational abilities among children with autism and children with developmental delays. *Autism, 2*, 325–344.

Carter, A. S., Volkmar, F. R., Sparrow, S. S., Wang, J., Lord, C., Dawson, G., Fombonne, E., Loveland, K., Mesibov, G., & Schopler, E. (1998). The Vineland Adaptive Behavior Scales: Supplementary norms for individuals with autism. *Journal of Autism and Developmental Disorders, 28*, 287–302.

Devries, R. (1970). The development of role-taking as reflected by behavior of bright, average, and retarded children in a social guessing game. *Child Development, 41*, 759–770.

Dunn, L. M., & Dunn, L. M. (1997). *Peabody Picture Vocabulary Test, Third Edition.* Circle Pines, MN: American Guidance Service.

Elliott, C. D. (1990). *Differential Ability Scales.* San Antonio, TX: Psychological Corporation/Harcourt Brace.

Fombonne, E., Siddons, F., Achard, S., Frith, U., & Happé, F. (1994). Adaptive behaviour and theory of mind in autism. *European Child and Adolescent Psychiatry, 3*, 176–186.

Frith, U. (1989). *Autism: Explaining the enigma.* Oxford: Blackwell.

Frith, U., Happé, F., & Siddons, F. (1994). Autism and theory of mind in everyday life. *Social Development, 3*, 108–124.

Garfield, J., Peterson, C. C., & Perry, T. (2001). Social cognition, language acquisition, and the development of the theory of mind. *Mind and Language, 16*, 494–541.

Happé, F. (1994). *Autism: An introduction to psychological theory.* London: University College London Press.

Kavanaugh, R., Eizenman, D., & Harris, P. (1997). Young children's understanding of pretense expressions of independent agency. *Developmental Psychology, 33*, 764–770.

Kjelgaard, M. & Tager-Flusberg, H. (2001). An investigation of language impairment in autism: Implications for genetic subgroups. *Language and Cognitive Processes, 16*, 287–308.

Lord, C., Rutter, M., DiLavore, P. C., & Risi, S. (1999). *Autism Diagnostic Observation Schedule–WPS (ADOS-WPS).* Los Angeles, CA: Western Psychological Services.

Lord, C., Rutter, M., & LeCouteur, A. (1994). Autism Diagnostic Interview–Revised: A revised version of a diagnostic interview for caregivers of individuals with possible pervasive developmental disorders. *Journal of Autism and Developmental Disorders, 24*, 659–668.

Lord, C., Risi, S., Lambrecht, L., Cook, E.H., Lenventhal, B.L., DiLavore, P.S., Pickles, A., & Rutter, M. (2000). The Autism Diagnostic Obervation Schedule–Generic: A standard measure of social and communication deficits associated with the spectrum of autism. *Journal of Autism and Developmental Disorders, 30*, 205–223.

Loveland, K., & Tunali, B. (1993). Narrative language in autism and the theory of mind hypothesis: A wider perspective. In S. Baron-Cohen, H. Tager-Flusberg, & D. J. Cohen (Eds.), *Understanding other minds: Perspectives from autism* (pp. 247–266). Oxford: Oxford University Press.

Mant, C., & Perner, J. (1988). The child's understanding of commitment. *Developmental Psychology, 24*, 343-351.

Miller, J., & Chapman, R. (2000). *Systematic analysis of language transcripts (SALT)* [Computer software, SALT for Windows, research version 6.1]. Madison: University of Wisconsin, Language Analysis Lab.

Perner, J. (1988). Higher-order beliefs and intentions in children's understanding of social interaction. In J. Astington, P. L. Harris, & D. Olson (Eds.), *Developing theories of mind* (pp. 271–294). Cambridge: Cambridge University Press.

Perner, J., Leekam, S., & Wimmer, H. (1987). Three-year-olds' difficulty with false belief: The case for a conceptual deficit. *British Journal of Developmental Psychology, 5*, 125–137.

Pratt, C., & Bryant, P. (1990). Young children understand that looking leads to knowing (so long as they are looking into a single barrel). *Child Development, 61*, 973–982.

Shatz, M., Wellman, H., & Silber, S. (1983). The acquisition of mental verbs: A systematic investigation of the first reference to mental state. *Cognition, 14*, 301–321.

Sparrow, S., Balla, D., & Cicchetti, D. (1984). *Vineland Adaptive Behavior Scales*. Circle Pines, MN: American Guidance Service.

Sullivan, K., Winner, E., & Hopfield, N. (1995). How children tell a joke from a lie: The role of second-order mental state attributions. *British Journal of Developmental Psychology, 13*, 191–204.

Sullivan, K., Zaitchik, D., & Tager-Flusberg, H. (1994). Preschoolers can attribute sec-ond-order beliefs. *Developmental Psychology, 30*(3), 395–402.

Tager-Flusberg, H. (1992). Autistic children talk about psychological states: Deficits in the early acquisition of a theory of mind. *Child Development, 63*, 161–172.

Tager-Flusberg, H. (1996). Current theory and research on language and communication in autism. *Journal of Autism and Developmental Disorders, 26*, 169–172.

Tager-Flusberg, H. (2000). Language and understanding minds: Connections in autism. In S. Baron-Cohen, H. Tager-Flusberg, & D. J. Cohen (Eds.), *Understanding other minds: Perspectives from developmental cognitive neuroscience* (2nd ed., pp. 124–149). Oxford: Oxford University Press.

Tager-Flusberg, H., & Anderson, M. (1991). The development of contingent discourse ability in autistic children. *Journal of Child Psychology and Psychiatry, 32*, 1123–1134.

Travis, L., Sigman, M., & Ruskin, E. (2001). Links between social understanding and social behavior in verbally able children with autism. *Journal of Autism and Developmental Disorders, 31*, 119–130.

Turner, M. (1997). Toward an executive dysfunction account of repetitive behaviour in autism. In J. Russell (Ed.), *Autism as an executive disorder* (pp. 57–100). New York: Oxford University Press.

Turner, M. (1999). Repetitive behaviour in autism: A review of psychological research. *Journal of Child Psychology and Psychiatry, 40*, 839–849.

Wellman, H., Cross, D., & Watson, J. K. (2001). Meta-analysis of theory-of-mind development: The truth about false-belief. *Child Development, 72*, 655–684.

Wellman, H. M., & Lagattuta, K. H. (2000). Developing understanding of mind. In S. Baron-Cohen, H. Tager-Flusberg, & D. J. Cohen (Eds.), *Understanding other minds* (2nd ed., pp. 21–49). New York: Oxford University Press.

Wellman, H. M., & Woolley, J. D. (1990). From simple desires to ordinary beliefs: The early development of everyday psychology. *Cognition, 35*, 245–275.

Williams, K. T. (1997). *Expressive Vocabulary Test*. Circle Pines, MN: American Guidance Service.

Wimmer, H., & Perner, J. (1983). Beliefs about beliefs: Representation and constraining function of wrong beliefs in children's understanding of deception. *Cognition, 13,* 103–128.

Yuill, N. (1992). Children's production and comprehension of trait terms. *British Journal of Developmental Psychology, 10,* 131–142.

10

Mind Reading and Social Functioning in Children with Autistic Disorder and Asperger's Disorder

CHERYL DISSANAYAKE
KATHLEEN MACINTOSH
School of Psychological Science, La Trobe University

*T*he inability to represent and reason about the mental states of others has been viewed as a core feature of individuals with autism ever since Baron-Cohen, Leslie, and Frith (1985) first charted this deficit. There is now a wealth of evidence confirming this impairment in a theory of mind (ToM) among those with a diagnosis of autism (see Baron-Cohen, 2000, for a review), and wide consensus as to its utility in explaining many of their manifest social difficulties (Baron-Cohen, 1989; Baron-Cohen, Tager-Flusberg, & Cohen, 2000; Frith, 1989; Happé, 1994). Nonetheless, there has been a surprising lack of work directly investigating the association between ToM and social functioning in individuals with autism.

As noted above, only a few studies have attempted to investigate whether and how social functioning might be related to ToM in individuals with autism. Furthermore, the majority of these studies have focused on caregiver reports of social behavior. Prior, Dahlstrom, and Squires (1990) failed to find any relationship between ToM ability (assessed using false-belief tasks) and parent ratings of social behavior (using the Social Behavior Rating Scale, SBRS; Dawson & Fernald, 1987) in their sample of children with autism. Similarly, Frith, Happé, and Siddons (1994) found that individuals with autism who passed ToM tasks (using two false-belief tests) performed no better on the Socialization domain of the Vineland Adaptive Behavior Scales (VABS; Sparrow, Balla, & Cicchetti, 1984) than those who failed. Differences between the two groups only became apparent when the Socialization domain was supplemented with items designed to distinguish behaviors that necessitate a ToM (e.g., engages in elaborate make-believe activities; apologizes for hurting others' feelings). Not surprisingly, those individuals who passed the ToM tasks scored higher on these items that were a priori categorized as likely to rely on mental state understanding. It should be noted, however, that the "passers" in this study had a higher verbal mental age than those individuals who failed the ToM tasks (7.9 years vs. 6.0 years, respectively). When Fombonne, Siddons, Achard, Frith, and Happé (1994) partialed out the influence of verbal ability (and chronological age) in an almost identical study, the differences in social behavior were no longer significant. However, Tager-Flusberg (this volume), using a large battery of tasks to assess ToM, found that the best predictor of the Vineland Socialization domain score (without supplemental items) was ToM performance (even after partialing out the influence of language).

To date, Travis, Sigman, and Ruskin (2001) have conducted the only study exploring the relationship between ToM and observational measures of social behavior in children with autism. They found no association between ToM and either the proportion of time participants spent in high-level social play with their peers in the schoolyard (Peer Play scale; Howes, 1980) or a combined prosocial measure of helping and sharing in a structured laboratory setting. The authors speculated that the use of observational measures may not be as sensitive to the social impairments experienced by individuals with autism as are caregiver reports that are based on much larger samples of behavior. They also suggested that the failure to find significant associations may be because ToM abilities have an impact on a relatively narrow and well-defined range of behaviors; that is, behaviors that a priori require a ToM (e.g., engaging in deception). However, Tager-Flusberg's (this volume) finding of an association between ToM and scores on the Socialization domain of the VABS argues against this view. In order to clarify the discrepant findings, it is necessary to explore the association between ToM ability and both observational and caregiver report measures of social functioning in the one sample.

The first aim in the study reported here was to systematically investigate the purported link between ToM and social functioning in children with autism by including a wider range of measures and informants than has previously been used to assess the social abilities of this group. Thus, in addition to the parent interview version of the VABS, which is a measure of adaptive functioning, naturalistic observations were conducted to assess children's spontaneous social interactions with their peers in the schoolyard. Furthermore, children's social skills were rated by both their parents and teachers using Gresham and Elliot's (1990) Social Skill Rating System (SSRS). It was anticipated that the use of multiple sources (experimenter, parent, teacher) and multiple methods (interview, observation, questionnaire) would begin to clarify the relationship between ToM abilities and social functioning in autism. Given that many of the social deficits in autism are, at least theoretically, well explained by the difficulty these children have in attributing mental states to other people, it was hypothesized that some positive associations would be found between the various measures of social functioning and ToM.

Another pervasive developmental disorder that shares many similarities with autism is Asperger's disorder. Like autistic disorder, Asperger's disorder is characterized by deficits in reciprocal social interaction, communication, and restricted and/or repetitive activities, behaviors, and interests. However, although up to 70% of children with autism have an intellectual disability, children with Asperger's disorder are of mostly normal intellect. Furthermore, the language of children with Asperger's disorder, although odd, is much more developed than in children with autism. Indeed, this is the main differentiating criterion between these conditions, with both *DSM IV–R* (APA, 1994) and ICD-10 (WHO, 1993) stating that children with Asperger's disorder, unlike those with autism, do not experience significant delays in language. To date, however, the empirical evidence has been quite mixed (Eisenmajer et al., 1996; Prior et al., 1998) so this criterion is somewhat controversial.

Given the similarities between the two clinical groups, there has been an ongoing debate since the late 1980s about whether these are separate disorders or, instead, form part of the same spectrum of disorder (Bishop, 1989; Gillberg & Ehlers, 1998; Wing, 1991). This debate has largely centered on comparisons of clinical, neuropsychological, and cognitive profiles (e.g., Manjiviona & Prior, 1999; Miller & Ozonoff, 2000; Szatmari, 2000; Szatmari, Tuff, Allen, Finlayson, & Bartolucci, 1990), as well as comparisons of motor skills (e.g., Ghaziuddin & Butler, 1998; Smith, 2000). However, there has been little systematic exploration of the similarities and differences in the social impairments associated with autistic and Asperger's disorder. The paucity of comparative studies on the social deficits in the two groups is remarkable given their central role in the expression of both conditions. Moreover, the few studies that have been conducted tend to rely on parent and teacher report (Gillberg, 1989; Szatmari, Archer, Fisman, Streiner, & Wilson, 1995; Szatmari, Bartolucci, & Bremner, 1989; Szatmari, Bremner, & Nagy, 1989), with only two including observational data (collected in a clinic setting) (Gilchrist et al., 2001; Ozonoff, South, & Miller, 2000).

When differences in social skills have been reported between the two groups, these have most frequently been in the direction of individuals with Asperger's disorder manifesting fewer social deficits in comparison to those with high-functioning autism, particularly during early childhood. For example, on the basis of parent report, Szatmari et al. (1995) found that in comparison to children with high-functioning autism, children with Asperger's disorder demonstrated more social intentions, social reciprocity, greetings, and pleasure/

excitement in social interactions. In addition, based on parent report, the children with Asperger's disorder scored higher on the Socialization domain of the VABS. On the other hand, many similarities have also been reported in the social behavior of individuals with Asperger's disorder and high-functioning autism, particularly during later childhood and adolescence (e.g., Gilchrist et al., 2001; Ozonoff et al., 2000). Of particular interest in the context of the current study is the finding by Ozonoff et al. (2000) of no differences between their participants with high-functioning autism and Asperger's disorder on the social subscales of the SSRS, based on parent report. Also noteworthy is the consistent finding, across *all* studies, of impoverished social functioning manifest in *both* Asperger's disorder and autistic disorder relative to control children without these diagnoses.

The findings of fewer social deficits in Asperger's disorder are in keeping with some reports that these individuals are also less deficient in their mental state reasoning in comparison to those with a diagnosis of autism. Ozonoff, Rogers, and Pennington (1991) compared 13 participants with high-functioning autism and 10 participants with Asperger's disorder (ranging in age from 8 to 20 years) to 20 nonautistic control participants on first-order (i.e., "X thinks that . . .") and second-order (i.e., "X thinks that Y thinks . . .") ToM tasks. They found that the children with high-functioning autism performed more poorly on these tasks than the other two groups. In addition, there was no significant difference in the ToM performance of the control participants and those with Asperger's disorder. Ziatas, Durkin, and Pratt (1998) replicated these findings with somewhat younger samples of children with autism (mean age: 8 years 3 months) and Asperger's disorder (mean age: 6 years 11 months). The failure to find ToM deficits among children with Asperger's disorder is corroborated in the adult literature. Bowler (1992), for example, found no difference in performance on first- or second-order ToM tasks in adults with Asperger's disorder compared to control participants with schizophrenia and participants with no handicaps. Together, these findings are consistent with reports of less severe social impairment in Asperger's disorder.

Bowler (1992) suggested that the more advanced ToM abilities among individuals with Asperger's disorder may be an outcome of the higher cognitive and verbal skills that characterize this disorder. More specifically, individuals with Asperger's disorder may be capable of logically deriving appropriate solutions to first- and second-order ToM tasks. Bowler hypothesized, however, that these individuals may continue to have difficulty in rapidly and intuitively understanding other people's mental states in the course of their everyday lives. One might assume that it is for this reason that, despite less social impairment in comparison to individuals with autism, individuals with Asperger's disorder continue to be awkward and impaired in their social interactions. Bowler's view is similar to the thesis put forward to explain how a small proportion of individuals with autism pass ToM tests. That is, like Bowler (1992), Frith, Morton, and Leslie (1991) and others (e.g., Eisenmajer & Prior, 1991) suggested that autistic "passers" may not use a ToM per se, but instead adopt alternative, nonmentalistic strategies or rules to succeed. Moreover, Happé (1995) proposed that these strategies may be verbally mediated.

A few studies have provided some evidence for Bowler's (1992) hypothesis that individuals with Asperger's disorder, in spite of good performance on standard ToM tasks, have some underlying difficulties in reasoning about other minds. Studies that have included adults with high-functioning autism and Asperger's disorder using more advanced mind-reading tasks such as the Strange Stories Task (Jolliffe & Baron-Cohen, 1999), the Eyes Task (Baron-Cohen, Jolliffe, Mortimore, & Robertson, 1997; Baron-Cohen, Wheelwright, Hill, Raste, & Plumb, 2001; Baron-Cohen, Wheelwright, & Jolliffe, 1997), and a Social Attribution Task (Klin, 2000) each revealed marked deficits in these clinical groups. However, it is pertinent that when comparisons have been made between high-functioning autism and Asperger's disorder, the groups with autism generally showed the poorest performance on these advanced ToM tasks.

In direct contrast to the findings just reported, Dahlgren and Trillingsgaard (1996) failed to find deficits on first- and second-order ToM tasks not only in their young participants with Asperger's disorder (aged 7–12 years) but also among those with high–functioning autism (aged 6–15 years), in comparison to 20 matched control children. Moreover, the two clinical groups were not differentiated from one another. On the basis of these findings, Dahlgren and Trillingsgaard argued that ToM deficits may not be central to autism. However, a possible explanation for these discrepant findings may be the very high verbal mental ages of each of the clinical groups in this study (high-functioning autism: 10.14; Asperger's disorder: 11.03). Happé (1995), in a review of ToM performance in 70 individuals with autism, reported that verbal mental age was highly correlated with ToM performance in this group, such that all children with a verbal mental age of above 11.7 years passed the (first-order) ToM tasks.

In light of the evidence for superior ToM abilities among individuals with Asperger's disorder, in comparison to those with autism, and the scant evidence of less-severe social impairments in the former group, it was of interest to investigate the association between these abilities in children with Asperger's disorder. To date, there have been no studies of ToM and social functioning in this group. This was the second aim addressed here. Given Bowler's (1992) hypothesis that individuals with Asperger's disorder may acquire their ToM competence via a different developmental route, it was difficult to hypothesize about the relationship between ToM understanding and social functioning in this group. For example, if individuals with Asperger's disorder are using verbally mediated strategies to succeed on ToM tasks, then it seems unlikely that their success will generalize to everyday social functioning. However, if their performance on these ToM tasks does in fact reflect social insight, one might then expect some associations with real-life social abilities.

The third and main aim in conducting the research reported here was to compare children with a diagnosis of high-functioning autism to those with a diagnosis of Asperger's disorder on their social understanding and behavior. Given the paucity of empirical data on the social abilities of children with Asperger's disorder, and the ongoing debate about the diagnostic boundaries between this condition and Autistic disorder, children in the two groups were compared to each other on the measures of social understanding and social functioning. In order to determine the form and severity of the social impairments in the clinical groups, a group of typically developing children was also studied here. It was hypothesized that although the children in each of the clinical groups would show impairments in their social functioning relative to the normal controls, the children with Asperger's disorder would generally show less-severe impairments in comparison to those with high-functioning autism. This latter hypothesis was based, in part, on the established ToM deficits in autism and the evidence that individuals with Asperger's disorder generally succeed on such tasks. In keeping with this evidence, it was further hypothesized that the children with autism would show greater ToM deficits in comparison to those with Asperger's disorder and the typically developing children.

METHODS AND SAMPLE

Three groups of children participated in this study: children diagnosed with high-functioning autistic disorder (HFAD; n = 21), children diagnosed with Asperger's disorder (ASD; n = 19), and typically developing children (TD; n = 20). The clinical diagnoses were made on the basis of *DSM IV–R* (APA, 1994) criteria by either a clinical psychologist and/or a psychiatrist. All children were male, between 5 and 11 years of age, and all had IQs above 70 (Stanford–Binet Intelligence Scales–Short Form; Thorndike, Hagen, & Sattler, 1986). The two clinical groups were matched on chronological age (CA) but were significantly older than children in the TD group (see Table 10.1). The three groups were matched on overall mental age, but the mean verbal mental age of the HFAD group was lower than that of the other two groups (see Table 10.1). Thus, CA and VMA were covaried as appropriate in the between-group analyses reported next.

TABLE 10.1. Sample Characteristics

	HFAD n = 21	ASD n = 19	TD n = 20
Chronological age	96.2 (19.1)[a]	97.8 (19.1)[a]	80.0 (20.9)
Verbal mental age	85.4 (18.1)[a, b]	102.0 (24.6)	104.3 (22.4)
Overall mental age	89.7 (17.2)	100.7 (24.6)	99.5 (23.2)

[a]Significantly different from TD, p < .05.
[b]Significantly different from ASD, p = .055.

Theory of Mind. Children's understanding of first-order false beliefs was assessed using two unexpected transfer tasks (the Sally–Ann task; Wimmer & Perner, 1983) and two unexpected contents tasks. In one version of the unexpected transfer task, the experimenter enacted the following scenario with two hand puppets: Bert places a ball in a basket and leaves the scene. Ernie arrives, moves the ball into a box, and leaves. The child was then asked, "Where is the ball really?" (reality control question) and "Where did Bert put the ball?" (memory control question). Bert then returns to the scene. The false-belief test question was then given (i.e., "Where will Bert first look for his ball?"). In the "real person" version of this task, the roles of the puppets were enacted by two familiar experimenters.

The two unexpected contents tasks assessed not only children's ability to attribute a false belief to another person, but also their ability to recognize their own false beliefs. In the Smarties task (adapted from Perner, Frith, Leslie, & Leekam, 1989), the child was shown a candy box and asked, "What's in here?" The contents of the box (pencils) were then revealed. Upon closing the box, the child was asked "Can you remember what's inside here?"(memory control question); "When I first showed you the box, what did you think was in here before we opened it?" ("self" false-belief question); and "Your mum has never looked inside this box. When I ask her, what will she say is in the box before I open it?" ("other" false-belief question). The second unexpected contents task was adapted from Bartsch and Wellman (1989). The experimenter showed the child a Band-Aid box and an unmarked box of the same dimensions. The child was asked: "Which box has Band-Aids in it?" It was then revealed that the Band-Aid box was empty and that the unmarked box contained Band-Aids. After closing the boxes, the experimenter enacted a scenario with Tigger, a hand puppet, who falls down. The child was told, "He has cut his chin. He wants to put a Band-Aid on it. He's never seen these boxes before. Now where will Tigger look for a Band-Aid?" ("other" false-belief question). The child was then asked, "Where are the Band-Aids really?" (reality control question), followed by the "self" false-belief question (i.e., "In the beginning before we opened the boxes, where did you think the Band-Aids were?").

All of the children passed the control questions for each task. Children received a score of 0 (incorrect) or 1 (correct) for their responses to each of the six false-belief questions. For each child, these scores were summed to give a composite first-order false-belief score, with a potential range from 0 to 6.

Baron-Cohen's (1989) ice cream task was also administered to assess children's higher order mental state reasoning. After setting up a model village and introducing a series of toy characters, the experimenter told a story about two characters who were playing in a park. One child (Mary) is led to have a false belief about the contents of another child's mind (John). Following a series of control questions designed to test participants' memory and comprehension of the narrative, children were asked to predict where Mary will *think* that John has gone to buy an ice cream, thereby testing their reasoning about second-order false beliefs. Children who failed one or more of the five control questions from this task were excluded from analysis. Each of the remaining participants received an aggregate ToM score based on the number of questions answered correctly across the first- and second-order tasks (potential range 0–7).

Social Behavior Measures

Adaptive Behavior. The Vineland Adaptive Behavior Scales (Survey Form; Sparrow et al., 1984) were administered to the parent during a structured interview. These scales assessed participants' everyday adaptive functioning in the areas of Communication, Daily Living Skills, and Socialization. For each domain, a norm-referenced standardized score was calculated based on the participant's chronological age.

Social Participation. Social participation was coded during observations of spontaneous peer interactions during unstructured free-time in the schoolyard. All children attended mainstream elementary schools, thus enhancing comparability across the three groups in the composition and characteristics of the school population. An observational schedule was designed (Macintosh, 2001) to measure social and play activity, the number of partners in each interaction, the direction of the interaction, and the quality of the interaction (see Appendix A), as well as a range of other behaviors not considered here. One–zero time sampling was used to capture the behaviors of interest at 30-second intervals. Each child was observed twice at school during free-play until a minimum of 40 minutes of data was collected. The observer was blind to the diagnostic status of the participants. All social participation data were transformed to proportion (of total observation intervals) scores in order to account for slight differences in observation times. Moderate to high interrater reliabilities (r of .74 or above) were obtained for the social participation categories.

Social Skills. A standardized questionnaire (SSRS—Elementary Level; Gresham & Elliott, 1990) was used to obtain both teacher and parent reports of the frequency with which various social skills were displayed at school or in the home and community. Both the Teacher and Parent versions of the SSRS contain the subscales of Cooperation, Assertion, and Self-Control. The Parent form also includes the Responsibility subscale.

SUMMARY OF GROUP COMPARISONS

Theory of Mind. Children's performance on the first-order tasks and their total ToM scores are presented in Table 10.2 (means adjusted for the effects of the covariates). Controlling for CA and VMA, the analysis of covariance (ANCOVA) revealed a significant difference between the groups in their scores

TABLE 10.2. Adjusted Means (and Standard Deviations)
for the First-Order Tasks and ToM Aggregate

	HFAD	ASD	TD
First-order	4.0 (1.7)	5.2 (0.7)[a]	5.1 (0.9)[a]
false beliefs	n = 21	n = 18	n = 20
ToM aggregate	5.3 (1.4)	6.0 (0.9)	6.0 (1.0)
	n = 13	n = 15	n = 19

[a]Significantly different from HFAD, $p < .05$.

on the first-order false-belief tasks, $F(2,54) = 4.39$, $p < .05$. Post hoc analyses indicated that the children with HFAD performed poorly relative to those with ASD and the TD children ($p < .05$). The latter two groups did not differ from each other and, unlike the children with autism, they performed significantly above chance on the first-order tasks ($ps < .001$). This latter result may be an outcome of a ceiling effect for the TD group, where 12 of the 20 children passed all six attribution questions (see Figure 10.1 for the distribution of scores across groups). In examining Figure 10.1, it is also worth noting that the children with autism performed at chance on the four false-belief tasks, whereas the other two groups were significantly above chance (both $ps < .001$)

When the second-order task was included in the analysis, a somewhat different pattern of results emerged. Despite having the lowest mean ToM aggregate, children with HFAD were not significantly different from the other groups (after controlling for VMA). This latter finding is most likely due to the exclusion of eight children with HFAD who failed one or more of the control questions on the ice cream task (in comparison to only three ASD and one TD child). These children had also performed poorly on the first-order tasks and their

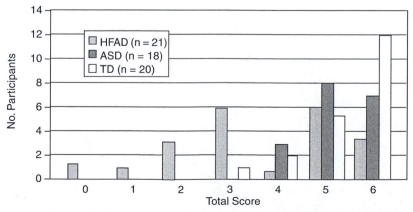

FIGURE 10.1. Distribution of scores on the first-order false-belief tasks.

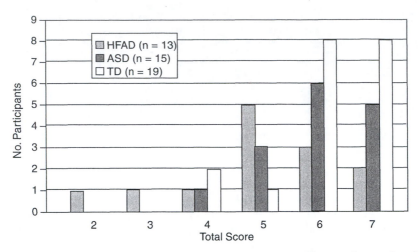

FIGURE 10.2. Distribution of scores on the ToM aggregate (first- and second-order false-belief tasks).

exclusion probably served to minimize the group differences. It is noteworthy, however, that once again there was a different distribution of scores for the HFAD group (see Figure 10.2) on these combined tasks in comparison to the other two groups.

· *Adaptive Behavior.* Children's mean standard scores on the Vineland domains of Communication, Daily Living Skills, and Socialization are presented in Figure 10.3. MANCOVA revealed a significant main effect of group, $F(6,104)$

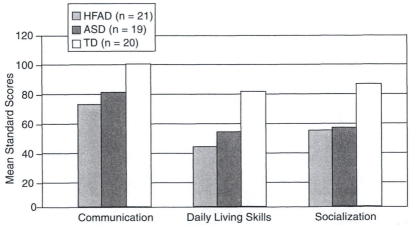

FIGURE 10.3. Mean standard scores on the domains of the Vineland Adaptive Behavior scales.

= 14.09, p < .001, with each of the domains contributing to this effect (all ps < .01). Post hoc analyses indicated that, in each domain, the TD children obtained significantly higher scores than the children with either HFAD or ASD (all ps < .01). The two clinical groups were similar across all of the domains (all ps > .10).

Social Participation. The proportions of time that children engaged in various social and play activities during the observation period are presented in Figure 10.4. A MANCOVA revealed a significant main effect of group, $F(16, 82)$ = 3.31, p < .001, with five of the eight behavior categories contributing to this main effect (all ps < .05). Children in the TD group spent significantly less time unoccupied than either those with HFAD or ASD (both ps < .001). They were also less engaged in activities classified as "other," that is, purposeful but nonsocial activity (both ps < .05) The two clinical groups spent considerable, and statistically comparable, proportions of the free play periods unoccupied or engaged in other activity. The children with HFAD also spent a greater proportion of time in solitary/proximity play and less time in simple social play in comparison to the TD children (both ps < .05). The only behavior category that differentiated the HFAD from the ASD group was their participation in Conversation. Post hoc comparisons revealed that children with ASD engaged in Conversation more often than those with HFAD (p = .001).

The mean proportions of the observation period spent in social interaction with zero to three or more partners are presented in Figure 10.5. The MANCOVA revealed a significant main effect of Group, $F(8, 96)$ = 6.50, p < .001. The TD children spent a greater proportion of the observation sessions interacting with three or more children simultaneously, in comparison to the clinical groups (both ps < .001). In contrast, the children with HFAD and ASD were more likely than the TD children to spend time alone (both ps < .001). There were no differences between the two clinical groups.

The mean proportions of the observation period during which children initiated interaction, were approached for interaction, and continued their interaction with others is presented in Figure 10.6. A significant multivariate group effect was found, $F(6, 98)$ = 5.28, p < .001. The children with ASD made more social initiations toward peers than did those with HFAD (p = .015) and the TD group (p = .055). Interestingly, there was no difference between the TD and HFAD groups in the frequency of initiations. The TD children also spent a greater proportion of the free-play periods engaged in enduring, reciprocal interactions in comparison to both the HFAD and the ASD groups (both ps < .001). Children in the two clinical groups spent an equal amount of time in continuing interaction. The three groups were not differentiated with regard to the frequency with which others directed social bids toward them. In other words, participants' peers initiated interactions with them equally regardless of their clinical status.

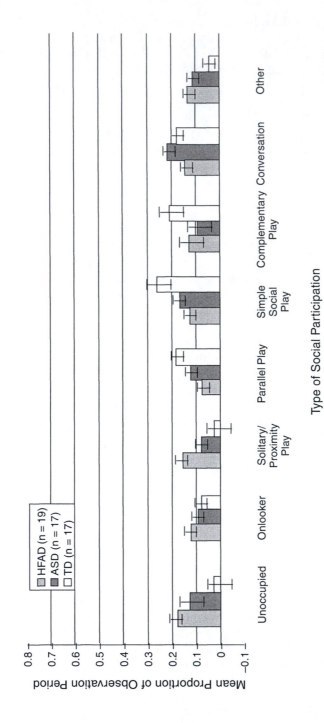

FIGURE 10.4. Mean proportion of the observation period spent in each Social Participation subcategory.

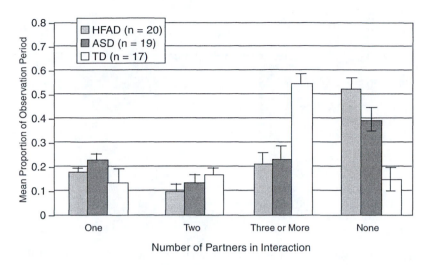

FIGURE 10.5. Mean proportion of the observation period spent interacting with zero to three or more children.

When the children in each group were interacting with others, the majority of their interactions were coded as positive or neutral (see Figure 10.7). Negative and/or aggressive styles of interaction, both from and toward participants, were rare in all groups. The Kruskal–Wallis one-way ANOVAs indicated that there were no group differences in the quality of the child's interactions or the quality of the other's interactions.

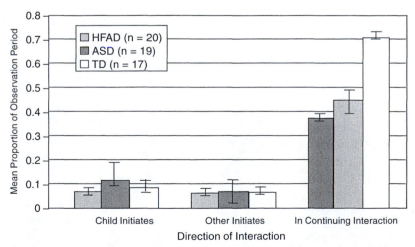

FIGURE 10.6. Mean proportion of the observation period during which children were recorded as initiating interaction, approached for interaction, and in continuing interaction with others.

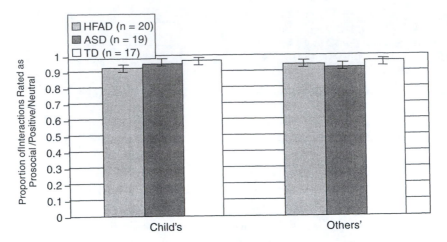

FIGURE 10.7. Mean proportion of the children's and other's interactions that were positive/neutral in quality.

Social Skills Ratings. Children's mean raw scores on each of the social subscales of the Teacher and Parent SSRS are presented in Figures 10.8 and 10.9. The MANCOVA conducted on the Teacher SSRS subscales revealed a significant group effect, $F(6, 90) = 4.76, p < .001$, with each of the three subscales contributing to this effect (all $ps < .05$). In comparison to each of the clinical groups, teachers reported that the TD children demonstrated higher levels of

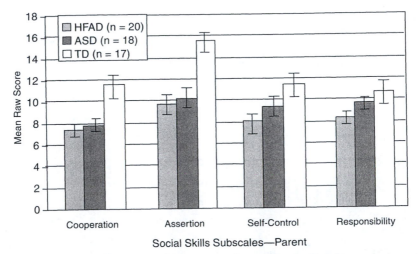

FIGURE 10.8. Mean raw scores on the Parent SSRS.

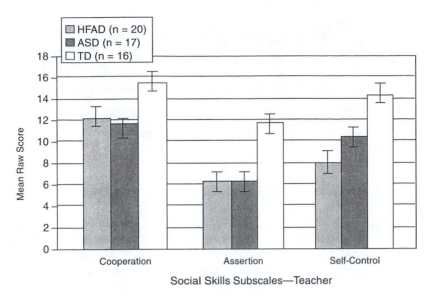

FIGURE 10.9. Mean raw scores on the Teacher SSRS.

Cooperation, Assertion, and Self-Control (all $ps < .05$) There were no significant differences between the children with HFAD and ASD for any of these subscales.

A MANCOVA conducted on the Parent SSRS largely replicated the teachers' reports. There was a significant overall group difference, $F(8, 94) = 6.28, p < .001$, with each of the social skills subscales contributing to this main effect (all $ps < .05$). In keeping with the teacher reports, parental ratings indicated that the TD children were perceived to be more socially competent (i.e., cooperative, assertive, and self-controlled) than children with HFAD or ASD (all $ps < .05$). The TD children were rated as more responsible than those with a diagnosis of HFAD ($p = .01$) but were similar to the ASD group. Once again, no differences were found between the clinical groups for any of the subscales.

INDIVIDUAL DIFFERENCE ANALYSES: THEORY OF MIND AND SOCIAL FUNCTIONING

Pearson product–moment correlation coefficients were used to examine the relationships between ToM and each measure of social functioning. The first-order false-belief scores were used to explore these relationships, given the larger subject numbers associated with this measure, particularly in the clinical groups. However, because many of the TD children performed at ceiling on this measure, and all but one child passed the control questions on the higher-

TABLE 10.3. Correlations Between Theory of Mind
(ToM) and Verbal Mental Age (VMA)

	HFAD First-order false beliefs (n = 21)	ASD First-order false beliefs (n = 18)	TD First-order false beliefs (n = 20)	ToM aggregate (n = 19)
VMA	.30	.29	.37	.54[a]

[a]Significant, p < .05.

order task, associations with the ToM aggregate score are also reported for this group.

Given the established associations between performance on false-belief tasks and verbal mental age in both clinical (e.g., Dahlgren & Trillingsgaard, 1996; Eisenmajor & Prior, 1991; Happé, 1995; Prior et al., 1990) and normal samples (e.g., Astington & Jenkins, 1995, 1999), the relations between these variables were examined for each group (see Table 10.3). Somewhat surprisingly, only one significant association was found, that between the ToM aggregate score and VMA in the TD group ($r = .54$, $p = .014$). Consequently, partial correlations between the social behavior measures and the ToM aggregate (controlling for VMA) will be reported for this group.

Theory of Mind and Adaptive Behavior. There were no significant relationships between theory-of-mind ability and the domain scores of the Vineland Scales (see Table 10.4).

Theory of Mind and Social Participation. In order to limit the number of analyses, only the relationships between the ToM scores and children's social/play activity behaviors were examined (see Table 10.5). No significant relationships emerged between these measures for the children with HFAD. However, in the ASD and TD groups, engagement in parallel play was negatively correlated with children's ToM ability. In addition, those children in the TD group

TABLE 10.4. Correlations Between Theory of Mind (ToM)
and the Domain Standard Scores of the Vineland Adaptive
Behavior Scales (VABS)

VABS domains	HFAD first-order false beliefs (n = 21)	ASD first-order false beliefs (n = 18)	TD First-order false beliefs (n = 20)	ToM aggregate (n = 19)
Communication	.06	−.13	−.19	−.01
Daily Living Skills	.19	−.25	.21	.26
Socialization	.22	−.13	.17	.32

TABLE 10.5. Correlations Between Theory of Mind (ToM) and Social/Play Activity Subcategories

	HFAD first-order false beliefs (n = 19)	ASD first-order false beliefs (n = 17)	TD	
			First-order false beliefs (n = 17)	ToM aggregate (n = 16)
Unoccupied	.05	.35	.08	.04
Onlooker	.34	.16	.30	.37
Solitary/proximity play	.24	.03	−.47[a]	−.54[b]
Parallel play	.20	−.49[b]	−.51[b]	−.55[b]
Simple social play	−.40	−.20	−.16	−.15
Complementary play	.06	.07	.16	.17
Conversation	−.27	.51[b]	.44	.37
Other	.16	.10	−.13	−.20

[a]Significant at $p < .10$.
[b]Significant at $p < .05$.

who spent more time in solitary/proximity play had lower scores on the ToM aggregate measure. However, when VMA was partialed out, these associations with the ToM aggregate were no longer significant (parallel play: $r(13) = −.38$, solitary/proximity play: $r(13) = −.38$, both $ps > .10$). Conversation, the most frequently observed behavior among the children with ASD, was also significantly correlated with their ToM ability. Those children with higher first-order false-belief scores engaged their peers in conversation for a greater proportion of the observation period.

Theory of Mind and Social Skills. The correlations between parents' and teachers' ratings of children's social skills and ToM are presented in Table 10.6.

TABLE 10.6. Correlations Between Theory of Mind (ToM) and Raw Scores of the Parent and Teacher Social Skills Rating System (SSRS) Subscales

Parent SSRS	HFAD first-order false beliefs (n = 20)	ASD first-order false beliefs (n = 16)	TD	
			First-order false beliefs (n = 17)	ToM aggregate (n = 16)
Cooperation	−.25	.00	.28	.27
Assertion	−.24	−.38	.67[b]	.68[b]
Responsibility	.03	−.23	.40	.38
Self-Control	−.05	−.40	.29	.37
Teacher SSRS	(n = 19)	(n = 16)	(n = 17)	(n = 16)
Cooperation	−.24	−.06	.02	.08
Assertion	−.22	.14	.13	.15
Self-Control	.54[a]	−.25	.20	.10

[a]Significant at $p < .05$.
[b]Significant at $p < .01$.

The only significant relationship observed between parental report of social skills and ToM ability was in the TD group. The TD children who performed better on the first-order false-belief tasks were rated as more assertive. Furthermore, the association between Assertion and the aggregate ToM score was significant, even after partialing out VMA, $r(13) = .66$, $p = .007$. With one exception, teacher ratings of children's social skills were not significantly correlated with performance on the ToM tasks. The children in the HFAD group with better theory-of-mind abilities were rated by their teachers as showing more self-control.

DISCUSSION

Some confirmation was found for the hypothesis that children with Asperger's disorder would demonstrate superior theory-of-mind ability in comparison to children with high-functioning autism. Indeed, not only did they outperform this clinical group, but they performed as well as typically developing children on both the first- and second-order false-belief tasks.[1] These results are consistent with those of Ozonoff et al. (1991) and Ziatas et al. (1998) and replicate Bowler's (1992) finding that individual's with Asperger's disorder perform well on these basic theory-of-mind measures. On the other hand, these results contradict Dahlgren and Trillingaard's (1996) finding of no differences between children with Asperger's disorder, high-functioning autism, and nondisabled control children on first- and second-order false-belief tasks. However, as noted earlier, the very high verbal mental age of their high-functioning autistic group (10.14 years compared with 7.11 years in the current sample) may account for their sample's unusually good performance on these tasks.

Although the children with Asperger's disorder were more competent in their ToM task performance than those with autism, the two groups were similar on the majority of the social functioning measures used in this study. Thus, contrary to our original expectations, the children with high-functioning autism and Asperger's disorder were largely indistinguishable on parent reports of their adaptive behavior and ratings (both teacher and parent) of their social skills. Moreover, with a few exceptions, their social participation with peers in the schoolyard was also very similar. However, as predicted, both clinical groups were impaired in their social functioning relative to the typically developing control children, who showed the highest level of social competence on nearly all of the measures reported here. These findings confirm that impaired social functioning is a hallmark of both high-functioning autism and Asperger's disorder (APA, 1994; WHO, 1993).

Only two of the social functioning variables differentiated the children with autistic disorder from those with Asperger's disorder. The most common social activity engaged in by the children with Asperger's disorder in the schoolyard was conversation, and in comparison to the children with autism, they spent significantly more time conversing with their peers. This propensity to engage in language-based forms of interaction highlights the typically higher verbal abilities of individuals with Asperger's disorder compared to those with high-functioning autism (Ehlers et al., 1997; Klin, Volkmar, Sparrow, Cicchetti, & Rouke, 1995; Manjiviona & Prior, 1999; Ozonoff et al., 2000; Ramberg, Ehlers, Nyden, Johansson, & Gillberg, 1996; Szatmari et al., 1995). It is of interest that despite using analyses of covariance to control for the slight difference in VMA between the clinical groups (HFAD: 7.11 years; AD: 8.5 years), this difference in conversation remained significant.

The children with Asperger's disorder also initiated interactions with peers more frequently than the children with autism. This finding reflects the increased social interest reported in this group relative to those with autism (Eisenmajer et al., 1996; Gillberg, 1989; Klin & Volkmar, 1997; Szatmari et al., 1989, 1995). It is also in keeping with clinical accounts that social motivation, as demonstrated by active (albeit sometimes awkward) efforts to initiate social interaction with peers, is a common characteristic of Asperger's disorder (Klin & Volkmar 1997; Wing, 1996, 1998). However, despite the greater number of social overtures directed toward their peers, the children with Asperger's disorder in the current study were no different from the children with autism in the amount of time they spent in ongoing interactions. In addition, both clinical groups were in continuing interactions for substantially less time compared to the typically developing children, which presumably reflects their comparable inability to sustain reciprocal social interactions.

The failure to differentiate the children with Asperger's disorder from those with autism on the each of the Socialization, Communication, and Daily Living Skills domains of the Vineland contrasts with the findings of Szatmari et al. (1995), who likewise used the VABS. Moreover, the impaired adaptive functioning among the children with Asperger's disorder relative to the typically developing controls is inconsistent with *DSM IV–R* (APA, 1994), which states that there are no clinically significant delays in the development of age-appropriate self-help skills and adaptive behavior in Asperger's disorder. The similarity in the adaptive behavior of the clinical groups relative to the nondisabled control group was corroborated by both parent and teacher ratings of the participants' social skills, using the SSRS. Unlike the Vineland, which measures adaptive behavioral skills that are required to function independently in a social environment, the SSRS measures the frequency with which various social skills are used by the child across various settings such as in the home and at school. The similarity between the two clinical groups on the SSRS is consistent with the findings of Ozonoff et al. (2000).

The caregiver reports of similar adaptive and social skills in both clinical groups were substantiated by the observational measures of social participation included in this study, providing further evidence of the extensive similarities in the social functioning of these two groups of children. Moreover, the pattern of results reveals that the social functioning of elementary school aged children with high-functioning autism and Asperger's disorder is similar not only at the quantitative level but also in terms of the range of behaviors engaged in. Although these findings are not in keeping with some of the recent comparative work (e.g., Szatmari et al., 1995), they are in accordance with the diagnostic criteria for qualitative social impairments in *DSM IV–R* (APA, 1994), which are identical for both conditions.

Given the aforementioned differences in performance on the theory-of-mind tasks between the children with high-functioning autism and Asperger's disorder, the extent of the similarities between the groups on the majority of measures of social functioning was surprising. Furthermore, despite equal performance on the false-belief tasks in comparison to the typically developing children, the children with Asperger's disorder were consistently differentiated from this control group in nearly all aspects of social competence measured here, as were the children with autism. This pattern of results lends some support to Bowler's (1992) thesis that, in spite of good performance on theory-of-mind tests, individuals with Asperger's disorder continue to show marked impairments within the social realm. It is in this context that the individual difference analyses are of particular interest.

No associations were found between the theory-of-mind abilities of children with high-functioning autism and parent reports of their adaptive behavior, nor the observational measures of their social participation with peers. Moreover, the failure to find a relationship between the Socialization domain of the Vineland and ToM performance is in direct contrast to Tager-Flusberg's recent findings (this volume), a point that will be returned to shortly. Indeed, teacher-rated Self-Control was the only social behavior significantly associated with theory-of-mind abilities in the group with autism. Interestingly, the Self-Control subscale of the SSRS targets behaviors such as appropriately managing teasing, engaging in turn taking, and developing compromises—all behaviors that, to some extent, require an understanding of another's perspective. However, given the failure to find a similar association with parental ratings on this subscale, the possibility that this single significant association may be spurious cannot be overlooked.

Similarly, very few associations were found between ToM and social functioning in the Asperger's group. The only significant relationships to emerge involved some of the observational measures of social participation. Specifically, those children who performed well on the first-order false-belief tasks were more likely to participate in conversation with their peers[2] and engage in less parallel play during the observation sessions.

The failure to find many associations between ToM ability and social functioning in the two clinical groups is in keeping with the "hacking" hypothesis put forward to explain why children with Asperger's disorder and a minority of children with autism (typically high-functioning) pass false-belief tasks (Bowler, 1992; Frith et al., 1991). According to this hypothesis, those children with good cognitive, and especially verbal, abilities arrive at the solution to theory-of-mind tasks (and presumably other social-understanding tasks) via a nonmentalistic route. Their social knowledge is acquired through sheer cognitive effort and learning rather than any understanding of mentalistic concepts like false belief. This learning of compensatory strategies by high-functioning individuals, be they with Asperger's disorder or autism, can often mask their social-cognitive deficits. However, these deficits become increasingly apparent in more natural- istic contexts where they are required to respond "live" without the benefit of time to enlist compensatory strategies. That is, these cognitively able children are unable to use their (hard-gained) knowledge in real-life social settings be- cause they cannot readily understand and respond to others' social and affec- tive behaviors, which occur in real time (as opposed to answering key questions at their own pace in a structured laboratory test situation). Real-life situations involve a number of background variables, which may not only distract the child, but also make it unclear what the important cues are. Together, this may make it difficult to apply a rule-based strategy.

Some support has recently been provided for this hacking hypothesis by Roeyers, Buyusse, Ponnet, and Pichal (2001) in a mixed sample of high- functioning adults with autism and pervasive developmental disorder—not other- wise specified (PDD–NOS). Although these two groups were unimpaired on advanced "static" theory-of-mind tasks (the Strange Stories Task and the Eyes Task) relative to matched normal controls, Roeyers et al. found impairments on an empathy task that required "on-line" inferences about another's thoughts and feelings within an interpersonal context that more readily matched real-life social situations. Klin's (2000) finding of deficits among individuals with Asperger's disorder and high-functioning autism on a social-attribution task that was designed to index social-cognitive deficits (while reducing factors thought to facilitate theory-of-mind performance such as the reliance on verbal media- tion, the explicit definitions of the task, and its dichotomous nature) also pro- vides support for the hacking hypothesis. If the individual difference results for the two clinical groups are reliable, they imply that simply teaching children theory-of-mind skills does not mean that they will necessarily be able to use them. There is already some evidence that these skills can be learned by indi- viduals with autism; however, it appears that they are not easily generalized to other social contexts. That is, studies that have attempted to teach ToM skills to people with autism have found that although there is some improvement on experimental tests of ToM, little improvement is evident on tests of social (Ozonoff & Miller, 1995) and communicative competence (Hadwin, Baron- Cohen, Howlin, & Hill, 1996). Indeed, Hadwin et al. used their findings to argue that children with autism pass social-cognition tasks using rules rather than any genuine understanding of the concepts involved.

Although the hacking explanation can account for the failure to find associations between theory-of-mind ability and social functioning in the two clinical groups, it cannot account for the failure to find many associations between these abilities among the typically developing children. That is, mental state understanding, as assessed using false-belief tasks, in the typically developing group was not associated with parent reports of adaptive behavior nor with teacher ratings of social skills. The only significant correlations were with parental reports of assertiveness on the SSRS and with low-level social participation. Thus, typically developing children with higher ToM scores were described by their parents as being more assertive and were observed less frequently in solitary/proximity and parallel play

An alternative explanation for the lack of significant associations in each of the groups, including the typically developing group, is that theory-of-mind ability influences only a relatively narrow range of social behaviors (e.g., those that have as their basis the understanding of another's intentions and point of view) and not social competence in the broader sense. It is possible that each of the measures used here to assess social functioning were too broad and general. Indeed, the Frith et al. (1994) findings support this view, where no differences were found between those individuals with autism who passed and failed the false-belief task and what they referred to as "simple sociability" (e.g., "initiates social contacts," "responds appropriately when introduced"). The two groups only differed on social items that a priori required a theory of mind such as "chooses appropriate presents" and "makes confidences." On the other hand, no relationship was found between false-belief task performance and the social behavior items that were a priori categorized as requiring a ToM in their group of typically developing control children. Unlike the group with autism, who were aged between 7 and 19 years, these were young children aged between 4 and 5 years, which is typically the age during which children develop a ToM. Thus, as Frith et al. argue, those children who fail do not entirely lack the ability to understand mental states. Unlike those with autism, they can still "understand true beliefs, can pretend and distinguish mental states from physical entities, can use mental state terms correctly and can pass non-standard theory of mind tasks" (p. 111). Thus, it is less likely that the typically developing passers and failers would differ on the social measures. After all, these typically developing children show social adaptation appropriate to their developmental level.

Studying typically developing preschoolers, Lalonde and Chandler (1995) found that false-belief understanding was related to items on a teacher-rated social competence questionnaire that required an understanding of mental states (e.g., able to comment on differences between his/her own wishes and those of another). However, no relationship was found with the social convention items on this questionnaire (e.g., says please when asking for something) that did not require such understanding. Astington (this volume) replicated this finding after controlling for the influence of language ability. Thus, she argues that false-belief understanding is related to some but not all aspects of social competence. Similarly, although performance on false-belief tests by young preschoolers was related to specific types of pretense such as role assignment and making joint plans, it was not related to overall amounts of pretend play or to popularity with peers, aggression, or empathy (as rated by peers). However, Astington does report some significant relationships between more global teacher ratings of social behavior and early theory-of-mind ability, as have some other researchers studying typical samples (e.g., Capage & Watson, 1999; Watson, Nixon, Wilson, & Capage, 1999).

The preceding ("too broad") explanation also fails to account for Tager-Flusberg's finding (this volume) of a relationship between theory-of-mind ability and the Socialization domain of the VABS—a finding that was not replicated in the current study. This discrepancy raises the possibility that the current pattern of results may have been an outcome of the particular characteristics of the samples recruited here. In contrast to Tager-Flusberg, who included a group of 67 mixed-ability children with autism aged between 4 and 14 years, each of the clinical groups in the current study comprised a relatively small number of only high-functioning individuals (all IQs > 70) within a relatively narrow age range (5–11 years). These samples may have served not only to limit the variability but also, given the small sample sizes, the power necessary to detect relationships between theory of mind and social functioning. Moreover, Tager-Flusberg used a large battery of tests to assess theory-of-mind ability that were not specific to false-belief understanding. This battery may have been more sensitive to fluctuations in social understanding than the four false-belief tasks used here to assess theory-of-mind competence.

At present, it is not possible to determine which of the three explanations put forward best accounts for the failure to find many associations between theory of mind and social functioning in each of the groups studied here. On the basis of the current results, it is concluded that there is no relationship between theory of mind, as measured here, and the social functioning of the children with autistic disorder, Asperger's disorder, and the typically developing children. That is, individual differences in the ability to predict the false beliefs of a protagonist, by and large, are not related to changes in real-world behavior. It is also concluded that the real-world behavior of children with high-functioning autism and Asperger's disorder is largely identical. There was no indication in the results of any real qualitative or quantitative differences in the social functioning of the two clinical groups, either on the basis of caregiver report or direct observation of their social skills. These results are supportive of the hypothesis that Asperger's disorder is on a continuum with autistic disorder. Thus, any difference between autistic disorder and Asperger's disorder is likely to be an outcome of severity rather than because these are distinct diagnostic entities. The implication of this outcome is that if the ToM deficit is indeed central to autism, then it must also account for the manifestations of Asperger's disorder. Given the demonstrated ability of children with Asperger's disorder to succeed on tests of ToM, the ToM hypothesis would only be feasible if the hacking hypothesis entertained here is true. It now remains necessary to systematically explore the specific processes by which high-functioning individuals with an autism spectrum disorder (be it autistic disorder or Asperger's disorder) are able to succeed on mind-reading tasks.

ACKNOWLEDGMENTS

This study was partly funded by an Australian Research Council Small Grant (8928). We gratefully acknowledge the assistance of Melanie Taylor in conducting this study, which would not have been possible without the generous cooperation of the study participants and their families.

NOTES

1. This pattern of results has recently been replicated in our laboratory in a younger sample of 4- to 7-year-old children with high-functioning autism, Asperger's disorder, and typically developing controls, matched on verbal and overall mental age.
2. It is noteworthy that conversation was the most common playground activity for this group of children, and was one of the two social-functioning behaviors that differentiated them from the group with high-functioning autism.

REFERENCES

American Psychiatric Association. (1994). *Diagnostic and statistical manual of mental disorders* (4th ed.). Washington, DC: American Psychiatric Association.

Astington, J. W., & Jenkins, J. M. (1995). Theory of mind development and social understanding. *Cognition and Emotion, 9,* 151–165.

Astington, J. W., & Jenkins, J. M. (1999). A longitudinal study of the relation between language and theory of mind development. *Developmental Psychology, 35,* 1311–1320.

Baron-Cohen, S. (1989). The autistic child's theory of mind: A case of specific developmental delay. *Journal of Child Psychology and Psychiatry, 30,* 285–287.

Baron-Cohen, S. (2000). Theory of mind and autism: A review. In L. M. Glidden (Ed.), *International review of research in mental retardation: Autism* (Vol. 23, pp. 170–184). San Diego: Academic Press.

Baron-Cohen, S., Leslie, A. M., & Frith, U. (1985). Does the autistic child have a "theory of mind"? *Cognition, 21,* 37–46.

Baron-Cohen, S., Jolliffe, T., Mortimore, C., & Robertson, M. (1997). Another advanced test of theory of mind: Evidence from very high functioning adults with autism or Asperger's syndrome. *Journal of Child Psychology and Psychiatry, 38,* 813–822.

Baron-Cohen, S., Tager-Flusberg, H., & Cohen, D. (Eds.). (2000). *Understanding other minds: Perspectives from developmental cognitive neuroscience* (2nd ed.). Oxford: Oxford University Press.

Baron-Cohen, S., Wheelwright, S., Hill, J., Raste, Y., & Plumb, I. (2001). The "reading the mind in the eyes" test revised version: A study with normal adults, and adults with Asperger's syndrome or high-functioning autism. *Journal of Child Psychology and Psychiatry, 42,* 241–251.

Baron-Cohen, S., Wheelwright, S., & Jolliffe, T. (1997). Is there a "language of the eyes"? Evidence from normal adults and adults with autism or Asperger's syndrome. *Visual Cognition, 4,* 311–331.

Bartsch, K., & Wellman, H. M. (1989). Young children's attribution of action to beliefs and desires. *Child Development, 60,* 946–964.

Bishop, D. V. M. (1989). Autism, Asperger's syndrome and semantic-pragmatic disorder: Where are the boundaries? *British Journal of Disorders of Communication, 24,* 107–121.

Bowler, D. (1992). "Theory of mind" in Asperger's syndrome. *Journal of Child Psychology and Psychiatry, 33,* 877–893.

Capage, L., & Watson, A. C. (2001). Individual differences in theory of mind, aggressive behavior, and social skills in young children. *Early Education and Development, 12,* 613–628.

Dahlgren, S. O., & Trillingaard, A. (1996). Theory of mind in non-retarded children with autism and Asperger's syndrome: A research note. *Journal of Child Psychology and Psychiatry, 37,* 759–763.

Dawson, G., & Fernald, D. (1987). Perspective-taking ability and its relationship to the social behavior of autistic children. *Journal of Autism and Developmental Disorders, 17,* 487–498.

Ehlers, S., Nyden, A., Gillberg, C., Dahlgren, S. A., Dahlgren S. O., Hjelmquist, E., & Oden, A. (1997). Asperger syndrome, autism and attention disorders: A comparative study of the cognitive profiles of 120 children. *Journal of Child Psychology and Psychiatry, 38,* 207–217.

Eisenmajer, R., & Prior, M. (1991). Cognitive linguistic correlates of "theory of mind" ability in autistic children. *British Journal of Developmental Psychology, 9,* 351–364.

Eisenmajer, R., Prior, M., Leekam, S., Wing, L., Gould, J., Welham, M., & Ong, B. (1996). Comparisons of clinical symptoms in autism and Asperger's disorder. *Journal of the American Academy of Child and Adolescent Psychiatry, 35,* 1523–1531.

Fombonne, E., Siddons, F., Achard, S., Frith, U., & Happé, F. (1994). Adaptive behavior and theory of mind in autism. *European Journal of adolescent Psychiatry, 3,* 176–186.

Frith, U. (1989). *Autism: Explaining the enigma.* Oxford: Blackwell.

Frith, U., Happé, F., & Siddons, F. (1994). Autism and theory of mind in everyday life. *Social Development, 3,* 108–123.

Frith, U., Morton, J., & Leslie, A. (1991). The cognitive basis of a biological disorder: Autism. *Trends in Neuroscience, 14,* 433–438.

Ghaziuddin, M., & Butler, E. (1998). Clumsiness in autism and Asperger's syndrome: A further report. *Journal of Intellectual Disability Research, 42,* 43–48.

Gilchrist, A., Green, J., Cox, A., Burton, D., Rutter, M., & Le Couteur, A. (2001). Development and current functioning in adolescents with Asperger's syndrome: A comparative study. *Journal of Child Psychology and Psychiatry, 42,* 227–240.

Gillberg, C. (1989). Asperger syndrome in 23 Swedish children. *Developmental Medicine and Child Neurology, 31,* 529–531.

Gillberg, C., & Ehlers, S. (1998). High-functioning people with autism and Asperger syndrome: A literature review. In E. Schopler, G. B. Mesibov, & L. J. Kunce (Eds.), *Asperger's syndrome or high functioning autism?* (pp. 79–106). New York: Plenum Press.

Gresham, F. M., & Elliot, S. N. (1990). *Social Skills Rating System.* Circle Pines, MN: American Guidance Service.

Hadwin, J., Baron-Cohen, S., Howlin, P., & Hill, K. (1996). Can we teach children with autism to understand emotions, belief, or pretense? *Development and Psychopathology, 8,* 345–365.

Happé, F. (1994). *Autism: An introduction to psychological theory.* Cambridge, MA: Harvard University Press.

Happé, F. (1995). The role of age and verbal ability in the theory-of-mind task performance of subjects with autism. *Child Development, 66,* 843–855.

Howes, C. (1980). Peer play scale as an index of complexity of peer interaction. *Developmental Psychology, 16,* 371–372.

Jolliffe, T., & Baron-Cohen, S. (1999). The Strange Stories Test: A replication with high functioning adults with autism or Asperger syndrome. *Journal of Autism and Developmental Disorders, 29*, 395–406.

Klin, A. (2000). Attributing social meaning to ambiguous visual stimuli in higher functioning autism and Asperger's syndrome: The social attribution task. *Journal of Child Psychology and Psychiatry, 41*, 831–846.

Klin, A., Volkmar, F. R., Sparrow, S. S., Cicchetti, D. V., & Rouke, B. P. (1995). Validity and neuropsychological categorization of Asperger's syndrome: Convergence with nonverbal learning disabilities syndrome. *Journal of Child Psychology and Psychiatry, 36*, 1127–1140.

Klin, A., & Volkmar, F. R. (1997). The pervasive developmental disorders: Nosology and profiles of development. In S. S. Luthar (Ed.), *Developmental psychopathology: Perspectives on adjustment risk and disorder* (pp. 208–226). Cambridge, MA: Harvard University Press.

Lalonde, C. E., & Chandler, M. (1995). False belief understanding goes to school: On the social-emotional consequences of coming early or late to a first theory of mind. *Cognition and Emotion, 9*, 167–185.

Macintosh, K. (2001). *An observational study of the spontaneous peer interactions of children with high functioning autism, children with Asperger's disorder and children developing normally*. Unpublished doctoral dissertation, La Trobe University, Bundoora.

Manjiviona, J., & Prior, M. (1999). Neuropsychological profiles of children with Asperger's syndrome and autism. *Autism, 3*, 327–356.

Miller, J. N., & Ozonoff, S. (2000). The external validity of Asperger's disorder: Lack of evidence from the domain of neuropsychology. *Journal of Abnormal Psychology, 109*, 227–238.

Ozonoff, S., & Miller, J. N. (1995). Teaching theory of mind: A new approach to social skills training for individuals with autism. *Journal of Autism and Developmental Disorders, 23*, 415–433.

Ozonoff, S., Rogers, S. J., & Pennington, B. F. (1991). Asperger's syndrome: Evidence for an empirical distinction from high functioning autism? *Journal of Child Psychology and Psychiatry, 32*, 1107–1122.

Ozonoff, S., South, M., & Miller, J. N. (2000). DSM-IV-defined Asperger syndrome: Cognitive, behavioral, and early history differentiation from high-functioning autism. *Autism, 4*, 29–46.

Perner, J., Frith, U., Leslie, A., & Leekam, S. (1989). Exploration of the autistic child's theory of mid: Knowledge, belief, and communication. *Child Development, 60*, 689–700.

Prior, M., Dahlstrom, B., & Squires, T. L. (1990). Autistic children's knowledge of thinking and feeling states in other people. *Journal of Child Psychology and Psychiatry, 31*, 587–601.

Prior, M., Eisenmajor, R., Leekam, S., Wing, L., Gould, J., Ong, B., & Dowe, D. (1998). Are there subgroups within the autistic spectrum? A cluster analysis of a group of children with autism spectrum disorders. *Journal of Child Psychology and Psychiatry, 39*, 893–902.

Ramberg, C., Ehlers, S., Nyden, A., Johansson, M., & Gillberg, C. (1996). Language and pragmatic functions in school-age children on the autism spectrum. *European Journal of Disorders of Communication, 31*, 387–414.

Roeyers, H., Buysse, A., Ponnet, K., & Pichal, B. (2001). Advancing advanced mind-reading tests: Empathic accuracy in adults with a pervasive developmental disorder. *Journal of Child Psychology and Psychiatry, 42*, 271–278.

Smith, I. M. (2000). Motor functioning in Asperger syndrome. In A. Klin, F. R. Volkmar, & S. S. Sparrow (Eds.), *Asperger syndrome* (pp. 97–124). New York: Guilford Press.

Sparrow, S., Balla, D., & Cicchetti, D. (1984). *Vineland Adaptive Behavior Scales (Survey Form)*. Circle Pines, MN: American Guidance Service.

Szatmari, P. (2000) Perspectives on the classification of Asperger's syndrome. In A. Klin, F. R. Volkmar, & S. S. Sparrow (Eds.), *Asperger syndrome* (pp. 403–417). New York: Guilford Press.

Szatmari, P., Archer, L., Fisman, S., Streiner, D. L., & Wilson, F. (1995). Asperger's syndrome and autism: Differences in behavior, cognition and adaptive functioning. *Journal* of the American Academy of Child and Adolescent Psychiatry, 34, 1662–1671.

Szatmari, P., Bartolucci, G., & Bremner, R. (1989). Asperger's syndrome and autism: Comparison of early history and outcome. Developmental Medicine and Child Neurology, 31, 709–720.

Szatmari, P., Bremner, R., & Nagy, J. (1989). Asperger's syndrome: A review of clinical features. Canadian Journal of Psychiatry, 34, 554–560.

Szatmari, P., Tuff, L., Allen, M., Finlayson, J., & Bartolucci, G. (1990). Asperger's syndrome and autism: Neurocognitive aspects. Journal of the American Academy of Child and Adolescent Psychiatry, 29, 130–136.

Thorndike, R. L., Hagen, E. P., & Sattler, J. M. (1986). The Stanford–Binet Intelligence Scale (4th ed.). Chicago: Riverside.

Travis, L., Sigman, M., & Ruskin, E. (2001). Links between social understanding and social behavior in verbally able children with autism. Journal of Autism and Developmental Disorders, 31, 119–130.

Watson, A. C., Nixon, C. L., Wilson, A., & Capage, L. (1999) Social interaction skills and theory of mind in young children. Developmental Psychology, 35, 386–391.

Wing, L. (1991). The relationship between Asperger's syndrome and Kanner's autism. In U. Frith (Ed.), Autism and Asperger's syndrome (pp. 93–121). Cambridge, UK: Cambridge University Press.

Wing, L. (1996). The autism spectrum: A guide for parents and professionals. Suffolk, UK: St. Edmundsbury Press.

Wing, L. (1998). Past and future research on Asperger's syndrome. In A. Klin, F. R. Volkmar, & S. S. Sparrow (Eds.), Asperger syndrome (pp. 11–28). New York: Guilford Press.

Wimmer, H., & Perner, J. (1983). Beliefs about beliefs: Representation and constraining function of wrong beliefs in young children's understanding of deception. Cognition, 30, 239–277.

World Health Organization. (1993). International classification of diseases (10th ed.). Geneva: Author.

Ziatas, K., Durkin, K., & Pratt, C. (1998). Belief term development in children with autism, Asperger syndrome, specific language impairment, and normal development: Links to theory of mind development. Journal of Child Psychology and Psychiatry, 39, 755–763.

APPENDIX A

SOCIAL PARTICIPATION[3]

All Social Participation subcategories were mutually exclusive. For each 30-second interval, the activity occupying the majority of the child's time was coded.

Social and Play activity subcategories: unoccupied; onlooker; solitary/ proximity play; parallel play; simple-social play; complementary play; conversation; other

Number of Partners subcategories: one; two; three or more; none

Direction of Interaction subcategories: child initiates; other initiates; in continuing interaction

Quality of Interaction subcategories: positive/neutral

---

3. Operational definitions of each of the Social Participation subcategories can be obtained from the authors.

11

Theory of Mind and Social Dysfunction
Psychotic Solipsism Versus Autistic Asociality

ROBYN LANGDON
*Macquarie Centre for Cognitive Science,
Macquarie University*

*P*remack and Woodruff (1978) coined the term *theory of mind* to refer to an ability to impute causal mental states in order to explain and predict behavior. Other authors prefer the terms "mind reading" (Baron-Cohen, 1995) and "mentalizing" (Frith, Morton & Leslie, 1991) because this capacity to "read minds" may or may not rely primarily upon the acquisition and use of a knowledge base about mental states and rules of inference concerning how mental states relate to behavior (i.e., a *theory* of mind).[1] The empirical standard traditionally used to assess whether an individual has an intact theory of mind is demonstrated understanding that intentional agents can act on the basis of beliefs that misrepresent the true state of affairs (Dennett, 1978; Pylyshyn, 1978). For example, in a classic false-belief task, a research participant must predict that another person can act on the basis of a belief that that participant knows to misrepresent the true state of affairs. Likewise, in a standard deception task, a research participant must, in order to gain some strategic advantage, manipulate an opponent into forming a belief that that participant knows to misrepresent the true state of affairs.

When we move out of the laboratory and go back into the real world, what we take the core of mind reading to be is that seemingly spontaneous capacity to appreciate both ourselves and others as subjective beings, each with a unique set of beliefs and desires about the world that govern our consequent actions and thoughts. That there should be a connection between social understanding of this type and everyday social functioning seems obvious. Responding appropriately and flexibly to other people in diverse and dynamic real-world situations must rely, if only in part, upon a fluid capacity to infer what thoughts another person is likely to have in the circumstances and to make appropriate allowances for those thoughts when formulating one's own course of action.

Theory-of-mind researchers have always been interested in the connection between mind reading and social functioning. Comparative studies have investigated the evolution of social behavior, with ongoing debate about the level of mind reading (if any) possessed by nonhuman higher primates (e.g., Heyes, 1998). Child-development studies have investigated the acquisition of increasingly sophisticated mind-reading skills as young children grow into full social adulthood, with ongoing debate about the necessary, if not sufficient, precursors to full-fledged mind reading such as executive function capacities or language (e.g., Astington, this volume; Perner & Lang, 1999). Finally, the theory of mind model of autism has been highly influential in explaining core autistic symptoms (e.g., autistic aloneness) as reflecting mindblindness—that is, a blindness to the subjective lives of people caused by a failure to develop the normal capacity to represent mental states (Baron-Cohen, 1995; Baron-Cohen, Tager-Flusberg, & Cohen, 1993; Frith, 1989). Debate continues, however, about the functional specificity of mind-reading impairments in autism and about the primacy of those impairments in explaining the core nature of the disorder (e.g., Hobson, 1993; Tager-Flusberg, this volume).

Recently, some new perspectives have emerged concerning the putative links between mind reading and social functioning. Ethnographers have begun to question whether mind reading (more specifically, predicting and explaining a person's behavior in terms of that person's inner states) is really a universal feature of human society (Avis & Harris, 1991; Lillard, 1998). Awareness has also been growing that mind reading is not an all-or-nothing ability. Individual differences in mind-reading ability have been observed both within cohorts of healthy young children and within clinical groups who demonstrate relatively poor mind reading when compared (as a group) to appropriately matched healthy controls. The question of interest then is whether these individual differences in mind reading predict individual differences in social functioning, within nonclinical groups (e.g., Astington, this volume) and/or clinical groups (e.g., Tager-Flusberg, this volume).

Individual differences in mind reading are not confined to young children or to clinical groups. Healthy adults with a complete conceptual understanding of mental state causation also show variations in mind-reading ability as a function of: (a) age (the younger the adult, the poorer the mind reading; Happé, Winner, & Brownell, 1998); (b) attributional style (the greater the propensity to blame other people, rather than circumstances, for negative events, the poorer the mind reading; Kinderman, Dunbar, & Bentall, 1998); and (c) self-reported schizotypal personality traits[2] (the higher the rating on such traits, the poorer the mind reading; Langdon & Coltheart, 1999; Pickup & Frith, 2001a).

Other researchers have begun to focus in more detail on the direction of causation in the relationship between poor mind reading and impaired social functioning. For example, whereas a lack of mind reading may be the primary cause of autistic asociality, relatively poor mind reading in some young children may reflect those young children's limited opportunities for crucial social interactions (e.g., with siblings; Peterson, 2000).

The very concept of "disturbed mind reading" may need to be fractionated to explain qualitatively distinct types of social dysfunction. For example, whereas an absence of mind reading may explain the "a"-sociality seen in autism, "anti"-social behaviors might be better explained by: (a) social misuse of normal (perhaps superior) mind-reading skills when these are coupled with other impairments (e.g., a lack of empathy; Blair, this volume) or by (b) a distorted theory about how other people's minds work, as may be the case in Machiavellian individuals (e.g., McIlwain, this volume).

The focus of this chapter is the relationship between poor mind reading and yet another type of social dysfunction. Here I refer to individuals with schizophrenia who, as part of their illness, adopt an alternate reality—that is, these individuals are asocial in the sense that they no longer share the same intersubjective real world inhabited by the rest of society. Later in the chapter, more is said about the phenomenology of schizophrenia and about the evidence for poor mind reading in these individuals. For now, the focus is on some other groups of adults, who, like psychiatric patients with schizophrenia, show mind-reading impairments much later in life, long after the development of normal mental state concepts.

ACQUIRED MIND-READING DEFICITS

Evidence of a link between poor mind reading and asociality in an early-onset neurodevelopmental disorder such as autism may say more about the role that normal mind reading plays in the acquisition of a knowledge base of social rules and a set of social skills than it does about the role that normal mind reading plays in the online processes that underpin everyday social interactions. That is why findings of mind-reading impairments that have been acquired later in life (e.g., in a late-onset neurodevelopmental disorder such as schizophrenia, or in an acquired neurological disorder such as stroke) are so compelling. And evidence that such acquired disorders of mind reading do occur is mounting. We now know, for example, that right-hemisphere and/or frontal brain damage in adults can produce mind-reading deficits, as assessed using a range of story and cartoon versions of traditional theory-of-mind tasks and a less traditional perspective-taking test of mind reading (Bach et al., 1998; Bach, Happé, Fleminger, & Powell, 2000; Happé, Brownell, & Winner, 1999; Happé, Malhi, & Checkley, 2000; Price, Daffner, Stowe, & Mesulam, 1990; Siegal, Carrington, & Radel, 1996; Stone, Baron-Cohen, & Knight, 1998; Winner, Brownell, Happé, Blum, & Pincus, 1998). We also know that acquired mind-reading deficits can be selective. For example, Rowe, Bullock, Polkey, and Morris (2001) found that acquired mind-reading deficits in frontal patients, although concurrent with acquired executive deficits, could not be completely explained by the latter dysfunction. The implication here is that co-occurring executive and mind-reading deficits in frontal patients may reflect the disruption of neuroanatomically close but functionally dissociable modules.

Neurological patients with frontal and/or right-hemisphere brain damage show not only acquired mind-reading deficits, but also acquired deficits in their social functioning. For example, frontal-lobe brain damage has been implicated in a range of social impairments, including social disinhibition, lack of empathy, poor social judgment, flat affect, and idiosyncratic behaviors (see Bach et al., 2000, and Blair, this volume, for reviews). Patients with right-hemisphere brain damage also display a range of social impairments, most notably in the area of communication (see Happé et al., 1999, for a review).

These findings are important for two reasons. First, acquired mind-reading deficits in brain-damaged adults are unlikely to reflect the selective loss of a domain-specific knowledge base about mental states (i.e., a *theory* of mind). Instead, it seems far more likely that what has become disrupted in these individuals is a premorbidly intact domain-specific cognitive system for representing and working out what mental states another person is likely to have in particular circumstances. In other words, what is impaired here is a theory-of-mind *processing* module rather than a theory-of-mind *knowledge* module (see Coltheart, 1999, for more on this distinction between processing modules and knowledge modules).[3] Second, evidence for the co-occurrence of acquired mind-reading deficits and acquired social deficits supports the view that normal everyday social functioning in healthy adults is sustained by the intact, online operation of this domain-specific cognitive system for mind reading. As such, the study of mind reading lends itself well to a cognitive-neuropsychological approach.

Cognitive neuropsychology has two main aims: (1) to explain disturbances of behavior and other symptoms (e.g., out-of-the-ordinary experiences such as delusions) in terms of selective patterns of cognitive disruption or selective difficulties in acquiring particular cognitive abilities, and (2) to evaluate cognitive models in terms of how well these can explain observed patterns of spared and dysfunctional cognitive capacities (Coltheart, 2001). The advantage of a cognitive-neuropsychological approach, in the present context, is that it provides a theoretical framework for hypothetically "lesioning" the cognitive system for mind reading in different ways in order to explain qualitatively different types of social dysfunction. Nowhere is that more important than when it comes to explaining poor mind reading in autism and schizophrenia—two distinct clinical groups who show remarkably similar patterns of poor performances on mind-reading tasks and yet strikingly dissimilar types of clinical asociality.

POOR MIND READING IN SCHIZOPHRENIA

Schizophrenia affects approximately 1 in every 100 individuals. It is the most severe of the psychotic disorders,[4] affects males and females equally, has an onset that is typically in late adolescence or early adulthood, and occurs in all cultures at similar prevalence rates. According to the American Psychiatric Association's *Diagnostic and Statistical Manual of Mental Disorders* (DSM–IV, APA,1994), diagnosis is confirmed by the presence of any two of the following characteristic symptoms: delusions, hallucinations, disorganized speech, disorganized behavior, and negative symptoms. The latter include flat affect, social withdrawal, alogia (i.e., poverty in the amount or the content of speech), apathy, and anhedonia (i.e., a loss of pleasure in life).

Although some negative symptoms of schizophrenia (e.g., social withdrawal and flat affect) are similar to autistic symptoms, schizophrenia and autism are considered quite distinct clinical disorders based, in part, on differences in family history, perinatal history, age of onset, and course of illness (Kolvin, Ounsted, Humphrey, & McNay, 1971; McKenna, Gordon, & Rapoport, 1994; Rutter, 1972).[5] The phenomenological characteristic that diagnostically differentiates schizophrenia from autism is the presence versus absence of delusions and/or hallucinations. Delusions (along with auditory hallucinations) are first-rank markers of schizophrenia and have been considered so since the 1950s (Schneider, 1959). Although the diagnostic criteria for schizophrenia list the presence of any two or more of the characteristic symptoms, the presence of delusions alone is enough to confirm diagnosis, if these are of the bizarre type typically found in schizophrenia. The point here is that delusions are characteristic of schizophrenia, but are not characteristic of autism.

Despite these differences, individuals with schizophrenia reliably show the same patterns of poor performances on mind-reading tasks that have been observed in autistic individuals. People with schizophrenia demonstrate: (a) a poor understanding of false beliefs and deception on story comprehension tasks (Doody, Gotz, Johnstone, Frith, & Cunningham Owens, 1998; Drury, Robinson, & Birchwood, 1998; Frith & Corcoran, 1996); (b) a lack of appreciation of visual jokes when understanding the humor depends upon inferred mental states (Corcoran, Cahill, & Frith, 1997); (c) a difficulty with inferring appropriate intentions of comic-strip characters (Sarfati & Hardy-Bayle, 1999; Sarfati, Hardy-Bayle, Besche, & Widlocher, 1997; Sarfati, Hardy-Bayle, Brunet, & Widlocher, 1999); (d) an impaired ability to infer complex mental states (such as thoughtfulness or boredom) from facial expressions (Kington, Jones, Watt, Hopkin, & Williams, 2000); (e) a difficulty with sequencing picture-card stories, which require inferences of false beliefs in story characters in order to determine the logical order of events (Langdon et al., 1997; Langdon, Coltheart, Ward, & Catts, 2001a, 2002); and (f) an impaired ability to go beyond literal meanings of words in order to infer speakers' thoughts when speakers are using either indirect hints (Corcoran, Mercer, & Frith, 1995) or verbal irony (Drury et al., 1998; Langdon, Davies, & Coltheart, 2002; Mitchley, Barber, Gray, Brooks, & Livingston, 1998). Nonclinical adults assessed as putatively at higher risk of psychosis on the basis of self-reported schizotypal personality traits (i.e., high-schizotypal adults) also show difficulties on mind-reading tasks of this type (Langdon & Coltheart, 1999; Pickup & Frith, 2001a). Furthermore, the mind-reading impairments found in clinical patients with schizophrenia and in nonclinical psychosis-prone adults appear to be highly selective, just as they do in frontal patients. For example, Langdon and colleagues found that domain-general executive impairments such as executive planning deficits and/or poor inhibitory control could not adequately explain poor mind reading in either patients with schizophrenia (Langdon et al., 2001a, 2002) or nonclinical psychosis-prone adults (Langdon & Coltheart, 1999).

THE COGNITIVE NEUROPSYCHOLOGY OF POOR MIND READING

Findings of poor mind reading in patients with schizophrenia and nonclinical psychosis-prone adults seem initially surprising, for two reasons. First, the psychopathological consequence of poor mind reading has always been taken to be autistic symptomatology. That in itself would not be so surprising if the proposal were that poor mind reading causes autisticlike symptoms (e.g., social withdrawal and flat affect), whether these occur in the context of schizophrenia or in the context of autism. Cognitive neuropsychology is interested in explaining symptoms; it is not interested in explaining syndromes or diagnostic entities and, as mentioned earlier, there are autisticlike features to schizophrenia. However, more than that has been proposed. Chris Frith (1992) suggested that poor mind reading may have a primary role to play in the explanation of schizophrenic delusions (in particular, persecutory delusions[6]), the very symptoms that, when present, clinically differentiate individuals with schizophrenia from individuals with autism. Second, patients with schizophrenia (or, at least, paranoid patients) cannot be mindblind in the same way that autistic individuals are. A person who believes that other people are harboring hostile or persecutory thoughts about them can hardly be thought of as mindblind—that is, as someone with an inability to represent mental states.

Frith and colleagues (Frith, 1992; Frith & Frith, 1991) sought to resolve this apparent paradox by drawing a distinction between an early-onset mind-reading deficit, said to explain autism, and a late-onset mind-reading deficit, said to explain the qualitatively different symptoms found in schizophrenia. In brief, the idea here is that early disruption to the normal mind-reading system in autistic individuals prevents these individuals from ever developing a fully functional theory of mind in the first place. In contrast, there may be other individuals, for whom the mind-reading system was intact earlier in life, thus enabling them to develop normal mental state concepts. However, later in life, these individuals lose full control of their ability to use behavioral data appropriately in order to infer the contents of mental states. As a result, these individuals will continue to use mental state concepts to explain events but now there will be misuse of these concepts, as in the unfounded inferences about other people's thoughts and intentions that are said to form the basis of paranoid delusions.[7]

But this only takes us part of the way toward explaining why different types of mind-reading impairment might be associated with qualitatively different types of social dysfunction (i.e., autistic asociality vs. paranoid distrust). A cognitive neuropsychological approach also requires that any theory of this type be modeled in terms of a modular system for mind reading that can be conceptually "lesioned" in different ways in order to determine whether a model based on that theory, although plausible on the surface, could ever be computationally instantiated in the mind.

The modular mind-reading account proposed by Leslie and colleagues (Leslie & Roth, 1993; Leslie & Thaiss, 1992) provides a starting point. Within this model, two components are critical for normal mind reading: (1) a domain-specific cognitive module (a theory-of-mind mechanism: ToMM) dedicated to inferring and representing mental states in order to reason causally about subsequent behavior; and (2) a domain-general selection processor (SP) responsible for selecting appropriate information and inhibiting inappropriate information when making inferences. The ToMM does its job by computing agent-centered representations of the form "Fred believes of y that x is true" or "John intends of y that x is true." Agent-centered representations link an agent to some aspect of a situation via an attitude to the truth of a proposition about that situation. In other words, the ToMM is computationally specialized to use propositional attitudes in order to represent the relationship between epistemic mental states (such as beliefs and intentions) and reality.

According to this model, autistic individuals may show the symptoms that they do because of an undeveloped ToMM,[8] whereas the symptoms displayed by paranoid schizophrenic patients may reflect some late-onset disruption to the SP itself, or to the interface between the SP and an otherwise intact ToMM. The ToMM must itself be intact in paranoid schizophrenic patients since these individuals actively infer other people's hostile thoughts. It seems most likely that the actual site of disruption in these individuals is the interface between the SP and the ToMM. This follows because damage to the SP would impair equally the ability to mind read and the ability to perform a range of executive function tasks and because mind-reading impairments in schizophrenia have been found to be independent of executive planning deficits[9] and/or difficulty with inhibiting "prepotent" inappropriate information (Langdon et al., 2001a, 2002). Pickup and Frith (2001b) also found that patients with schizophrenia perform just as well as psychiatric controls and healthy controls on a "false-map" task (testing understanding of nonmentalistic representation), despite performing more poorly than both control groups on an analogous false-belief task. These results are inconsistent with damage to the SP, which should impair performances on both types of false-representation task.

Localized disruption to the interface between the SP and an otherwise intact ToMM would leave affected individuals capable of representing that other people have beliefs and intentions, while at the same time making those affected individuals vulnerable to drawing inappropriate and unfounded inferences about the contents of other people's thoughts—precisely the story that Frith (1992) tells to explain the link between poor mind reading and paranoid delusions. But it is not just delusions with paranoid content that are associated with poor mind reading in people with schizophrenia. Although some studies report evidence of a link between selective mind-reading impairments and paranoid delusions (Corcoran et al., 1995; Frith & Corcoran, 1996), other studies report that poor mind-reading, when found in acute psychotic individuals, is associated with delusional-hallucinatory states in general, rather than paranoid delusions in particular (Drury et al., 1998). Examples of nonparanoid delusions include grandiose delusions (e.g., the belief that one is God) and somatic delusions (e.g., the belief that one has no internal organs). A view that is emerging now is that selective mind-reading impairments in clinical patients with schizophrenia and in nonclinical psychosis-prone adults may indicate a cognitive vulnerability that predisposes individuals toward magical thinking and delusions (of all types), which can then be exacerbated in the context of an acute psychotic episode (Langdon et al., 2001a).

The ToMM model does a reasonably good job of explaining why poor mind reading of a selective kind (i.e., not due to a damaged SP) might lead to paranoid delusions in people with schizophrenia. However, it fares less well in explaining why selective mind-reading impairments should also be associated with nonparanoid delusions. Initially, one might want to speculate that paranoid delusions reflect localized disconnection to an otherwise intact ToMM, whereas nonparanoid delusions reflect a more fundamental type of theory-of-mind impairment, that is, central damage to the ToMM itself. Damage of this second type would leave affected individuals impaired in their ability to represent the content of a deluded thought as belief—that is, they would have difficulty reflecting "I only think 'I have no internal organs.'"[10]

However, there are two difficulties for this account. First, the paradox that

Frith and colleagues were trying to avoid resurfaces: How could central damage to a ToMM cause nonparanoid delusions in people with schizophrenia when the failure to develop a ToMM does not have the same consequence in autistic individuals? Perhaps delusions only manifest when central damage to the ToMM co-occurs with some other deficit, found in schizophrenia, but not found in autism.[11] Even allowing that argument, there is still a second problem: If a person with a nonparanoid delusion suffers central damage to the ToMM, then it follows that such a person should be impaired in their ability to infer mental states, including other people's hostile thoughts. Hence, nonparanoid delusions should not co-occur with paranoid delusions. That is not the case. Paranoid delusions commonly co-occur with all sorts of other delusions in people with schizophrenia.[12]

That it is proving difficult to adapt a ToMM model to explain the symptoms that are characteristic of schizophrenia (i.e., delusions) hints that some feature of this model, perhaps engineered to address key findings in the autism literature, is wide off the mark when it comes to explaining the core nature of schizophrenia. A key feature of the ToMM model is its focus on propositional attitudes.

MIND READING, VISUAL PERSPECTIVE TAKING, AND PROPOSITIONAL ATTITUDES

Mindblind autistic individuals, who fail to appreciate that other people can *believe* something that differs from what they themselves believe, nevertheless appear to understand that other people can *see* a visual array in ways that differ from what they themselves see (see Baron-Cohen, 1993, for a review). For example, Hobson (1984) found that mindblind autistic individuals performed as well as intellectually matched controls when asked to infer the visual perspective of a doll facing a cube with different colored sides. Findings of this type have been highly influential in promoting the idea that what must be specifically impaired in autistic individuals is a domain-specific capacity to represent *epistemic* mental states, such as believing, in a way that allows for "referential opacity." The contrast here is with nonepistemic mental states, such as seeing, which can be understood transparently (or situationally). Propositional attitudes allow for referential opacity. For example, the meta-representational proposition "I *believe* (attitude) 'It is Wednesday' (proposition)" can be true even if it is really Tuesday. In contrast, "I *saw* a mouse" is true only if I did indeed see one. Hence "perception is transparent and not opaque" (Baron-Cohen, 1993, p. 65). From this it follows that selective damage to a putative theory-of-mind module dedicated to representing epistemic mental states using propositional attitudes will impair mind reading but will leave intact transparent understanding of seeing, including visual perspective taking.

Baron-Cohen (1988) further justified the idea that visual perspective taking requires only a transparent understanding of seeing on the grounds that visual perspectives can be inferred "using a strategy of mental rotation on *primary* representations" (p. 394). In other words, all that one needs to do when making judgments about another visual perspective is to mentally rotate a three-dimensional (3-D) object-centered representation of an array (a primary representation) about an object-relative axis. If this is so, then it follows that the ability to meta-represent an agent's attitude to the truth of a proposition is not needed for visual perspective taking. Hence, if autistic individuals are poor mind readers because they lack this type of meta-representational capacity, then visual perspective taking should be intact in these individuals.

However, what holds for autistic individuals may not hold for patients with schizophrenia or, for that matter, nonclinical psychosis-prone adults. An early report (Anthony, 1958) of visual perspective-taking impairments in a sample of so-called "psychotic" children, most likely a mixed group of individuals, some of whom would now be diagnosed autistic and some of whom would now be diagnosed with childhood-onset schizophrenia, raises some suspicions. If the group, as a whole, was poor at visual perspective taking, and one assumes that the purely autistic members of that group (by today's *DSM–IV* criteria) were normal at visual perspective taking, then it follows that the visual perspective-taking impairments were showing up in the individuals who were manifesting psychotic symptoms and might now be diagnosed with childhood-onset schizophrenia.

INTERIM SUMMARY

Acquired mind-reading deficits, independent of acquired executive deficits, have been found in adults with normal mental state concepts who sustain right-hemisphere and/or frontal brain damage. Acquired deficits of social functioning co-occur with acquired mind-reading deficits. These findings support the view that online mind-reading processes underpin the day-to-day social functioning of healthy adults and that there exists a domain-specific processing module for normal mind reading that can be selectively compromised, resulting in social dysfunction.

Poor mind reading is associated with qualitatively distinct types of social dysfunction (autistic asociality vs. psychotic solipsism). An impairment of precisely the same type cannot explain qualitatively distinct symptoms. Hence, Frith and colleagues proposed that autistic symptoms reflect an early-onset impairment of mind reading, whereas the symptoms that are characteristic of schizophrenia (i.e., delusions) reflect a late-onset disruption to normal mind reading in adults who have acquired normal mental state concepts earlier in their life.

A cognitive neuropsychological approach requires that any theory of this type be modeled in terms of a modular system for mind reading that can be dissociably impaired in order to evaluate whether a model based on that theory, although plausible on the surface, could ever be computationally instantiated in the mind.

The theory-of-mind mechanism (ToMM) model of Leslie and colleagues is a prominent modular account of mind reading. This model does a reasonably good job of explaining why selective mind-reading impairments might cause paranoid delusions in people with schizophrenia. However, it fares less well in explaining why selective mind-reading impairments should also cause nonparanoid delusions.

At the heart of the ToMM model is a domain-specific cognitive module (the ToMM) dedicated to inferring and representing epistemic mental states, such as believing and intending. The contrast here is with nonepistemic mental states, such as seeing, which can be understood transparently. The ToMM does its job by computing agent-centered representations using propositional attitudes. Propositional attitudes allow for referential opacity. For example, the meta-representational proposition "I *believe* (attitude) it is Wednesday (proposition)" can be true even when the embedded proposition is false. Domain specificity of this type allows for a selective disruption to mind reading that can impair appreciation of false belief, while leaving intact transparent understanding of seeing. Transparent understanding of seeing is sufficient to perform successfully on visual perspective-taking tasks. Evidence that visual perspective taking is intact in mindblind autistic individuals supports this particular conception of domain specificity.

However, what holds for autism may not hold for psychotic or psychosis-prone individuals. An early report of visual perspective-taking impairments in a sample of psychotic children raises doubts. If those doubts prove justified, investigation of the visual perspective-taking abilities of psychotic and psychosis-prone individuals may offer insights concerning the link between poor mind reading and psychotic delusions. The following section reviews recent findings of a selective kind of visual perspective-taking impairment in nonclinical adults assessed as putatively at higher risk of psychosis on the basis of self-reported schizotypal traits. The advantage of starting here is that potential confounds inherent in work with clinical psychiatric patients (e.g., medication and institutionalization) can be avoided.

VISUAL PERSPECTIVE TAKING IN NONCLINICAL ADULTS

Langdon and Coltheart (2001) tested visual perspective taking in two groups of nonclinical adults who reported no history of psychiatric illness, using both "item" and "appearance" questions. Item questions required participants to judge the locations of array features relative to another viewer position, whereas appearance questions required judgments about how an array would appear from a different perspective. In order to comprehensively examine visual perspective-taking under a number of conditions, both types of question were paired with viewer- and array-rotation instructions. The former instructed participants to imagine moving themselves to another viewer position (e.g., "what would the array look like if you sat in that chair over there?"), and the latter directed them to imagine rotating a turntable on which an array of objects stands so as to align a different side of the turntable to be directly in front of them (e.g., "what would the array look like if the stand turned so that the edge of the stand now over there were directly in front of you?").[13]

Study 1

In the first study (Experiment 1, Langdon & Coltheart, 2001), the participants were 40 first-year psychology students (26 females and 14 males; mean age of 23.1 years). Exclusion criteria included history of head injury, central nervous system disease, or psychiatric illness. These participants were subdivided into a group of high-schizotypal (hi-S) adults and a group of low-schizotypal (lo-S) adults on the basis of a median split of their total score on the Raine (1991) Schizotypal Personality Questionnaire (SPQ).[14] The hi-S adults in this sample had shown evidence of poor mind reading when required to infer causal mental states in order to sequence false-belief picture cards (Langdon & Coltheart, 1999).

When performing the visual perspective-taking task, participants sat in front of a small table on which stood a square flat white stand. Four colored blocks (red, green, blue, and yellow) were arranged on the stand in a square layout. Beyond the table was a desk with a computer monitor displaying questions (see Figure 11.1). The stand was mounted on a turning platform (not visible to participants) that allowed the stand to be rotated when explaining array-rotation instructions. Prior to that, participants were unaware the stand could rotate. Participants saw three types of instructions (simple, array rotation, and viewer rotation) paired with both item and appearance questions. During array-rotation instructions, three small lever arms (normally concealed under the white stand) were extended to label the three sides of the stand (one dot at 90°, two dots at 180°, and three dots at 270°). During viewer-rotation instructions, the lever arms were concealed and three similarly labeled chairs were placed around the table. During the simple instructions, the lever arms were hidden and there were no chairs placed around the table.

Each participant responded to six types of questions:

(a) *Item question with simple instructions*: "Look at the blocks as they appear directly in front of you. What color do you see in the FRONT on your RIGHT?"

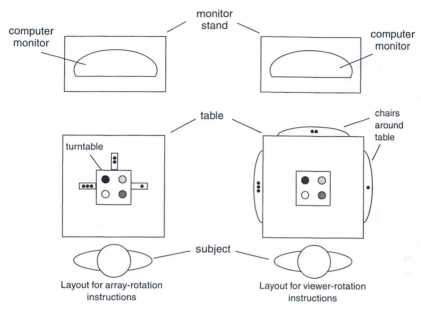

FIGURE 11.1. On the left, the layout for array-rotation instructions with lever arms extended to label the three sides of the turntable (one dot at 90°, two dots at 180°, three dots at 270°); and, on the right, the layout for viewer-rotation instructions with lever arms concealed and three labeled chairs placed around the table. Reprinted from Langdon and Coltheart (2001), with permission from Elsevier Science.

(b) *Appearance question with simple instructions:* "Look at the blocks as they appear directly in front of you. Do the blocks look like this?"[15]

(c) *Item question with array-rotation instructions:* "Imagine turning the stand so that the single dot is in front of you. What color would you see in the FRONT on your RIGHT?"

(d) *Appearance question with array-rotation instructions:* "Imagine turning the stand so that the single dot is in front of you. Would the blocks look like this?"

(e) *Item question with viewer-rotation instructions:* "Imagine moving to sit in the chair with the single dot. What color would you see in the FRONT on your RIGHT?"

(f) *Appearance question with viewer-rotation instructions:* "Imagine moving to sit in the chair with the single dot. Would the blocks look like this?"

The simple instructions always came first. Order of presentation of array- and viewer-rotation instructions was then counterbalanced, as was the order of presentation of item and appearance questions. Participants wore a microphone headset. The computer recorded voice-activated response latencies, and errors were recorded manually.

Initial analyses treated instruction type as a within-subjects factor and revealed significant carryover effects—that is, the strategies adopted with the first set of instructions influenced how participants performed with the second set of instructions. Results were therefore reanalyzed treating instruction type as a between-subjects factor—that is, the visual perspective-taking abilities of lo- and hi-S adults on item and appearance questions were compared *when participants saw each instruction for the first time*[16] (see Figure 11.2). In brief, there were no differences between lo- and hi-S adults judging item questions. Differences were restricted to accuracy scores on appearance questions. The lo-S adults judged appearance questions with equal accuracy whether given array- or viewer-rotation instructions, $F(1,36) = .71, p = .40$. In contrast, the hi-S adults were significantly less accurate under the viewer-rotation instructions, $F(1,36) = 4.76, p = .03$. There was also a tendency for the hi-S adults to be less accurate than the lo-S adults judging appearance questions under the viewer-rotation instructions, $F(1,36) = 3.30, p = .07$, but not under the array-rotation instructions, $F(1,36) = 1.34, p = .25$.

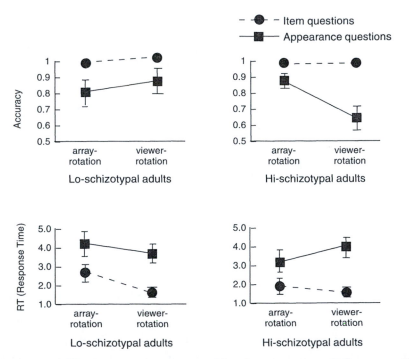

FIGURE 11.2. Accuracy (proportion correct) and response times (RTs, expressed as a ratio of baseline RT responding to simple instructions) of lo- and hi-S adults judging item and appearance questions under viewer- and array-rotation instructions (based on Experiment 1, Langdon & Coltheart, 2001).

Regardless of their schizotypy rating, a participant's accuracy judging appearance questions under viewer-rotation instructions tended to predict his or her mind-reading ability[17] (in the group who saw viewer-rotation instructions first: $r = .40$, $p = .07$), whereas accuracy judging appearance questions under array-rotation instructions was unrelated to mind reading (in the group who saw array-rotation instructions first: $r = .00$, $p = .99$). There was no relationship between mind reading and item questions under either instruction.

After the first study, a second experiment was carried out for the following reason: If lo- and hi-S adults differ on appearance questions (mediated by instruction type), but not on item questions, then the theoretical interpretation of that dissociation depends upon what the crucial distinction between these questions is. Although it seems likely that the critical distinction here is the different strategies cued by the two types of questions (geometric reasoning in the case of item questions vs. imaging what it would be like, firsthand, to view another perspective in the case of appearance questions), the item and appearance questions used in the first study differed in other ways. First, these questions differed in their level of complexity; item questions focused on the location of a single block, whereas appearance questions asked participants to take account of all four block locations. Second, item questions asked participants to name colors, whereas appearance questions required yes/no decisions.

Study 2

The aim of the second study was to replicate the pattern of results found in Study 1, using more directly comparable item and appearance questions. The participants were 28 first-year psychology students (16 females and 12 males; mean age of 22.1 years) who were subdivided into a group of hi-S adults and a group of lo-S adults on the basis of a median split of their total schizotypy score. Exclusion criteria were the same as in Study 1. These individuals had participated in Experiment 2 of Langdon and Coltheart (1999) and had provided evidence that relatively poor mind reading in hi-S adults cannot be explained by executive planning impairments and/or poor inhibitory control.

Response type was equated by asking participants to make yes/no decisions for both item and appearance questions. Response latencies and errors were recorded by the computer. In order to equate for level of complexity, appearance questions were redesigned to vary in complexity with the simplest appearance questions being asked about arrays where three blocks were of the same color (e.g., three yellow blocks and one blue block), thus allowing participants to focus on the location of a single, distinctly colored block (as is the case for item questions) when answering the appearance question. For more complex appearance questions, participants were then shown arrays where two blocks were of the same color (e.g., two yellow blocks, one red, and one green) and then arrays with four distinctly colored blocks (as in Study 1). In all other ways the procedure and analyses were similar to Study 1.

Figure 11.3 illustrates results for item questions and the simplest level of appearance questions (i.e., those where responses could be based on the relative location of a single distinctive block)[18] when each instruction was seen for the first time. In brief, lo- and hi-S adults did not differ in their ability to judge item questions regardless of instruction. Differences between lo- and hi-S adults were restricted to response latencies judging appearance questions. The lo-S adults judged appearance questions at similar rates whether given array- or viewer-rotation instructions, $F(1,24) = .41$, $p = .53$. In contrast, the hi-S adults were significantly slower under the viewer-rotation instructions, $F(1,24) = 11.18$, $p = .003$. There was also a tendency for the hi-S adults to be faster than the lo-S adults judging appearance questions under the array-rotation instructions, $F(1,24) = 3.66$, $p = .07$, but slower than this group under the viewer-rotation instructions, $F(1,24) = 3.76$, $p = .06$.

Regardless of their schizotypy rating, a participant's speed judging appearance questions under the viewer-rotation instructions tended to predict his or

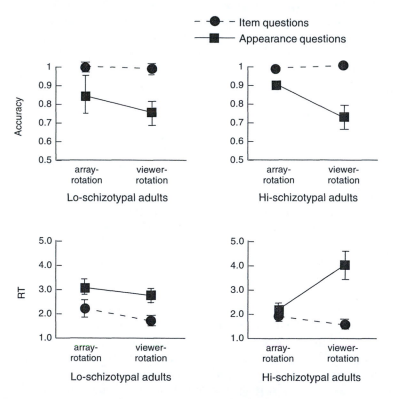

FIGURE 11.3. Accuracy (proportion correct) and RTs (expressed as a ratio of baseline RT) of lo- and hi-S adults judging item and stage-one appearance questions under array- and viewer-rotation instructions (Experiment 2, Langdon & Coltheart, 2001).

her mind-reading ability (in the group who saw viewer-rotation instructions first: $r = -.49$; $p = .06$), whereas speed judging appearance questions under the array-rotation instructions was unrelated to mind reading (in the group who saw array-rotation instructions first: $r = .17$; $p = .90$). There was no relationship between mind reading and the item questions under either instruction.

OVERVIEW OF STUDIES 1 AND 2

Nonclinical high-schizotypal adults, who show relatively poor mind reading when compared to low-schizotypal adults, showed no signs of visual perspective-taking difficulty when required to make judgments about relative spatial locations of array-features (i.e., on item questions). Their difficulties only became apparent when participants were required to imagine how an array would appear from a different perspective (i.e., on appearance questions), and then, only when instructed to imagine relocating as viewer, relative to a fixed array (i.e., under viewer-rotation instructions). In contrast, the high-schizotypal adults sometimes outperformed the low-schizotypal adults when required to image a change of visual perspective by imagining an array rotating while they stayed fixed as viewer (i.e., under array-rotation instructions). Of interest now is whether poor mind reading co-occurs with this selective kind of visual perspective-taking impairment in clinical patients with schizophrenia.

VISUAL PERSPECTIVE TAKING IN PATIENTS WITH SCHIZOPHRENIA

Using the same paradigm that had been used to test visual perspective taking in Study 2, Langdon et al. (2001b) investigated visual perspective taking in a group of clinical patients with schizophrenia who had elsewhere shown evidence of poor mind reading[19] that could not be completely explained by intellectual deterioration and/or generalized executive dysfunction (Langdon et al., 2001a). Thirty-two patients took part in the study; 30 had a diagnosis of schizophrenia and 2 were diagnosed with schizoaffective disorder. Age of illness onset ranged from 17 to 50 years (mean 24.3 years) and duration of illness ranged from 10 months to 34 years (mean 12.9 years). All but one patient were receiving medication. Twenty-four healthy controls, matched to the patient group on age, sex, and educational level, were recruited and screened for the presence of psychotic and/or affective disorders.

Visual memory span, spatial working memory, and visual perspective-taking were tested in patients and controls. As has been found elsewhere, the patients showed reduced memory spans and a poorer capacity for spatial working memory. The visual perspective-taking abilities of patients and controls[20] were therefore compared, making appropriate adjustments for visual memory span and spatial working memory capacity. Figure 11.4 shows adjusted means for item questions and the simplest level of appearance question (i.e., those where responses could be based on the relative location of a single distinctive block)[21] when each instruction was seen for the first time. In brief, the patients and the controls were equally capable of judging item questions regardless of instruction. In contrast, the patients made significantly more errors than the controls judging appearance questions, but only under the viewer-rotation instructions, $F(1,50) = 5.84, p = .019$, and not under the array-rotation instructions, $F(1,50) = .46, p = .42$.

That the patients also tended to be faster than the controls judging appearance questions under the viewer-rotation instructions raised the possibility of a speed–accuracy trade-off. However, if the patients had made more errors when appearance questions were paired with viewer-rotation instructions simply because they gave up, then that would predict an increase in random responding

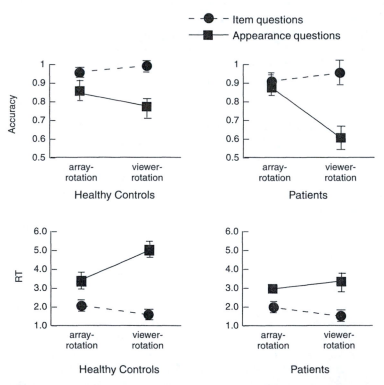

FIGURE 11.4. Adjusted means for patients and controls of accuracy (proportion correct as a ratio of baseline accuracy) and RTs (expressed as a ratio of baseline RTs) judging item questions and stage-one appearance questions under array- and viewer-rotation instructions (Langdon et al., 2001b).

and, hence, an increase in all types of errors. That was not the pattern found. Patients made more errors judging appearance questions under the viewer-rotation instructions (compared to how well they performed under the array-rotation instructions), but only when required to accept the correct perspective or to reject a depiction of their own viewpoint, $ps < .02$. In contrast, the patients rejected other incorrect perspectives and impossible arrangements of blocks equally well under the two instructions, $ps > .30$. In other words, the patients were clearly trying to do the task when given the viewer-rotation instructions, but they were trying in an inappropriate way. Under the viewer-rotation instructions (but not under the array-rotation instructions), the patients' responses were influenced by how the array appeared directly to them—that is, they made more egocentric errors.

For the group of 16 patients and 12 controls who saw viewer-rotation instructions first, mind reading was significantly correlated with accuracy in judging appearance questions under viewer-rotation instructions, $r = .42$, $p = .02$. For the other group of 16 patients and 12 controls who saw array-rotation instructions first, mind reading was unrelated to accuracy judging appearance questions under array-rotation instructions, $r = .22$, $p = .26$.[22]

IMPLICATIONS: DOMAIN SPECIFICITY AND ALLOCENTRIC FRAMES OF REFERENCE

Doubts prompted by an early report (Anthony, 1958) of visual perspective-taking impairments in a sample of psychotic children have been justified. Visual perspective taking is not fully intact in either clinical patients with schizophrenia or nonclinical high-schizotypal adults who show selective mind-reading impairments when compared to appropriate controls. Whether or not visual perspective taking is truly intact in mindblind autistic individuals, as is currently thought, is an open question. This is because the impairments of visual perspective taking observed in psychotic and psychosis-prone adults only became apparent when research participants were required to image a change of visual perspective (i.e., on appearance questions), and then only when instructed to imagine relocating as viewer, relative to a fixed array (i.e., under viewer-rotation instructions). In contrast, the psychotic and the psychosis-prone adults showed no signs of visual perspective-taking difficulty when required to make judgments about relative spatial locations (i.e., on item questions), regardless of instruction type.

In the case of autistic individuals, intact visual perspective taking has most often been demonstrated using item questions, possibly because these are easier to understand. For example, Reed and Peterson (1990) found no differences between autistic individuals and controls when participants were asked to move a turntable, on which an object stood side-on to the experimenter, so that the experimenter could see the "nose" or "tail" (i.e., the object's front or back). Likewise, Tan and Harris (1991) found no differences between autistic individuals and controls when participants were asked which of two objects another observer would identify as being "in front." In contrast, Yirmiya, Sigman, and Zacks (1994) found that high-functioning autistic children performed more poorly (as a group) than controls on a visual perspective-taking task when instructions were more like appearance questions—that is, the participants were asked to "turn it (referring to a turntable on which an array of objects stood) around until you see it in the same way that I see it now from where I am standing" (p. 267). Yirmiya and colleagues concluded, however, that most of their autistic participants showed good visual perspective taking. It is intriguing to note though that the question used by Yirmiya and colleagues combines aspects of viewer- and array-rotation instructions—that is, the participants were asked to rotate an array (somewhat like array-rotation instructions) until they saw it like an experimenter saw it from another viewer position (somewhat like viewer-rotation instructions).

Whether or not autistic individuals will continue to show intact visual perspective taking when asked appearance questions under viewer-rotation instructions is something that we need to know. The current practice of using item questions to test visual perspective taking in these individuals may not be the most appropriate way to determine whether or not they really do appreciate that other people can see a visual array in ways that differ from what they themselves see. That is, item questions can be solved geometrically by representing relative spatial locations; in contrast, appearance questions may tap a capacity to image the visual perceptual experience of a person viewing a 3-D array[23] from a point in space other than where the self is currently located. Later in this chapter, more is said concerning the distinction between item and appearance questions. For now, the focus is on findings of a selective kind of visual perspective-taking impairment in psychotic and psychosis-prone adults. Those findings require explanation.

Psychotic and psychosis-prone adults who are poor mind readers show difficulties with judging appearance questions under viewer-rotation instructions (but not under array-rotation instructions), despite performing as well as controls when judging item questions, regardless of instruction. The latter result is a challenge to any account that focuses primarily on propositional attitudes. To clarify, the results for item questions indicate that psychotic and psychosis-prone adults are perfectly capable of representing the relationship between an agent's position in space and a description of (or a proposition about) the location of array features (e.g., "Person in chair x sees 'feature z to the front-right' about the array"). If this is so, why do these individuals have a difficulty with formulating the same type of representation in order to judge appearance questions under viewer-rotation instructions, which they do poorly, and why do they have a difficulty with representing an agent being connected to reality via a decoupled proposition (e.g., "Fred believes 'proposition x' is true about situation y") in order to carry out false-belief tasks, which they also do poorly?

A lot depends on how one interprets the verb "*sees*" in "Person in chair x *sees* 'feature z to the front-right' about the array." Correct responses to item questions do not require an intact ability to represent "seeing" as a visual experience; instead, these questions can be solved correctly as long as a participant is capable of representing "seeing" spatially—that is, in terms of geometric line of sight and relative spatial locations. In contrast, appearance questions may tap a capacity to represent "Fred" as visually experiencing the sight of an array in a way that is uniquely determined by where Fred stands in the world relative to that array. However, it is unclear why propositional attitudes are the best way to conceptualize that sort of relationship between Fred and the world.

Langdon and colleagues (Langdon & Coltheart, 2001; Langdon et al., 2001b) proposed, instead, that psychotic and psychosis-prone adults show performance deficits on theory-of-mind tasks because of an impairment of cognitive and/or visual perspective taking (i.e., perspective taking is impaired in these individuals whether they are required to appreciate what another person might think in particular circumstances or they are required to image another visual perspective by relocating self, in imagination, relative to a fixed world). This perspective-taking impairment occurs, Langdon and colleagues proposed, because psychotic and psychosis-prone individuals have a difficulty with stepping outside the tunnel of their own subjectivity in order to position self as only one subject among many other subjects, all apprehending an independent reality. In other words, these individuals are selectively impaired in their ability to use an *allocentric* frame of reference in order to engage in intersubjective perspective taking.

Although novel in this context, the allocentric/egocentric distinction is well known to researchers investigating the psychology of spatial navigation, where the term *allocentric* is used to describe a "*map-like* representation, from a detached point of view, from which the subject figures as one object among many. . . . The contrast here is with a more subjective or idiosyncratic way of locating things around one, which is essentially dependent upon one's own perspective . . . (*egocentric*) spatial representation somehow tied to one's own point of view, which therefore has difficulty in capturing the idea of a world which is there anyway . . . independently of the way it currently seems" (Brewer & Pears, 1993, p. 26). To illustrate, there is a distinction between learning to get from home to work via a fixed route (egocentric referencing) and learning to get to work from anywhere in the city (allocentric referencing).

The findings reviewed in this chapter suggest that allocentric frames of reference are needed not only to perform some types of spatial reasoning tasks but also to engage in intersubjective perspective taking. Psychotic and psychosis-prone adults appear to be perfectly capable of mapping themselves as only one *object* among many other objects onto an allocentric frame of reference (allocentric spatial representation) in order to judge item questions under viewer-rotation instructions (which ask about spatial locations of array features relative to another point in space). In contrast, these individuals appear to have a selective difficulty with mapping themselves as only one *subject* among many other subjects all apprehending a shared objective reality that stands independent of each and every viewpoint (an allocentric representation of intersubjectivity). It is the latter capacity that is tapped by appearance questions under viewer-rotation instructions, but not by appearance questions under array-rotation instructions. This follows because only the former require participants to step outside the tunnel of their own subjectivity in order to represent the viewed object as the independent focus of multiple arbitrary first-person viewpoints.

In terms more compatible with traditional theory-of-mind research, what is being suggested here is that we need to move beyond the current focus on agent-centered representations in order to consider the processes required to position agent-centered representations relative to an allocentric frame of reference. This is not so radically different from Baron-Cohen's (1995) idea of a Shared Attention Mechanism, which "triangulates" agents relative to each other and each agent relative to an object, although now we're talking about more than just attention. Perhaps this notion of positioning an agent relative to a world map has always been implicit in ideas about meta-representation. Nevertheless, the findings reviewed in this chapter suggest that this now needs to be made explicit in order to develop a full account of the processes required for normal mind reading and the dissociable ways in which normal mind reading can be disrupted.

The normal cognitive system for mind reading may depend on the interaction of two dissociable cognitive processes: (1) an intact ability to decouple subjectivity from objectivity using propositional attitudes so as to appreciate that belief can misrepresent reality (a capacity that appears to be impaired in autistic individuals but is intact in psychotic and psychosis-prone adults), and (2) an intact ability to map agent-centered representations onto an allocentric frame of reference so as to appreciate that each subjective view of the world (including our own) is tied to a unique vantage point. It is the latter capacity that is selectively impaired in psychotic and psychosis-prone individuals. At this point, it is an open question whether or not this second capacity is also impaired in autistic individuals. If autistic individuals have type 1 impairment in the absence of type 2 impairment, then perhaps these individuals will still continue to perform normally on visual perspective-taking tasks, even when required to judge what an array will *look like* from another point in space.

CONCLUSIONS

This chapter began by reviewing evidence of acquired mind-reading deficits, independent of acquired executive deficits, in brain-damaged adults with normal mental state concepts. Acquired mind-reading deficits co-occur with acquired deficits in social functioning. These findings support the existence of a domain-specific processing module for mind-reading that sustains normal adult social interactions. Qualitatively distinct types of social dysfunction are associated with poor mind reading. Attempting to dissociably "lesion" the ToMM model in order to provide a coherent account of the clinical distinction between autistic asociality and delusions (with either paranoid or nonparanoid content, or sometimes both) in people with schizophrenia had proved problematic. At the heart of the ToMM model is a domain-specific cognitive module dedicated to representing epistemic mental states using propositional attitudes. This conception of domain specificity developed, in part, to explain a putative dissociation in autism between impaired mind reading and intact visual perspective taking. Evidence of a selective kind of visual perspective-taking impairment in psychotic and psychosis-prone adults who are poor mind readers casts doubt on this dissociation, even in autistic individuals.

Impairments of visual and/or cognitive perspective taking in psychotic and psychosis-prone adults were attributed to a selective difficulty with mapping self as only one subject among many other subjects onto an allocentric frame of reference. This led to the proposal that the normal cognitive system for mind reading comprises (1) an intact ability to decouple mental states from reality so as to represent false belief and (2) an intact ability to represent the "aspectuality" of subjective life (i.e., that each subjective representation of the world is tied to a unique vantage point). It is the latter capacity that is selectively impaired in psychotic and psychosis-prone individuals, leading them to slide into psychotic solipsism—but why, precisely? Perhaps type 2 mind-reading capacity is critical when confronted with discordant information (e.g., when the things we take for fact are at odds with the things that other people tell us are fact) in order to represent those conflicting pieces of information as equally possible ways of apprehending an independent reality, each contingent upon a unique vantage point. An intact ability to represent information in this way (information that might be about the state of one's own body or about the plotting of neighbors) may provide a means of reconciling discordant information that is quite different to the way in which acutely psychotic patients "reconcile" discordant information. This they do by simply discounting what other people think as blatantly wrong and maintaining their own view as unequivocally right, as opposed to being able to reflect "it seems this way to me" and "it seems that way to someone else," where neither viewpoint automatically acquires the status of absolute truth.

ACKNOWLEDGMENTS

I am grateful to participants of the MACCS (Macquarie Centre for Cognitive Science) funded workshop "Mindreading and Behaviour: Individual Differences in Theory of

Mind and Implications for Social Functioning," held at Macquarie University in July 2001, for helpful discussion of many issues raised in this chapter.

NOTES

1. "Simulation" theorists take the view that mind reading is primarily a process of disengaging from how we ourselves apprehend the world in order to "step into the mental shoes" of another person so as to *simulate* (imaginatively) the consequent thoughts and actions that would follow from being in that other person's situation (see Davies & Stone, 1995a, 1995b, for an overview of theory–theory versus simulation theory).

2. Schizotypal personality traits form part of the normal diversity of healthy personality expression found within adults, which, although not considered pathological, may mark a cognitive vulnerability that predisposes toward psychosis (i.e., delusional/hallucinatory experience). This vulnerability may remain dormant, never manifesting in psychotic breakdown, unless triggered and exacerbated by adverse physical, social, and/or environmental factors (Claridge, 1987, 1994; Claridge & Beech, 1995).

3. It also seems far more likely that graded impairment of a processing module, rather than a knowledge module, will better explain the individual differences in mind-reading ability observed in healthy adults who function adequately enough in normal society not to have come to the notice of clinicians.

4. The term *psychosis* derives from *psyche* meaning "the mind" and *osis* meaning "illness," hence "illness of the mind." Over the years, the term has been used in a number of ways—for example, at one point, to distinguish disorders of the brain (psychoses) from nervous conditions (neuroses). Today, the term is generally taken to apply to conditions where an individual adopts an alternate reality, defined primarily by the presence of delusions and/or hallucinations.

5. For example, even those relatively rare cases of childhood onset schizophrenia develop after years of normal, or near-normal, development.

6. Frith (1992) originally conceptualized different types of schizophrenic symptoms as reflecting poor mind reading in different domains: (1) negative symptoms (e.g., apathy) were seen to reflect a theory-of-mind difficulty with representing one's own goals; (2) alien control delusions and other "loss of boundary" experiences (e.g., thought insertion) were seen to reflect a theory-of-mind difficulty with representing one's own intentions; and (3) delusions of persecution and reference were seen to reflect a theory-of-mind difficulty with inferring the appropriate thoughts and intentions of other people. More recently, Frith and Corcoran (1996) focused on a link between selective theory-of-mind impairments in schizophrenia and persecutory delusions.

7. A full account of paranoid delusions also requires a motivational bias to explain why unfounded inferences always take the form of inferring that other people have harmful intentions. Kinderman and Bentall (2000) proposed just such a model whereby paranoia manifests when a theory-of-mind deficit is coupled with an externalizing–personalizing bias (i.e., a tendency to externalize blame for negative

events coupled with a tendency to target other people rather than situational factors when avoiding self-blame).

8. According to this model, young children prior to four or five years have a functional ToMM and an undeveloped SP. That is why these individuals succeed on simple mind-reading tasks that test understanding of desire and yet perform poorly on false-belief and false-photograph tasks, both of which require inhibition of current reality. In contrast, autistic individuals have an intact SP and an undeveloped ToMM. That is why these individuals perform poorly on false-belief tasks (testing understanding of the representational nature of mental states), despite succeeding on false-photograph tasks (testing understanding that nonmentalistic representations can misrepresent current reality).

9. Part of the job of the SP is to inhibit current reality when reasoning strategically about sequences of hypothetical moves in order to solve executive planning tasks.

10. Another way to think about this is that a patient with grandiose delusions may have difficulty representing first-order beliefs, whereas a patient with paranoid delusions only has difficulty representing second-order beliefs (e.g., to shift from "They *intend* to harm me" to "I only *think* 'They *intend* to harm me.'" I thank Betty Repacholi for this suggestion.

11, Alternatively, some deficit, present in autism but not present in schizophrenia, may "protect" autistic individuals from developing delusions.

12. One patient interviewed by Robyn Langdon had the grandiose delusion that he owned every company in the world as well as the paranoid delusion that the government was plotting with his parents to stop him from receiving the royalties he was due. This patient also believed that hidden cameras were monitoring his every movement and that this surveillance was organized by government officials who thought he was dangerous.

13. Huttenlocher and Presson (1973, 1979) were the first to combine both types of instructions with both types of questions when investigating visual perspective taking in children.

14. See Bentall, Claridge, and Slade (1989) and Claridge (1994) for reviews of past studies providing evidence that psychoticlike traits vary within normal adults and that individual differences in psychosis proneness, or schizotypy, can be measured using self-report scales such as the SPQ, a self-report scale of 74 yes/no questions comprising nine subscales based on the criteria for diagnosis of schizotypal personality disorder.

15. For all appearance questions, a graphic image appeared beneath the question depicting an array of colored blocks on a white stand, as if seen in perspective.

16. In other words, the 10 lo- and 10 hi-S adults who saw the viewer-rotations instructions first were compared to the 10 lo- and 10 hi-S adults who saw the array-rotation instructions first.

17. Mind-reading ability was indexed by speed and accuracy in sequencing false-belief picture-card stories relative to control stories.

18. Appearance questions showed a main effect of increasing complexity. However, the pattern of results for more complex appearance questions was identical to that found for the simplest level of appearance questions.

19. Mind reading in this patient group was assessed using the same false-belief picture-

sequencing task that had been used to test mind reading in the nonclinical groups described in Studies 1 and 2.

20. Patients showed poorer baseline visuo-spatial abilities than controls when responding to the simple instructions (whether indexed by accuracy or RT measures). Both the accuracy and RT measures of visual perspective-taking ability were therefore computed as ratios of corresponding baseline performances under the simple instructions.

21. As with Study 2, there was a main effect of complexity for appearance questions, but this did not alter the basic pattern of results for patients and controls.

22. No correlations were significant when patients and controls were treated separately, possibly due to heterogeneity in the patient group and limitations of power.

23. I am grateful to Helen Tager-Flusberg, Janet Astington, and other participants at the 2001 Macquarie Centre for Cognitive Science Workshop: Mindreading and Behaviour: Individual Differences in Theory of Mind and Implications for Social Functioning, for helpful discussion on this point.

REFERENCES

American Psychiatric Association. (1994). *Diagnostic and statistical manual of mental disorders DSM–IV* (4th ed.). Washington DC: APA.

Anthony, E. J. (1958). An experimental approach to the psychopathology of childhood: Autism. *British Journal of Medical Psychology, 31*, 211–225.

Avis, J., & Harris, P. (1991). Belief-desire reasoning among Baka children: Evidence for a universal conception of mind. *Child-Development, 62*(3), 460–467.

Bach, L., Davies, S., Colvin, C., Wijeratne, C., Happé, F., & Howard, R. (1998). A neuropsychological investigation of theory of mind in an elderly lady with frontal leucotomy. *Cognitive Neuropsychiatry, 3*(2), 139–159.

Bach, L., Happé, F., Fleminger, S., & Powell, J. (2000). Theory of mind: Independence of executive function and the role of the frontal cortex in acquired brain injury. *Cognitive Neuropsychiatry, 5*, 175–192.

Baron-Cohen, S. (1988). Social and pragmatic deficits in autism: Cognitive or affective? *Journal of Autism and Developmental Disorders, 18*, 379–402.

Baron-Cohen, S. (1993). From attention-goal psychology to belief-desire psychology: The development of a theory of mind and its dysfunction. In S. Baron-Cohen, H. Tager-Flusberg, & D. J. Cohen (Eds.), *Understanding other minds: Perspectives from autism* (pp. 59–82). Oxford: Oxford University Press.

Baron-Cohen, S. (1995). *Mindblindness: An essay on autism and theory of mind*. Cambridge, MA: MIT Press.

Baron-Cohen, S., Tager-Flusberg, H., & Cohen, D. J. (1993). *Understanding other minds: Perspectives from autism*. Oxford: Oxford University Press.

Bentall, R. P., Claridge, G. S., & Slade, P. D. (1989). The multidimensional nature of schizotypal traits: Factor analytic study with normal subjects. *British Journal of Clinical Psychology, 28*, 363–375.

Brewer, B., & Pears, J. (1993). Frames of reference. In N. Eilan, R. McCarthy, & B. Brewer (Eds.), *Spatial perception*. Oxford: Blackwell.

Claridge, G. (1987). "The schizophrenias as nervous types" revisited. *British Journal of Psychiatry, 151*, 735–743.

Claridge, G. (1994). Single indicator of risk for schizophrenia: Probable fact or likely myth? *Schizophrenia Bulletin, 20*(1), 151–168.

Claridge, G., & Beech, T. (1995). Fully and quasi-dimensional constructions of schizotypy. In A. Raine, T. Lencz, & S. A. Mednick

(Eds.), *Schizotypal personality* (pp. 192–216). New York: Cambridge University Press.

Coltheart, M. (1999). Modularity and cognition. *Trends in Cognitive Sciences, 3,* 115–120.

Coltheart, M. (2001). Assumptions and methods in cognitive neuropsychology. In B. Rapp (Ed.), *Handbook of cognitive neuropsychology* (pp. 3–21). Philadelphia: Psychology Press.

Corcoran, R., Cahill C., & Frith, C. D. (1997). The appreciation of visual jokes in people with schizophrenia: A study of mentalizing ability. *Schizophrenia Research, 24*(3), 319–327.

Corocoran, R., & Frith, C. D. (1996). Conversational conduct and the symptoms of schizophrenia. *Cognitive Neuropsychiatry, 1,* 305–318.

Corcoran, R., Mercer, G., & Frith, C. D. (1995). Schizophrenia, symptomatology and social inference: Investigating "theory of mind" in people with schizophrenia. *Schizophrenia Research, 17,* 5–13.

Davies, M., & Stone, T. (1995a). *Folk psychology: The theory of mind debate.* Oxford: Blackwell.

Davies, M., & Stone, T. (1995b). *Mental simulations: Evaluations and applications.* Oxford: Blackwell.

Dennett, D. C. (1978). *The intentional stance.* Cambridge, MA: MIT Press.

Doody, G. A., Gotz, E. C., Johnstone, E. C., Frith, C. D., & Cunningham Owens, D. G. (1998). Theory of mind and psychosis. *Psychological Medicine, 28,* 397–405.

Drury, V. M., Robinson, E. J., & Birchwood, M. (1998). 'Theory of mind' skills during an acute episode of psychosis and following recovery. *Psychological Medicine, 28,* 1101–1112.

Frith, C. D. (1992). *The cognitive neuropsychology of schizophrenia.* Hove, UK: Lawrence Erlbaum.

Frith, C. D., & Corcoran, R. (1996). Exploring "theory of mind" in people with schizophrenia. *Psychological Medicine, 26,* 521–530.

Frith, C. D., & Frith, U. (1991). Elective affinities in schizophrenia and childhood autism. In P. E. Bebbington (Ed.), *Social psy-*

chiatry: Theory, methodology, and practice (pp. 65–88). New Brunswick, NJ: Transaction Publishers.

Frith, U. (1989). *Autism: Explaining the enigma.* Oxford: Blackwell.

Frith, U., Morton, J., & Leslie, A. M. (1991). The cognitive basis of biological disorder: Autism. *Trends in Neurosciences 14*(10), 433–438.

Happé, F. G. E., Brownell, H., & Winner, E. (1999). Acquired "theory of mind" impairments following stroke. *Cognition, 70,* 211–240.

Happé, F., Malhi, G. S., & Checkley, S. (2000). Acquired mind-blindness following frontal lobe surgery? A single case study of impaired "theory of mind" in a patient treated with stereotactic anterior capsulotomy. *Neuropsychologia, 39,* 83–90.

Happé, F., Winner, E., & Brownell, H. (1998). The getting of wisdom—Theory of mind in old age. *Developmental Psychology, 34*(2), 358–362.

Heyes, C. M. (1998). Theory of mind in non-human primates. *Behavioral and Brain Sciences, 21,* 101–134.

Hobson, R. P. (1984). Early childhood autism and the question of egocentrism. *Journal of Autism and Developmental Disorders, 14*(1), 85–104.

Hobson, R. P. (1993). *Autism and the development of mind.* Hove, UK: Lawrence Erlbaum.

Huttenlocher, J., & Presson, C. C. (1973). Mental rotation and the perspective problem. *Cognitive Psychology, 4,* 277–299.

Huttenlocher, J., & Presson, C. C. (1979). The coding and transformation of spatial information. *Cognitive Psychology, 11,* 375–394.

Kinderman, P., Dunbar, R., & Bentall, R. P. (1998). Theory-of-mind deficits and causal attributions. *British Journal of Psychology 89*(2), 191–204.

Kinderman P., & Bentall, R. P. (2000, March). *Delusions as motivated beliefs.* Paper presented at the Annual Conference of the British Psychological Society.

Kington, J. M., Jones, L. A., Watt, A. A., Hopkin, E. J., & Williams, J. (2000). Impaired eye expression recognition in schizophrenia. *Journal of Psychiatric Research, 34,* 341–347.

Kolvin, I., Ounsted C., Humphrey, M., & McNay, A. (1971). Studies in the childhood psychoses: II. The phenomenology of childhood psychoses. *British Journal of Psychiatry, 118*(545), 385–395.

Langdon, R., & Coltheart, M. (1999). Mentalising, schizotypy, and schizophrenia. *Cognition, 71*, 43–71.

Langdon, R., & Coltheart, M. (2001). Visual perspective-taking and schizotypy: Evidence for a *simulation*-based account of mentalising in normal adults. *Cognition, 82*, 1–26.

Langdon, R., Coltheart, M., Ward, P. B., & Catts, S. V. (2001a). Mentalising, executive planning, and disengagement in schizophrenia. *Cognitive Neuropsychiatry, 2*, 81–108.

Langdon, R., Coltheart, M., Ward, P. B., & Catts, S. V. (2001b). Visual and cognitive perspective-taking impairments in schizophrenia: A failure of allocentric simulation? *Cognitive Neuropsychiatry, 6*, 241–270.

Langdon, R., Coltheart, M., Ward, P. B., & Catts, S. V. (2002). Disturbed communication in schizophrenia: The role of poor pragmatics and poor mind reading. *Psychological Medicine, 32*, 1273–1284.

Langdon, R., Davies, M., & Coltheart, M. (2002). Understanding minds and understanding communicated meanings in schizophrenia. *Mind & Language, 17*(1&2), 68–104.

Langdon, R., Michie, P., Ward, P. B., McConaghy, N., Catts, S. V., & Coltheart, M. (1997). Defective self and/or other mentalising in schizophrenia: A cognitive neuropsychological approach. *Cognitive Neuropsychiatry, 2*(3), 167–193.

Leslie, A.M, & Roth, D. (1993). What autism teaches us about metarepresentation. In S. Baron-Cohen, H. Tager-Flusberg, & D. J. Cohen (Eds.), *Understanding other minds: Perspectives from autism* (pp. 83–111). Oxford: Oxford University Press.

Leslie, A.M., & Thaiss, L. (1992). Domain specificity in conceptual development: Neuropsychological evidence from autism. *Cognition, 43*, 225–251.

Lillard, A. (1998). Ethnopsychologies—Cultural variations in theory of mind. *Psychological Bulletin, 123*(1), 3–32.

McKenna, K., Gordon, C. T., & Rapoport, J. L. (1994). Childhood-onset schizophrenia: Timely neurobiological research. *Journal of the American Academy of Child and Adolescent Psychiatry, 33*(6), 771–781.

Mitchley, N. J., Barber, J., Gray, J. M., Brooks, N., & Livingston, M. G. (1998). Comprehension of irony in schizophrenia. *Cognitive Neuropsychiatry, 3*(2), 127–138.

Perner, J., & Lang, B. (1999). Development of theory of mind and executive control. *Trends in Cognitive Sciences, 3*, 337–344.

Peterson, C. C. (2000). Influence of siblings' perspectives on theory of mind. *Cognitive Development, 15*, 435–455.

Pickup, G. J., & Frith, C. D. (2001a). Schizotypy, theory of mind and weak central coherence. *Schizophrenia Research, 49*(1–2 Suppl.), 118.

Pickup, G. J., & Frith, C. D. (2001b). Theory of mind impairments in schizophrenia: Symptomatology, severity and specificity. *Psychological Medicine, 31*, 207–220.

Premack, D., & Woodruff, G. (1978). Does the chimpanzee have a theory of mind? *Behavioral and Brain Sciences 1*(4), 515–526.

Price, B., Daffner, K., Stowe, R., & Mesulam, M. (1990). The compartmental learning disabilities of early frontal lobe damage. *Brain, 113*, 1383–1393.

Pylyshyn, Z. W. (1978). When is attribution of beliefs justified? *Behavioral and Brain Sciences, 1*, 592–593.

Raine, A. (1991). The SPQ: A scale for the assessment of schizotypal personality based on DSM-III–R criteria. *Schizophrenia Bulletin, 17*, 55–64.

Reed, T., & Peterson, C. (1990). A comparative study of autistic subjects' performance at two levels of visual and cognitive perspective taking. *Journal of Autism & Developmental Disorders, 20*, 555–567.

Rowe, A. D., Bullock, P. R., Polkey, C. E., & Morris, R. G. (2001). "Theory of mind" impairments and their relationship to executive functioning following frontal lobe excisions. *Brain, 124*(3), 600–616.

Rutter, M. (1972). Childhood schizophrenia reconsidered. *Journal of Autism and Childhood Schizophrenia, 2*, 315–337.

Sarfati, Y., & Hardy-Bayle M. C. (1999). How

do people with schizophrenia explain the behaviour of others? A study of theory of mind and its relationship to thought and speech disorganization in schizophrenia. *Psychological Medicine, 29*(3), 613–620.

Sarfati, Y., Hardy-Bayle, M. C., Besche, C., & Widlocher, D. (1997). Attribution of intentions to others in people with schizophrenia: A non-verbal exploration with comic strips. *Schizophrenia Research, 25*, 199–209.

Sarfati, Y., Hardy-Bayle, M. C., Brunet, E., & Widlocher, D. (1999). Investigating theory of mind in schizophrenia: Influence of verbalization in disorganized and non-disorganized patients. *Schizophrenia Research, 37*(2), 183–190.

Schneider, K. (1959). *Clinical psychopathology*. New York: Grune & Stratton.

Siegal, M., Carrington, J., & Radel, M. (1996). Theory of mind and pragmatic understanding following right hemisphere damage. *Brain & Language, 53*(1), 40–50.

Stone, V. E., Baron-Cohen, S., & Knight, R. T. (1998). Frontal lobe contributions to theory of mind. *Journal of Cognitive Neuroscience, 10*(5), 640–656.

Tan, J., & Harris, P. L. (1991). Autistic children understand seeing and wanting. *Development & Psychopathology, 3*, 163–174.

Winner, E., Brownell, H., Happé, F., Blum, A., & Pincus, D. (1998). Distinguishing lies from jokes—Theory of mind deficits and discourse interpretation in right hemisphere brain-damaged patients. *Brain & Language, 62*(1), 89–106.

Yirmiya, N., Sigman, M., & Zacks, D. (1994). Perceptual perspective-taking and seriation abilities in high-functioning children with autism. *Development & Psychopathology, 6*, 263–272.

12

Theory of Mind in Autism and Schizophrenia
A Case of Over-optimistic Reverse Engineering

PHILIP GERRANS
University of Adelaide

VICTORIA McGEER
Australian National University

CONSTRAINTS ON MODULAR THEORIES: HORIZONTAL INTEGRATION, VERTICAL INTEGRATION, AND THE THEORY-OF-MIND MODULE

Although autism and schizophrenia present as widely differing disorders, there are intriguing connections between them, which have led to a number of speculative attempts at theoretical unification. First, the term *autism*, now confined to autistic subjects, was first coined by Eugene Bleuler in the 19th century to capture the social isolation and lack of impetus to engage with the world characteristic of schizophrenics experiencing what today would be called "negative symptoms." Second, both autistics and schizophrenics have sensory-motor disorders including perceptual abnormalities, stereotypy and disorganization, unusual patterns of affect, attentional and executive deficits, and social problems. Third, these are both disorders where the range of symptoms extends in a characteristic pattern across many cognitive domains, although general intelligence is sometimes spared.

Explaining these disorders, either separately or together, poses a two-staged challenge of horizontal and vertical integration (Robbins, 1997). *Horizontal integration* means accounting for and so unifying a pathological set of behavioral and phenomenological symptoms by reference to a cognitive model of normal function. *Vertical integration* refers to the way in which the symptoms thus unified are linked to neurobiology by a theory that shows how the relevant cognitive function is normally implemented, hence pathologically manifested, in human neurobiology. Thus cognitive models initially constructed by abstracting from neurobiology at the stage of horizontal integration are ultimately mapped to neurobiological function at the stage of vertical integration via an implementation theory. This two-staged project of horizontal and vertical integration is complicated by the developmental dimension of neurocognitive disorders (Karmiloff-Smith, 1998; Thomas & Karmiloff-Smith, in press). In disorders acquired during adulthood, theorists can be more confident of the ways in which distinctive abnormalities result from damage to, or disruption of, normally articulated cognitive systems, whereas the distinctive abnormalities of developmental neurocognitive disorders inevitably reflect a long history of organismic adaptation and compensation.

In this chapter, we examine a theory of cognitive function that aims to resolve these difficulties for both autism and schizophrenia. This theory proposes, first, a cognitive account of the core symptoms of each disorder, thereby meeting the goal of horizontal integration. Second, it suggests a way of mapping a range of diverse symptoms onto a highly specific neural substrate, thereby meeting the goal of vertical integration. The theory, originally proposed by Simon Baron-Cohen and collaborators for autism and extended by Chris Frith for schizophrenia, is that both disorders result from the malfunction of a single cognitive system, incorporating, most importantly, the "theory-of-mind" module (or ToMM) (Baron-Cohen, Leslie, & Frith, 1985; Frith, 1992). According to these theorists, the ToMM is required for an understanding of intentional agency because it underwrites autistic peoples' capacity to conceptualize mental states, specifically beliefs and desires, as part of a theory of behavioral explanation. In brief, ToMM theorists suggest that if this specific cognitive module fails to develop properly (perhaps due to failure of subsidiary cognitive modules that play an important role in triggering ToM), the result is autism; if it fails in maturity, the result is schizophrenia. The idea is that the autistic child's specifically social failures and the schizophrenic person's disrupted sense of agency may have a common causal-cognitive structure basis in malfunction of a module specialized for the representation of mental-state concepts. There are, of course, many differences between these disorders despite the similarities just noted. However, as Christopher Frith reminds us, this need not tell against the project of finding a unified theory encompassing both. Given that autism is a developmental disorder, whereas schizophrenia usually occurs first in adulthood, we might reasonably expect significant (although cognitively related) differences in their typical symptoms. As Frith put it:

It is likely that the cognitive deficit in autism is present from birth, although not reliably detectable until about the third year (Schopler & Mesibov, 1988). As a consequence the whole course of development must be abnormal. There is evidence that a proportion of schizophrenic patients show signs of social abnormalities during childhood (Castle, Wessely, & Murray, submitted). However in most cases of schizophrenia development appears to be entirely normal until the first breakdown, typically in the early 20s. My proposal is that people with schizophrenia resemble people with autism in that they too have impairments in the mechanism that enable them to empathize. However in most cases this mechanism was functioning adequately until their first breakdown. Given these very different developmental histories this defect will be manifest in different ways. The autistic person has never known that other people have minds. The schizophrenic knows well that other people have minds but has lost the ability to infer the contents of these minds: their beliefs and intentions. They may even lose the ability to reflect on the contents of their own mind. However they still have available ritual and behavioural routines for interacting with people which do not require inferences about mental states. (Frith, 1992, p. 121)

Despite its initial appeal, we argue that the ToMM theory of autism and schizophrenia fails. There is no single ToM module responsible for successful social reasoning and behavior in normal subjects; hence there is no dedicated module, realized in neural substrate, that fails to develop in autism or breaks down in schizophrenia. In other words, we argue that the ToMM theory fails at the first stage of horizontal integration.

CONSTRAINTS ON MODULAR THEORIES

Cognitive Domains: Actual or Virtual

Our objection to the ToM modularity hypothesis does not hinge on evidence for or against neural localization. We accept that cognitive functions can be realized in distributed neural architectures. In our view, the only structural constraint modularity hypotheses must meet is the following: In order for there to be an *actual* cognitive domain subserved by a dedicated module for processing information specific to that domain, it must be realized in a functionally specific neural assembly—that is, an assembly that serves no other cognitive function(s). If this constraint cannot be met, then even supposing a particular disorder comprises a pathological behavioral domain, the domain specificity of the underlying cognitive disorder is merely *virtual*: There may be an appearance of modularity but the appearance is misleading. In both autism and schizophrenia, the *apparent* ToM deficits are a consequence of a disunified array of cognitive and (possibly) noncognitive malfunctions. This implies that whatever unity obtains in the domain of social cognition is merely virtual, the result of a number of interacting subsystems whose interaction is not governed by the operations of a single "theory-of-mind" mechanism.

Cognitive Capacities: Developmentally Set or Developmentally Constructed

To say that a cognitive domain is actual—that is, subserved by a dedicated module—is a synchronic hypothesis about cognitive architecture. It does not depend on claims about the diachronic history of cognitive development. Thus objections to modular nativism should be disentangled from objections to modularity per se (Karmiloff-Smith, 1998; cf. Elman et al., 1996). A cognitive capacity may be modular in the sense of functionally discrete without such modularity being genetically predetermined. If so, there can be failure of typical modularization without failure of a genetically specified module.

To illustrate this difference, consider two alternative explanations of specific language impairment (SLI), a deficit in language ability that spares other cognitive capacities. The classical approach to this disorder, on which nativist theories of ToM deficits are modeled, is one of straightforward reverse engineering: In order to account for the unified and specific behavioral deficit, classical theorists posit a genetically prespecified dedicated language module for deriving grammatical rules that fails to mature normally. Evidence of heritability is often taken as further support for the innate modular theory (Gopnik & Goad, 1997; Van der Lely, 1997).

Another possibility is that SLI is not the result of failure in a genetically prespecified modular language capacity at all. It is, rather, the absence of a modularized capacity—hence, a specific language impairment—due to the developmental impact of a subtle hearing deficit (Donnai & Karmiloff Smith, 2000; Tallal, 1985, 1988; Thomas & Karmiloff-Smith, in press). In order to read linguistic structure into the acoustic stream, children need to be able to detect significant acoustic variation in that stream, but the SLI subject is unable to do this. For example, the SLI child might just hear "ough" instead of "D" "O" "G" where "dog" comes in the middle of an acoustic stream. Wright, Lombardino, Puranik, Leonard, and Merzenich (1997) found that in order for SLI subjects to distinguish linguistically significant variations against the masking effects of surrounding sounds, they needed to be amplified 45 dB above the surrounding stream (see also Tallal, Miller, & Fitch, 1995, on the ameliorating effects of lengthening phonemic transitions). The hearing of these subjects would not show up as abnormal in standard tests because it is their ability to overcome masking effects that is the problem, not auditory function per se. (Subjects can hear the sounds perfectly well as long as they are not masked by preceding and succeeding sounds.) If this explanation is right, then the link between SLI as a behavioral domain and the underlying cognitive domain is not, as it initially appears, the result of an impairment in native linguistic capacity. Instead SLI is the product of a developmental cascade based on a subtle perceptual deficit which has nothing to do with language per se (Wright et al., 1997). Thus, theses like that of Stephen Pinker that SLI is evidence for the presence of a genetically specified module devoted to syntactic processing are undermined (Gerrans, 2002; Karmiloff-Smith, 1998; Karmiloff-Smith et al., 2003; Thomas & Karmiloff-Smith, in press). This explanation will naturally complicate the project of vertical integration for SLI as a developmental disorder: Instead of searching for the neural substrate of a specific grammatical capacity in early stages of linguistic development, theorists ought to be looking for the neural substrate of a cognitive system dedicated to processing phonological distinctions.

We call a cognitive capacity *developmentally set* insofar as it is achieved by a module whose cognitive architecture is genetically prespecified. By contrast, a cognitive capacity is *developmentally constructed* if the mechanism or mechanisms that achieve it are progressively structured in consequence of an organism's environmentally interactive developmental history. Thus it counts against a dedicated modularity hypothesis as a developmental thesis about high-level cognitive capacities such as syntax or ToM if it can be shown that such specialized competencies fail to develop as a result of the way organisms interact with their environment in consequence of lower order abnormalities. However, as in the case just described, it may be that some cognitive capacity is still an actual cognitive domain, capable of being selectively impaired in adulthood, even if it depends developmentally on mediating systems that are cognitively unrelated to the capacity in question.

Cognitive Versus Mechanical Explanations: Guarding Against Methodological Bias

Explaining any cognitive disorder begins with its behavioral profile: the distinctive pattern of disabilities and spared (or sometimes superior) abilities. From there, theorists hypothesize underlying structures that account for this behavioral profile, testing these hypotheses against further external and/or internal sources of evidence (e.g., cognitive-behavioral and/or neurological studies, as well as computational models), and then modifying or replacing their theories. This methodological practice of reverse engineering is indispensable yet introduces a bias in explanation toward theories that postulate dedicated higher order cognitive structures. This bias is not necessarily a bad thing, because the theories it favors may be on the right track. However, we note that this methodologically induced bias can easily slide into a reverse-engineering fallacy if alternative explanations are not appropriately considered. This is particularly true if alternatives seem theoretically more complicated and empirically less tractable when it comes to experimental design. Still, although it may be more elegant to postulate an X-module to explain a set of symptoms, the truth for any particular disorder may often lie in a complex multiplicity of overlapping cognitive and noncognitive causes. To keep the full range of conceptual possibilities in mind, we think a distinction between cognitive and purely mechanical explanations of cognitive function can be usefully clarified.

Cognitive Explanations.   An explanation for a disorder counts as genuinely cognitive if it makes essential or theoretically ineliminable reference to a system's design by way of invoking a malfunctioning cognitive mechanism or mechanisms (Dennett, 1978). For example, we lose explanatory power if we explain visual neglect purely in neural terms without reference to the visual task the neural system implicated normally performs. Of course, because cognitive mechanisms are realized in neural substrate, cognitive malfunctions are inevitably problems at the level of neuronal functioning. However, a cognitive theory initially abstracts from neural realization in identifying a cognitive function and then maps that function to its neural substrate via an implementation theory. Consider an analogous case: A computer malfunction is correctly explained at the design or programming level (analogous to the cognitive level) if its occurrence is contingent upon some flaw in the program no matter how that program is physically realized—differently, as it may be, in two different computer systems (cf. below note 1).

Thus, in terms of the taxonomy introduced earlier, a cognitive module, putatively identified as the cause of a disorder, may be actual or virtual. If it is actual, then there is selective damage to a dedicated cognitive mechanism, making the reverse engineering inference from behavior to mechanism relatively straightforward. In this case, the module implicated in the disorder is architecturally real (see Figure 12.1). By contrast, the postulated unifying cognitive function may be virtual: It gives the appearance of being achieved by a dedicated mechanism, but the underlying architectural reality is of a number of interacting, possibly lower order, quasi-independent cognitive subsystems. The proposed cognitive function is descriptively too abstract to serve as an implementation theory and, in this sense, the modularity hypothesis misdescribes the organization of the agent's cognitive system (see Figure 12.2).

What kind of evidence could distinguish between these two alternatives? One important piece of evidence exploits the putative link between autism and schizophrenia. For, should it turn out as we suspect in schizophrenia, that postdevelopmental abnormalities in lower order systems suffice to produce the pathological symptoms, this is good reason to question the existence of a module specialized for cognizing that domain, hence one that could be differentially affected in the course of autistic development.

Mechanical Explanations.   So far, we have claimed that reasoning backward from a behavioral profile may misleadingly invite high-level modularity hypotheses for specific cognitive disorders, either diachronically, as a developmental

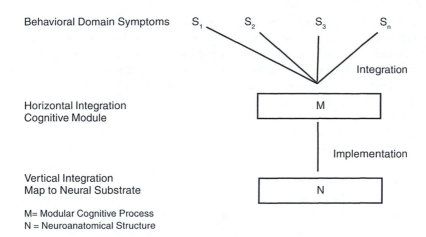

FIGURE 12.1. Reverse engineering: Mapping symptoms to neural substrate via a cognitive model.

hypothesis, or synchronically, as a hypothesis about contemporary architectural organization. However, the postulation of dedicated cognitive entities can also mislead if it turns out that the disorder is not cognitive at all. This is the case with structureless neuropathologies such as Alzheimer's disease. The interest of this type of case for our purposes is that structureless neuropathology can sometimes produce behavioral outcomes that misleadingly invite cognitive unification at higher levels and so constitute architecturally virtual domains.

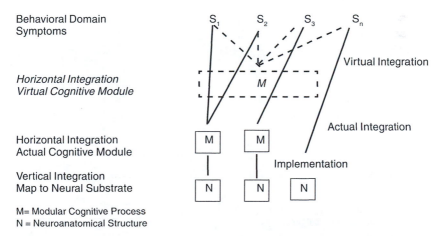

FIGURE 12.2. Reverse engineering fallacy 1: Lower level cognitive explanation.

Consider, for instance, the disorder *phenylketonuria* (PKU). Although PKU has many symptoms that are similar to autism, it is produced not by the failure of a specific cognitive module, but by the absence of an enzyme that synthesizes an amino acid. In this case, postulating the failure of a higher order mechanism is ultimately mistaken, not because the postulated module fractures into a subset of cognitively or developmentally more basic ones, but because the cause of the disorder is essentially noncognitive: It does not arise through the breakdown of any cognitive system *qua* cognitive system. Because there is no cognitive story to tell in this case, the correct approach for achieving vertical integration is bottom up: We explain the neural malfunction and treat the resultant behavior as the outcome of haphazard interference with the development of a number of arbitrarily involved cognitive functions. The correct explanation, as illustrated in Figure 12.3, is entirely at the level of neural mechanism.[1]

Autism and schizophrenia are interesting cases precisely because their diversity of symptoms and lack of uniformity from case to case continue to encourage the idea, popular among pioneers of neurology, that the deficits in question may be essentially mechanical rather than cognitive. Nonetheless, clinicians are reluctant to endorse this conclusion because the disorders do seem to form a pathological domain, rather than a random collection of symptoms. Hence, unifying cognitive theories, such as ToMM, continue to be attractive. However, ToM theorists go too far in proposing that high-level processing of social information constitutes a developmentally set or, indeed, architecturally real cognitive system whose malfunction is implicated in both autism and schizophrenia.

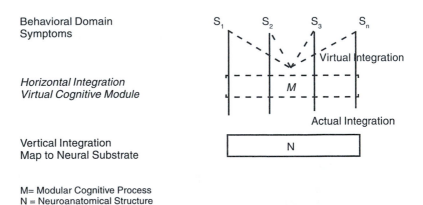

FIGURE 12.3. Reverse engineering fallacy 2: Mechanical explanation.

STRONG AND WEAK TOMM HYPOTHESIS

In both autism and schizophrenia we propose that the symptoms unified under theToMM hypothesis can be explained in either one of two ways: (a) as a result of malfunction at sensorimotor or perceptual levels (i.e., in terms of malfunction of a lower order cognitive module), or (b) as a result of purely mechanical malfunction.

In the case of autism, we remain neutral between the two alternatives because determining whether the type of sensorimotor disorder we identify as a developmental precursor to autism is low-level cognitive or mechanical is not a simple matter. However, we do think that a developmental cascade consequent on early sensorimotor malfunction is a sufficient explanation of mentalizing abnormalities, especially once the role of social interaction, modulated by sensory experience, is given its due in characterizing the development of higher order social cognition. In the case of schizophrenia, there are two well-developed alternatives to a ToMM account that fit the pattern we outlined. In keeping with option (a), the motor control account locates the malfunction that produces a significant set of symptoms in a lower order cognitive subsystem whose neural substrate is the premotor cortex. In keeping with option (b), the misconnection account treats schizophrenia as a mechanical malfunction with diffuse cortical and subcortical effects.

These arguments are directed at a strong version of the ToMM hypothesis, which claims that a malfunctioning ToM module accounts for all significant symptoms of these disorders. The ToMM theorist may also defend a weaker claim that autism and schizophrenia involve a congery of cognitive capacities of which only an essential core, typically having to do with social cognition, are ToMM deficits. However, this weaker claim is open to the following objections: First, if the affected capacities are genuinely independent, then there should be some evidence of dissociation between so-called core and peripheral symptoms occurring in both these disorders. This has yet to be established. But even were there convincing evidence of dissociation, the ToMM hypothesis could no longer play an explanatory role in autism (or schizophrenia) per se, but only for so-called core (i.e., ToM) aspects of the disorder. This only postpones the question of why these "core" problems are often enough conjoined with other problems to constitute an autistic (or schizophrenic) behavioral type. Moreover, if the core deficits can be produced in either of the ways we suggest, then there is no reason to save the ToMM hypothesis at all. This in effect replays the argument against strong ToMM for the more restricted set of "core" symptoms.

In light of these difficulties, the weak ToMM theorist may revert to the claim that all symptoms, core and peripheral, are connected even though they are not dependent on the same module. But this is to concede that however specific the cognitive abnormalities seem in autism (or schizophrenia), the disorder involves a number of subsystems linked by neural architecture or neurochemical modulation. In other words, as in the case of PKU or "misconnection" explanations of schizophrenia, the correct level of explanation is mechanical.

In sum, the weak ToMM hypothesis is not a stable fallback position. But the strong ToMM hypothesis—that all significant symptoms of these disorders are in fact cognitively unified by the ToM module—is far too strong to remain defensible, even in the eyes of some of its main proponents. We conclude that although the ToMM hypothesis has generated much valuable research, it is in the end an instance of overly optimistic reverse engineering.

THE CASE OF AUTISM[2]

Autistic individuals share a distinctive triad of impairments in social, communicative, and imaginative capacities (the latter demonstrated by the absence of pretend play in childhood and restricted interests and activities that persist throughout life) (Rutter & Schopler, 1987; Wing & Gould, 1978, 1979). Although 75% of individuals diagnosed with autism are intellectually handicapped in a general way (as reflected in low IQ scores), the remaining 25% have normal to high IQs and often perform well, and sometimes better than average, on reasoning tasks that do not require any understanding of the mental life of agents. In contrast, on so-called "theory-of-mind" tests, these "high-functioning" autistic children are significantly impaired when compared with normal children and even those with Down's syndrome who are matched with them by mental age (for a review of research, see Baron-Cohen, 2001). For instance, on first-order false-belief tasks, which require subjects to predict another's behavior on the basis of attributing them to a false belief, children will normally pass by a mental age of 4 to 5 years (Wimmer & Perner, 1983).[3] Autistic individuals, if they pass at all, only do so when they are considerably older: on average, at a verbal mental age of 9 (Happé, 1995).

A prime example of this dissociation between social and nonsocial reasoning skills involves the Zaitchik "false-photograph" task, which is modeled on the standard false-belief task except insofar as it tests children's ability to reason about physical (photographic) instead of mental representation (Zaitchik, 1990). Using a simplified version of this task, Leekam and Perner (1991) tested a group of high-functioning autistic teenagers in two conditions, one testing false-belief understanding and the other, photographic "misrepresentation." In both conditions, participants were shown a doll (Judy) wearing a red dress. In the false-belief condition, a second doll (Susan) sees Judy in the red dress and then leaves the room. Judy's dress is changed from red to green, and subjects are asked: "What color does Susan think that Judy is?" In the false photograph condition, a Polaroid photo is taken of Judy in the red dress. While the photo is developing, her dress is again changed from red to green, and subjects are asked: "In the picture, what color is Judy?" Only 25% of autistic participants were correct on the false-belief question, but almost all those tested passed the false-photograph question (Leekam & Perner, 1991). Similar results were obtained by Leslie and Thais (1992). This pattern of dramatically failing false-belief while passing false-photograph tasks does not occur in normal 4-year-olds.[4]

Results like these strongly suggest that autistic individuals are not generally impaired in their reasoning abilities, but rather have a specific inability to reason about, and perhaps even conceptualize, mental states and processes—hence the idea that autism results from the developmental failure of a so-called ToM module, an "innate, isolable component of the mind which embodies a *theory* of the nature and the operations of mind" (Carruthers, 1996, p. 258; see also Baron-Cohen, 1995; Leslie & Thaiss, 1992). Moreover, as an important extension of their theory, ToMM theorists argue that a dysfunctional ToM module can account not just for the deficits identified experimentally, but for the clinical profile collected under the headings of social, communicative, and imaginative abnormalities.[5]

Consider, for instance, the characteristic social abnormalities associated with autism. These might easily be connected with an inability to attribute mental states to others, especially if these abnormalities reflect an apparent indifference or insensitivity to what others are thinking and feeling. Thus, autistic children show no interest in, and even a positive aversion to, meeting another's eyes. They show no tendency to engage in social referencing behaviors, that is, directing another's attention toward an object in order to share their interest in it or gather information about it. They show little understanding of how their actions affect others or how others' actions are meant to affect them. They may often be confused by what other people do, but show little capacity to be hurt by intentionally malicious behavior, or touched by intentionally kind behavior whether or not the behavior is experienced as beneficial. They may be amused by other people's physical "antics," even when those antics betray extreme distress or pain. They understand sabotage, but are blind to deceit and other forms of slyness.

Communicative abnormalities may also be rooted in this mentalizing deficit. Language skills vary widely across the autistic population. But even among those who develop fair linguistic capacity, typical problems remain. These are connected in particular with communicative and pragmatic aspects of language use that depend on the speaker's awareness of the conversational situation, including especially the listener's point of view: abnormal prosody (rhythm, stress, tone), abnormal shifts in topic, inability to give and receive conversational cues, abnormal accompanying gestures and facial expressions, pronoun reversals ("I" for "you"), idiosyncratic use of words, abrupt interruptions and terminations of conversation, insensitivity to taboos on personal topics, and so forth. Autistic individuals also tend toward extreme literal-mindedness—showing an insensitivity to metaphor, irony, sarcasm, even idioms as idioms: To autistic individuals, "he went the whole nine yards" means, literally, "he went nine whole yards." There is little or no understanding that others may intend to convey by their words something more or other than just what their words mean.

Some of these communicative abnormalities are closely related to the final element in this triad of deficits: autistic lack of imagination. From early childhood, autistic individuals show a notable absence of spontaneous pretend play, as if it never occurs to them to think about things (represent them) other than as they are. Instead, they will engage in repetitive, stereotyped activities such as sorting objects or lining them up in rows. They also tend to show limited or absent interest in the larger meaning of things (function, associations, symbolic properties) but focus instead on superficial details, with obsessive interests that are circumscribed accordingly. It may be memorizing bus routes, timetables, birth dates, or even door colors. Many autistic individuals are notable for their rote memory skills, even though they show little concern with focusing on what's worth remembering for other cognitive purposes. Perhaps this is because they have a limited capacity for imagining what those purposes might be, hence a limited capacity for opportunistic planning (for a discussion of planning deficits as connected with theory-of-mind capacities, see Currie, 1996; for an alternative perspective, see Russell, 1997).

So prima facie ToMM is a very attractive unifying hypothesis, but we should note that there are other autistic abnormalities that seem to have little to do with "theory-of-mind" capacities. These include sensory-motor problems: for example, extreme and unusual physical sensitivities and insensitivities; slowed orienting of attention; oddities of posture and gait; tics, twitches, and unusual mannerisms; and stereotypies such as rocking, hand-flapping, spinning, thumb-twiddling, and echolalia. They also include abnormalities in perceptual processing, leading to a characteristic autistic profile of assets and deficits on various perceptual tasks: for example, insusceptibility to certain perceptual illusions, superior performance on finding embedded figures within a larger design, superior visual memory and capacity for rendering scenes in precise detail, perfect pitch, difficulties with "gestalt" perception—seeing whole figures or scenes as opposed to their parts, absence of perceptual "switching" with ambiguous figures such as the duck-rabbit, and so on.

How can ToMM theorists account for these additional symptoms? As we saw in the introduction, a weak ToMM view would involve conceding that these abnormalities are fundamentally unrelated to the core ToMM deficit, so that autism is, in effect, an association of relatively independent disorders resulting from multiple failures across a variety of distinct neurological systems. However, if these neurological systems are genuinely independent, then either we should expect some evidence of dissociable breakdown or, in lieu of that, some explanation for why breakdowns in multiple systems co-occur. The weak ToMM theorist encounters trouble either way: The first possibility seems empirically unvindicated and the second undercuts the explanatory power of the weak ToMM hypothesis.

Consider the first possibility: If ToM deficits are essentially unrelated to other characteristic symptoms in autism, then we should expect to see a relatively pure ToM-impaired autistic type. Such autistics would most nearly resemble individuals who have developed normally but show impairments in so-cial cognition because of acquired neurological damage in their frontal or tem-poral lobes. Yet there seems to be no evidence of such specific abnormalities in the autistic population. Whatever range of symptoms autistics manifest, their profile is quite unlike that of brain-damaged adults, especially with regard to sensory-motor and perceptual difficulties. However, as Tager-Flusberg reminded us, these differences in profile should not be surprising given that autism is a neurodevelopmental disorder:

> Interestingly, neurodevelopmental disorders are more often associated with *diffuse* cortical damage, which suggests the impact of such disorders is more widespread, affecting complex neural systems rather than simple localized areas. Furthermore, across a range of developmental syndromes, we find that not only are particular cortical systems affected but often associated atypical subcortical structures are involved as well. For example, in autism both the cerebellum and limbic system show significant abnormalities. These findings suggest deviations in brain development that begin early in embry-ology and cannot be easily classified and interpreted as later acquired focal lesions. Our theories of structural brain abnormalities in neurodevelopmental disorders will have to incorporate these kinds of developmental complexities rather than relying on more established studies from work with adults. (Tager-Flusberg, 1999, p. 3)

More likely, then, is the second possibility: Autism involves multiple fail-ures across various distinct neurological systems that co-occur for a reason. If these systems are functionally unrelated, as the weak ToMM theorist avers, then it seems the only kind of account that would make sense of this multiple failure is a mechanical one. As with PKU, autistic behavior might be the result of haphazard interference with the development of a number of arbitrarily in-volved cognitive functions, including those supporting social cognition. If so, hypothesizing a particular deficit in the putative ToM module does no explana-tory work in autism, whatever it may do for explaining acquired disorders in social cognition. (This is not to say we endorse such a hypothesis, only that it plays no role in the explanation of autism even under the assumption that social cognition is normally accomplished by a modularized neural system.)

Faced with these difficulties, the ToMM theorist might well consider the stronger claim: Many if not all "peripheral" autistic symptoms can be explained in terms of a malfunctioning ToM module, in which case they are not periph-eral to defects in social cognition at all, since they too are produced by failure to metarepresent mental states. Uta Frith and Francesca Happé (1999) recently made this suggestion,[6] building on an idea repeatedly emphasized by Alison Gopnik: that a ToM capacity implies no asymmetry between first- and third-person ascriptions of mental states.[7] Thus, the autistic subject's understanding of her own mind would be just as impoverished as her understanding of other minds.

Frith and Happé speculated that because autistic subjects cannot metarepresent their sensory and perceptual processes as states of their own mind, they are at the mercy of them in a way that could produce the characteristic profile of autistic abnormalities. For instance, on motor tests involving monitoring and correction of action, autistics perform poorly when compared with normal controls (Russell & Jarrold, 1998, 1999). Frith and Happé offered the following ToM explanation: "without self-awareness, an individual might not know how she is going to act until she acted, nor why she acted as she did. . . . A person who lacks self-consciousness may be unable to distinguish between her own willed and involuntary actions" (Frith & Happé, 1999, p. 8). Alternatively, there might be improved performance on tasks where action without in-depth conscious reflection is superior to consciously performed action. This might explain autistic individuals' relatively good capacity to perform routinized action coupled with a poor capacity to act flexibly and imaginatively (ibid., p. 10). It might also account for autistic insusceptibility to certain visual illusions, such as the Titchener circles (or Ebbinghaus illusion), where subjects' "superior performance in verbal response is not contaminated by conscious reflection" (ibid., p. 10). [In support of this contention, recent evidence shows that when even normal subjects respond motorically (and apparently unconsciously) in their reaching behavior to the correct size of the circles, nevertheless they continue to (consciously) judge the size of the circles incorrectly (Aglioti, DeSouza, & Goodale, 1995)].

One notable and particularly salient characteristic of autism is extreme and unusual sensory experience. Frith and Happé relate this to a dysfunctional ToM as follows:

> If low-functioning autistics are unable to reflect on their inner experiences, then they would be unable to develop over time the richly connected semantic and experiential associations which normally pervade our reflective consciousness. Observation by parents suggests that the awareness of sensations and experiences may be peculiar in children with autism. Anecdotal reports of abnormal sensory and pain experiences are on occasion quite extreme. . . . One anecdotal example is the case of a young girl with autism who was found to have suffered acute appendicitis, but had not complained of pain and, when asked how she felt, did not report anything wrong. Abnormal response to heat and cold, as well as hypo- and hyper-sensitivity to sound, light or touch are frequently reported. . . . Such responses might be expected if there was an inability to reflect on inner experiential states. Of course, normal pain perception is greatly affected by attribution and expectation. These individuals might feel immediate pain in the same way as everyone else, but would not be able to attribute to themselves the emotional significance that normally accompanies pain. This might explain why they do not complain about it. We may speculate that the self-conscious person reflects not only on the pain but also on the experience of pain. This person is feeling "misery" in addition to feeling pain. (Frith & Happé, 1999, pp. 10–11)

Frith and Happé's view implies that autistic subjects would be rather unreflective about their sensory experiences. But, as they themselves noted, autistic hypersensitivity is as dramatic as autistic hyposensitivity. In fact, both third-person observation and first-person report indicate that autistic subjects are abnormally aware of their sensory experiences, and aware of them mainly because their sensory experiences are extreme and persistently captivating. Furthermore, they are aware of them *as* mental experiences. It's hard to see how this can be accounted for in terms of a general deficit of self-consciousness stemming from a dysfunctional ToM mechanism. And, of course, if there is no general deficit of self-consciousness; accounting for autistic motor and perceptual abnormalities in these terms becomes equally suspect (as opposed to accounting for them in terms of local motor and perceptual system dysfunctions).

Our conclusion is that Frith and Happé's strong ToMM hypothesis encounters these difficulties because it reverses, temporally and conceptually, the correct direction of explanation between lower and higher order cognitive capacities. Reverting to the SLI case, it is as if someone tried to explain auditory failures and related behavior as the consequence of defective grammatical processing rather than defective grammatical processing as the consequence of early auditory difficulties. The higher order cognitive difficulties of autism and other developmental disorders are far more likely to be the cascading effects of relatively early, lower order sensory and perceptual abnormalities than lower order abnormalities are to be the result of a failure in higher cognition (Karmiloff-Smith, 1998; cf. Tager-Flusberg, 1999). If this developmental connection makes theoretical (and empirical) sense, then the explanatory difficulty of integrating the various symptoms of the disorder disappears.

To make theoretical sense of this approach, we need to consider how early sensory and perceptual disturbances could generate the autistic profile of social deficits. The first step involves restoring the emphasis, sometimes lost in reverse engineering reasoning, of the role intersubjective encounters play in developing a child's capacity for normal agency. Reciprocal, affectively patterned interactions with others are important determinants of infant experience and a necessary condition for the development of higher order cognitive capacities, especially those relating to "mind reading" (here, minimalistically conceived as a capacity for understanding others as psychological agents like oneself). In our view, developing a capacity for "mind reading" goes hand in hand with developing the capacity to *be minded* like others—that is, with acquiring habits of psychological self-regulation and behavior that conform to shared norms of sensible (predictable, rational) agency. If the infant's sensory-motor and perceptual systems are abnormal, his or her motivation and ability to engage with others in the types of interaction that lead to developing such capacities of agency will be disrupted from the very beginning. Hence, the difference between autistic and normal individuals may not be so much the lack of some specifically social capacity as the failure to develop their capacities within an intensely social context (for more detailed and somewhat complementary developments of this view, see Gerrans, 1998; McGeer 2001).

This fits with, although does not precisely repeat, a theme emphasized by Hobson and other theorists that what matters to a child's normal social cognitive development is the affective quality of his or her intersubjective experience (Hobson, 1991; Stern, 1985; Trevarthen, 1979; Trevarthen & Hubley, 1978). That is to say, the initial innate bridge between self and other is sustained by perceiving and reproducing the bodily expressed feelings of others: smile for smile, frown for frown, fearful look for fearful look. This makes others potentially significant for the infant in two respects at once: Not only do they provide information about the world and human experience; they also serve as a critical source of sensory-affective regulation. Thus, for instance, a mother may comfort a distressed child by, first, adopting in face and voice expressions that are recognizable to the child as mirroring its own distress, then modulating these in a way that expresses the easing of distress. The child, carried along by its innate proclivities for imitation, will often follow the direction of the mother's expressive modulation, experiencing the easing of its own distress in consequence (Gergely & Watson, 1995). Indeed, the regulative benefits of imitation may be so critical to an infant's well-being that it is they, rather than any direct epistemic rewards, that drive the infant's interactions with responsive others.

In learning how to be like others, the infant is learning how to be itself in tolerable contact with the world. Of course, these structured interactions, first with others, then later with objects and situations via the mediation of others, become enormously rewarding on the epistemic front as well, for they allow the growing child to metabolize its experiences in ways that are conducive to developing a picture of the world as a stable, predictable place. The normal child who becomes well-regulated in the manner of other people thus derives a double epistemic benefit from this process: The world, including the progressively more complex and differentiated behavior of other people, is made open to manageable exploration, while, at the same time, other people become known to the child inside and out in a way that underwrites his or her "mind-reading" capacities.

If this is a reasonable sketch of what happens in normal development, it suggests a clear connection between autistic sensory disturbances and their failure to engage with others in ways that lead to developing normal capacities of agency. Autistic individuals need not lack a basic social capacity, or even drive to imitate others, as is sometimes suggested (Meltzoff & Gopnik, 1993). Indeed, some autistics show extraordinary if oddly selective parroting tendencies. Nor need it be true that they have a basic affective disorder, as Hobson and others propose. Their capacity to imitate and so engage in intersubjective encounters would hardly be evoked in a sustained way if autistics find their contact with others, on the whole, far too stimulating to be tolerated. Indeed, in an effort to manage their sensory experiences, autistic individuals might need to shut other people out in a fairly pointed way. But far from indicating that they lack any specialized machinery for attending to others, this may well show that they *have* such machinery, with the consequence that others constitute a disproportionately powerful source of stimuli that quickly become overwhelming for them. In any case, the devastating effects of finding in others an abnormal source of sensory dysregulation rather than a normal source of helpful regulation are two-fold: (1) Autistic individuals would be cast back on their own resources for managing their sensory experiences perhaps by reducing, repeating or drowning out incoming sensory stimuli in ways they can control. This could explain a number of characteristic autistic behaviors that range from being seemingly dull and repetitive to bizarrely self-stimulatory and even self-abusive: lining up blocks, counting and calculating, repetitively flushing toilets, examining grains of sand, chewing things regardless of taste or danger, spinning, hand-flapping, rocking, echolalia, head-banging, biting and slapping oneself, and so forth. (2) Being excluded from the regulative influences of other people, autistics will not develop habits of agency that conform to shared norms of what it is to experience, think, and act in recognizably normal ways. Hence, they will be deprived of the very kinds of interactions that give rise to ordinary capacities of agency, a disability reflected in the perplexing nature of their own behavior as well as in their own perplexity at the behavior of others.

In sum, we think that strong ToMM theorists are right to emphasize the connection between a capacity to know other minds and the sorts of capacities for self-awareness and self-governance that make for normal agency. As against weak ToMM theorists, we also think strong ToMM theorists are right to emphasize the connection between higher order cognitive abnormalities in autism and so-called peripheral symptoms. However, in postulating a single higher order cognitive deficit, they neglect to consider how basic sensory and perceptual problems can have cascading developmental effects, particularly with respect to sociocognitive development, by disrupting an infant's normal environment of regulative interactions with others. From this perspective, autistic mentalizing deficits are part of a more general pattern of deficits that constitute from birth to maturity an abnormal developmental trajectory that leads to a distinctive cognitive style or set of cognitive styles. In some cases, depending on the severity of the initial problems, the child's compensatory abilities, and the kind of environmental supports he or she may find, this developmental trajectory may even produce capacities that are sufficient to pass some, if not all, "theory-of-mind" tasks. Such capacities have been found amongst high-functioning autistics, although they vary widely and do not lead to normal social behavior. Are these autistic individuals then not genuine mentalizers? Certainly they are not mentalizers in the usual sense. However, in our view, this is not because their ToM module is inoperative or only partially operative; rather, it is because the capacities they develop bear only, and to varying degrees, a family resemblance to capacities that characterize the cognitive styles of normally developing individuals.

There are a number of advantages to the bottom-up developmental approach we suggest. We have discussed two of them and alluded to a third. These include: (1) respecting the distinction between "peripheral" (or lower order) and "core" (higher order cognitive) abnormalities, and yet accounting in an integrated way for their comorbidity; (2) making sense of the neurofunctional differences between a disorder like autism and acquired pathologies consequent upon localized brain damage; and (3) providing a natural way to account for the range of mentalizing capacities found amongst high-functioning autistics without having to posit a late-developing ToM mechanism that is only partially operative.[8]

A fourth and final advantage of our approach bears special mention because it makes sense of an otherwise puzzling phenomenon. If autistic sensory disturbances do indeed lie at the developmental core of later "mindblindness" and other higher order cognitive abnormalities, then other clinical populations with early sensory problems ought to show similar kinds of deficits. And indeed this is the case. Deaf children of hearing parents as well as congenitally blind children show autistic-like abnormalities in social, communicative, and imaginative skills, as well as selective incapacity to pass reasoning tasks with a mentalistic component (Brown et al., 1997; Hobson, 1993; Peterson & Siegal, 1998, 1999; Peterson, Peterson, & Webb, 2000).[9] We think the parallels among these populations are so stunning as to call for a unifying explanation. It follows from the account developed here that any child will be unable to develop mind reading as long as it is impossible for him or her to make good regulative use of other people. This may stem from having a missing sensory avenue to others, as much as it may stem from having one's sensory avenues to others overwhelmed by the overstimulation involved in sustained exposure to them.

In terms of the taxonomy we laid out in our introductory remarks, we have argued that the mentalizing deficits of autism constitute at the very least a developmentally constructed cognitive domain. Whatever neural specialization for social reasoning occurs in normally developing children, we believe this is the outcome of an ongoing process of functional development in which these higher order cognitive capacities depend on a child's normal engagement with others in a structured social environment. Such normal engagement is naturally mediated by a child's sensory-motor and perceptual systems, among other things, so if profound disruptions occur in these systems, it is not surprising that subsequent neurofunctional developmental will be dramatically affected. Do we therefore think that normal development leads to the kind of modularization of "theory-of-mind" capacities that nonnativistic ToMM theorists suggest? Do we think, in other words, that normal ToM capacities constitute an actual cognitive domain, subserved by an architecturally real neural system? Nothing we have said so far argues strongly against this possibility. However, we do think that the ToMM account of an adult-onset disorder like schizophrenia, with symptoms that are interestingly similar to and interestingly distinct from autism, is sufficiently problematic that it points to the general conclusion that social reasoning constitutes an architecturally virtual as well as a developmentally constructed domain.

THE CASE OF SCHIZOPHRENIA

In its strong form, the ToMM theory of schizophrenia hypothesizes that all symptoms of the disorder derive from an acquired deficit in ToM function. It is certainly true that schizophrenics perform very poorly on standard ToM tests (Langdon & Coltheart, 1999) and that their social interactions, especially in cases of severe negative symptoms, are severely impaired. However, the real impetus (and challenge) for the ToMM theory derives less from giving an adequate account of these ToM deficits than to providing an integrated account of the range of disparate symptoms not obviously connected with problems in social cognition. For example, it is not clear how hallucinations and delusions, formal thought disorder, and inappropriate affect and the psychomotor poverty (alexia, avolition, apathy, flat affect) could all be attributable to one underlying cognitive problem.

The first stage in achieving horizontal integration of schizophrenic symptoms is to focus on the nature of the delusions and hallucinations characterizing the disorder. Typically these concern the subject's sense of agency—that is, the feeling that the subject is the author of his or her own thoughts or actions. In some cases the schizophrenic feels as if auditory experiences ("hearing voices") that are, so to speak, "in her mind" are nevertheless not produced by her. She is the owner of these experiences but not the author of them (Gallagher, 2000a, 2000b; Gerrans, 2001). Similarly, schizophrenics may feel as if their occurrent thoughts are being influenced by someone else (someone else is making them think certain thoughts) or actually being inserted into their minds by a kind of psychokinesis. In the reverse case, schizophrenics may feel as if they are inserting their thoughts into the minds of others (thought broadcast).

A similar dissociation between ownership and authorship is characteristic of the schizophrenic experience of action. Schizophrenics may feel as if their body is not under their own volitional control, as if they were a kind of inert marionette moving at the will of someone else. Once again, they own these actions in the sense of knowing that the movements are movements of their own bodies. But because they are not aware of intending to perform the movements or of their voluntary control, they do not feel as if they author them. Voluntary control of action can also fail in a way that is analogous to thought broadcast. In these cases the schizophrenic may feel as if the movements of others, or in some cases of objects in the external world, are caused by the schizophrenic herself. Bovet and Parnas (1993) reported a case of a subject who thought that his urinations launched bombing raids, and the delusion that the universe is expanding or contracting according to the subject's own bodily peristalsis is well known to clinicians.

These phenomena are all "first rank" (core) symptoms of schizophrenia described by Carl Schneider as a "loss of ego boundaries." These Schneiderian symptoms concern the subject's awareness of her own cognitive or practical agency, which seems to affect her ability to correctly discern who is the author of particular experiences/thoughts or actions.

Once the cases are described in this way, ToMM theorists claim that their hypothesis gains plausibility due to the conceptual structure of folk psychological ascriptions of agency (Frith, 1992; Leslie, 1994). According to a philosophical analysis of this structure, agency is the intentional control of bodily movement: What distinguishes an action from mere bodily movement is that the agent's intentions play a causal role in producing the action. So attributing agency involves a cognitive act of attributing intentions to the author of the relevant bodily movement, whether the author is oneself or someone else. Further, because intentions decompose into constituent beliefs and desires, attributing intentions requires a cognitive capacity to attribute beliefs about the world in which an agent's desires are to be realized, and desires to change the state of the world. The desires give the ends, and the beliefs give the means.

Support for this view comes from picture sequencing ToM tests. Schizophrenics, like autistic subjects, are good at completing sequences where the relevant movements can be captured in nonintentional terms (as in someone's being pushed off a seat and starting to cry, a strictly causal chain of events); but they are poor at completing sequences in which the story requires interpreting the characters' intentions, as in stories of deception. Further clinical and experimental data show that the schizophrenic ability to attribute agency, internal (self) or external (other), is very fragile. Perhaps then the schizophrenic makes an observation or has an experience that stands in need of belief/desire interpretation in order to be correctly attributed to an agent but lacks the cognitive capacity to do so. Hence the schizophrenic will be very poor at linking action to its governing intention in both internal and external cases, because the schizophrenic has an acquired deficit in the module that represents the constituents (beliefs and desires) of an intention.

Such a deficit might also explain so-called negative symptoms of the disorder in terms of an inability to generate the requisite intentions or to make use of them to terminate or adjust an action (failures of willed action, perseveration, Parkinsonianism). Finally, and most speculatively, if we conceive of thought itself as intentionally guided, a deficit in the device that monitors intentions might explain formal thought disorder and inappropriate affect. Perhaps the schizophrenic who initiates a train of thought "loses" access to its guiding intention, with the consequence that that sequence of thoughts becomes rambling, incoherent, or fixated and disconnected from the appropriate emotions (Campbell, 1999; Frith, 1992; Gallagher, 2000a).

The foundational idea behind all these speculations is that an agent who cannot (meta)represent beliefs and desires, the task supposedly performed by the ToM module, will be unable either to determine agency in conditions where attribution is an issue or to exert appropriate agential control in cases where she needs access to her original governing intentions. As Christopher Frith put it in

1992, "resolution may be achieved at the theoretical level if we can show that defects of will and defects in inferring the intentions of others reflect a similar cognitive deficit" (Frith, 1992, p. 122). At the time, Frith described this framework as "no doubt overinclusive." But he said that postulating a unifying cognitive domain subserved by the ToM module is the first step in a cognitive explanation of a pathological behavioral domain.

One prominent refinement of this "overinclusive" formulation owes much to Frith himself, and from our point of view, it is interesting that it involves both a weakening of the ToMM hypothesis (a dysfunctional ToM does not account for all schizophrenic symptoms) and a shift of explanatory emphasis from higher order to lower order cognitive systems. Frith now claims that an important subset of Schneiderian symptoms is likely produced at a much lower cognitive level than that initially postulated by ToMM theory: namely, the motor control system. Various "misconnection" or "dysmetric" theories of schizophrenia go even further: They explain the variety of symptoms at a mechanical level, bypassing the need for cognitive explanations at all.

It is worth pointing out that, depending on the actual mechanisms involved, these mechanical and cognitive accounts could be made to fit together. If, for example, the mechanism of misconnection is neurochemical transport between cortical areas, then one consequence might be local over- or underactivation of the premotor cortex, an architecturally discrete subsystem. As we explained in our introduction, we would still consider the ultimate cause of schizophrenic positive symptoms to be a basic noncognitive mechanism that happens to selectively affect one subsystem first en route to its more global disabling effect. Another example might be a dopamine failure in the basal ganglia, characteristic of Parkinson's disease, which, en route to its more global manifestation, produces the unusual grammatical disorders characteristic of Parkinsonians (Pinker, 2000).

We now describe the motor control and misconnection approaches in slightly more detail, showing how they explain important schizophrenic symptoms without implicating a dysfunctional ToM module.

Forward Models and the Sense of Agency

Frith originally argued that delusions of control or influence in schizophrenia are essentially failures to correctly attribute authorship of actions resulting from failures to correctly cognize intentions.

However, a more economical explanation of problems with the attribution of authorship implicates a more basic cognitive subsystem dedicated to the control of action. That subsystem, neurally realized in the premotor cortex, is the forward model for motor control.

The idea of a forward model goes back at least to the 19th century and it is captured in Figure 12.4. This model builds on the idea that any bodily move-

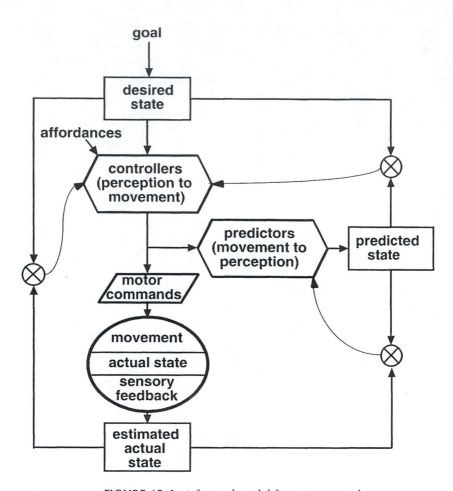

FIGURE 12.4. A forward model for motor control.

ment will generate perceptual and sensory (afferent) feedback. In order to control the movement, the system compares that feedback with a prediction about that feedback generated when the movement was initiated. When the afferent feedback matches the prediction, the system computes that the movement has been successful. When there is a mismatch, the system can send another motor instruction, which, in effect, corrects for the degree of discrepancy sensed. The system operates dynamically and in real time. For example, when someone decides to pick up a glass, the motor system must first calculate the movement(s) required to realize that goal (the desired state). The result of this calculation is the inverse model. The system then produces an instruction to the motor subsystem, which, if successfully completed, will realize the goal. A copy of that instruction (efference copy) is stored together with a prediction of the anticipated (bodily) consequences of the movement (for instance, that a movement of the hand 15 degrees to the left will produce a corresponding change in visual and proprioceptive information representing its orientation). This is the forward model. Now if the hand moves too far, say 20 degrees to the left, the reafferent information can be compared to the prediction, thereby yielding an error of 5 degrees. The system then generates a new inverse model, motor instruction, and efference copy to initiate and control a corrective movement of 5 degrees to the right.

The forward model is a computational solution to problems of motor control. Although not all of its elements have been decisively mapped to neural substrates, there is a large body of convergent research to show that the basic idea captures the essential cognitive properties of the motor control system (Blakemore, Goodbody, & Wolpert, 1998; Frith, Blakemore, & Wolpert, 2000; Jahanshahi & Frith, 1998; Decety et al., 1994). In particular, there is good evidence to suggest that current and predicted states of limbs are represented in parietal regions, and that actions are initiated in frontal brain regions. The most likely mechanism for the comparator system, then, is the inhibition of parietal areas by activity in frontal areas (Jeannerod, 1994).

Apart from its empirical credentials, the forward model is theoretically well placed to explain the way in which we establish ownership and authorship of actions. For any action, it will be ours if it corresponds to an efference copy that our motor system has generated (Frith, 1987; Frith & Done, 1989). Schizophrenic misattribution of agency might then arise at this level of processing in one of two ways:

Option 1: The schizophrenic performs an action but the forward model system contains no matching prediction—in such cases the schizophrenic attributes the action to someone else.

Option 2: The schizophrenic might activate the prediction system by observing the action of another. Note that this phenomenon has been established in macaque monkeys as part of the normal observation of action. It seems that merely observing an action can provoke neural activity in that part of the monkey's control system that signals that a movement is an action: namely, the forward model (Gallese, Fadiga, Fogassi, & Rizzolatti, 1996; Gallese, Fadiga, Fogassi, Luppino, & Murata, 1997; Rizzolati, Fadiga, Gallese, & Fogassi, 1996). Due to hypoactivity in the inhibitory system, or lack of connectivity between controllers and predictors, the normal signals that tell the system that the action is not self-initiated are unavailable to the system. The schizophrenic then attributes the observed action to herself (Figure 12.5) (Dapriati et al., 1997; Georgieff & Jeannerod, 1998).

These hypotheses are supported by experiments with schizophrenics who experience delusions of influence. They show unusual patterns of activity and connectivity between frontal and parietal areas and failures of attribution in motor control tasks. For example, schizophrenics report vivid sensations of alien control when asked to move a joystick. In other cases, when provided with am-

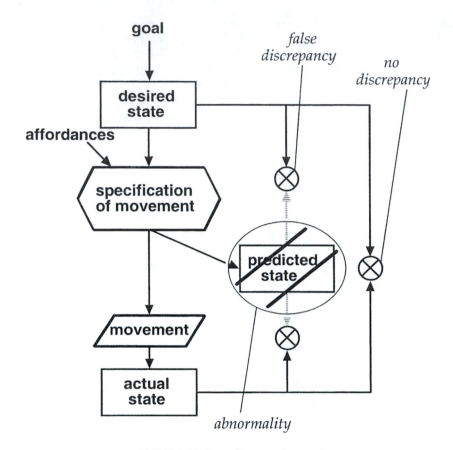

FIGURE 12.5. Delusions of control.

biguous visual feedback concerning bodily movement, schizophrenics that report alien influence are far worse than normal and noninfluenced schizophrenic controls at correctly attributing authorship (Dapriati et al., 1997; Spence et al., 1997).

Motor control theorists of schizophrenic delusion disagree over the precise details of experimental interpretation (Frith et al., 2000; Georgieff & Jeannerod, 1998). However, there is broad agreement on the idea that the primary cognitive failure is of the motor control subsystem. Over- or underactivation of implicated neural areas produces aberrant sensations of volitional control. The schizophrenic feels as if she is not in volitional control of her body or, alternatively, as if she is in volitional control of actions or events external to her. If this is correct, then the source of at least these positive symptoms has nothing to do with a ToM module but results from malfunction in a more basic sensorimotor mechanism.

If the positive symptoms of schizophrenia can be explained in this way, then it seems that a weak ToMM hypothesis has not much role to play in accounting for the disorder. After all, Schneiderian symptoms are generally held to constitute the core of the disorder. Of course, another way to defend a weak ToMM hypothesis (explored by Frith, 1992) is to argue that the core of the disorder is actually the *negative* symptoms (psychomotor poverty, avolition, apathy), now interpreted as *failures of willed action*, and attempt to explain these as a result of ToM malfunction—for example, as failures to form, metarepresent, and act on intentions. However, as we show, the negative symptoms are prime candidates for a mechanical explanation. If so, then the weak ToMM hypothesis is left without any real work to do.

In any case, to repeat our arguments made in the introduction, if positive and negative symptoms are not cleanly dissociable, this suggests that the cognitive system or systems implicated in schizophrenia are affected together. Either this is because there is only one system involved (as the discredited strong ToMM hypothesis suggested), or it is because more than one system is involved (as the weak ToMM hypothesis suggests). But then the problem becomes one of accounting for the connection between them: Why do they fail together? The most obvious hypothesis is one of mechanical failure: Some neurological process causes disruption in a number of cognitive systems, which produces the characteristic array of positive and negative symptoms. If this is genuinely the case (see the misconnection theory described next), then the explanation for schizophrenia is ultimately not cognitive at all, despite the suggestive pattern of cognitive disabilities. Most importantly from our point of view, mechanical failures of this sort dramatically undermine straightforward reverse engineering theorizing. The reason is this: Given the number of systems that are likely to be involved in any such mechanical failure, reasoning backward from a pattern of cognitive and other behavioral disabilities to the functional architecture of the system is an Herculean task. In particular, there is no good reason to assume that seemingly discrete domains at the cognitive level will correspond to actual domains in the architecture of the system. As we put it earlier, these may not be real, but only architecturally virtual cognitive domains.

Misconnection and Dysmetria

Motor control theories of misattributed agency undermine the strong ToMM hypothesis for schizophrenia by accounting for a significant—some say "core"— subset of symptoms in terms of a malfunctioning lower level sensorimotor subsystem, rather than one that is devoted to higher level cognitive processes. A second way of opposing the strong ToMM hypothesis would be more radical still, by seeking to explain schizophrenia as an essentially mechanical disorder. In this case, even if the sensorimotor system is affected, it is not a problem specific to the sensorimotor system per se—that is, a cognitive problem relating to the generation and use of motor predictions. It is, rather, a noncognitive problem that affects, among a variety of functionally unrelated things, the generation and use of motor predictions.

Some recent theories of schizophrenia take this approach. Although differing in many details, both Nancy Andreasen and Peter Liddle share the view that schizophrenia involves disruption to a circuit integrating functionally diverse cognitive processes whose neural substrates are located in different areas of the brain. As Liddle put it, "the evidence indicates that the abnormality characteristic of schizophrenia is impaired coordination of activity at the diverse sites engaged during mental processing rather than a static loss of function at any site" (Liddle, 2001, p. 72).

For Liddle, the relevant circuit involves a series of linked cortico-striato-thalamo-cortical feedback loops whose activation affects the diverse regions implicated by neuroimaging studies of schizophrenia. He suggests that the cause of this *misconnection* is most likely dopaminergic regulation of this circuit.

For Andreasen, the explanatory strategy is to identify the neural substrates of cognitive malfunction in schizophrenia and investigate possible linking circuitry. The circuit she identifies is a cortico-cerebellar-thalamo-cerebellar-cortical loop. For Andreasen, however, the misconnection is explained as a lack of temporal integration of activation across distributed brain regions. Hence she dubs the misconnection syndrome a case of *dysmetria* (Andreasen, Paradisio, & O'Leary, 1998; Andreasen et al., 1999).

Patients suffering from schizophrenia have a misconnection syndrome that leads them to make abnormal associations between mental representations; they lack the ability to distinguish between self and nonself, and, due to an incapacity to suppress the multiple stimuli normally bombarding human consciousness, they are further unable to distinguish between the important and the trivial. In light of these difficulties, a number of problems follow: Internal representations may be attributed to the external world, leading to hallucinations. Perceptions or other information will be misconnected with inappropriate associations leading to delusional misinterpretations. Online monitoring of language or thoughts will be impaired or mistimed, leading to disorganized speech and disorganized thinking. Behavior will not be adequately monitored, leading to social awkwardness, excessive aggressiveness or shyness, or other abnormalities in behavioral activities. The inability to monitor may also lead to the "freezing" characteristic of catatonic immobility or a failure to inhibit expressed as catatonic excitement. Difficulties in inhibiting or prioritizing may also lead to the various negative symptoms such as avolition or anhedonia, much as a computer locks when it cannot match signals sent at an incorrect rate or to an incorrect place (Andreasen et al., 1999, p. 4).

Andreasen calls her theory "cognitive" rather than "mechanical." But we should note that exactly the same explanation could be offered by someone who focuses on finding the mechanical link between diffusely affected systems. The only thing missing would be the *coda* of cognitive unification provided by suggesting a functional role for the linking circuit that Andreasen proposes is disrupted in schizophrenia.

Why, then, does Andreasen accord the CCTCC circuit a functional role in cognition? No doubt it is because schizophrenic symptoms seem to mark a disintegration of the mind, rather than structureless neuropathology. To account for this difference, Andreasen introduces an extra function the brain must accomplish for normal functioning—namely, "synchrony," the neural substrate of which is the proposed CCTCC circuit. Malfunction of this circuit (due to widespread mechanical breakdown) is "dysmetria."

Although we think Andreasen is right to emphasize that schizophrenia involves functional disintegration (and so, effectively, a disintegration of mind), she goes too far in supposing it needs a cognitive explanation. What distinguishes schizophrenia from a structureless neuropathology is the anatomical (rather than functional) integrity of the proposed CCTCC circuit. Schizophrenic symptoms are the result of mechanical damage to the CCTCC circuit, so are not accidentally distributed throughout the brain.

Ultimately, Andreasen's theory is eliminative of higher cognitive and intentional explanations for schizophrenia, not just because dysmetria "cuts across" cognitive explanations, but for a deeper reason shared by all eliminative explanations. It suggests that the anatomical level exhausts explanation of schizophrenic symptoms. Although Andreasen postulates "synchrony" as a cognitive function, she is simply imposing unnecessary higher order unification on functionally disparate symptoms. As a higher order cognitive concept, "synchrony" does not work, not least because it is implicated in all cognitive functions because they all involve the synchronized firing of sets of neurons. In particular, it does not suggest progressive decomposition into finer and more basic cognitive structures terminating in an implementation theory. Instead it leads straight to the mechanical level via a search for a circuit whose *location* would link all the symptoms, and an account of the functioning of that circuit not in cognitive terms but rather in the vocabulary of neuroscience. Hence this is a case where the postulation of cognitive unity is merely virtual, and such unity as the disorder possesses is at a purely mechanical level.

Our purpose here is not to argue for a particular theory of schizophrenia but to point out that persuasive accounts of the origin of schizophrenic symptoms do not require their unification at a high level. Co-occurrence of symptoms is, here, most likely the result of neuroanatomical processes that are essentially noncognitive.

CONCLUSION

Both autism and schizophrenia present a distinctive profile of spared abilities and disabilities, with "core" symptoms that invite unification in terms of discretely impaired cognitive function. By the principles of reverse engineering, such unification suggests there may be a single underlying cognitive entity that is differentially affected. However, although such reasoning is not always fallacious, it may inhibit research into more basic underlying cognitive and/or mechanical explanations of "core" symptoms. In our view, this research becomes especially important if there is no explanation of a range of further symptoms with which these core symptoms are characteristically comorbid. ToMM theorists have generally recognized the need to widen the explanatory scope of their accounts, but have failed to do so in any convincing way. Admittedly, their proposals are often speculative, awaiting further empirical investigation. But it may be that they persist in this approach partly because it seems unlikely that such distinctive higher order cognitive abnormalities could be explained except by way of selective impairment to dedicated higher order cognitive systems. In this chapter, we have argued that such cognitive abnormalities may in fact be caused—developmentally or, indeed, architecturally—by damage to lower order cognitive mechanisms and/or mechanical malfunction, and there are good reasons to prefer such explanations for both autism and schizophrenia. In any case, we propose that theorists should only retain high-level cognitive hypotheses where these function as theoretically ineliminable constraints on implementation theories for cognitive capacities. In the case of both autism and schizophrenia, continuing research suggests that, even though ToM deficits constitute a clinically interesting set of related symptoms, their explanation will not involve a dedicated ToM module. In fact, our bet is that this module will prove to be eliminable as the deeper cognitive and noncognitive structure of both disorders becomes more fully understood.

NOTES

1. Mirroring our earlier point, because mechanical malfunction inevitably produces cognitive malfunction, some might doubt the viability of distinguishing between mechanical and cognitive explanations for various disorders. Although we think the distinction between PKU and, say, prosopagnosia is clear enough, we reinforce the idea by considering another computer analogy. Suppose some instability in the microcircuitry of a PC causes a particular, resource-hungry, program to crash first. The program is indeed a discrete computational entity identified by its selective malfunction, but the ultimate cause is not computational but mechanical. The reason is simply this: The solution is not to reinstall the program, but to fix the microcircuitry.
2. Some of the material in this section draws heavily on ideas developed in McGeer (2001) and McGeer (forthcoming). For additional arguments against the ToM approach to autism, see Gerrans (1998).
3. There are a number of variations of this task, but one simple version that has been used on autistic populations is the so-called "Sally–Ann" task (Baron-Cohen, Leslie, & Frith, 1985; cf. Wimmer & Perner, 1983): Children are shown two dolls, "Sally" and "Ann." Sally has a basket in which she places a marble. Then, she goes away

leaving her basket behind. Ann takes Sally's marble out of the basket and puts it in a box. Sally returns, and the children are asked "where will Sally look for her marble?" To pass, children must correctly predict that Sally will look in the basket where *she* believes the marble to be, as opposed to the box where they know the marble is themselves.

4. Although some studies indicate normal children may show weak superiority on false-photo tasks (Slaughter, 1998) or dissociation in the opposite direction (passing false belief and failing false photograph; Leslie & Thaiss, 1992; Zaitchik, 1990), more recent studies suggest this may be an artefact of experimental design. Normal 4-year olds do equally well on both tasks once incidental conversational and linguistic differences between them have been eliminated. Autistic subjects, on the other hand, continue to show the dramatic physical–mental dissociation seen in earlier studies (Peterson & Siegal, 1998).

5. For a defence of this perspective and for details of autistic abnormalities from which the following limited summary is culled, see the collected papers in Baron-Cohen, Tager-Flusberg, & Cohen (2000). See also Frith (1989) and Happé (1994).

6. The theoretical perspective advocated in this paper stands in some contrast to other work done by these authors. Although both have been friendly to a ToM account of social deficits, Uta Frith in particular has advocated a "weak central coherence" (WCC) view of autism in contrast to the ToM approach on grounds that the latter cannot account for autistic abnormal capacities in areas unrelated to social cognition (for instance, autistic savant talents). According to WCC, autistics lack a capacity to process incoming information in context, thereby using contextual cues to deliver higher level meanings. For an explanation and defense of this approach, see Frith (1989) and Happé (1999). At one time, Frith seemed to reject the ToM approach on the grounds that autistic assets and deficits are likely to have the same origin. Recently, she seems to have leaned more toward a multiple deficit approach involving WCC, ToM, and executive dysfunction (affecting planning, working memory, impulse control, shifting tasks, and the initiation and monitoring of action; Frith, 1997). Happé herself has also advocated something like a weak ToM (multiple dysfunction) stance in her writing: "To date, the experimental findings suggest that weak central coherence and theory of mind are somewhat independent. . . . However, it is likely that these two aspects of autism interact, and failure to integrate information in context might contribute to everyday social difficulties. Featural processing might play a part in certain social impairments. Piecemeal processing of faces, for example . . . could hamper emotion recognition" (Happé, 1999, p. 220). This theoretical vacillation with respect to ToM may well indicate that the authors have no settled views as yet, due precisely to the kinds of explanatory difficulties we are highlighting in this chapter.

7. This is not to suggest that Gopnik endorses the kind of modularity approach to ToM capacities discussed in this article. In Gopnik's view (and the view of her collaborators), theory of mind is—as the term suggests—a theoretical competence. Its acquisition is to be explained in terms of a child's native capacity for theory building put to work on progressively elaborating an innate proto-theory of agency in the face of new evidence (see, e.g., Gopnik, Capps, & Meltzoff, 2000).

8. As yet ToMM theorists give no explanation for why a late-developing ToM mechanism should not work as reliably as one that develops on schedule, other than its

lateness. Perhaps to avoid this problem, some suggest that high-functioning autistics that are able to pass theory-of-mind tests do so by means of "compensatory mechanisms"—general problem-solving capacities deployed in the social realm. However, it is hard to see how this use of "general problem-solving capacities" would not require some specialized knowledge about psychological matters, in which case the expertise of normal subjects might well be explained by the vast difference in their knowledge base acquired through years of training, rather than by the presence of any specialized mechanism for psychological reasoning.

9. It is interesting to compare these various clinical populations with Down's syndrome children who do pass false-belief tasks at the same mental age as normal children. Hence, Down's syndrome children are developmentally retarded, but they seem to follow a normal developmental trajectory (see, e.g., Baron-Cohen, Leslie, & Frith, 1985). By contrast, congenitally blind children and deaf children of hearing parents follow the same abnormal developmental trajectory as autistic children: They are unusually delayed in passing theory-of-mind tasks compared with non-social reasoning tasks. They also show autisticlike abnormalities in social, communicative, and imaginative abilities; but, as is not the case with autistic children, these abnormalities tend to disappear as they become more able to relate to others through developing skills that overcome their handicaps in a context of able and responsive others (Brown et al., 1997; Peterson & Siegal, 1998). It is also notable that deaf children whose parents are native signers, and who therefore have rich proto-conversational and conversational interactions with others from an early age, do not show any "autistic" social or cognitive abnormalities in the nature of their conversational behavior (Meadow, Greenberg, Erting, & Carmichael, 1981). In particular, they do not have any difficulty passing "theory-of-mind" reasoning tasks. These comparative results are discussed in Peterson and Siegal (1999).

REFERENCES

Aglioti, S., DeSouza, J., & Goodale, M. (1995). Size-contrast illusions deceive the eye but not the hand. *Current Biology, 5*(6), 679–685.

Andreasen, N. C., Paradisio, S., & O'Leary, D. (1998). "Cognitive dysmetria" as an integrative theory of schizophrenia: A dysfunction in cortical-subcortical-cerebellar circuitry? *Schizophrenia Bulletin, 24,* 203–217.

Andreasen, N. C., Nopoulos, P., O'Leary, D. S., Miller, D. D., Wassink, T., & Flaum, M. (1999). Defining the phenotype of schizophrenia: cognitive dysmetria and its neural mechanisms. *Biological Psychiatry, 46*(7), 908–920.

Baron-Cohen, H., Tager-Flusberg, H., & Cohen, D. (Eds.). (2000). *Understanding other minds: Perspectives from developmental cognitive neuroscience* (2nd ed.). Oxford: Oxford University Press.

Baron-Cohen, S. (1995). *Mindblindness: An essay on autism and theory of mind.* Cambridge, MA: MIT Press.

Baron-Cohen, S. (2001). Autism: A review. *International Review of Research in Mental Retardation, 23,* 169–184.

Baron-Cohen, S., Leslie, A. M., & Frith, C. D. (1985). Does the autistic child have a theory of mind?" *Cognition, 21,* 37–46.

Blakemore, S.-J., Goodbody, S. J., & Wolpert, D. M. (1998a). Predicting the consequences of our own actions: The role of sensorimotor context estimation. *Journal of Neuroscience, 18,* 7511–7518.

Bovet, P., & Parnas, J. (1993). Schizophrenic delusions, a phenomenological approach. *Schizophrenia Bulletin, 19,* 579–597.

Brown, R., Hobson, R. P., Lee, A., & Stevenson, J. (1997). Are there "autistic-like" features in congenitally blind children?" *Journal of Child Psychology and Psychiatry,* 38(6), 693–703.

Campbell, J. (1999). Schizophrenia, the space of reasons and thinking as a motor process. *Monist, 8,* 609–625.

Carruthers, P. (1996). Autism as mind-blindness: An elaboration and partial defense. In P. Carruthers & P. Smith (Eds.), *Theories of theories of mind* (pp. 22–38). Cambridge: Cambridge University Press.

Currie, G. (1996). Simulation theory, theory-theory and the evidence from autism. In P. Carruthers & P. Smith (Eds.), *Theories of theories of mind* (pp. 242–256). Cambridge: Cambridge University Press.

Daprati, E., Franck, N., Georgieff, N., Proust, J., Pacherie, E., Dalery, J., & Jeannerod, M. (1997). Looking for the agent: An investigation into consciousness of action and self-consciousness in schizophrenic patients. *Cognition, 65,* 71–86.

Decety, J., Perani, D., Jeannerod, M., Bettinardi, V., Tadary, B., Woods, R., Mazziotta, J. C., & Fazio, F. (1994). Mapping motor representations with PET. *Nature, 371,* 600–602.

Dennett, D. (1978). *Brainstorms: Philosophical essays on mind and psychology.* Montgomery, VT: Bradford Books.

Donnai, D., & Karmiloff-Smith, A. (2000). Williams syndrome: From genotpe through to the cognitive phenotype. *American Journal of Medical Genetics: Seminars in Medical Genetics, 97*(2), 164–171.

Elman, J., Bates, E., Johnson, M., Karmiloff-Smith, A., Parisi, D., & Plunkett, K. (1996). *Rethinking innateness: A connectionist perspective on development.* Cambridge, MA: MIT Press.

Frith, C. D. (1987). The positive and negative symptoms of schizophrenia reflect impairments in the perception and initiation of action. *Psychological Medicine, 17,* 631–648.

Frith C. D. (1992). *The cognitive neuropsychology of schizophrenia.* Hove: Lawrence Erlbaum.

Frith, C. D., Blakemore, S. J., & Wolpert, D. M. (2000). Abnormalities in the awareness and control of action. *Philosophical Transactions of the Royal Society of London B, 355,* 1771–1788.

Frith, C. D., & Done, D. J. (1989). Experiences of alien control in schizophrenia reflect a disorder in the central monitoring of action. *Psychological Medicine, 19,* 359–363.

Frith, U. (1989). *Autism: Explaining the enigma.* Oxford: Blackwell.

Frith, U. (1996). Cognitive explanations of autism. *Acta Paediatrica, 85,* 63.

Frith, U. (1997). The neurocognitive basis of autism. *Trends in the Cognitive Sciences, 1*(2), 73–77.

Frith, U., & Happé, F. (1999). Theory of mind and self-consciousness: What it is like to be autistic?" *Mind and Language, 14*(1), 1–22.

Gallagher, S. (2000). Philosophical conceptions of the self: Implications for cognitive science. *Trends in Cognitive Science, 4*(1), 14–21.

Gallagher, S. (2000). Self-reference and schizophrenia: A cognitive model of immunity to error through misidentification. In D. Zahavi (Ed.), *Exploring the self: Philosophical and psychopathological perspectives on self-experience* (pp. 203–239). Philadelphia: John Benjamins.

Gallese, V., Fadiga, L., Fogassi, L., & Rizzolatti, G. (1996). Action recognition in the premotor cortex. *Brain, 119,* 593–609.

Gallese, V., Fadiga, L., Fogassi, L., Luppino, G., & Murata, A. (1997). A parieto-frontal circuit for hand grasping movements in the monkey: Evidence from reversible inactivation experiments. In P. Thier & H. O. Karnath (Eds.), *Parietal lobe contributions to orientation in 3-D space* (pp. 255–269). Heidelberg: Springer-Verlag.

Georgieff, N., & Jeannerod, M. (1998). Beyond consciousness of external reality: A "who" system for consciousness of action and self-consciousness. *Consciousness and Cognition, 7*(3), 465–477.

Gergely, G., & Watson, J. (1996). The social biofeedback theory of parental affect mirroring: The development of emotional self-awareness and self-control in infancy. *International Journal of Psychoanalysis, 77,* 1181–1212.

Gerrans, P. (1998). The norms of cognitive development. *Mind and Language, 13,* 56–75.

Gerrans, P. (2002). Theory of mind in evolutionary psychology. *Biology and Philosophy, 17,* 305–321.

Gerrans, P. (2001). Authorship and ownership of thoughts. Critical notice of C. Lynn Stephens and George Graham, *When Self-Consciousness Breaks. Alien Voices and Inserted Thoughts. Philosophy Psychology and Psychiatry, 8,* 231–237.

Gopnik, A., Capps, L., & Meltzoff, A. (2000). Early theories of mind: What the theory theory can tell us about autism. In S. Baron-Cohen, H. Tager-Flusberg, & D. J. Cohen (Eds.), *Understanding other minds: Perspectives from developmental cognitive neuroscience* (pp. 50–72). Oxford: Oxford University Press.

Gopnik, M., & Goad, H. (1997). What underlies inflectional error patterns in genetic dysphasia? *Journal of Neurolinguistics, 10,* 109–137.

Happé, F. (1994). *Autism: An introduction to psychological theory.* Cambridge, MA: Harvard University Press.

Happé, F. (1995). The role of age and verbal ability in the theory of mind task performance of subjects with autism. *Child Development, 66,* 843-55.

Happé, F. (1999). Autism: Cognitive deficit or cognitive style? *Trends in the Cognitive Sciences, 3*(6), 216–222.

Hobson, R. P. (1991). Through feeling and sight to self and symbol. In U. Neisser (Ed.), *Ecological and interpersonal knowledge of the self* (pp. 254–279). New York: Cambridge University Press.

Hobson, R. P. (1993). Understanding persons: The role of affect. In S. Baron-Cohen, H. Tager-Flusberg, & D. J. Cohen (Eds.), *Understanding other minds: Perspectives from autism* (pp. 204–227). Oxford, Oxford University Press.

Jahanshahi, M., & Frith, C. D. (1998). Willed action and its impairments. *Cognitive Neuropsychology, 15,* 483–533.

Jeannerod, M. (1994). The representing brain—Neural correlates of motor intention and imagery. *Behavioral and Brain Sciences, 17,* 187–202.

Karmiloff-Smith, A. (1998). Development itself is the key to understanding developmental disorders. *Trends in Cognitive Sciences, 2*(10), 389–398.

Karmiloff-Smith, A., Scerif, G., & Ansari, D.

(2003). Double dissociations in developmental disorders? Theoretically misconceived, empirically dubious. *Cortex, 39,* 161–163.

Langdon, R., & Coltheart, M. (1999). Mentalising, schizotypy, and schizophrenia. *Cognition, 71,* 43–71.

Leekam, S., & Perner, J. (1991). Does the autistic child have a metarepresentational deficit? *Cognition, 40,* 203–218.

Leslie, A. (1994). Pretending and believing: Issues in the theory of ToMM. *Cognition, 50*(1–3), 211–238.

Leslie, A., & Thaiss, L. (1992). Domain specificity in conceptual development: Evidence from autism. *Cognition, 43,* 225–251.

Liddle, P. (2001). Is disordered cerebral connectivity the core problem in schizophrenia? *Neuroscience News, 4,* 62–74.

McGeer, V. (2001). Psyche-practice, psyche-theory and the contrastive case of autism—How practices of mind become second-nature. *Journal of Consciousness Studies, 8*(5–7), 109–132.

McGeer, V. (forthcoming). Out of the mouths of autistics: Subjective report and its role in cognitive theorizing. In A Brook & K. Akins (Eds.), *Cognition and the brain: The philosophy and neuroscience movement.* Cambridge: Cambridge University Press.

Meadow, K. P., Greenberg, M. T., Erting, K., & Carmichael, S. (1981). Interactions of deaf mothers and deaf preschool children: Comparison with three other groups of deaf and hearing dyads. *American Annals of the Deaf, 126,* 454–468.

Meltzoff, A., & Gopnik, A. (1994). The role of imitation in understanding persons and developing a theory of mind. In S. Baron-Cohen, H. Tager-Flusberg, & D. Cohen (Eds.), *Understanding other minds: Perspectives from autism* (pp. 335–366). Oxford: Oxford University Press.

Peterson, C. C., Peterson, J., & Webb, J. (2000). Factors influencing the development of a theory of mind in blind children. *British Journal of Developmental Psychology, 18,* 431–447.

Peterson, C. C., & Siegal, M. (1998). Changing focus on the representational mind: Concepts of false photos, false drawings and false beliefs in deaf, autistic and normal children.

British Journal of Developmental Psychology, 16, 301–320.

Peterson, C. C., & Siegal, M. (1999). Insights into theory of mind from deafness and autism. *Mind and Language, 15*(1), 77–99.

Pinker, S. (1999). *Words and rules: The ingredients of language.* London: Phoenix.

Rizzolatti, G., Fadiga, L., Gallese, V., & Fogassi, L. (1996). Premotor cortex and the recognition of motor actions. *Cognitive Brain Research, 3,* 131–141.

Robbins, T. W. (1997). Integrating the neurological and neuropsychological dimensions of autism. In J. Russell (Ed.), *Autism as an executive disorder* (pp. 21–53). Oxford: Oxford University Press.

Russell, J. (Ed.). (1997). *Autism as an executive disorder.* Oxford: Oxford University Press.

Russell, J., & Jarrold, C. (1998). Error correction problems in autism: Evidence for a central monitoring impairment? *Journal of Autism and Developmental Disorders, 28*(3), 177–188.

Russell, J., & Jarrod, C. (1999). Memory for actions in children with autism: Self versus other. *Cognitive Neuropsychiatry, 4*(4), 303–331.

Rutter, M., & Schopler, E. (1987). Autism and pervasive developmental disorders: Conceptual and diagnostic issues. *Journal of Autism and Developmental Disorders, 17,* 159–186.

Schopler, E., & Mesibove, G. B. (Eds.). (1988). *Diagnosis and assessment in autism.* New York: Plenum Press.

Slaughter, V. (1998). Children's understanding of pictorial and mental representations. *Child Development, 68*(2), 321–332.

Stern, D. (1985). *The interpersonal world of the infant.* New York: Basic Books.

Spence, S. A., Brooks, D. J., Hirsch, S. R., Liddle, P. F., Meehan, J., & Grasby, P. M. (1997). A PET study of voluntary movement in schizophrenic patients experiencing passivity phenomena (delusions of alien control). *Brain, 120,* 1997–2011.

Tager-Flusberg, H. (Ed.). (1999). *Neurodevelopmental disorders.* Boston: MIT Press.

Tallal, P. (1985). Children with language impairment can be accurately identified using temporal processing measures: A response to Zhang and Tomblin. *Brain and Language, 65,* 395–403.

Tallal, P., Miller, S., & Fitch, R. (1995). Neurobiological basis of speech: A case for preeminence of temporal processing. *Irish Journal of Psychology, 16*(3), 194–219.

Tallal, P., Sainburg, R., & Jernigan, T. (1991). The neuropathology of developmental dysphasia: Behavioral, morphological, and physiological evidence for a pervasive temporal processing disorder. *Reading and Writing, 3*(3–4), 363–377.

Tallal, P., Stark, R., & Mellits, D. (1985). The relationship between auditory temporal anaylsis and receptive language development: Evidence from studies of developmental language disorder. *Neuropsychologia, 23*(4), 537–534.

Thomas, M., & Karmiloff-Smith, A. (in press). Are developmental disorders like cases of adult brain damage? Implications from connectionist modelling. *Behavioral and Brain Sciences.*

Trevarthen, C. (1979). Communication and cooperation in early infancy: A description of primary intersubjectivity. In M. Bullowa (Ed.), *Before speech: The beginning of interpersonal communication* (pp. 321–347). New York: Cambridge University Press.

Trevarthen, C., & Hubley, P. (1978). Secondary intersubjectivity: Confidence, confiding and acts of meaning in the first tear. In A. Lock (Ed.), *Action, gesture and symbol: The emergence of language* (pp. 183–229). London: Academic Press.

Van der Lely, H. (1997). Language and cognitive development in a grammatical SLI boy: Modularity and innateness. *Journal of Neurolinguistics, 10,* 75–107.

Wimmer, H., & Perner, P. (1983). Beliefs about beliefs: Representation and the constraining function of wrong beliefs in young children's understanding of deception. *Cognition, 13,* 103–128.

Wing, L., & Gould, J. (1978). Systematic recording of behaviours and skills of retarded and psychotic children. *Journal of Autism and Childhood Schizophrenia, 8,* 79–97.

Wing, L., & Gould, J. (1979). Severe impairments of social interactions and associated abnormalities in children: Epidemiology and classification. *Journal of Autism and Developmental Disorders, 9,* 11–29.

Wright, B., Lombardino, L., King, W., Puranik, C., Leonard, C., & Merzenich, M. (1997). Deficits in auditory temporal and spectral resolution in language impaired children.

Nature, 387(6629), 176–178.

Zaitchik, D. (1990). When representations conflict with reality: The preschooler's problem with false belief and "false" photographs. *Cognition, 35,* 41–68.

13

Synthesis
Psychological Understanding and Social Skills

MARTIN DAVIES
Australian National University

TONY STONE
South Bank University

*S*uppose we use the term *theory of mind* in a neutral and inclusive way, so that having a theory of mind is simply having an ability to engage in our everyday folk psychological practices of attribution, interpretation, and prediction. This use of the term is noncommittal as to how the ability is to be explained. Perhaps the explanation is to be given in terms of possession of a substantive theory about how the psychological world works; perhaps in terms of a capacity to identify with others in imagination and to simulate their mental lives; or perhaps in terms of a mixture of these things. The neutral and inclusive use of *theory of mind* is also noncommittal as to whether the basis of our folk psychological abilities resides in a special-purpose module of the mind.

Once we abstract away from questions about theory versus simulation and from questions about modularity, it can seem truistic that having a theory of mind—being able to engage in our everyday folk psychological practices or having *psychological understanding*—is fundamental to social functioning. Thus, for example, at the beginning of *The Child's Theory of Mind*, Henry Wellman said (1990, p. 1): "Arriving at some sort of understanding of mind is an important accomplishment of childhood. . . . An understanding of the mind is . . . fundamental to an understanding of the social world." Indeed, it seems natural to suppose that, just as a naïve or everyday understanding of physics enables us to negotiate the physical world, so also a naïve or everyday under-standing of psychology enables us to negotiate the mental, and in particular the social, world.[1] In a similar spirit, Simon Baron-Cohen said (1995, p. 30): "Mindreading [the ability to imagine or represent states of mind that we or others might hold] is good for a number of important things, including social understanding, behavioral prediction, social interaction, and communication."

The truistic-seeming idea that having a theory of mind is fundamental to social functioning might suggest that individual differences in theory of mind will go neatly in step with differences in social functioning. However, as the chapters in this book make clear, the relationship between psychological under-standing and social skills is very much more complicated. One indication of the complexity of the relationship is that there are striking mismatches between psychological understanding as evidenced in experimental tasks—including, centrally, false-belief tasks—and social skills as evidenced in daily life. In some individuals, social skills outrun psychological understanding. Other individuals have a high level of psychological understanding even while their social skills leave much to be desired. We begin with a mismatch of the first kind.

MISMATCHES BETWEEN UNDERSTANDING AND SKILLS: DUNN'S PARADOX

In line with the neutral and inclusive use of the term *theory of mind*, Janet Astington[2] says that having a theory of mind is a matter of attributing mental states to people so as to interpret their behavior. The core of this interpretive practice is 'that we assume that people's actions are motivated by their desires in light of their beliefs' (p. 14). So, having a theory of mind involves understand-ing the relations among the three core notions—belief, desire and action—and the relations between these and intention, attention, perception, emotion, and the rest.

Although it seems obvious that having this kind of understanding of the mental domain is a fundamental requirement for functioning well socially, there is a paradox here, pointed out by Judy Dunn.[3] Even very young children are social creatures who show a measure of understanding of the actions and feel-ings of other people. But children up to the age of 5 years are apt to fail at experimental tasks that are designed to assess their folk psychological under-standing. Why, in these children, do social engagement and interaction outrun experimental performance?

In general, mismatches between psychological understanding and social skills invite a variety of explanatory strategies. Where real-life social skills out-run experimentally tested psychological understanding, at least three possibili-ties suggest themselves. First, it might be that the aspects of psychological understanding tested by the experimental tasks are indeed absent but that they are not centrally relevant to everyday social life. After all, many people who fluently negotiate their physical environment have a flawed understanding of how the physical world works. Second, it might be that the experimental tests reveal the absence of aspects of psychological understanding that normally play a central role in social life but that subjects are able to make up for this deficit by employing rules and work-arounds. Third, it might be that the experimental tasks test central aspects of psychological understanding that are actually present, but that these aspects of understanding are manifested more readily in real-world performance than in laboratory performance. That is, it might be that the real-world situation imposes fewer demands, or offers more resources in support, than does the laboratory situation. So, in the case where skills manifested in the real world outrun understanding manifested in the laboratory (S > U), we can summarize the three explanatory strategies as follows: (S > U)1, irrelevance; (S > U)2, compensation by rules; and (S > U)3, difference in demands or resources.

Now, the experimental tasks by which young children's theory of mind is assessed mainly test understanding of the fact that people's thoughts, actions, and feelings flow from beliefs that may not represent reality accurately. But it will not do to say, as the first strategy, (S > U)1, irrelevance, would suggest, that understanding of false beliefs simply has nothing to do with the social life of a 3-year-old. Even if an understanding of desires and emotions is more centrally relevant to the preschooler, there is still the fact that, by 3 years of age, children engage in deceptive behavior that seems to manifest an appreciation of the possibility of false belief. So why does this aspect of social interaction outrun performance on false-belief tasks? The second strategy, (S > U)2, compensation by rules, is not adequate to explain this mismatch since these children do not seem to be just relying on learned deceptive routines (pp. 16–17).

Astington mentions at least two factors that may help to explain the mismatch in a way that is more in line with the third strategy, (S > U)3, difference in demands or resources. A child's developing understanding of false belief may be more readily manifested in real-world social behavior than in an experimental task, first, because the child's social behavior is very often "supported by more competent others" (p. 33) and, second, because in a real-world social situation the child is likely to be emotionally involved and to "have the motivation to act in an appropriate manner" (p. 34). In short, the real-world situation offers supporting resources that are missing from the laboratory situation. (For the purposes of our simple taxonomy of explanatory strategies, we treat factors that provide motivation as "resources.")

In the title of her chapter, Astington says that false-belief understanding is "never sufficient" for social competence. Factors other than false-belief understanding, including familiar settings, emotional significance, interaction with parents and others, interest, motivation, and emotional understanding, make essential contributions to social competence. We have just seen that the "never sufficient" claim helps to solve Dunn's paradox because some of the factors that are required if understanding is actually to be manifested may be present in real-world situations but absent from the experimental situation.

But what the "never sufficient" claim primarily suggests is a strategy for explaining a low level of social skills in subjects with a high degree of false-belief understanding (S < U). For it may be that social competence in a real-world situation imposes additional demands by comparison with an experimental test of false-belief understanding. For example, acting appropriately in a social situation may require understanding of both false belief and emotion. This is (S < U)3, difference in demands or resources. And we can rapidly see that there are at least two other strategies for explaining cases in which understanding manifested in the laboratory outruns skills manifested in the real world.

First, if experimentally tested psychological understanding is not centrally relevant to real-life social skills then the two may vary fairly independently, so skills may be low while understanding is high. This is (S < U)1, irrelevance. Second, the understanding manifested in the laboratory might not be systematic or deep. Even in the absence of genuine psychological understanding, a subject might be able to work out the correct responses to experimental tasks such as false-belief tasks, using rules and work-arounds. But laboriously reasoning one's way to solutions for problems posed in the laboratory does not make for fluent negotiation of the social domain. This is (S < U)2, compensation by rules.

NORMAL DEVELOPMENT, AUTISM, AND ASPERGER'S SYNDROME

The proposed solution to Dunn's paradox is that real-world social behavior is likely to be supported and facilitated by resources that are absent from the laboratory. This still leaves it open that understanding of false beliefs may be only occasionally relevant to preschool social life. But the complex relations between false-belief understanding and social behavior in normally developing children are very much clarified by the research of Astington and her colleagues in Toronto. False-belief understanding is "never sufficient" but it is "sometimes necessary" for social competence.

Normal Development

Astington reports that although false-belief understanding is not related to mere frequency of pretend play, it is related to specific aspects of sophisticated pretend play: role assignment and joint planning. It is also related to certain pragmatic aspects of language use having to do with informativeness and to aspects of social competence that involve recognizing and taking account of other people's mental states (all this independently of age and language ability.) Furthermore, in the case of role assignment and joint planning in pretend play, there is evidence that the direction of causation is from development of false-belief understanding to these features of pretend play. So the aspects of psychological competence tested by false-belief tasks are causally relevant to preschool social life in the real world—and not only in respect of deceptive behavior.

At the beginning of his chapter, Thomas Keenan[4] commends a framework for considering individual differences in the development of psychological understanding that was originally proposed by Karen Bartsch and David Estes (1996). According to their framework, there are three categories of research into individual differences in theory-of-mind development focusing on three kinds of differences:[5]

> Differences in the *antecedents* of theory-of-mind development that might facilitate or delay the acquisition of psychological understanding (e.g. differences in the number of siblings[6]).
>
> Differences in the developmental *consequences* of the specific timing— early or late—of acquisition of psychological understanding (e.g. differences in peer status).
>
> *Qualitative* differences in the child's theory of mind (e.g. a child might develop a "theory of nasty minds"[7] if raised in a hostile environment; Happé & Frith, 1996).

In the present volume, many of the chapters report investigations of the consequences of individual differences in psychological understanding for the development of social skills—a category of research described by Bartsch and Estes (1996, p. 287) as being still in its infancy.[8] Some chapters are concerned with the antecedents of psychological understanding, especially the role of language (see next section). And qualitative differences in children's theories of mind, especially attributional biases such as aggressive children's bias toward attributing hostile intentions to an agent, are important for the chapters that discuss the relationship between psychological understanding and antisocial behavior (see later sections).

Keenan himself reports an investigation into the relationships between psychological understanding (assessed by a false-belief task), peer acceptance or likeability, and social skills (as rated by a teacher) in 4- and 5-year-old children. The relationship between false-belief understanding and peer acceptance turned out to be complex, with a significant correlation (independent of language ability) when likeability was rated by girls but not when it was rated by the entire group or by boys. There were also significant correlations (again, independent of language ability) between false-belief understanding and social skills and between likeability (when rated by the entire group or by girls) and social skills.

Keenan also considers the prospects for a measure of psychological understanding that could detect continuing development beyond the age of 5 when a basic understanding of false beliefs is in place. He suggests that we borrow from research on social cognition the idea of "empathic accuracy" or everyday mind reading as a measure of the accuracy of a subject's attributions of thoughts and feelings to other people.[9] Although passing a test of false-belief understanding certainly requires accurate attribution of a thought to another person, tests of empathic accuracy typically draw on a rich set of resources going far beyond basic conceptual understanding of mental states. So, even when basic understanding is securely in place, empathic accuracy continues to develop. Keenan suggests that if existing empathic accuracy tasks could be adapted for use with younger children, then this measure would have a developmental span ranging from the preschool years right through into adulthood.

Because we later give a rather specific sense to the word *empathy*, we use the more neutral term *attributional accuracy* instead of *empathic accuracy*. But the idea remains the same. Attributional accuracy requires complex inferences about the mental states of other people, and these inferences may draw on observation, memory, and knowledge, including, for example, knowledge about the specific individual in question and knowledge about particular kinds of relationships.[10] The hope is that, by using attributional accuracy tasks alongside more familiar tasks including false-belief tasks, we could tease apart two rather different aspects of psychological understanding. On the one hand, there is the basic conceptual understanding of mental states of various types; not just beliefs but also desires, intentions, emotions, and so on. On the other hand, there is the further knowledge about the psychological world that is needed for accurate attributions of mental states to various people in various situations.

Tests of basic conceptual understanding of mental states, such as false-belief tasks, often require subjects to attribute mental states to the protagonist in a story. But, even in these cases, there is a difference between having a basic understanding of mental states and actually attributing mental states to people. It is a difference between competence and performance, in the sense of Chomsky (1965). Basic understanding of mental states—of belief, for example—is a kind of conceptual competence. Actually attributing a mental state—attributing to Sally a belief about the location of her marble, for example—is performance. Competence is never sufficient for performance, and there are many factors that could lead to an incorrect attribution even when basic conceptual understanding is in place. For example, actually giving the correct answer in a false-belief task may require inhibiting a prepotent response to indicate the position where the marble really is.

What is more important for Keenan's proposal, however, is that accurate attribution of mental states often requires not only basic conceptual understanding of beliefs, desires, intentions, emotions, and the rest, but also substantive empirical knowledge about mental states.[11] So, even when basic conceptual understanding is in place, and even when factors like prepotent responses are not at issue, still a flawed view about how the psychological world works may lead to incorrect attributions of mental states. The flawed view might not be articulated. It might just be an attributional bias, and Keenan makes the helpful suggestion that such biases can be conceived as implicit theories about people and their psychological properties (p. 137–138). Someone who has a bias toward attributing hostile intentions to other people does not have an inability to represent intentions or an impaired conceptual understanding of what intentions are. But such a person is likely to have an impaired ability to attribute intentions accurately.[12]

We can connect the issues in the last couple of paragraphs with the multiple uses of the term *theory of mind*. Some theory-of-mind tasks assess psychological understanding in the sense that they assess basic conceptual understanding of one or another type of mental state. Other theory-of-mind tasks assess psychological understanding by probing the subject's knowledge about how the psychological world works. Either having a basic understanding of mental states or knowing how the psychological world works could be described as having a theory of mind. Either lacking a basic understanding of some or all mental states or having false empirical views about how the psychological world works could be described as having an impaired theory of mind. But it is important to recognize that, in these cases, the term *theory of mind* would be used in two different ways.

Furthermore, the neutral and inclusive use of the term *theory of mind* with which we began is different from both these uses. Having an ability to engage in our everyday folk psychological practices of attribution, interpretation, and prediction—especially if this is conceived as an ability to offer accurate attributions, interpretations, and predictions—requires both having a basic conceptual understanding of mental states and having some knowledge about how the psychological world works.[13]

Autism

From Astington's research, we have seen that, in normally developing children, the aspects of psychological understanding tested by false-belief tasks are related to social competence (at least where this involves appreciation of other people's mental states), to pragmatic aspects of language use (having to do with informativeness), and to aspects of sophisticated pretend play (role assignment and joint planning). It is particularly interesting to compare all this with the case of children with autism because they typically have a triad of impairments: in social skills, in communication, and in pretend play.

As Helen Tager-Flusberg explains,[14] a typical pattern in research on the "theory-of-mind hypothesis of autism" is that theory of mind as assessed by false-belief tasks is found to be related to some measure of social skills, but the relationship disappears once age and language ability are factored into the analysis. So, despite the evident explanatory power of the theory-of-mind hypothesis, there is still a genuine question whether a theory-of-mind deficit explains discourse deficits and impairments in everyday social functioning in people with autism.

One distinctive aspect of the research being carried out by Tager-Flusberg and her colleagues in Boston is that they assess psychological understanding with a test battery that is broader than just false-belief tasks. It includes at the lower end of the scale tests of pretence and of predicting action based on desire, and at the upper end tests of judging intentions given information about personality traits and of moral judgments. The range of this test battery corresponds, in normally developing children, to an age range from 18 months to early adolescence. In contrast, first-order false-belief tasks, such as the Sally–Ann task or the Smarties box task, correspond to an age range from 3 to 5 years (Wellman, Cross, & Watson, 2000).[15]

Psychological understanding assessed in this way is related, in children with autism, to a measure of social competence, to a pragmatic aspect of language use (namely, staying on topic), and to severity of autism diagnosis[16] (all this independently of language ability). In respect of both social and communicative functioning, these results provide a striking parallel with Astington's results for normally developing children, even though the specific measures of social competence and of language use differ between the two research programs.[17]

Tager-Flusberg's research improves on earlier work, and provides important support for the theory-of-mind hypothesis of autism. This is because the demonstrated relationships between psychological understanding, on the one hand, and social and communicative functioning and severity of diagnosis, on the other, remain even when factors such as age, IQ, and—most important—language ability, are factored into the analysis. She attributes this improvement to the wider developmental span of her theory of mind test battery. But perhaps it is worth observing that the test battery is broader than just first-order false-belief tasks in two ways. On the one hand, it covers a greater developmental span—as it would, although to a lesser extent, if it included the false-belief explanation task, at the lower end of the scale, and second-order and other more complex false-belief tasks, at the upper end of the scale. On the other hand, it assesses understanding of a wider range of psychological phenomena, including pretence, the role of desire in action, character traits, and moral commitment.[18]

Asperger Syndrome

The research reported by Cheryl Dissanayake and Kathleen Macintosh[19] sheds some further light on the social skills of children with autism and also of children diagnosed with Asperger's disorder. On a test battery of four first-order false-belief tasks, the children with autism performed significantly less well than typically developing children and also significantly less well than the children with Asperger's disorder.[20] But despite this difference in performance on false-belief tasks, on various measures of social skills the two clinical groups did not differ from each other.[21] Nor, for the most part, were individual differences in false-belief performance within the groups related to social skills.

Dissanayake and Macintosh consider various possible explanations for these negative findings. Some of these concern the relatively narrow range of tasks used to test psychological understanding and the relatively broad range of measures used to assess social functioning. In the case of the mismatch found in the children diagnosed with Asperger's disorder, between experimentally tested psychological understanding and real-life social skills, these explanations belong in the category (S < U)3, difference in demands or resources. The basic idea here is that many aspects of good social functioning impose demands that go beyond anything required for understanding of false beliefs.

But Dissanayake and Macintosh also consider a different kind of explanation, the so-called "hacking" hypothesis (Bowler, 1992), which belongs in the category (S < U)2, compensation by rules. In the case of the children with Asperger's disorder, the idea would be that their success on false-belief tasks is not the result of real psychological understanding but rather of laborious compensatory strategies that do not make for fluent negotiation of the social domain. This kind of explanation seems to be broadly in line with the following description of individuals with Asperger's syndrome offered by Uta Frith and Francesca Happé (1999, p. 7)[22]:

> There is reason to believe that the understanding of mental states developed by these individuals is rather different from the effortless automatic ToM of the normal preschooler. First, they require much higher verbal ability to pass ToM tasks than do normal children, and do so at later stages (typically in adolescent, not preschool, years). Second, even as adults they are prone to making tell-tale slips in mental state attribution. . . . Third, their approach to social tasks has been said to resemble slow, conscious calculation. They appear to do better with written than spoken communication, where the fast to and fro of mental state appraisal is avoided.

Frith and Happé regard people with Asperger's syndrome as belonging within the autistic spectrum, differing from other people with autism in being able to "pass tests of mental state attribution" and in having "higher social and communication abilities than those without ToM ability" (ibid., p. 6). In apparent contrast, Dissanayake and Macintosh's two clinical groups are contrasted as children with high-functioning autistic disorder, on the one hand, and children with Asperger's disorder on the other. But Dissanayake and Macintosh note that the "hacking" hypothesis could also be used to explain how some high-functioning children with autism are able to pass false-belief tests and they regard their results as supporting the claim that "Asperger's disorder is on a continuum with autistic disorder" (p. 235).

In fact, it is not easy to obtain a clear picture of Asperger's syndrome. One diagnostic criterion is normal language development, but impairments in pragmatic aspects of language use are often present. People with Asperger's syndrome are reckoned to have higher social abilities than do most people with autism, but still show impaired social understanding and abnormal, inappropriate, and gauche social interactions.[23] The combination of relatively high language abilities and abnormal social interactions is seen in the two measures of social functioning on which children with Asperger's disorder differed from children with autism in Dissanayake and Macintosh's study. In the school playground, they spent more time conversing with their peers and they initiated interactions with peers more frequently, even though this resulted in no more time spent in ongoing interactions.

THE ROLE OF LANGUAGE

In order to explore the contribution that psychological understanding makes to social skills, we need to take into account that the development of both the understanding and the skills will be correlated with factors such as age. So experimenters need either to choose subjects matched for age but differing in psychological understanding or else to use statistical methods to determine whether psychological understanding makes a contribution to the prediction of social skills that is independent of age. What goes for age goes also for language ability, and Astington and Tager-Flusberg both stress the importance of controlling for language ability when investigating the relationship between psychological understanding and social skills. However, we are also interested in the role that language ability plays in the development of psychological understanding and of social skills.[24] To what extent is language ability a causal factor in the development of psychological understanding or social skills and to what extent is it a causal consequence?

If we view language ability from the perspective of Paul Grice (1989), then it may seem that language ability must rest on prior psychological understanding. According to Grice, understanding an utterance is a matter of discerning the intentions and beliefs of the speaker, so linguistic understanding would be impossible for someone utterly unable to attribute mental states to others. But, although it is correct that some degree of psychological understanding is required even to understand literal utterances as speech acts, it is not obviously correct that the kind of psychological understanding that is assessed by false-belief tasks, for example, is required for the basic communicative use of language.[25] Thus, it remains open that language ability may be an important causal factor in the development of psychological understanding and Astington provides evidence that in 3-year-old children, language ability does indeed play a causal role in the development of false-belief understanding, rather than the other way around (p. 7).

In an illuminating discussion of the time lag between understanding of desires and understanding of beliefs, Paul Harris (1996) proposes a specific role for conversation in the development of belief understanding. The basic idea is that children are involved in planned actions and in conversation. Planning and acting together with others, and coming to understand other people as agents, puts goals or desires center stage. But exchanging information through conversation involves understanding other people as epistemic subjects, so it puts beliefs and knowledge center stage (Harris, 1996, p. 208):

> My central claim is that children's understanding of other people as epistemic subjects develops in the context of their increasing proficiency at conversation involving the deliberate exchange of such information. Hence, my explanation for the lag is that a critical precondition for understanding beliefs but not desires—participation in the exchange of information through conversation— is not attained by most children until the third year.

According to Harris's hypothesis, it is conversational abilities and not verbal abilities as such, pragmatic aspects of language use rather than knowledge of syntax or vocabulary size, that are the crucial causal factors in the development of an understanding of beliefs. If this is right, then it will be important to investigate which pragmatic aspects are causal factors in the development of belief understanding and which are causal consequences.[26]

Harris's paper originated in a conference held in 1994, before the work of Candi Peterson and Michael Siegal with deaf children was widely known. He notes that if his hypothesis is correct, then we should expect "that children with limited or delayed exposure to conversation (e.g. deaf children) should show difficulties on tests of belief understanding."[27] As we now know, this is just how it turned out.

In a review of 11 separate studies, Peterson and Siegal (2000) found that false-belief understanding in deaf children from hearing families is delayed in comparison with hearing children. It is also delayed in comparison with "native signers" (that is, deaf children of signing deaf parents or those who have a native speaker of sign language in their immediate household). Indeed, deaf native signers seem to develop false-belief understanding at the same age as children of normal hearing, whereas the performance of deaf children from hearing families is markedly similar to that of autistic children of similar mental age.

Peterson and Siegal proposed that the explanation of this delay in developing false-belief understanding is that (2000, p. 132):

> until they enter a signing (or Total Communication) primary school, many profoundly deaf children have no readily available means of conversing with any of their hearing family members, especially about topics like mental states which have no obvious visual referent.

This explanation seems to be roughly in line with Harris's hypothesis. But the situation is really quite complex.

Harris's hypothesis is that it is participation in conversation as such—as the exchange of information—that is crucial for the development of an understanding of beliefs, and not for the development of an understanding of desires, goals, and plans, for example. He distinguishes this from the hypothesis that what is crucial is participation in conversations about mental states (Harris, 1996, p. 211). Conversation about mental states—about beliefs or thoughts, desires or plans, itches, or tickles—typically requires the use of specific lexical items. And where these lexical items are propositional attitude verbs, such as *believes, desires, hopes,* and the like, their use typically involves a characteristic syntactic construction: "*x* Vs that *p*" ("Sally believes that the marble is in the box"; "Sally desires that Anne should come and play"; "Sally hopes that she will find the marble soon").[28] So, the "conversation about mental states" hypothesis is connected with hypotheses about specific lexical items and syntactic constructions, and it is concerned not only with beliefs, but also with other propositional attitudes. In contrast, the "conversation as such" hypothesis is not connected with hypotheses about lexical items or syntactic constructions, and it is concerned specifically with beliefs, not with other propositional attitudes such as desires or hopes.

It seems clear that the explanation proposed by Peterson and Siegal is intended to be in line, not so much with Harris's "conversation as such" hypothesis, as with the competing "conversation about mental states" hypothesis. So important questions arise about the development, in deaf children, of an understanding of desires and other mental states. It is to such questions that Peterson turns in her chapter.[29] The experiments that she reports confirm, once again, that deaf children from hearing families lag behind hearing children in their development of false-belief understanding. The results also show that the deaf children with an average age between 9 and 10 years are less successful than hearing children with an average age between 4 and 5 years in tests of desire and emotion understanding.

These results seem to be broadly consistent with Peterson's proposal that "the present group of deaf children may have lacked the opportunities often available to hearing preschoolers in hearing-speaking families for querying, commenting on, or justifying seemingly false or deviant beliefs, feelings and desires" (p. 189). And the results do not sit as comfortably with Harris's hypothesis that participation in conversation makes a contribution specifically to the development of belief understanding. However, the situation remains somewhat unclear because the discrepancy between the deaf children and the hearing children is greater in the case of belief understanding than in the case of desire and emotion understanding. One possibility is that the developmental sequence is the same in deaf children as in hearing children—belief understanding lags behind desire understanding—and that the overall delay is to be explained in terms of the limited opportunity for participation in conversation about mental states. Another possibility is that the limited opportunity for conversation as such results in a specific delay in the development of belief understanding by comparison with desire understanding, and that the overall delay—including the delay in understanding desires different from one's own—is attributable to some other factor. Perhaps both possibilities will figure in a full explanation of these phenomena.

UNDERSTANDING, EMPATHY, AND ANTISOCIAL BEHAVIOR

We began from the truistic-seeming idea that having an ability to engage in our everyday folk psychological practices of attribution, interpretation, and prediction is fundamental to social functioning. But Dunn's paradox highlights the fact that social skills manifested in the real world may outrun experimentally tested psychological understanding; and Astington's claim, "Sometimes necessary, never sufficient," leads us to expect mismatches in the opposite direction as well. Various strategies are available for explaining these mismatches; one is an appeal to differences in demands or resources. Thus, where real-world skills outrun understanding manifested in the laboratory, this may be because the real-world situation imposes fewer demands, or offers more resources in support, than does the laboratory situation. Equally, where experimentally tested understanding outruns skills manifested in the real world, this may be because social competence in a real-world situation imposes additional demands by comparison with an experimental test of psychological understanding. This is especially clear if the experimental test battery includes only false belief tasks. Appropriate behavior in a social situation may surely require understanding, not only of beliefs and desires, but also of emotions.

One of the findings of Astington's research is that, although false-belief understanding is related to aspects of social competence, language use, and pretend play, it is not related to empathy, to popularity, or to aggression. So we should keep separate the ideas of belief understanding, on the one hand, and emotion understanding and empathy, on the other. But it is also important to distinguish between emotion understanding and at least two notions of empathy. Astington's measure of empathy involved asking children to nominate classmates who are kind when others are sad.[30] But empathy in this sense, which is perhaps better called "sympathy," is different from understanding of emotions. Someone who understands sadness and understands kindness might be kind, unkind, or indifferent toward another person who is sad. Furthermore, both understanding of emotions and kindness to sad people (sympathy) should be distinguished from the more common notion of empathy as feeling with, or identifying in imagination with, another person. First, although the imaginative process of empathy may enhance emotional understanding, understanding of emotions, particularly third-person understanding, does not require empathy. Second, although empathy may lead to sympathy, it is neither necessary nor sufficient for sympathy.

Sympathy, manifested by kindness toward people who are sad, is thus several steps removed from false-belief understanding. Belief understanding does not guarantee emotion understanding; emotion understanding does not guarantee empathy; and empathy does not guarantee sympathy.[31] This last point was well explained by Peter Goldie (2000, p. 215):

> [Imaginative processes such as empathy] are consistent with at least three kinds of response which do not involve the sort of ethical motivation that is involved in sympathy. First, they are consistent with indifference: you can imagine the other's suffering, yet simply disregard it. . . . Secondly, they are consistent with a response which is the *opposite* of sympathetic, involving *rejoicing* in the other's suffering, or even, like the subtle and imaginative inquisitor, exploiting your sensitivity to the other's feelings to help you exacerbate his suffering. And thirdly, they are consistent with motivations and actions aimed at alleviation of one's own suffering, rather than the other's. For example, one might turn away at the sight of blood.

So, third-person understanding of emotions and even the kind of first-person (or "from the inside") understanding that is connected with empathy can be deployed for good (e.g., sympathy) or ill (e.g., cruelty).

Several of the chapters in this volume look at the relationship between psychological understanding and antisocial behavior, defined by James Blair[32] as "any action that impinges on the rights and welfare of others" (p. 146). It includes the behavior of children and adults who bully others, children and adults who are Machiavellian, and individuals who are classified as psychopathic. The Bartsch and Estes (1996) framework for considering individual differences in the development of psychological understanding is also helpful for thinking about the relationship between theory-of-mind development and antisocial behavior. In particular, one question that has been prominent in the literature is whether antisocial behavior is a *consequence* of delayed or impaired psychological understanding.

The thought here might be this. Psychological understanding is required for socially competent behavior; bullying, Machiavellianism, and psychopathy are incompetent social behaviors; so bullies, manipulators, and psychopaths must be deficient in psychological understanding. But as the distinctions between psychological understanding, empathy, and sympathy reveal, and as Jon Sutton[33] points out in his chapter, this is not really a promising line of thought. It confuses social competence or social skills, on the one hand, with social conformity or moral correctness, on the other; and it pathologizes rather than explains psychological differences (pp. 102–103). Sutton recommends—as do Betty

Repacholi, Virginia Slaughter, and their colleagues[34] (this volume)—that psychological understanding should be regarded as a collection of neutral social tools to be assessed by tests that are "value free" (p. 116). With psychological understanding seen in this way, there can then be an investigation of the motivations and other factors that influence how the neutral tools of psychological understanding are put to use for good or ill in social interaction.

Bullying

This leaves the theory-of-mind abilities of bullies, Machiavellians, and psychopaths as an open empirical question, and the consensus view of the authors in this volume is that those abilities are not impaired. In the case of bullies, for example, Sutton remarks that "there is little empirical evidence to support the popular stereotype of a bully as physically powerful yet intellectually simple or backward" (p. 102).

If the psychological understanding of those engaging in antisocial behavior is not deficient, might it actually be better than average? Perhaps a successful bully, manipulator, or psychopath requires theory-of-mind abilities that are superior to those that result from the typical course of development. On this question, the evidence does not allow an unequivocal answer. Sutton reports a study in which bullies demonstrate better false-belief understanding than other children—better, in particular, than children classified as victims—even when the tasks require some understanding of the role of displays of emotion in the production of beliefs. But he agrees that, overall, the literature does not reveal such a straightforward picture of the relationship between psychological understanding and bullying. Similarly, the studies of Machiavellianism reported by Repacholi, Slaughter, and their colleagues and the studies of psychopaths reported by Blair reveal normal, but not superior, theory-of-mind abilities.

If the theory-of-mind abilities of these people are normal, then where should we look to explain their antisocial behavior? If psychological understanding is a collection of neutral social tools, then why does one person use the tools antisocially and another not? Recalling again the Bartsch and Estes framework mentioned in Keenan's chapter, we might ask: Are there antecedents in a child's development of psychological understanding that might result in its differential use? Sutton asks, in particular, whether certain features of children's family environments might have a tendency to result in their using theory-of-mind abilities to bully. He notes that the families of children who are bullies are "often characterized by a lack of cohesion and an imbalance of power between the parents" and that "ringleader bullying appears to be associated with insecure attachment." But the question that remains is whether these features of family relationships actually impair the development of psychological understanding or rather encourage a "cold, manipulative" way of deploying that psychological understanding (p. 108).

There are several possibilities to be teased apart here. If bullies show normal psychological understanding on test batteries that are dominated by false-belief tasks, it remains possible that they have an impaired understanding of mental states other than beliefs. Perhaps they do not understand emotions. On the other hand, it might be that bullies have a normal third-person understanding of emotions but do not attribute the correct emotions to their victims because they are not good at recognizing emotions from the facial and bodily expressions of other people.[35] But Sutton does not regard either of these possibilities as being generally the case: "It is as if some children who bully understand the emotions their actions cause and go ahead not only despite that, but because of that" (p. 109).

Other options that need to be distinguished include the possibility that bullies lack empathy in the sense that they do not identify with, or share, the joy or sadness of other people and the possibility that they do not understand what Sutton calls the "moral emotions," such as guilt, love, remorse, sympathy, and shame. Finally, there is the possibility that, whether or not they empathize with other people's joy or sadness, bullies do not experience, and do not show, sympathy or remorse when it would be appropriate to do so. In this last case, it may be that exercises in excusing oneself are important for sustaining the lack of guilt, remorse, or shame, and it is plausible that these exercises would draw on psychological understanding. We might, then, expect that lack of remorse, for example, would be related to some measure of psychological understanding, and Sutton briefly mentions some evidence that this is indeed so (Sutton, Reeves and Keogh, 2000).

Machiavellianism

The overall picture that is suggested by Sutton's chapter is that bullies deploy their psychological understanding in a way that is skilful but cynical, manipulative and morally unattractive. In short, bullies seem to be rather Machiavellian and bullies do indeed score higher than control children on a questionnaire designed to assess Machiavellianism in children as young as nine years of age (the Kiddie-Mach scale).[36]

As Doris McIlwain[37] explains in her chapter, Machiavellianism has several components, including a cynical view of others, a willingness to manipulate and exploit others to the point of harm, and a distinctive "cool" affective style (pp. 46–48). The cynicism component amounts to a belief that other people are untrustworthy; the Machiavellian expects the worst of others and gets in first. In his own eyes, his actions are no worse than what other people would do to him, given the chance. The cool affective style has two aspects. First, the Machiavellian lacks empathy. Indeed, McIlwain suggests that the combination of normal or superior psychological understanding with impaired empathy lies at the heart of the Machiavellian personality style. The second aspect of the affective coolness is that the Machiavellian betrays little in the way of emotion or affect. Because of this second aspect, he is well placed to escape detection as he engages in manipulation and exploitation.

Successful manipulation and exploitation require an accurate view of the mind of the other person and here the Machiavellian's lack of empathy may present a potential problem. So the second aspect of the cool style is important in part because tactics such as deception and flattery can be used in an information-gathering project that compensates for the first aspect, that is, for the Machiavellian's inability to use empathy or imaginative identification to understand the mind of another person.

Machiavellianism is, then, characterized by cynicism, manipulativeness, and cool affect. But McIlwain also mentions another way of seeing Machiavellianism as having a multidimensional nature: It involves beliefs, tactics, and morality. The central belief is that other people are untrustworthy. This is a cynical belief, but it also attributes cynicism to other people. The Machiavellian's tactics include deception and flattery. And the Machiavellian's morality is that it is better to exploit than to be exploited. It is the morality of getting one's retaliation in early. But there is a little more that can be said about the moral aspect of Machiavellianism, for the personality style includes lack of "empathic concern" (pp. 44–45).

We take this to mean, first, that Machiavellians do not show the moral emotions of sympathy, remorse, and so on and, second, that this is plausibly explained in terms of the lack of empathy or "feeling with" the person who is being manipulated. McIlwain makes use of a distinction between hot and cold empathy here. Cold empathy is a matter of being able to work out the mental state, particularly the emotional state, of another person. It is a kind of third-person emotional understanding, and Machiavellians are not impaired in this respect. Hot empathy is assessed by measures of personal distress to another's negative experience and an affective response for the distressed other (p. 44). In other words, hot empathy encompasses what we have called empathy and what we have called sympathy. It is also implicit in the use of the term "hot empathy" that empathic personal distress is normally involved in bringing forth the affective response, that is, the moral emotion. On McIlwain's account, it is in these connected respects of empathy and sympathy that Machiavellians are impaired.

Because Machiavellianism is a multifaceted personality style, it is natural to ask why the facets go together. To a considerable extent, the combination of normal or superior psychological understanding with impaired empathy, stressed by McIlwain, does help to make sense of the co-occurrence of the beliefs, the tactics, and the morality—the cynicism, the manipulativeness, and the coolness of affective response. But, partly because empathy is not strictly speaking necessary for sympathy, it seems possible to imagine people with normal or superior psychological understanding and impaired empathy who are, nevertheless, not inclined to antisocial behavior. What else might explain the use of psychological understanding for antisocial purposes?

Repacholi, Slaughter, and their colleagues investigated whether young Machiavellians have social-cognitive biases that would support the use of psychological understanding for antisocial purposes. They found that 9- to 12-year-old children who scored highly on the Kiddie-Mach scale were more likely to attribute negative intent to story characters in ambiguous social situations, and more likely to predict that the situations would lead to negative outcomes, than children with low Mach scores. These biases might lead to the cynical Machiavellian belief that other people are untrustworthy and, indeed, cynical themselves and to the Machiavellian morality of getting one's retaliation in early. There would remain the question of what antecedent factors might figure in the etiology of these social-cognitive biases.[38]

Repacholi, Slaughter, and their colleagues also investigated whether the high-Mach children showed any impairment in empathy.[39] They did find a negative correlation between Mach scores and empathy scores, but this was explained by the fact that female children scored higher on empathy and lower on Mach than male children. Once the effects of gender were taken into account, the negative correlation was no longer significant. Given the image of a Machiavellian as someone with normal or superior psychological understanding but impaired empathy, this is a somewhat surprising result. But Repacholi, Slaughter, and their colleagues suggest an interesting and important possible explanation. In respect of empathy proper, they suggest that Machiavellians might not be impaired, but might be able to regulate their emotional feelings, especially when these could interfere with their personal goals. In addition, empathic personal distress might be offset by the positive emotional feelings associated with a personal goal. In respect of the moral emotions, such as sympathy, guilt, or remorse, they suggest that these might be absent, not because of an impairment—not because of impaired sympathy resulting from impaired empathy—but because the cynical Machiavellian belief and its associated morality provide justifications for manipulative and exploitative actions, even actions that lead to harm.

If this explanation is correct then it remains the case that "the Machiavellian presumably knows how their manipulative behavior will impact another person's feelings, but this knowledge is not accompanied by any feelings of concern, sympathy or compassion." It may also be true that "without this emotional arousal [the moral emotion], antisocial behavior is less likely to be inhibited" (p. 85). But the primary explanation of the absence of the moral emotion would not go via a presumed connection between empathy and sympathy. Instead, the absence of the moral emotion would be the result of an exercise in self-justification. The Machiavellian's psychological understanding would thus enter the picture twice over, in the project of manipulation and in the project of excusing. This might seem to suggest that Machiavellians need to have not just typical but superior psychological understanding. But in this study there was no significant difference in psychological understanding between high- and low-Mach children.[40]

It is an open question whether Machiavellianism properly so-called can be present in children below the age for which the Kiddie-Mach scale is appropriate. In their chapter, Repacholi, Slaughter, and their colleagues report on pioneering research with children between the ages of four and six years, using a new Mach rating scale. Here, as with the older children, there was no relation between Mach scores and psychological understanding as assessed by false-belief tasks. And, as with older children tested in other laboratories, Mach scores were found to be positively correlated with aggression scores and negatively correlated with prosocial behavior scores. Finally, Mach scores were not related to social preference scores (a measure of the extent to which a child is among other children's most liked, rather than least liked, classmates). But they were related to social impact scores (a measure of the extent to which a child is among other children's most liked *or* least liked classmates). Machiavellians are noticed, favorably or unfavorably, by their peers. Overall, these first results with the new Mach scale are consistent with the idea that young Machiavellians, or proto-Machiavellians, deploy average psychological understanding in a distinctive antisocial way.

A DOUBLE DISSOCIATION: AUTISM AND PSYCHOPATHY

Several of the chapters in this volume report the use of correlational analyses to investigate the relationship between psychological understanding and social skills. But, as James Blair[41] notes at the beginning of his chapter, the existence of correlations may not tell us very much about functional architecture (p. 147).

It is a familiar point that correlation is one thing and causation is another. But, even if a correlation between measures of two cognitive abilities X and Y is the result of a causal relationship, there remain questions about the nature of this relationship. The direction of causation may be from X to Y or from Y to X; or it may be that both X and Y depend causally on some third factor Z. And even when the direction of causation is settled, that still leaves us some distance from a conclusion about functional architecture. For example, if there is causation in the direction from X to Y, that still does not show that the cognitive system that underpins X is a component of the system that underpins Y. It might be, for example, that possession of ability X is crucial for the acquisition of ability Y but is not directly implicated in the exercise of ability Y. That is, X might be a distal, but not a proximal cause of Y. Equally, if X and Y both depend on some third factor, this factor might be crucial for the acquisition of both X and Y but directly implicated in the exercise of neither.[42]

Developmental Cognitive Neuropsychology

Because of the questions that can be raised about correlational analyses,[43] Blair adopts the approach of developmental cognitive neuropsychology instead. But in cases where cognitive neuropsychology delivers only findings of associations between deficits, important questions remain. If abilities X (e.g., psychological understanding) and Y (e.g., some social skill) are impaired together then this may only reflect facts about neuroanatomy. But suppose that there is a functional explanation for the co-occurrence of deficits. Suppose, for example, that both deficits result from some third impairment to ability Z (e.g., a linguistic ability or an executive ability). Still, just as in the case of a correlation between measures of X and Y, this might not tell us much about the structure of the cognitive systems that underpin X and Y. In particular, the cognitive system that underpins ability Z might not be part of the cognitive system for ability X or the system for ability Y.

It is a very familiar point that neuropsychological findings of dissociations between impairments are apt to impose more constraints on functional architecture than do findings of associations. Blair's strategy is thus to use dissociations to investigate the relationship between psychological understanding and social skills. For example, if there are subjects in whom psychological understanding is absent or severely impaired while a particular social skill Y is intact, then this counts against the hypothesis that psychological understanding is normally necessary for the possession of Y.[44]

However, when we discussed Dunn's paradox we noted three possible ways of explaining cases in which real-life social skills outrun experimentally tested psychological understanding. It may be that the aspects of psychological understanding tested by the experimental tasks are absent but that they are not centrally relevant to Y. Alternatively, it may be that psychological understanding normally plays a central role in Y but that the subjects with impaired psychological understanding employ rules or work-arounds in order to manifest social skill Y. Or again, it may be that the real-world situations in which Y is manifested impose fewer demands, or offer more resources in support, than does the laboratory situation in which psychological understanding is tested. So, even given cases in which psychological understanding is impaired while social skill Y is intact, we need to rule out two kinds of explanation—(S > U)2, compensation by rules, and (S > U)3, difference in demands or resources—before we conclude that psychological understanding is not normally implicated in the social skill.

In a neuropsychological context, the explanation in terms of demands or resources can be ruled out, or rendered highly implausible, by presenting cases of the reverse dissociation; that is, psychological understanding intact but social skill Y impaired.[45] So the evidence that Blair reviews takes the form of a double dissociation. On the one hand, people with autism are usually thought to have a severe impairment of psychological understanding while certain social functions are intact. On the other hand, psychopathic individuals are impaired in those social functions but have intact psychological understanding. Examining these two groups, people with autism and people with psychopathy, is an important way of investigating the relationship between theory-of-mind abilities and antisocial behavior.

Two of the social functions on which Blair focuses are empathic responding and moral development.[46] People with autism orient toward adults who display signs of distress, and they show autonomic responses to distress cues (sad faces) just as normally developing children do. Furthermore, the balance of evidence is that people with autism are able to recognize emotional expressions on faces. This is not yet to say that people with autism show normal empathy, or normal sympathy, as we have been using those terms. But the evidence certainly does not suggest a total lack of empathy, despite the severe impairment to psychological understanding.

In addition, people with autism understand the difference between moral and merely conventional transgressions. Across cultures, normally developing children make this distinction from around 39 months of age, and what is crucial for the distinction is the presence or absence of a victim. For example, children's classification of an unknown transgression (signified by a nonsense word) as moral or conventional depends on the consequences of the transgression. If it has a victim ("X has done dool and made Y cry"), then it is classified as moral; if it has no victim ("X has done dool and the teacher told him off") it is classified as conventional. In Blair's experiments, children with autism—even children who failed all false-belief tasks—made this distinction. So, although this is not yet to say that people with autism show the moral emotion of sympathy to those who are experiencing distress, it does suggest that they "generate appropriate aversion to acts that typically result in harm to others" (p. 153).

The reverse pattern of dissociation is found in individuals diagnosed with psychopathy: "a disorder characterized in part by callousness, a diminished capacity for remorse, impulsivity, and poor behavioral control" (p. 154). These people have intact psychological understanding. But they are impaired in their autonomic responses specifically to distress cues, in recognizing sad and fearful expressions on faces, and in making the distinction between moral and conventional transgressions. The cases of autism and psychopathy thus provide a double dissociation between psychological understanding and appropriate responses to distress; it is impairments in the latter, rather than the former, that are associated with antisocial behavior.

The Violence Inhibition Mechanism

The connection between the impairments shown by psychopathic individuals and their antisocial behavior is made by Blair's (1995) theory of a violence inhibition mechanism (VIM). In healthy subjects, this mechanism initiates a withdrawal in response to signs of distress such as a sad facial expression. So an observer—and, in particular, an aggressor—who sees a victim's distress cues will be predisposed to withdraw from the situation. In the course of normal development, a child "will be negatively reinforced by the distress cues every time he engages in any aggressive activity" (Blair, 1995, p. 5). As Blair summarized the VIM theory (p. 155):

> Sad and fearful facial and vocal expressions act as punishing stimuli that, when experienced, reduce the probability that a healthy individual will engage in any action associated with the display of these expressions. In other words, the healthy individual is punished for engaging in antisocial activity by the distress of the victims.

Indeed, Blair suggests, even the thought of aggression may come to trigger the VIM, so that the child will become less likely to engage in violent actions. The VIM is also implicated in the development of the moral emotions and of the distinction between moral and conventional transgressions.

According to the VIM theory, absence of the violence inhibition mechanism has several consequences in addition to the absence of an aversive response to distress cues. Violent action is not inhibited; moral emotions such as sympathy, guilt, and remorse are lacking; and the distinction between moral and conventional transgressions is not drawn. Furthermore, if empathy is conceived simply as "an emotional reaction to a representation of the distressed internal state of another," then the VIM normally plays a role in the development of empathy. Where the VIM is absent, empathy is missing as well. Thus, the constellation of impairments found in psychopathic individuals—impairments in autonomic responses to distress cues, in recognizing sad and fearful expressions on faces, and in making the distinction between moral and conventional transgressions—is just what would be expected if, for physiological or social reasons, the VIM is absent. And, of course, if the VIM is absent then antisocial behavior is liable to be forthcoming.

However, it is important not to oversimplify the relationship between the violence inhibition mechanism and actual behavior. The presence of the VIM in healthy subjects does not guarantee withdrawal from a situation in which distress cues are present. Despite the predisposition to withdraw, an aggressor may be motivated to overrule the aversion generated by the VIM; or a bystander may approach and help the distressed victim. Equally, the absence of the VIM does not guarantee antisocial behavior. The absence does not, of itself, provide any motivation for aggression and, in any case, other systems may serve to inhibit aggressive behavior.[47] Nevertheless, it is clear in outline how the absence of the VIM could, given other factors, lead to the antisocial behavior of psychopathic individuals.

Psychological Understanding, the VIM, and Antisocial Behavior

Having in mind Blair's account of the antisocial behavior of psychopathic individuals, we can return briefly to bullying and Machiavellianism. From Sutton's chapter, recall two points. First, bullies do not have impaired psychological understanding. Second, "It is as if some children who bully understand the emotions their actions cause and go ahead not only despite that, but because of that" (Sutton, this volume, pp. 108–109). This does not suggest any impairment in recognizing sad or fearful expressions on faces. On the other hand, Sutton notes that "young bullies frequently ignore the submissive behavior of their victims and carry on inflicting pain" (ibid.). This sounds like the absence of a predisposition to withdraw and to that extent it suggests an impaired or absent VIM. But, as Blair says, an aggressor with an intact VIM may overrule the aversion that it generates. So it would be interesting to know whether bullies are impaired in their autonomic responses to the distress of others and also whether they have any difficulties with the distinction between moral and conventional transgressions. For the time being, we should leave open the possibility that bullies engage in antisocial behavior despite having an intact VIM.

In the case of Machiavellianism, McIlwain's discussion of an impairment to "hot empathy" is broadly in line with the idea that Machiavellians have an impaired or absent VIM. In contrast, Repacholi, Slaughter, and their colleagues suggest an account that is more in line with the idea that Machiavellians overrule the deliverances of an intact VIM because of their own goals and because of the cynical Machiavellian belief and its associated morality. Once again, further information would be useful.

The Machiavellian belief that other people are untrustworthy and the associated bias toward attributing negative intent and expecting a negative outcome might be described as impaired psychological understanding. But it is not an impairment of the kind that is associated with autism; it is not an inability to represent and understand the nature of psychological states. Machiavellians are in general able to represent and understand other people's intentions, but there is a bias in their assessments of what these intentions are likely to be.

The overall picture seems to be that psychological understanding, particularly belief understanding, is necessary for the antisocial behavior seen in bullying, Machiavellianism, and psychopathy. Also, antisocial behavior does not seem to be the product of impaired emotion understanding, especially if this is conceived as third-person understanding of emotions. In addition, it is not clear that antisocial behavior in bullies and Machiavellians is the product of impaired empathy or sympathy. It appears that a good understanding of beliefs, desires, intentions, emotions, and other mental states may be deployed in a way that leads to antisocial behavior, especially in cases where an attributional bias has the result that the mental states attributed to others tend to have negative connotations. This may happen as the result of a child's experience of a developmental environment in which the attribution of negative mental states to others is often adaptive.[48]

A different route to antisocial behavior does involve impaired empathy or sympathy. Blair's theory of the violence inhibition mechanism makes very good sense of the antisocial behavior of psychopathic individuals. More work is required to assess its applicability to the cases of bullying and Machiavellianism. Also, more work of an interdisciplinary kind is needed in order to relate the theory of the VIM to more philosophical accounts of empathy, sympathy, and the moral emotions more generally.[49]

In this, we might begin with the role that Hume assigns to "sympathy" in the production of moral approval and disapproval. For Hume, sympathy is a disposition to feel what others are feeling, so it is close to what we have been calling empathy. Its operation is the business of imagination rather than reason[50]:

> When I see the *effects* of passion in the voice and gesture of any person, my mind immediately passes from these effects to their causes, and forms such a lively idea of the passion as is presently converted into the passion itself.

That is, when I perceive the vocal and bodily signs of an emotion, I form a representation of the emotion, and hence experience the same emotion myself. "In like manner, when I perceive the *causes* of any emotion, my mind is conveyed to the effects, and is actuated with a like emotion." That is, when I perceive a situation that would bring forth an emotion in another person, I experience the same emotion myself. Hume provides some vivid examples:

> Were I present at any of the more terrible operations of surgery, it is certain that, even before it begun, the preparation of the instruments, the laying of the bandages in order, the heating of the irons, with all the signs of anxiety and concern in the patient and assistants, would have a great effect upon my mind, and excite the strongest sentiments of pity and terror.

THE THEORY-OF-MIND HYPOTHESIS OF AUTISM AND SCHIZOPHRENIA

A number of authors in this volume discuss the theory-of-mind hypothesis of autism that is associated particularly with Simon Baron-Cohen and his colleagues. This hypothesis concerns the cognitive explanation of many of the symptoms of autism, especially of the characteristic impairments in imaginative play, social functioning, and communication. According to the theory-of-mind hypothesis, this explanation can be provided in terms of a deficit in psychological understanding that results from damage to a domain-specific module or neurocognitive mechanism—or, perhaps better, damage to one or two components of a network of mechanisms. On Baron-Cohen's account, our normal ability to "mindread"—that is, "to imagine or represent states of mind that we or others might hold" (1995, p. 2)—is subserved by a network of four mechanisms: the intentionality detector, the eye-direction detector, the shared-attention mechanism, and the theory-of-mind module proper. He suggests that in autism there is an impairment to the shared-attention mechanism and a consequent dysfunction in the theory-of-mind module.

As we have already seen, Tager-Flusberg provides support for the theory-of-mind hypothesis of autism by showing that in children with autism, psychological understanding is related to severity of the autism diagnosis, to a measure of social competence, and to a pragmatic aspect of language use. On the other hand, Peterson shows that in development, impaired psychological understanding is not specific to children with autism. In the case of deaf children, the impairment seems to be the result of their limited opportunities for participation in conversation. So this raises the possibility of an explanation of autism in which impaired psychological understanding is not the manifestation of a deficit in a cognitive module but rather a consequence of more basic linguistic and social difficulties.[51]

The theory-of-mind hypothesis of autism offers a unified cognitive explanation of many of the symptoms of autism, and it grounds this cognitive explanation in neurobiology.[52] Christopher Frith proposed a similar theory-of-mind hypothesis of schizophrenia (1992, p. 121): "My proposal is that people with schizophrenia resemble people with autism in that they too have impairments in the mechanism that enables them to mentalise." So we can consider a unified theory-of-mind hypothesis of autism and schizophrenia according to which both disorders result from damage to a single neurocognitive mechanism, the theory-of-mind module. In the early-onset developmental disorder of autism this mechanism never develops properly; in the late-onset disorder of schizophrenia the mechanism malfunctions after achieving its mature state.

This bold hypothesis aims at what Philip Gerrans and Victoria McGeer[53] call "horizontal integration" and "vertical integration" (pp. 271–272). Horizontal integration is the within-level unification provided by a single cognitive functional explanation of various symptoms. Vertical integration is the cross-level unification provided by an account of the neural basis of that explanatory cognitive function. In their chapter, Gerrans and McGeer critically assess and ultimately reject the hypothesis for the fundamental reason that "there is no single ToM [theory of mind] module responsible for successful social reasoning and behavior in normal subjects" (p. 273). That is, there is no module or neurocognitive mechanism that, on the one hand, explains our ability to do the things that mind reading is supposed to be good for, such as "social understanding, behavioral prediction, social interaction, and communication" (Baron-Cohen, 1995, p. 30), and, on the other hand, could be damaged, early or late, so as to give rise to most or many of the symptoms of autism or schizophrenia.

Their argument for rejecting the theory-of-mind hypothesis of both autism and schizophrenia comes in two stages. First, they argue that the case of autism does not support the idea of a genuine cognitive domain of psychological understanding or mind reading that is subserved by an innate module specific to that domain. This first stage of the argument leaves it open that the cognitive capacity for mind reading may be underpinned by a dedicated cognitive mechanism. The point of the first stage is to make it plausible that, even if the capacity for mind reading is subserved by a dedicated module, still it is a developmentally constructed capacity rather than one that is "achieved by a module whose cognitive architecture is genetically prespecified" (p. 275). Second, they argue that the case of schizophrenia makes it plausible that the capacity to do the things that mind reading is supposed to be good for is not only developmentally constructed but also architecturally virtual rather than architecturally real. That is, "it gives the appearance of being achieved by a dedicated mechanism [albeit a developmentally constructed one] but in fact the underlying architectural reality is of a number of interacting, possibly lower order, quasi-independent, subsystems" (p. 276).

In the case of autism, a starting point for the argument is that there are symptoms of autism that do not have a satisfying explanation in terms of impaired psychological understanding. The symptoms that are problematic for the theory-of-mind hypothesis are not just the "restricted repetitive and stereotyped behaviors, interests, or activities" that Tager-Flusberg (this volume, p. 208) found to be not significantly related to psychological understanding, but include also sensory-motor problems and abnormalities in perceptual processing. Gerrans and McGeer suggest that we make better sense of the co-occurrence of symptoms if we see the symptoms that do fit the theory-of-mind hypothesis as resulting from early sensory and perceptual disturbances. These disturbances could have severe consequences for the social interactions and interpersonal engagement of a child with autism. The explanation of impaired psychological understanding in people with autism is thus structurally similar to the explanation offered by Peterson in the case of deaf children from hearing families.

The explanation is also structurally similar to the explanation of specific language impairment (SLI) that is offered by Paula Tallal (1988). According to this account, SLI is the result of a hearing deficit that makes it difficult for children to gather the information that would be needed for learning about rules of language such as the rules of inflectional morphology. This kind of account does not appeal to a genetic impairment in an innately specified language module; indeed, the postulated cause of SLI does not have any intrinsic connection with language. But the account still leaves it open that inflectional morphology is a real cognitive domain and that in normal mature language users the capacity to negotiate this domain is an architecturally real capacity grounded in the presence of a dedicated piece of cognitive machinery.

Thus, the state of play at the end of the first stage of the argument is as follows. There are symptoms of autism that are problematic for the theory-of-mind hypothesis. The co-occurrence of these symptoms with impaired psychological understanding can be explained if the theory-of-mind impairment is a causal consequence of the problematic symptoms. This explanation would still allow that psychological understanding is a genuine cognitive domain.

In the case of schizophrenia, Gerrans and McGeer point out that, alongside the theory-of-mind hypothesis of schizophrenia, Frith more recently developed a rather different style of explanation for the experiences, and corresponding delusions, of alien control and thought insertion. Both styles of explanation appeal to a disorder of self-monitoring; in particular, an inability to monitor one's own intentions (Frith, 1992, pp. 114–115); but there is a crucial difference. According to the theory-of-mind hypothesis of schizophrenia, the breakdown in the representation of one's own intentions results from an impairment of the mechanism that supports the representation of mental states in general, the theory of mind module. But in the alternative explanation, the key idea is that internal monitoring of self-initiated action is lost as a result of a breakdown in the component of the motor control system that compares feedback from a limb movement with a forward model or efference copy. This more recent explanation does not make any essential appeal to a general problem with representing mental states. The experience of alien control—which leads, in the delusion of alien control, to an incorrect attribution of intention—results from the breakdown of a comparator in the motor control system rather than from a malfunction in the theory-of-mind module.

If, as Gerrans and McGeer suggest, the second kind of explanation is to be preferred then in the case of schizophrenia, as in the case of autism, the theory-of-mind hypothesis does not really meet the requirement of horizontal integration. It does not provide a single cognitive functional explanation of the symptoms.

Now, in the case of autism, Gerrans and McGeer suggested that the symptoms that do not receive a satisfying explanation in terms of impaired psychological understanding might play a role in the disturbed course of development that results in that very impairment. But, in the case of schizophrenia, the challenge of explaining the co-occurrence of symptoms must be met in a different way. It is not plausible that impaired psychological understanding—which is indeed found in people with schizophrenia—is a causal product of factors such as the breakdown of a comparator. Nor is it plausible that impaired psychological understanding accounts for all the symptoms that are left unexplained by the hypothesis about a failure of self-monitoring.[54]

Gerrans and McGeer propose that the most likely explanation of the co-occurrence of symptoms in schizophrenia will be neurobiological rather than cognitive. Strictly speaking, this would still leave it open that normal mind-reading ability is an architecturally real capacity. But the crucial point is that even if psychological understanding were underpinned by a cognitive module, we would not have a horizontally integrated cognitive explanation of schizo-phrenia.[55] So once it is allowed that the unification of symptoms is to be achieved neurobiologically rather than cognitively, the reality or virtuality of the capacity for psychological understanding or mind reading becomes substantially irrelevant.

For the purposes of explaining the symptoms of schizophrenia, the apparent unity of the domain of psychological understanding might as well be regarded as virtual. We might as well suppose that mind reading is the manifestation of a collection of disparate cognitive systems. Thus, Gerrans and McGeer arrive at their main claim: "[Theory-of-mind-module] theorists go too far in proposing that high-level processing of social information constitutes a developmentally set or, indeed, [even an] architecturally real cognitive system whose malfunction is implicated in both autism and schizophrenia" (p. 278).

DISTAL CAUSES AND ONLINE PROCESSES

Correlation is one thing and causation is another. But where there are correlations between aspects of psychological understanding, as evidenced in experimental tasks, and social skills, as evidenced in daily life, it is natural to ask whether there is a causal relationship and, if so, in what direction the causal explanation runs. Some researchers stress that both language and social experience play a role in the development of psychological understanding.[56] If this is right, then the development of some social skills is plausibly explanatorily prior to the development of some aspects of psychological understanding. On the other hand, some kinds of social interaction clearly require psychological understanding. It seems to us, beyond dispute, that negotiating the social world is, in part, negotiating a world in which people have beliefs, desires, and emotions that are different from our own and that successful negotiation of such a world may, on occasion, require an understanding of these mental phenomena.[57] If this is right, then the development of some aspects of psychological understanding is plausibly explanatorily prior to the development of some social skills.

If a cognitive ability Y depends causally on another cognitive ability X in the course of normal development, we can ask a further question. Does the development of X operate as a distal cause of the development of Y—perhaps contributing to the conditions in which Y can be effectively learned—or is X a proximal cause, directly implicated in the exercise of Y at a given time?[58] For an example where the answer to this question is intuitively clear, consider again Tallal's account of SLI. There is evidence that knowledge of inflectional morphology depends causally on specific aspects of hearing (having to do with the detection of acoustic changes over very short time intervals). It seems clear that these aspects of hearing operate as a distal cause of the development of knowledge of inflectional morphology by contributing to the conditions in which the rules of morphology can be learned. The crucial aspects of hearing are not directly implicated in the presence or use of morphological knowledge at a given time. Suppose, for example, that a subject gains the morphological knowledge and is able to use it and then suffers a hearing impairment of the crucial type. Intuitively, there is no reason to expect that the subject's performance on morphological tasks will immediately be impaired. Or suppose that a subject has impaired knowledge of morphology because of a hearing impairment. The morphological impairment is distally caused by, but not presently constituted by, the hearing impairment. If the subject's hearing were to be instantaneously improved there would, intuitively, be no reason to expect the subject immediately to perform at normal levels on morphological tasks.[59]

When we first considered the example of SLI, it was in the context of discussing the role of social interactions and interpersonal engagement in the etiology of psychological understanding. But we can consider psychological understanding as a cause as well as an effect. Thus, consider some aspect of psychological understanding, such as false-belief understanding, and some social skill. We can ask whether the development of false-belief understanding is a distal cause of the development of the social skill, as crucial aspects of hearing are a distal cause of the development of morphological knowledge and as certain kinds of social interactions are a distal cause of the development of psychological understanding. Or is false-belief understanding a proximal cause, directly implicated in the existence of the social skill at a given time? Is false-belief understanding actually exercised online in the day-to-day manifestations of the social skill?

This kind of question also arises, for example, in the case of psychological understanding and pragmatic aspects of language use. There is considerable evidence of the co-occurrence, in people with autism, of impaired psychological understanding and impairments in pragmatic aspects of language use. We have already seen (Tager-Flusberg, this volume) that there is a relationship between psychological understanding and the ability to stay on topic. Also, people with autism show a poor understanding of metaphorical and ironical utterances (Happé, 1991, 1993, 1995) and a difficulty with distinguishing the different intentions of speakers who make jokes and speakers who lie (Leekam and Prior, 1994).[60] But evidence of an association, a correlation, or even a causal relation between poor psychological understanding and poor pragmatics in autism may tell us rather little about the role that psychological understanding plays in the online processes that underpin pragmatic aspects of language use in normal adults. An argument for the claim that day-to-day exercises of communicative skills involve the online deployment of psychological understanding could be strengthened considerably by evidence about disorders of cognition that result from brain injury or a late-onset disorder such as schizophrenia, after the attainment of mature psychological understanding. Thus, for example, the claim is supported by findings that disorders that impair the ability to interpret other minds also impair pragmatic aspects of language use.[61]

In the case of people with schizophrenia, Robyn Langdon and her colleagues report that patients are impaired in false-belief understanding, and that this impairment cannot be accounted for in terms of more general problems that are evident in patients' performance on a picture-sequencing task. Patients also have difficulty identifying appropriate uses of irony and metaphor, though they do not differ significantly from control subjects in their ability to recognize appropriate literal uses of expressions (Langdon, Davies, and Coltheart, 2002). But their problems with irony and metaphor do not reflect a single impairment in pragmatics. For Langdon's results also show that interpretation of irony and interpretation of metaphor involve distinct cognitive processes. Relatively sophisticated psychological understanding, of a kind that is disrupted in patients with schizophrenia, is implicated in the interpretation of irony. But only a more basic ability to attribute mental states, which is intact in patients with schizophrenia, is necessary for the interpretation of metaphor. The difficulty with metaphor interpretation that people with schizophrenia have is the result of something other than their impaired psychological understanding.

If we are to learn more about the contribution of psychological understanding to social skills then there is clearly much to be gained by the parallel investigation of psychological understanding—and, in particular, of individual differences in psychological understanding—in several populations. These include normally developing children, children with autism, deaf children, and blind children, normal adults, people who have suffered brain injury, and people with schizophrenia.

PSYCHOLOGICAL UNDERSTANDING AND DELUSIONAL THINKING IN SCHIZOPHRENIA

As Langdon explains in her chapter,[62] people with autism and with schizophrenia both show impaired psychological understanding. But, although some of the negative symptoms of schizophrenia are similar to symptoms of autism, there are marked differences between the two disorders. The most striking of these is the presence of delusions in schizophrenia. Also, it may well be that impaired psychological understanding in autism is the result of a conceptual or representational deficit. That is, children with autism may be unable to represent representational mental states such as beliefs, intentions or pretendings. But, whether or not that is the correct account in the case of autism, it certainly cannot be the correct account of poor psychological understanding in the case of schizophrenia. For schizophrenic delusions often involve the attribution of quite elaborate beliefs and intentions to other people—consider, in particular, persecutory delusions.

The occurrence of persecutory delusions in schizophrenia is enough to show that patients' poor psychological understanding is not the result of an inability to represent representational mental states. But it appears that flawed psychological understanding in people with schizophrenia, or in healthy adults with a high rating on schizotypal personality traits, may be related not just to persecutory delusions but to delusional thinking more generally. So the question arises whether there is some aspect of impaired psychological understanding in people with schizophrenia that could explain the tendency toward delusions.[63] Is there something that might explain the "solipsism," or the private world, of a delusional patient with schizophrenia in contrast to the asocial "aloofness" of a person with autism?

Langdon addresses this question by examining visual perspective taking in high-schizotypal healthy adults and in patients with schizophrenia. Now, one of the tasks included in Peterson's test battery involved visual perspective-taking. The deaf children did not perform significantly differently from hearing children on this task even though they were impaired relative to hearing children on various measures of psychological understanding involving beliefs, desires, and emotions. This same pattern—understanding of visual perspective intact, but understanding of false belief impaired—is found in children with autism and in blind children.[64] But, in apparent contrast to these results for children with autism, and deaf or blind children, high-schizotypal healthy adults and patients with schizophrenia do show a problem with visual perspective-taking. And their performance on the visual perspective taking task is related to their performance on a picture-sequencing task used to assess false-belief understanding.

The particular visual perspective-taking task that presents difficulties for Langdon's subjects involves judgments about how an array of colored blocks would look when viewed from a different position.[65] Answering the question "Imagine moving to sit in the chair [90 degrees to the right]. Would the blocks look like this?" is equivalent to answering the question "Imagine turning the array [90 degrees to the left]. Would the blocks look like this?" But it is only the first question, that asks the subject to imagine adopting a different perspective, that presents a problem. Given this striking result, it is natural to suggest that these subjects show poor psychological understanding because they find it difficult to adopt in imagination a different point of view and, in particular, the point of view of another person. That is, it is natural to suggest that the co-occurrence of the visual perspective-taking problem with poor psychological understanding counts in favor of a simulation-theory account of psychological understanding (Langdon and Coltheart, 2001).

But Langdon moves beyond this natural suggestion to a proposal that draws on ideas about egocentric and allocentric frames of reference.[66] When we represent a place in an egocentric frame of reference, this representation is closely linked with perception and action. I hear a sound as coming from a direction 45 degrees to the left of straight ahead and I turn in that direction. I see a drink as being about a meter away to the right and I move and reach toward it. But we also have a more detached way of representing places by using a cognitive map of a region. Quite independently of where I am or, indeed, of any facts about me, Macquarie University is very much further from the Sydney Opera House than the Harbour Bridge is, but in (roughly) the same direction.

It is a familiar thought in philosophy that this maplike style of representation is crucial for our objective conception of the world. One aspect of this objective conception is that I have a general, although highly fallible, ability to integrate egocentric and allocentric frames of reference so as to be able to make use, in my own actions, of the information provided by a cognitive map. Thus, the objective conception involves an appreciation that I am one *object* among others. I and the objects in my egocentric space have locations that can be represented on a cognitive map. Conversely, in virtue of my location, I have a subjective perspective or point of view on a region of objective space.[67]

Another aspect of the objective conception often stressed in philosophical discussions is that I appreciate that the course of my experience over time is determined jointly by what is happening at various places and by where I am located from time to time.[68] This means that facts about worldly occurrences cannot be wholly woven out of facts about my own experience and it allows for the possibility of existence unperceived. An event may occur unperceived by me because it happens at a place different from where I am located.

The conditions that are required for such an objective conception were famously explored by Peter Strawson in *Individuals*. For the most part, Strawson carried out his exploration by considering the conceptual scheme of a single subject. Under what conditions can a subject conceive of particular things as existing independently of himself and his experiences? Or, as Strawson put it, under what conditions can the conditions of a "nonsolipsistic consciousness" be fulfilled? Here, a nonsolipsistic consciousness is defined as "the consciousness of a being who has a use for the distinction between himself and his states on the one hand, and something not himself or a state of himself, of which he has experience, on the other" (Strawson, 1959, p. 69). But Strawson also noted that it is tempting to gloss the notion of something "objective" as something "public," so that an objective conception comes to involve "the ideas of other enjoyers of experience and of shared surroundings" (ibid., p. 68). He briefly indicated a line of thought that might support the idea that objectivity requires publicity though he did not commit himself on the issue.

Here, we do not need to decide on the merits of the somewhat controversial philosophical theory that an objective conception absolutely requires a plurality of subjects. What is important is just to recognize that, in my ordinary thinking about the world, I appreciate that I am not only one object among others but also one *subject* among others. I am one of many subjects, each with a point of view onto a common world that exists independently of all of us. This is the idea that Langdon appeals to in order to explain the striking finding that psychotic and psychosis-prone adults have a selective impairment in visual perspective taking when this is tested by questions of the form: "Imagine moving to sit in the chair [90 degrees to the right]. Would the blocks look like this?" Her proposal is that the psychotic or psychosis-prone subject has a flawed appreciation of the fact that he or she is one subject among others and, similarly, that his or her present subjective point of view is one among many.

This proposal also promises to contribute to an account of delusional thinking in schizophrenia. The appreciation that I am one subject among others provides me with a way of understanding disagreement and a way of "reconciling discordant information," as Langdon puts it (p. 263). So a breakdown in this appreciation could leave schizophrenic patients less able to adopt a critical stance toward their own view of the world, less able to engage with others in a joint assessment of the real truth of the matter,[69] and so more prone to delusional thinking.

TWELVE QUESTIONS ABOUT PSYCHOLOGICAL UNDERSTANDING AND SOCIAL SKILLS

Many issues have been raised in this volume, but there is no single issue that dominates over all others. There are many questions to which we would like to know the answers. But no question seems to have a unique claim to be pivotal for future research. In this final section, we briefly review and connect some of the issues that seem to us to be important, deep, and fascinating. Along the way, we pose a dozen questions.

Correlation and Causation

Many of the chapters describe correlational studies that explore the relationships between aspects of psychological understanding and communicative and social skills. We have half a dozen questions about these studies. In general, correlational studies do not settle questions about causation. But, in some cases, the correlational studies presented in this volume do include evidence for causal relationships—for example, Astington presents evidence from a longitudinal study to support the claim that the direction of causation is from development of false-belief understanding to certain features of pretend play. So our first question is this:

- Do correlational studies provide any evidence of a causal relationship between false-belief understanding and pragmatic aspects of language use or social competence?

There might, of course, be a causal relationship even though correlational studies provide no evidence of it. If there is in fact a causal relationship in the direction from false-belief understanding to some aspects of social competence, then we follow up with this question:

- Does the development of false-belief understanding operate as a distal cause of these social skills or is it a proximal cause, directly implicated in the exercise of the skills at a given time?

Some earlier studies have failed to find even correlations between psychological understanding and pragmatic aspects of language use or social skills, once language ability is taken into account. Tager-Flusberg assesses psychological understanding in children with autism using a test battery that is broader than just first-order false-belief tasks in two ways. It covers a greater developmental span and it assesses understanding of a wider range of psychological phenomena. We have a question about this test battery:

- What properties of Tager-Flusberg's psychological understanding test battery give rise to her findings of correlations with a pragmatic aspect of language use (namely, staying on topic) and a measure of social competence (Vineland socialization score)?[70]

Keenan suggests that attributional accuracy tasks could provide another developmentally extended measure of psychological understanding. But accurate attributions of mental states often require much more than just basic conceptual understanding; they may require substantial empirical knowledge about how the psychological world works. If people with autism have an impaired ability even to represent mental states such as beliefs and desires, then it may be that their performance on attributional accuracy tasks will vary less than their performance on tests of basic understanding because of a floor effect. So we ask:

- If we were to use attributional accuracy tasks as a measure of psychological understanding in people with autism, should we expect to find correlations with social competence and pragmatic aspects of language use?

Dissanayake and Macintosh find that in children diagnosed with Asperger's disorder, experimentally tested psychological understanding outruns real-life social skills. They consider more than one kind of explanation for this finding. The mismatch might be the result of the relatively narrow range of tasks used to assess psychological understanding, or it might indicate that these children succeed on false-belief tasks without real psychological understanding. So we ask:

- If psychological understanding in people with Asperger's syndrome were to be assessed using Tager-Flusberg's broader test battery, or using a test of attributional accuracy as proposed by Keenan, how would it then be related to social skills?

False-belief understanding in deaf children from hearing families is delayed by comparison with both hearing children and "native signers." This finding is consistent with Harris's suggestion that participation in conversation as such is crucial for the development of belief understanding. But it is also consistent with Peterson's rather different proposal that participation in conversation about mental states is crucial for the development of an understanding of beliefs, desires and feelings. We might be able to resolve this disagreement in favour of either Peterson or Harris by using information about the time course of understanding of mental states other than belief, and especially understanding of desire, in normally developing children, in children with autism, and in deaf children of hearing parents. But our question is more basic:

- Might it be that Peterson and Harris are both right—that conversation about mental states facilitates the development of understanding of all mental states and that participation in conversation also plays a special role in the development of belief understanding?

Antisocial Behavior

Although we started out from the truistic-seeming idea that psychological understanding is fundamental to social functioning, it turns out not to be a promising line of thought to suppose that antisocial behavior is a consequence of impaired psychological understanding. Psychological understanding is best thought of as a collection of neutral tools that can be used for good or ill. Several of the chapters describe investigations of the additional factors that are at work in antisocial behavior.

Blair reports that psychopathic individuals have a specific impairment in their response to distress cues and in their recognition of sad and fearful emotional expressions on faces. Sutton reports that bullies score more highly than other children on false-belief tests, even when the tasks require recognition and understanding of emotions. This suggests that the explanation of antisocial behavior in bullies is different from the explanation of antisocial behavior in psychopathic individuals. To confirm this, we ask:

- Do Sutton's data show that bullies do not have the specific impairment in recognition of sad and fearful emotional expressions that is characteristic of psychopathic individuals?

McIlwain provides a vivid account of Machiavellianism as a personality style characterized by an average or above average competence in theory of mind, but lacking in certain forms of empathy. Repacholi, Slaughter, and their colleagues report that children with high Kiddie-Mach scores did not show impaired empathy. So our eighth question is:

• Are there individual differences within the Machiavellian personality style with some Machiavellians impaired in empathy and others not?

Where there is no impairment to empathy, antisocial behavior may still be forthcoming; and (as Blair stresses), even where empathy is impaired, this is not sufficient for antisocial behavior. So, in either case, additional factors—such as cynical beliefs, attributional biases, or executive-function deficits—must be involved. This seems to suggest that there may be a good deal of variation within the category of individuals who are psychopathic. So we have a further question about individual differences:

• Are there individual differences in psychological understanding and empathy among psychopathic individuals, and what might be the consequences of these differences for remediation?

Simulation Theory

Over the last 15 years or so, the simulation theory of psychological understanding has been seen as an alternative to both the theory theory and the modular theory.[71] But in the 11 chapters that we have reviewed, the simulation theory is scarcely mentioned.

According to the simulation theory, our everyday folk psychological practices of attribution, interpretation, and prediction centrally involve identification in imagination with the other person. In the eyes of many, although certainly not all, simulation theorists, the position draws strength from the plausibility of the idea that identification with another person in imagination is involved in first-person, or "from the inside," emotional understanding and empathy. Mental simulation is supposed to be involved in all psychological understanding, but first-person emotional understanding and empathy are often regarded as especially favorable cases for the simulation theory. However, the chapters on antisocial behavior tend to drive a wedge between psychological understanding, on the one hand, and empathy, on the other. So our tenth question is:

• Does the investigation of antisocial behavior—particularly, the double dissociation between psychological understanding and empathy—pose a challenge for the simulation theory?

If the dissociation between psychological understanding and empathy does deprive the simulation theory of psychological understanding of the support that it was thought to gather from the case of empathy, this might motivate a hybrid theory. Indeed, the dissociation might provide a principle for formulating such a theory. The idea would be to combine a theory of psychological understanding with a simulation theory of empathy and the moral emotions. The mechanistic underpinnings of psychological understanding might include a theory-of-mind module. The mechanistic underpinnings of empathy might include the violence inhibition mechanism.

Psychological Understanding and Schizophrenia

Gerrans and McGeer offer a critical assessment of "a theory of cognitive function which aims to [meet the challenges of horizontal and vertical integration] for both autism and schizophrenia"—a theory that draws on the work of Baron-Cohen and Frith.[72] Frith introduces his theory-of-mind hypothesis of schizophrenia as being similar to the theory-of-mind hypothesis of autism. But here we need to recall that impaired attributional accuracy is not the same thing as impaired conceptual understanding of mental states. In the case of autism, the theory-of-mind hypothesis is that there is an impairment of the basic representation and conceptual understanding of mental states. But people with schizophrenia do not have a late-onset impairment of that same kind, for they are able to represent and understand mental states. People with schizophrenia may have an impaired theory of mind in the sense that they have false views about how the psychological world works. But they do not have an impaired theory of mind in the same sense that people with autism have an impaired theory of mind.

In any case, it seems clear that the theory-of-mind impairment in schizophrenia—whatever exactly may be its nature—cannot provide a cognitive unification of the symptoms of the disorder. So, Gerrans and McGeer argue, if the symptoms are to be unified, this must be a neurobiological unification, and for those purposes it is irrelevant whether psychological understanding constitutes a genuine cognitive domain.[73] This certainly removes one possible motivation for thinking that psychological understanding is a genuine domain. But removal of a motivation for saying something is not yet a reason for saying the opposite. So the question of whether psychological understanding has the status of a genuine, or a merely virtual, domain seems to remain open.

When we are considering schizophrenia, and particularly the theory-of-mind hypothesis of schizophrenia, we have to regard theory of mind, or psychological understanding, as encompassing more than just basic conceptual understanding of mental states. It includes also the substantive empirical knowledge about the psychological world that is needed for accurate attributions of mental states. In this inclusive sense, psychological understanding draws on the ability to construct certain kinds of representations, on knowledge about how the psychological world works, and on the ability to carry out inferences. It does not seem very likely that all this is underpinned by a single cognitive module. So if a genuine cognitive domain is one that is subserved by a single dedicated module, then it is independently not very plausible that psychological understanding is a genuine domain.[74] Our question here does not concern the correctness of this claim about psychological understanding but rather its theoretical connection with the unification of the symptoms of schizophrenia:

- If it turns out that the symptoms of schizophrenia can be unified neurobiologically but not cognitively, what does this tell us about the architectural reality or virtuality of the capacity for psychological understanding?

Langdon finds a relationship in patients with schizophrenia and high-schizotypal nonclinical adults, between false-belief understanding and a particular kind of visual perspective taking. If our aim were just to unify these two performance deficits, then it would be natural to suggest that, at least in these subjects, impaired false-belief understanding is the result of an impaired ability to take on in imagination the point of view of another person—that is, an impaired ability to engage in mental simulation. But Langdon's main concern is to understand the connection between performance deficits on theory-of-mind tasks, including false-belief tasks, and delusional thinking. To this end, she suggests that poor false-belief understanding and poor visual perspective taking co-occur in psychotic and psychosis-prone individuals because of a breakdown, in these individuals, of the ability to represent subjective experience as contingent on one among many subjective points of view. Such a breakdown of the appreciation that one is one subject among many may help to account for delusional thinking, because it may leave a schizophrenic patient less able to engage with other people in order to reconcile conflicting views of reality.

These suggestions raise a host of interesting issues. But, in order to move toward our final question, we consider just one. There is an apparent contrast between Langdon's results and results with children with autism, deaf children, and blind children. But in these latter experiments the visual perspective-taking task does not share the crucial features of Langdon's task, which asks a question about how an array would *look* if the *viewer* were to adopt a different position. Indeed, Langdon asks the subject to *imagine* adopting that different position. So, our final question links our end back to our beginning:

- How should we expect normally developing children, children with autism or Asperger's syndrome, and deaf children to perform on Langdon's visual perspective-taking task, and how should we expect their performance to be related to their psychological understanding?

Experiments might confirm that children with autism, and other children with impaired psychological understanding, are able to perform the visual perspective-taking task. If so then, as Langdon argues, this may help to explain the most striking difference between schizophrenia and autism; namely, the presence in schizophrenia but absence in autism of delusions.

Other possible outcomes would teach us something important about psychological understanding, imagination, and point of view. And if the visual perspective-taking task were included in test batteries for people who engage in antisocial behavior—bullies, Machiavellians, and psychopathic individuals—then we could also find out whether visual perspective taking forms patterns with psychological understanding, with empathy, or independently of both.

The 11 chapters that we have reviewed both indicate and instantiate the extraordinary richness, fertility, and promise of contemporary research on individual differences in theory of mind. The implications of this research extend beyond the psychology of typical and atypical development, into other disciplines including philosophy and psychiatry. Perhaps our dozen questions may provide a not wholly disconnected sample and summary of important, deep, and fascinating issues that have been raised:

1. Do correlational studies provide any evidence of a causal relationship between false-belief understanding and pragmatic aspects of language use or social competence?
2. Does the development of false-belief understanding operate as a distal cause of these social skills or is it a proximal cause, directly implicated in the exercise of the skills at a given time?
3. What properties of Tager-Flusberg's psychological understanding test battery give rise to her findings of correlations with a pragmatic aspect of language use (namely, staying on topic) and a measure of social competence (Vineland socialization score)?
4. If we were to use attributional accuracy tasks as a measure of psychological understanding in people with autism, should we expect to find correlations with social competence and pragmatic aspects of language use?
5. If psychological understanding in people with Asperger's syndrome were to be assessed using Tager-Flusberg's broader test battery, or using a test of attributional accuracy as proposed by Keenan, how would it then be related to social skills?
6. Might it be that Peterson and Harris are both right—that conversation about mental states facilitates the development of understanding of all mental states and that participation in conversation also plays a special role in the development of belief understanding?
7. Do Sutton's data show that bullies do not have the specific impairment in recognition of sad and fearful emotional expressions that is characteristic of psychopathic individuals?
8. Are there individual differences within the Machiavellian personality style, with some Machiavellians impaired in empathy and others not?
9. Are there individual differences in psychological understanding and empathy among psychopathic individuals, and what might be the consequences of these differences for remediation?

10. Does the investigation of antisocial behavior—particularly, the double dissociation between psychological understanding and empathy—pose a challenge for the simulation theory?
11. If it turns out that the symptoms of schizophrenia can be unified neurobiologically but not cognitively, what does this tell us about the architectural reality or virtuality of the capacity for psychological understanding?
12. How should we expect normally developing children, children with autism or Asperger's syndrome, and deaf children to perform on Langdon's visual perspective-taking task, and how should we expect their performance to be related to their psychological understanding?

NOTES

1. See Heider (1958, p. 5; quoted by Wellman, 1990, p. 2): "In the same way one talks about a naïve physics . . . one can talk about a 'naïve psychology' which gives us the principles we use to build up our picture of the social environment and which guides our reactions to it."
2. "Sometimes necessary, never sufficient: False-belief understanding and social competence," in this volume.
3. Astington says (p. 14): "At the [1988] Yale meeting mentioned earlier, Dunn pointed to a paradox that is at the heart of the issue. It is this: Babies and toddlers are fundamentally social creatures, who are tuned in to other people, seemingly well aware of other people's behavior and emotional reactions. Yet until the end of the preschool years, children fail at experimental tasks that are designed to assess their understanding of another person's point of view."
4. "Individual differences in theory of mind: The preschool years and beyond," in this volume.
5. The three kinds of differences mentioned by Bartsch and Estes are all inter-individual differences. Keenan adds a fourth category, namely, intra-individual differences. People may deploy their psychological understanding in different ways—for example, with different degrees of sophistication—in different contexts—for example, in relationships with different affective quality. See O'Connor and Hirsch (1999).
6. Perner, Ruffman, and Leekam, 1994; Jenkins and Astington, 1996.
7. Happé and Frith, 1996.
8. Bartsch and Estes refer to Astington and Jenkins (1995), Jenkins and Astington (1996), and Lalonde and Chandler (1995).
9. P. 135; see Ickes (1993, 1997).
10. Because of the rich variety of factors that are implicated in performance of these inferences—including not only knowledge about individuals and kinds of relationships, but also motivation, for example—we would expect attributional accuracy to be subject to intra-individual differences.
11. This is analogous to the situation in the study of language. Competence is linguistic knowledge; performance is the use of that knowledge. But linguistic performance,

such as utterance interpretation, also requires knowledge that goes beyond knowledge of language. Both linguistic knowledge (competence) and real-world knowledge are needed for utterance interpretation.

As Kim Sterelny pointed out to us, it is not straightforward to apply the competence–performance distinction in the context of a simulation-theory account of our folk psychological practices. Indeed, it is a substantive question whether simulation theory can furnish an account of our basic conceptual understanding of mental states. The authors in the present volume largely ignore simulation theory; but see pages 340–341.

12. Strictly speaking, being biased is one thing and being inaccurate is another. Someone who has a bias, in the sense of being far more likely than most subjects are to attribute hostile intentions to other people, may have a superior, rather than an impaired, ability to attribute intentions accurately, for a biased subject might be surrounded by people with hostile intentions.

13. Or perhaps a way of arriving at such knowledge, such as mental simulation.

14. "Exploring the relationship between theory of mind and social-communicative functioning in children with autism," in this volume.

15. Wellman, Cross, and Watson, 2001.

16. But, Tager-Flusberg suggests, psychological understanding is not related to all aspects of autism; in particular, not to "restricted repetitive and stereotyped behaviors, interests or activities" (p. 208).

17. Tager-Flusberg's work does not assess the relationship between psychological understanding and pretend play, presumably because a pretending task is already included in the theory of mind test battery.

18. Keenan's proposed measure of attributional accuracy would also have a wide developmental span and it would range over a variety of psychological phenomena. But it would be different from Tager-Flusberg's test battery in a significant respect, for it would test knowledge of how the psychological world works and not just basic conceptual understanding of mental states.

19. "Mind reading and social functioning in children with Autistic Disorder and Asperger's Disorder," in this volume.

20. The children with Asperger's disorder did not perform differently from the typically developing children, but this may be the result of a ceiling effect in the latter group.

21. "The children with high-functioning autism and Asperger's disorder were largely indistinguishable on parent report of their adaptive behavior, and on both parent and teacher ratings of social skills" (p. 230).

22. See also Raffman (1999).

23. For a brief review, see Ellis and Gunter (1999).

24. See the concluding section of Astington's chapter in this volume.

25. See Langdon, Davies and Coltheart (2002) and Sperber (2000).

26. See Peterson and Siegal (2000, pp. 139–140): "To the extent that a theory of mind is a necessary component of a skilled conversationalist's pragmatic understanding of an interlocutor's mind and intentions, impairments in pragmatic skill and mental state understanding are likely to be reciprocal and inextricably interconnected."

27. Harris (1996, p. 220, n. 7); the observation is credited to Peter Carruthers.

28. It is worth noting that desires and hopes, for example, are often expressed without

using the complement construction "Vs that *p*." Thus: "Sally wants Ann to come and play"; "Sally hopes to find the marble soon." On competence with the "*x* Vs that *p*" construction as a predictor of false-belief understanding, see de Villiers (2000). Note too the relevance to these issues of investigations of psychological understanding in children with specific language impairment.

29. "The social face of theory of mind: The development of concepts of emotion, desire, visual perspective and false belief in deaf and hearing children," in this volume.

30. Astington, this volume, p. 24.

31. There is considerable variation in the use of the terms *empathy* and *sympathy*. Alvin Goldman said (1993/1995, p. 197): "To empathize with someone, in its most frequent sense, is to sympathize or commiserate, which involves shared attitudes, sentiments, or emotions." But, strictly speaking, having an emotional experience of the same sort as someone else is one thing, and commiserating with someone is another thing. As we use the terms here, empathy is an imaginative process that leads to the first thing; sympathy is the second thing. But it is the distinction, rather than the terminology, that is important.

32. "Did Cain fail to represent the thoughts of Abel before he killed him? The relationship between theory of mind and aggression," in this volume.

33. "ToM goes to school: Social cognition and social values in bullying," in this volume.

34. "Theory of mind, Machiavellianism, and social functioning in childhood," in this volume.

35. Sutton, Smith and Swettenham (1999) show that bullies can answer questions about emotional expressions on faces. But, as McIlwain (this volume) notes, Machiavellians are impaired in recognizing emotional expressions.

36. Sutton and Keogh (2000). However, as Repacholi, Slaughter, and their colleagues point out (pp. 75–76), there are important differences between bullies and Machiavellians, both in the type of antisocial acts committed and in the underlying intentions and motivations.

37. "Bypassing empathy: A Machiavellian theory of mind and sneaky power," in this volume.

38. As in the case of bullying, we might naturally look to features of children's family environments to help explain these biases. Betty Repacholi reports (personal communication) that the high-Mach children in their study classified their parents as "permissive-neglectful." This parenting style is described as "disengaged parents who are motivated to do whatever is necessary to minimize the costs in time and effort of interaction with the child" (Maccoby & Martin, 1983, p. 49).

39. As measured by the Bryant Empathy Index; see Bryant (1982).

40. As Repacholi, Slaughter, and colleagues note, high-Mach children were simply those in the original sample with Mach scores in the upper quartile. In the absence of normative data, it remains open whether these children were high Mach by any more absolute criterion. So it remains a possibility that genuinely high-Mach children would show superior psychological understanding.

41. "Did Cain fail to represent the thoughts of Abel before he killed him? The relationship between theory of mind and aggression," in this volume.

42. See later section for the distinction between distal and proximal causes. Blair also mentions the possibility that a cognitive ability *X* might be implicated in perfor-

mance of tasks that are used to assess cognitive ability Y even though the cognitive system that underpins X is not a component of the cognitive system that underpins Y. For example, performance on false-belief tasks depends on executive ("inhibitory") systems (p. 147).

43. Blair explicitly mentions the problems faced by the correlational approach when it is adopted with normally developing individuals. But presumably the same point applies in the case of people with autism, for example. Thus, as we have noted earlier, both Astington—working with normally developing children—and Tager-Flusberg—working with people with autism—stress that it is important to control for language ability, as well as age and IQ, when investigating the relationship between psychological understanding and social skills. Of course, even with language ability controlled for, a correlation still does not settle questions about causation, let alone functional architecture.

44. A dissociation of the form "X impaired *at present* but Y intact at present" does not, in general, count against the hypothesis that *earlier* presence of X is normally necessary for the acquisition of Y. If X is a distal, rather than a proximal, cause of Y then it may be impaired after it has made its contribution to the acquisition of Y. For more on these issues, see later section. But, in the case of autism, psychological understanding is not, and never has been, present. So if a particular social skill Y is intact in people with autism, then this counts against the hypothesis that psychological understanding is normally necessary either as a distal or as a proximal cause of Y.

45. Also, in the case of the particular social functions under discussion, particularly autonomic responses to distress cues, the explanation in terms of compensation by rules is not plausible.

46. Another is inhibition of antisocial behavior. The apparent lack of instrumental antisocial behavior in people with autism is consistent with the claim that there is a dissociation here: theory of mind impaired but inhibition of antisocial behavior intact. However, the social interactions of people with autism are dysfunctional in any case (p. 153).

47. Blair (1995, p. 11): "a lack of VIM need not result in the individual becoming a psychopath. . . . A lack of VIM does not of itself motivate an individual to commit aggressive acts. A lack of VIM just means that one source of the interruption of violent action is lost. . . . It is perhaps possible that the development of the psychopath may require deficits within executive functioning as well as within VIM; that both sources of behavioral inhibition must be impaired for the child to develop as a psychopath."

48. See Keenan (this volume, pp. 127–128): "For a child growing up in an abusive or hostile environment, such a modification to one's theory of mind might be quite adaptive in the short term, helping to protect the child from aggressive acts. For example, a hypersensitivity to aggressive intents may prove to be a useful adaptation to their social environment, helping an abused child to avoid acts of aggression and abuse."

However, there are further complexities here because a bias toward attribution of hostile intentions is more closely associated with reactive aggression than with proactive aggression. For some discussion, see Sutton (this volume, p. 107) and Blair (this volume, p. 161).

49. See also Nichols (2001), for an account that postulates a concern mechanism (CM) to do some of the work that is done, on Blair's theory, by the VIM. The normal operation of the VIM is that distress cues activate predispositions to withdraw. On the input side, *representations of distress* come to activate the VIM only by way of *classical conditioning* as a result of pairings of distress cues with representations of distress. On the output side, the operation of the VIM gives rise to *moral emotions*, such as sympathy, and hence to caring behavior only by way of a process in which the arousal that is induced by the activation of the VIM is *interpreted* as a moral emotion (Blair, 1995, p. 156). In contrast, the basic operation of the CM is that representations of distress give rise either to empathic distress or else directly to the moral emotion of sympathy. Thus, the basic operation of the CM, unlike the basic operation of the VIM, requires representation of a mental state. But, according to Nichols, "basic altruistic motivation [provided either by a distinctive emotion of sympathy or else by empathic distress] requires only a minimal capacity for mindreading, the capacity to attribute negative affective or hedonic mental states like distress" (Nichols, 2001, p. 445).

50. The following three quotations are from Hume (1958, Book 3, Part 3, Section 1). See also Stroud (1977, chap. 9).

51. See again Peterson (this volume; Peterson and Siegal, 2000; Garfield, Peterson and Perry, 2001). Any putative explanation of autism along these lines must take into account that although deaf children's impaired psychological understanding persists even into late adolescence, it is usually described in terms of delay rather than deficit. Some high-functioning children with autism are able to pass tests of false-belief understanding, as are people with Asperger's syndrome, but there is some plausibility to the idea that this success reflects laborious compensatory strategies rather than systematic or deep psychological understanding (see again Dissanayake and Macintosh, this volume). So it would be interesting to know the results of a detailed and relatively demanding investigation of the psychological understanding of deaf adults who grew up in hearing families.

  Perhaps it is worth noting that even if impaired psychological understanding in autism is a consequence of more basic linguistic and social difficulties, this does not undermine Blair's double-dissociation argument discussed in the previous section.

52. Baron-Cohen (1995, chapter 6), suggested that the theory of mind module proper may be grounded in the orbito-frontal cortex (though see Blair, this volume, pp. 158–159). But, on his account, psychological understanding depends on a network of four mechanisms and he suggests that the neural basis for this network involves the superior temporal sulcus and the amygdala, as well as the orbito-frontal cortex.

53. "Theory of mind in autism and schizophrenia: A case of over-optimistic reverse engineering," in this volume.

54. The delusions of alien control and thought insertion are among the positive symptoms of schizophrenia. The analogue of the strategy followed in the case of autism would be to say that the impairment that explains the positive symptoms causes impaired psychological understanding and that this, in turn, explains the negative symptoms of schizophrenia, such as flattening of affect, poverty of speech, and social withdrawal. But Gerrans and McGeer say, "the negative symptoms are prime candidates for a mechanical [rather than cognitive] explanation" (p. 295).

55. That is, the explanation of the co-occurrence of symptoms would take the form of a vertically integrated account that unifies the symptoms neurobiologically. Speaking of the mechanical explanation of the disorder phenylketonuria, Gerrans and McGeer describe the strategy of vertical integration in the absence of horizontal integration (p. 278): "We explain the neural malfunction and treat the resultant behavior as the outcome of haphazard interference with the development of a number of *arbitrarily involved* cognitive functions."

56. See again Peterson (this volume); see also Garfield, Peterson, and Perry (2001). This kind of position is sometimes associated with Lev Vygotsky; see Astington (1996).

57. See Currie and Sterelny (2000, p. 145) for this point. It appears to be disputed by Garfield, Peterson and Perry (2001, p. 525).

58. For a general discussion of the importance of the distinction between distal and proximal causes for developmental cognitive neuropsychology, see Jackson and Coltheart (2001, chap. 2, "Proximal and Distal Causes of Individual Differences in Reading").

59. Improved hearing might, though, permit gradual linguistic improvement as a result of training. See Tallal et al. (1996).

60. See also the test battery used by Tager-Flusberg (this volume).

61. See, for example, see Happé, Brownell and Winner (1999) for a review of research with patients who have sustained right hemisphere brain damage.

62. "Theory of mind and social dysfunction: Psychotic solipsism versus autistic asociality," in this volume.

63. We can ask this question about the role of impaired psychological understanding in the etiology of delusions, such as the *delusion* of alien control, even if we accept that alien control *experiences* are caused by a breakdown of a component of the motor control system. See Davies et al. (2001).

64. For discussion, see Peterson and Siegal (2000, pp. 125–127); Garfield, Peterson and Perry (2001, pp. 512–513).

65. The question how the array would look is an *appearance* question, "Would the blocks look like this [as presented on a computer monitor]?" rather than an *item* question, "Would you see a yellow block in the front on your right?"

66. Eilan, McCarthy and Brewer (1993/1999); Evans (1982, chap. 6).

67. See Evans (1982, p. 163) on being able "to impose the objective way of thinking upon egocentric space."

68. See Evans (1980).

69. For several discussions of the role of this kind of breakdown in schizophrenic delusions, see the special issue of *Philosophy, Psychiatry, and Psychology*, volume 8, number 2/3, June/September 2001, "On Understanding and Explaining Schizophrenia," edited by Christoph Hoerl.

70. With this question in mind, it is interesting to note that even with one test in the battery that assesses understanding of desire, there is no relationship between psychological understanding as assessed by the test battery and the use of desire words. In contrast, there is a relationship with use of cognition words to refer to cognitive mental states.

71. For some of the seminal papers in this debate, see Davies and Stone (1995).

72. Pp. 271–272; see Baron-Cohen, Leslie and Frith (1985), Baron-Cohen (1995), and C. Frith (1992).

73. An evaluation of the significance of this claim about the possibility of unifying the symptoms of schizophrenia would need to take account of the fact that the symptoms do not always occur together, but dissociate.

74. For the notion of a module as dedicated to a domain, that is, as domain-specific, see Coltheart (1999).

REFERENCES

Astington, J. W. (1996). What is theoretical about the child's theory of mind?: A Vygotskian view of its development. In P. Carruthers & P. K. Smith (Eds), *Theories of theories of mind* (pp. 184–199). Cambridge: Cambridge University Press.

Astington, J. W., & Jenkins, J. M. (1995). Theory of mind development and social understanding. *Cognition and Emotion, 9,* 151–165.

Baron-Cohen, S. (1995). *Mindblindness: An essay on autism and theory of mind.* Cambridge, MA: MIT Press.

Baron-Cohen, S., Leslie, A., & Frith, U. (1985). Does the autistic child have a "theory of mind"? *Cognition, 21,* 37–46.

Bartsch, K., & Estes, D. (1996). Individual differences in children's developing theory of mind and implications for metacognition. *Learning and Individual Differences, 8,* 281–304.

Blair, R. J. R. (1995). A cognitive developmental approach to morality: Investigating the psychopath. *Cognition, 57,* 1–29.

Bowler, D. 1992: 'Theory of mind' in Asperger's syndrome. *Journal of Child Psychology and Psychiatry, 33,* 877–93.

Bryant, B. K. (1982). An index of empathy for children and adolescents. *Child Development, 53,* 413–425.

Chomsky, N. (1965). *Aspects of the theory of syntax.* Cambridge, MA: MIT Press.

Coltheart, M. (1999). Modularity and cognition. *Trends in Cognitive Sciences, 3,* 115–120.

Currie, G., & Sterelny, K. (2000). How to think about the modularity of mind-reading. *Philosophical Quarterly, 50,* 145–160.

Davies, M., Coltheart, M., Langdon, R., & Breen, N. (2001). Monothematic delusions: Towards a two-factor account. *Philosophy, Psychiatry and Psychology, 8,* 133–158.

Davies, M., & Stone, T. (Eds). (1995). *Folk psychology: The theory of mind debate.* Oxford: Blackwell.

de Villiers, J. G. (2000). Language and theory of mind: What are the developmental relationships? In S. Baron-Cohen, H. Tager-Flusberg, & D. Cohen (Eds.), *Understanding other minds: Perspectives from developmental cognitive neuroscience* (2nd ed., pp. 83–123). Oxford: Oxford University Press.

Eilan, N., McCarthy, R., & Brewer, B. (Eds). (1999). *Spatial representation: Problems in philosophy and psychology.* Oxford: Oxford University Press. (First published by Blackwell Publishers, 1993)

Ellis, H. D., & Gunter, H. L. (1999). Asperger syndrome: A simple matter of white matter? *Trends in Cognitive Sciences, 3,* 192–200.

Evans, G. (1980). Things without the mind: A commentary upon chapter 2 of Strawson's *Individuals.* In Z. van Straaten (Ed.), *Philosophical subjects: Essays presented to P. F. Strawson* (pp. 77–116). Oxford: Oxford University Press. Reprinted in *Collected Papers.* Oxford: Oxford University Press, 1985.

Evans, G. (1982). *The varieties of reference.* Oxford: Oxford University Press.

Frith, C. (1992). *The cognitive neuropsychology of schizophrenia.* Hove, UK: Lawrence Erlbaum/Taylor & Francis.

Frith, U., & Happé, F. (1999). Theory of mind and self-consciousness: What is it like to be autistic? *Mind and Language, 14,* 1–22.

Garfield, J. L., Peterson, C. C., & Perry, T. (2001). Social cognition, language acquisition and the development of the theory of mind. *Mind and Language, 16,* 494–541.

Goldie, P. (2000). *The emotions: A philosophical exploration.* Oxford: Oxford University Press.

Goldman, A. I. (1995). Empathy, mind, and

morals. In M. Davies & T. Stone (Eds.), *Mental simulation: Evaluations and applications* (pp. 185–208). Oxford: Blackwell Publishers. (Original work published 1993)

Grice, H. P. (1989). *Studies in the way of words*. Cambridge, MA: Harvard University Press.

Happé, F., & Frith, U. (1996) Theory of mind and social impairment in children with conduct disorder. *British Journal of Developmental Psychology, 14,* 385–398.

Happé, F., Brownell, H., & Winner, E. (1999)Acquired "theory of mind" impairments following stroke. *Cognition, 70,* 211–240.

Happé, F. G. E. (1991). The autobiographical writings of three Asperger syndrome adults: Problems of interpretation and implications for theory. In U. Frith (Ed.), *Autism and Asperger syndrome* (pp. 207–242). Cambridge: Cambridge University Press.

Happé, F. G. E. (1993) Communicative competence and theory of mind in autism: A test of relevance theory. *Cognition, 48,* 101–119.

Happé, F. G. E. (1995) Understanding minds and metaphors: Insights from the study of figurative language in autism. *Metaphor and Symbolic Activity, 10,* 275–295.

Harris, P. L. (1996). Desires, beliefs, and language. In P. Carruthers & P. K. Smith (Eds.), *Theories of theories of mind* (pp. 200–220). Cambridge: Cambridge University Press.

Heider, F. (1958). *The psychology of interpersonal relations*. London: Wiley.

Hume, D. (1958). *A treatise of human nature*. Oxford: Oxford University Press.

Ickes, W. 1993: Empathic accuracy. *Journal of Personality,* 61, 587–610.

Ickes, W. (Ed.). (1997). *Empathic accuracy*. New York: Guilford Press.

Jackson, N., & Coltheart, M. (2001). *Routes to reading success and failure*. Hove, UK: Psychology Press.

Jenkins, J. M., & Astington, J. W. (1996). Cognitive factors and family structure associated with theory of mind development in young children. *Developmental Psychology, 32,* 70–78.

Lalonde, C. E., & Chandler, M. (1995). False belief understanding goes to school: On the social-emotional consequences of coming early or late to a first theory of mind. *Cogni-*

tion and Emotion, 9, 167–185.

Langdon, R., & Coltheart, M. (2001). Visual perspective-taking and schizotypy: Evidence for a simulation-based account of mentalising in normal adults. *Cognition, 82,* 1–26.

Langdon, R., Davies, M., & Coltheart, M. (2002). Understanding minds and understanding communicated meanings in schizophrenia. *Mind and Language, 17,* 68–104.

Leekam, S. R., & Prior, M. (1994). Can autistic children distinguish lies from jokes?: A second look at second-order belief attribution. *Journal of Child Psychology and Psychiatry and Allied Disciplines, 35,* 901–915.

Maccoby, E. E., & Martin, J. A. (1983). Socialization in the context of the family: Parent-child interaction. In P. H. Mussen & E. M. Hetherington (Eds.), *Handbook of child psychology, Volume 4: Socialization, personality, and social development* (4th ed., pp. 1–101). New York: Wiley.

Nichols, S. (2001) Mindreading and the cognitive architecture underlying altruistic motivation. *Mind and Language,* 16, 425–455.

O'Connor, T. G., & Hirsch, N. (1999). Intra-individual differences and relationship-specificity of mentalizing in early adolescence. *Social Development,* 8, 256–274.

Perner, J., Ruffman, T., & Leekam, S. R. (1994). Theory of mind is contagious: You catch it from your sibs. *Child Development,* 65, 1228–1238.

Peterson, C. C., & Siegal, M. (2000) Insights into theory of mind from deafness and autism. *Mind and Language, 15,* 123–145.

Raffman, D. (1999). What autism may tell us about self-awareness: A commentary on Frith and Happé. *Mind and Language, 14,* 23–31.

Sperber, D. (2000). Metarepresentations in an evolutionary perspective. In D. Sperber (Ed.), *Metarepresentations: A multidisciplinary perspective* (pp. 117–137). Oxford: Oxford University Press.

Strawson, P. F. (1959). *Individuals: An essay in descriptive metaphysics*. London: Methuen.

Stroud, B. (1977). *Hume*. London: Routledge and Kegan Paul.

Sutton, J., & Keogh, E. (2000). Social competition in school: Relationships with bullying, Machiavellianism and personality. *British*

Journal of Educational Psychology, 70, 443–457.

Sutton, J., Reeves, M., & Keogh, E. (2000). Disruptive behavior, avoidance of responsibility and theory of mind. *British Journal of Developmental Psychology, 18,* 1–11.

Sutton, J., Smith, P. K., & Swettenham, J. (1999). Social cognition and bullying: Social inadequacy or skilled manipulation? *British Journal of Developmental Psychology, 17,* 435–450.

Tallal, P. (1988). Developmental language disorders. In J. F. Kavanagh & T. J. Truss Jr. (Eds.), *Learning disabilities: Proceedings of the national conference* (pp. 181–272). Parkton, MD: York Press.

Tallal, P., Miller, S. L., Bedi, G., Byma, G., Wang, X., Nagarajan, S. S., Schreiner, C., Jenkins, W. M., & Merzenich, M. M. (1996). Language comprehension in language-learning impaired children improved with acoustically modified speech. *Science, 271,* 81–84.

Wellman, H. M. (1990). *The child's theory of mind.* Cambridge, MA: MIT Press.

Wellman, H. M., Cross, D., & Watson, J. (2001). Meta-analysis of theory-of-mind development: The truth about false belief. *Child Development, 72,* 655–684.

Author Index

Subject Index